THE SCIENTIFIC SECRETS OF

BBC

DOCTOR WHO

SIMON GUERRIER AND
DR. MAREK KUKULA,
Public Astronomer,
Royal Observatory Greenwich, London

HARPER
DESIGN
An Imprint of HarperCollinsPublishers

HarperCollins books may be purchased for educational, business, or sales promotional use.
For information please e-mail the Special Markets Department at SPsales@harpercollins.com.

This book is published to accompany the television series entitled
Doctor Who, broadcast on BBC One. *Doctor Who* is a BBC Wales production.
Executive producers: Steven Moffat and Brian Minchin

First published by BBC Books in 2015.
BBC Books is an imprint of Ebury Publishing, part of the
Penguin Random House Group of companies.

First published in the United States and Canada in 2015 by
Harper Design
An Imprint of HarperCollins*Publishers*
195 Broadway
New York, NY 10007
Tel: (212) 207-7000
Fax: (855) 746-6023
harperdesign@harpercollins.com
www.hc.com

This edition distributed throughout the world by
HarperCollins*Publishers*
195 Broadway
New York, NY 10007

Library of Congress Control Number: 2015939502

ISBN 978-0-06-238696-0

First Printing, 2015

Printed and bound in the USA

CONTENTS

'I, too, used to believe in magic, but the Doctor has taught me about science. It is better to believe in science.'

Leela, *Horror of Fang Rock* **(1977)**

INTRODUCTION

'The TARDIS is outside.'

'So?'

'So, all of time and all of space is sitting out there.
A big blue box. Please, don't even argue.'

The Twelfth Doctor and Clara Oswald, *Last Christmas* **(2014)**

How could anyone resist a chance to explore all of time and space? The Doctor offers his companions – and us, watching at home – a chance to venture out into the universe and discover its extraordinary wonders.

On these journeys, we uncover the most astounding secrets. Somewhere out there are creatures made of pure energy and monsters that exist in only two dimensions. There are worlds made of diamond, and stars which are alive. You can rewrite history, regenerate from injuries and, best of all, you can travel to anywhere or when in a blue police box that is bigger on the inside than the outside...

At least, according to *Doctor Who*.

This *isn't* a book about what bits of science *Doctor Who* might have got right or wrong in the more than fifty years that it has been on TV. Getting the science right isn't necessarily the same thing as telling a good story – although, as we'll see, it's surprising how often bits of real science work their way into the Doctor's adventures. In fact, the series has occasionally been ahead of its time – using the latest scientific theories as the inspiration for stories such as *Earthshock* (1982), or, in stories such as *Planet of the Daleks* (1973), including outlandish-sounding ideas that scientists only later demonstrated to be real phenomena.

This book *won't* detail how you can build your own versions of the technological gadgets that we've seen in the series – robot dogs, sonic screwdrivers or fully working time machines. That said, there is a bit in Chapter 11 about growing your own potatoes.

And this book *isn't* about the intentions of the people who have made *Doctor Who* over the years, and whether or how much they cared about getting the science right. Though that does come up, for example when we discuss the creation of the Cybermen.

Instead, our hope is that the experience of reading this book will be a little like travelling in the TARDIS with the Doctor. Our fifteen thrilling, original *Doctor Who* stories are inspired by the latest and most boggling scientific ideas. Each story is followed by an examination of the real science involved. Using the stories in this book and from the Doctor's TV adventures, we'll explore the strangest, funniest and most astonishing elements of the cosmos.

We hope it's a book to thrill you, make you laugh and think, and ultimately see the world – and the universe – around you differently. *Doctor Who* has been taking us on adventures for more than fifty years, and science is also a great adventure, constantly revealing new things to amaze and astonish us. We hope this book will make you watch *Doctor Who* with new eyes. And we hope it will be just a first step – inspiring you to explore the world of *Doctor Who* and the equally extraordinary world of science still further.

A book, in fact, that's bigger on the inside…

Please note: This book uses examples from all 813 television episodes of *Doctor Who*, from *An Unearthly Child* (1963) to *Last Christmas* (2014). There will be spoilers. Scientific data and *Doctor Who* statistics are correct up to February 2015.

regen = 12

PART 1
SPACE

$$\partial^3 \sum' x^2$$

Fig 19.

Fight

Diamond

Regian

·9·

$X\| \simeq \textcircled{M} \text{ or } \textcircled{\Omega} ??$

SUNSET OVER VENUS

MARK WRIGHT

'Lovell Platform from *Genetrix*, we have a green board for descent. Await go confirm.'

An alert pinged in Lieutenant Devika Cullen's earpiece. She glanced across the cockpit to Probe Specialist Rick Attah, who flashed a reassuring grin, then yawned. He reclined in his chair, hands behind his head. They were hanging by a thread 54 kilometres above the surface of Venus, and he looked ready to take a nap. Devika shook her head. Space exploration: a game for the young, as Dad once said.

'*Genetrix* from Lovell,' crackled Valeriya Alexandrova over the comms. 'You have go confirm, cleared for umbilical detach.'

'Acknowledged, Lovell.'

'Hey Valeriya,' Rick broke in. 'Wanna crack open an alcohol-free tonight?'

The Russian sounded less than keen. 'You have job to do down there. Fraternising with mission co-ordinator is not part of that job.'

'See you in the mess at twenty hundred.'

Devika rolled her eyes. 'You two done?'

Rick grinned and sat up. His body language flowed from bored 24-year-old to alert mission specialist. Rick's fingers danced across the instrument panels before and above him. 'Pressure exchange nominal. Good to go.'

'Lovell from *Genetrix*, umbilical detach on my mark.'

'Acknowledged, *Genetrix*.'

Devika sat forward, restraining straps tightening. She glanced at the Heads Up Display, relaying the external camera feed. Below the linked struts and cluster of mission pods that made up International Aeronautical Space Agency Orbital Platform Lovell hung the *Genetrix* manned probe. A long, slender balloon, its surface glistening silver in the sunlight reflected off the thick Venusian cloud. The balloon's material was laced with a discrete dynastream compound, more than enough to deal with the conditions at the edge of the cloud layer. Slung below the balloon was the mission pod, packed with monitoring instruments, systems – and more importantly, herself and Rick.

'Let's ride the Venus Express,' whispered Rick, tensing. This was their third descent from Lovell in as many weeks. Yes, it was becoming routine, something the crew of any long-term space mission had to contend with. What was it Commander Sanford said? *Routine breeds contempt.* It had become a mantra of every member of the Venus mission crew. This might be their third descent but, to both Devika and Rick, it was as dangerous as the first, and they had to be alert.

'Umbilical release in five. Four. Three. Two. One.' Devika's fingers curled against the release trigger. She took a breath. 'Mark.'

The cockpit lurched. Instead of a sickening drop, the *Genetrix* began a smooth, swooping descent into the carpet of yellow-tinged cloud directly below.

Devika activated controls, her board a line of pleasing green status lights. 'Rick, how's it looking?'

'Check, check, check and check,' he said briskly. 'Systems at nominal.'

'Check that. Lovell from *Genetrix*, we are descending to cloud layer.'

'Acknowledged, *Genetrix*. Stay on comms, and happy fishing.'

'OK, Rick, take us down.'

'You got it.' Rick tapped out a sequence.

This was what Devika Cullen loved about her job. Space exploration was exciting, most people agreed, even nearly half a century after the

2049 Moon Crisis. But nothing could describe the feeling of floating down to skim through the upper cloud layer of a planet millions of kilometres from home. Looking out into the stars and taking the human race the next few steps.

But it was dangerous out there. A choking atmosphere, anathema to humans, blistering heat that could scorch flesh from bones. From those twentieth-century pioneers of the old USA and Soviet Union to her hero Adelaide Brooke and beyond, anybody who had ever strapped in and felt the crush of 3 gs as they blasted into orbit knew it was dangerous. But still they came.

Devika felt a flush of heat on her face, droplets of perspiration prickling her brow. She smiled. Environmental systems assured her it was a cool 20 degrees, but it never harmed to remember what was out there, literally inches away.

'Levelling out at 49 km above the surface of Venus,' reported Rick.

The HUD relayed an image of thick, sulphurous clouds, tendrils of vapour caressing the screen. They were now inside the cloud layer and perfectly safe at this altitude.

Devika unbuckled and strode to the controls ranged alongside the sealed hatch to the lower level. 'Atmospheric sifters online,' she announced. 'Deploying... now.'

She pulled down on the release triggers. Metallic clangs echoed round the cockpit, one after the other. On the HUD, four lozenge-shaped probes dropped away from the *Genetrix*, umbilical hoses snaking back to the mission pod as they vanished into the haze.

Devika toggled her comms. 'Lovell Platform from *Genetrix*, commencing atmospheric skim. Stand by.'

The comms silenced with a beep. Rick blew out a breath. Now, they waited.

Devika perched on the edge of her flight chair. Rick started to sing, tunelessly, under his breath.

'Don't give up the day job, Rick,' said Devika. 'What is that?'

Rick adjusted a control. '"Magic Carpet Ride". Steppenwolf.'

Devika snorted. 'Finger on the pulse, Granddad. Try The Beatles next, they're—'

Devika suddenly pitched forward, head smashing painfully against the metal deck plate. Lights flickered, alarms screamed, status indicators blinked from green to red.

Devika shook her head against the dizziness, vision blurring as she scrabbled onto her chair. 'What the—?' She stopped before completing the sentence, knowing every word they said was heard back on Lovell.

Rick's eyes darted over his control board. 'Pressure mismatch, power drains in all systems.' He turned to face Devika. 'We're dead in the water and dropping further into the cloud layer.'

The HUD screen choked with yellow-stained clouds.

'Lovell Platform from *Genetrix*. We have a problem. Power drain to all systems, pressure mismatch. Descending into cloud layer.' Despite her even, calm tone, Devika's elevated heartbeat would be giving away to her colleagues monitoring up on Lovell that they had a situation. 'Stand by while we investigate.'

Static crackled.

'Lovell Platform, please acknowledge.'

A calm took hold of Devika. Her eyes locked with Rick's. They both knew what this meant.

'Gah!' Rick gasped, the spell broken as something slammed hard against the sealed rear hatch. 'What was that?'

Devika stood. 'Plasma venting?' she offered unconvincingly.

A gentle buzzing penetrated the cockpit.

'Something's out there,' breathed Rick.

The light above the hatch flashed from red to green. Devika gripped the back of her chair so hard her knuckles bleached white.

The hatch slid open, white vapour streaming into the cockpit.

'Hey, how are ya?' barked the tall man who stepped through the venting gas, brandishing a slender probe. Its tip glowed green. He planted booted feet firmly on the deck and pocketed the device. Devika saw a flash of red beneath his long, dark-blue coat. He glared at the astronauts, extending a bony finger to each of them in turn. 'You. You. Blue box out there. In.'

The stunned pair didn't move.

'What the Doctor meant to say,' said a bright voice preceding the young woman peering around the man, 'is that I wanted to watch a Venusian sunset, so we were nearby in our ship when we saw your balloon-thing plunge into the atmosphere. Thought we'd drop in and offer you guys a lift.' She smiled, self-consciously pushing back a strand of dark-brown hair. Then, as an afterthought: 'Hi, I'm Clara.'

The man – the Doctor – cocked his head to one side. 'My version was quicker,' he murmured. 'Come on, shift yourselves!' He clapped his hands, gesturing through the hatch. 'You can say thank you later. If you're lucky, I might even say you're welcome.'

Rick looked at the newcomers, mouth open. Devika found her voice. 'We have valuable equipment and data aboard *Genetrix*. We can't just leave.'

The Doctor's brow furrowed. 'Fair enough,' he shrugged. 'Stay here and die.' With a curt wave, he turned smartly and made to stride through the hatch.

Clara yanked him back. 'Doctor, we have to help.'

'Do we?' asked the Doctor.

'Yes! Unless...' Clara looked up at him, innocent mischief flashing across her eyes. 'Unless you're saying you don't know how you could save the ship?'

The Doctor returned Clara's gaze, then sighed. 'I hate you sometimes.'

Clara grinned. 'No you don't.'

'Right then,' said the Doctor decisively, whipping out the probe-device in one fluid movement. At that second, it felt to Devika like their situation came crashing back in, the alerts shrill and deafening. Her head throbbed, limbs feeling like dead weights, a sickening plunging in her stomach. She ran a hand across her brow; it was slick with sweat and blood. Sweat. The heat, suddenly cloying and oppressive in the cockpit.

The Doctor waved the buzzing probe across a bank of controls, the green glow bright in the flickering half-light.

'What is that thing?' asked Devika, suspicious.

The Doctor gave her a withering look. 'Sonic screwdriver. Obviously.' He returned his attention to the controls. 'I don't know whether to admire the human race, or point and laugh. Bobbing along in your little kiddie's balloon above a meltingly hot world in the name of exploration. Indomitable or stupid, it's a fine line.'

Devika felt a rush of anger. 'Now listen…'

'No!' countered the Doctor, glaring back. 'You listen! Here's what's going to happen. We are plunging at –' he jumped up and down – '3 km per minute into the atmosphere of Venus. Below 30 km, it's going to get messy. Fact: the mean temperature on the surface of Venus is 735 degrees Kelvin. The pressure is 92 times that of Earth. Conclusion: the further we fall, we'll either be cooked or crushed. Your choice.'

As if to emphasise his point, a metal panel buckled in on itself.

'Sorry,' said Clara, trying to break the tension. 'He does this. Best to ignore him.'

Devika's gaze had not left the Doctor's watery-blue eyes. 'Instead of lecturing us, help us.'

The Doctor smiled, thinly. 'Better.'

Rick stepped forward. 'What can we do?'

The Doctor raised a finger to the young astronaut. 'Better.'

Clara grinned. 'Come on, Doctor. Let's get these guys home.'

The Doctor was galvanised into action. 'You!' he pointed at Rick, then seemed to look at him properly for the first time. 'How old are you?'

'24.'

'You don't look old enough to shave let alone wear an IASA uniform.' Before Rick could reply, the Doctor waved him away. 'Vent the thermo buffers.'

'Check.' Rick stepped to a rear control bank, his movements sluggish in the increasing pressure.

'Clara, be a pal.' The Doctor threw the probe to her.

'Yes, Doctor?'

'Second level down, control stack to the right of the ladder. Need you to regulate power flow to the pressure exchange. Just point and hope.'

'Gotcha.'

'And don't dilly-dally on the way,' he called after her as she disappeared.

It was now unbearably hot in the cockpit – though the Doctor didn't seem to feel it, even with that coat on. He flicked switches in quick order. 'Need to equalise the pressure exchange.' He glanced at Devika. 'Want to tell me what happened?'

'Systems went down, no rhyme or reason.'

'There's always a rhyme, always a reason.'

'Thermo buffers vented!' Rick's face shone with sweat.

'Good man.' The Doctor stepped back, eyes glinting as they darted across every control.

Devika jumped as a bulkhead panel buckled, vapour blasting into the cockpit. The *Genetrix* lurched, forcing her and Rick to steady themselves. The Doctor remained bolt upright, unaffected. 'Pressure's building,' he said, evidently relishing the danger.

Rick pinched the bridge of his nose, Devika feeling the same pain behind her eyes. 'We're dead, aren't we?'

The Doctor nodded. 'Probably.' He jabbed at a control. 'Clara? How's it coming down there?'

Static crunched. The Doctor frowned, hawkish eyebrows knitting together worriedly. 'Clara?'

Static hissed, then cleared. 'Doctor.' Clara's tinny voice sounded calm, but there was a wavering note of fear beneath. 'Get down here. Now.'

The Doctor was already moving, lanky frame vanishing through the hatch. 'Rick, come on!' Devika tried to sprint after the Doctor, but only managed a graceless stagger in the ever-increasing pressure.

Devika barely registered the tall blue box standing against a bulkhead before she saw the Doctor launch himself onto the ladder, pivoting round and sliding in one fluid motion to the deck below. 'Clara,' he shouted, looking around the stacks of scientific instruments. Devika jumped down next to him, feet slamming heavily to the deck plates. Rick clambered down behind. 'Clara!'

'Doctor.'

The Doctor's head whipped round. Clara stood with her back to an instrument bank, eyes wide. She held the Doctor's sonic device up, the tip pointing towards...

'Oh man,' whispered Rick. As her eyes followed the probe's direction, Devika could only agree.

Standing – or floating? – a few feet away was a... Devika's mind struggled to put the image into a context she understood. A cloud of dirty yellow vapour floating next to a control stack, constantly shifting tendrils of gas spiralling in a crude approximation of human form. A gaseous life form? Within the miasma, points of light sparkled, the crude humanoid shape completed by two points burning like coals where eyes should have been.

'Oh, look at you,' whispered the Doctor. He grinned, hard lines of his face softening with rapt fascination. 'Look at you.'

'Glad you're so impressed,' said an unmoving Clara.

'What's it doing?' asked Devika. A gaseous arm stretched out, wisps of vapour dissipating as it wafted over a panel. The controls sparked and burned.

'Stop it!' shouted Rick, stepping forward. 'It's screwing with the *Genetrix*.' The movement caused the creature to turn and face them. It hissed angrily, eyes burning brighter.

'Hey, wispy man!' called the Doctor, waving his arms. 'Over here!'

The creature turned with surprising speed. A gaseous arm lashed out, releasing a shower of viscous liquid towards the Doctor.

'Doctor!'

The Doctor whipped about, droplets of liquid spattering across the back of his coat. It began to smoke, the fabric deteriorating as holes formed across its surface.

The Doctor whipped the coat off and hurled it down. Seconds later all that remained were tattered rags of smoking blue and red.

'Oh, Wispy, that was rude,' said the Doctor. The creature turned back to the control stack. The Doctor sniffed at the dirty smoke curling up from the remains of his coat. 'Sulphuric acid. Of course!' He glanced up at his three companions. 'Fact: sulphuric acid was called "oil of vitriol" by eighth-century alchemists.'

'So?' shouted Rick.

'Man's got a point,' said Clara. 'Stop showing off.' She gestured to the creature. 'What is that?'

'Ladies and gentleman,' announced the Doctor with a theatrical flourish, 'you are looking at the indigenous life form of the planet Venus!'

Devika snorted. 'There can't have been life on Venus for billions of years.'

'You'd think, not since the oceans evaporated,' conceded the Doctor. 'Now, that was a day and a half. But look!' He pointed to the gas creature, the threat of the humans discarded for now. 'Bonded molecules of acidic gas, coalescing, forming and reforming in a pressure cooker of carbon dioxide, nitrogen and sulphuric acid. Life found a way!'

Devika jabbed a finger at the creature. 'And it's tearing my probe apart!'

'Doctor, I can hardly breathe,' said Clara, struggling. Her face flushed red, hair dripping with sweat.

The Doctor didn't seem to hear. He watched the creature spray a fine mist of acid, causing an instrument bank to bubble and melt. Its gaseous head turned to the Doctor. It hissed. Was that desperation?

'Perhaps you deserve it,' the Doctor said, glaring. 'That control bank. What does it do?'

'Regulates the atmospheric sifters,' said Rick. 'Deployment, analysis, everything. The *Genetrix*'s prime function is full-spectrum analysis of the Venusian cloud layer, studying the samples to assess terraforming potential.'

'Atmospheric...' mused the Doctor. 'Atmospheric sifters?' His face hardened. 'Tell me you didn't?'

'Are you saying what I think you're saying, Doctor?' asked Clara.

Devika looked from one to the other. 'What? Tell me!'

'You really are as stupid as I thought.' The Doctor's eyes blazed. 'Look at him! Bonded molecules of carbon dioxide, nitrogen and sulphuric acid.'

Realisation dawned on Rick's face. 'Oh, Dev.'

Devika tasted bile as sickening clarity hit her through the noise and chaos. The gas creature – this incredible, impossible life form – stood before them. Outside, the *Genetrix* tumbling towards the surface, atmospheric sifters trailing along with it. Atmospheric sifters sucking in carbon dioxide, nitrogen and sulphuric acid.

'Oh no. Please, no.'

'The penny drops! No wonder Wispy's none too happy. You've been hoovering up his relatives! Purge those sifters, now!'

'On it!' Rick stumbled to the control stack. The creature rounded on him.

'Wispy,' said the Doctor gently. 'May I call you Wispy?' His arms opened wide as he stepped closer. 'I'm not sure if you can understand me, but we need to get to that control bank. Make this right. What do you say? Want to help us out?'

The creature tilted its head in a strangely human pose. With every second that ached by, the temperature rose, breathing now painful, movement sluggish. Wispy began to move. The Doctor let out a relieved breath, face relaxing. He stepped towards the panel, but Wispy lashed out, shrieking in anger. The Doctor dodged back, arms raised protectively.

'Wispy, over here!' Clara staggered towards the creature, now-heavy arms waving as best she could manage. It wailed and moved towards her, away from the controls. Clara backed away. 'Do your work, Doctor!'

'Do it fast!' shouted Rick, jumping in next to Clara.

Wispy stalked after Clara and Rick. Devika was right behind the Doctor as he pounced on the sifter controls, seemingly unaffected by the pressure bearing down on them. Her vision blurred in the inferno-like heat, confused thoughts bouncing against each other through the stabbing needles of pain in her head. The Doctor snarled, slamming a fist repeatedly against the controls. 'It's fused!'

'We've got to… got to unlock them.'

'Doctor!' It was Clara. Both she and Rick were backed against a bulkhead, the gaseous creature bearing down on them. Above them, a viewport cracked. 'Catch!' She launched the sonic screwdriver across the control room, ducking as the life form sprayed a mist of sulphuric acid that fizzed and burned into the bulkhead above her.

The Doctor caught the device and brought it to bear on the control stack in one motion. 'One chance,' he said, mouth set determinedly. The air filled with an incessant buzzing as the tip glowed green. As her vision darkened, Devika was dimly aware of Wispy turning away from Clara and Rick, eyes incandescent in fury as it bore down on the Doctor.

'Come on, come on!'

The buzzing intensified. Devika slumped to the floor, feeling as if her head were about to explode. The vaporous alien raised both arms towards the Doctor, shrieking in hissing anger, then –

The control stack before the Doctor exploded in a shower of sparks that haloed round him for a split second. 'Got it! Sifter's purging!'

Wispy threw its head back, gaseous tendrils snaking around it, and let out an alien shriek, before its whole form dissipated to nothing. Smoking droplets of acid hissed to the floor, the only evidence it had ever been there.

The Doctor pulled Devika to her feet. Clara stumbled forwards, supporting Rick. The *Genetrix* shuddered.

'Still falling,' Devika wheezed. She slumped to the floor, pressure forcing her down, lungs burning as she tried to suck in air. The four huddled together beneath the ladder.

'Nothing I can do,' said the Doctor. A control panel buckled as if punched, sparks billowing and fizzing onto the deck plates 'Up the ladder, into the TARDIS.'

'The what?' asked Rick.

Clara heaved him forward. 'The big blue box! Move!'

'Quickly!' urged the Doctor. The whole craft shook, dirty yellow Venusian clouds billowing past the viewport, the heat now an unbearable, cloying haze. 'We've got seconds before—'

The shaking ceased. The Doctor stopped mid-sentence, one foot on the bottom rung. A serene calm took over, alarms silenced, warning lights blinked off one by one. Almost immediately it felt easier to breath, Devika sucking in a lungful of cooler air.

Rick tapped at a readout screen. 'We're rising,' he said, that grin spreading across his youthful features.

The Doctor looked dubious. 'Can't be. I haven't done anything.'

Devika let out a heavy breath. The temperature was cooling all the time.

Clara stood on tiptoe, peering out through the cracked viewport. 'Guys. You really need to see this.'

Devika crowded in behind Clara. She suddenly felt as light as air. The Venusian clouds still rolled and boiled in the void, but there was something else. Gas creatures, gliding and swooping around the *Genetrix*, their glowing eyes shining like fireflies. There must have been fifty or more, whirling in a circle beneath them, a vortex of these amazing life forms.

'They're taking us up,' breathed Devika.

The Doctor stood behind them, arms folded, face implacable. 'Good old Wispy.'

'… *trix*, please respond. *Genetrix* from Lovell Platform, please advise status.'

Devika and Clara continued to watch. Rick toggled the comms. 'Lovell Platform from *Genetrix*. We're fine, status… erm…? What do I say?'

Devika smiled, glancing at the Doctor. 'Tell them they'd never believe us.'

Two hours later, Devika Cullen, Rick Attah, Clara and the Doctor looked out from Lovell's observation deck. A thick carpet of yellow cloud stretched away in all directions. On the far horizon, a fuzzy yellow-orange orb was half submerged in the clouds, light stretching out to highlight the atmosphere in brilliant colour.

Clara sighed happily. 'I thought I was going to miss my sunset.'

'A day on Venus lasts 116.75 Earth days,' said the Doctor. 'The sunsets here are a sublimely leisurely experience. Plenty of time.'

'It looks like a melting ice cream.'

The Doctor rolled his eyes.

They continued to watch in silence. Below the platform hung the *Genetrix*, the silver balloon secure in its umbilical. Devika tried to retain the memory of their flight back to Lovell. The Wispies – as Clara now called them – pushing them up through the clouds, temperature and pressure receding by the second. Up and up, until Lovell came into sight and they were able to reattach to the umbilical. Seconds later, the Wispies plunged back towards Venus, diving through the cloud layer as if it were an ocean.

Devika turned to the Doctor. His face reflected the light from below. 'Commander Sanford is speaking to IASA Command on Earth about how we best protect this life form. We'll do better, I promise.'

The Doctor's expression didn't change. 'I'll be watching, so make sure you do. You got lucky today. Very lucky.'

'It was OK in the end, right?' said Clara.

'Just. But here's the thing.' The Doctor turned to face them, tall frame highlighted against yellow Venusian cloud and the inky black carapace of space above. 'Humanity needs to buckle up. You're expanding, setting off through the stars. I envy you the discovery, but out there...' He opened his arms wide, gesturing into space. 'Out there, beyond the Solar System, there are even more strange, fantastical, dangerous things to discover.'

The Doctor looked at each of them in turn, Devika and Rick hanging on his every word. Clara smiled as he continued.

'You thought today was scary – you just see what's waiting out there.' And he grinned.

ONE

ALIEN LIFE AND OTHER WORLDS

'I've had a life with you for 19 years, but then I met the
Doctor, and all the things I've seen him do for me,
for you, for all of us. For the whole stupid
planet and every planet out there.'

Rose Tyler, *Doomsday* (2006)

Until 24 August 2006 – a month after the first broadcast of the Tenth
Doctor episode, *Doomsday* – we didn't know what a planet was.

The word 'planet' means 'wanderer' and dates back thousands of years
to the ancient Greeks. But their ideas about what they saw when they
looked up in the sky were very different from what we understand now.
They thought the Earth was at the centre of the cosmos, surrounded by
a series of huge, revolving, crystal spheres. Each of the first seven spheres
had a planet fixed to it – and these seven 'planets' included the Sun and
Moon. On the eighth and outermost sphere were fixed all the stars.

OK, the ancient Greeks got it wrong, but – as *Doctor Who* shows us
when the TARDIS lands in the past – people in history weren't stupid.
They were just as clever and inventive as we are. Today, we have ever
more powerful telescopes to look deep into space. We send spacecraft
and robots to explore the planets near us – such as Venus – and gaze
further out into the universe. But for a long time, all people could use
to explore the heavens was the naked eye and some clever thinking.

The ancient Greek model of the planets

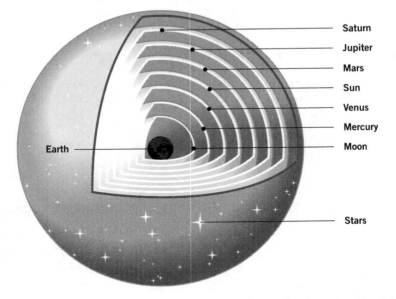

Imagine a room with a wheel fixed on the wall. The wheel is side-on, so it looks like a disc – a circle. The circle is spattered with blobs of white paint. Turn off the lights and you can't see the circle but the paint blobs glow in the dark. They look like a pattern of stars. Then the pattern of blobs starts to move, all together, spinning round and round.

What must be happening? The obvious answer is that the wheel is turning. It doesn't matter that you can't see the wheel in the darkness; you can work it out easily from the way the blobs move. If you'd never seen the wheel – if you'd only entered the room when the lights were already off – you'd still quickly work out that the glowing blobs were fixed to something that was spinning round.

What you probably *wouldn't* think is that the blobs were keeping still and *you* were the one who was spinning. That would be ridiculous! How could you be turning upside down but not feel you were moving at all?

Except, of course, that that is exactly what's happening when we look up at the stars. They slowly turn through the night sky, as if they're fixed on something like a wheel. But they look like that because our planet – Earth – is turning on its axis. We're the ones going round.

> 'It's like when you're a kid. The first time they tell you the world's turning and you just can't quite believe it because everything looks like it's standing still. I can feel it. The turn of the Earth. The ground beneath our feet is spinning at a thousand miles an hour, and the entire planet is hurtling round the Sun at 67,000 miles an hour, and I can feel it. We're falling through space, you and me, clinging to the skin of this tiny little world, and if we let go...'
>
> **The Ninth Doctor, *Rose* (2005)**

Frankly, a lot of what we now know about other planets – and our own – is a bit weird and unsettling. It's certainly not obvious. So how did we puzzle it out? Unlike the Doctor, we can't feel the turn of the Earth beneath us. We don't have a TARDIS to take us to other planets for a quick look round.

But what does the Doctor do when he lands on an alien world where something strange is happening? He explores, looks for clues and asks awkward questions (sometimes getting himself in trouble with whoever's in charge). That's also how, over thousands of years, we puzzled out what planets really are.

Let's go back to the beginning. Why did the ancient Greeks think the planets were fixed to glass spheres?

As we saw, it looks as if the pattern of stars is slowly turning round and round, fixed to something like a wheel that we can't see. But the stars aren't the only lights in the sky. There are the Sun and the Moon. Then there are a whole lot of things that, with the naked eye, look like the other stars but don't behave in the same way. Instead of turning round and round as part of one fixed pattern, these stars seem to 'wander' about from night to night. The ancient Greek word for wanderers was πλανῆται – 'planetai'.

The Sun was the easiest to see of these planetai, and its movements were the easiest to understand – or that was how it seemed. Every morning, the Sun rises in the east. It then gets slowly higher in the sky until midday, starts to sink again in the afternoon and finally sets in the west. We don't see it at night but it's back in the east by next morning. It seemed obvious that the Sun circled round us.

Less obvious was explaining why the Sun's position in the sky at midday was much higher in the summer than it is in winter. We now know that the Earth is slightly tilted as it spins round the Sun. When the tilt means we point towards the Sun, we get more hours and a greater density of sunlight – our summer. At the same time we have our summer, the other side of the Earth tilts away from the Sun so is in winter. But ancient civilisations thought the Sun went round the Earth, so they came up with different explanations.

The ancient Greeks knew that if you threw something up into the sky it fell back down to Earth. So, they asked themselves, why didn't the Sun fall to Earth? They decided that it had to be fixed to something. Since the Sun circled around us, they decided it was fixed to something round. Since the height of the Sun varied through the year, they decided the thing was a sphere, and the position of the Sun on this sphere was not quite aligned with Earth. Since we could see other planets and stars further away than the Sun, the sphere had to be made of something transparent. The only naturally occurring transparent material they knew of was crystal. So, in a series of logical steps, they concluded that the Sun was fixed to a huge crystal sphere, encircling and spinning round Earth.

'Logic, my dear Zoe, merely enables one to be wrong with authority.'
The Second Doctor, *The Wheel in Space* (1968).

Other ancient people had their own ideas about how the Sun moved round the Earth: the ancient Egyptians thought it was rolled through the sky by a gigantic (and invisible) scarab beetle – just the way that dung beetles in Egypt rolled balls of dung along the ground. In *The Aztecs*

(1964), the Doctor meets people who understand the movements of the Sun enough to know there's going to be an eclipse – but they think the Sun won't shine again afterwards unless it's offered lots of human blood.

These theories might not have been right, but they seemed to fit the observed movements of the Sun. More importantly, understanding that the Sun's position varied in a regular cycle – what we call a year – meant ancient people knew how the Sun would behave in future.

Until that point, human beings had themselves been wanderers. We hunted and foraged for food where we could find it. In the very first *Doctor Who* story – *An Unearthly Child* (1963) – the Doctor meets a tribe of people living a desperate existence in what seems to be the Stone Age. They're scared and cold and hungry because 'Orb' (the Sun) has left the sky. To eat, they must hunt dangerous animals – and do it every day. We're told many of the tribe have died.

But once people understood Orb's movements through the sky, life became a lot easier. For example, in about 4000 BC, people settled along the banks of the River Nile in Egypt. The river flooded every year, and the flooded, muddy ground was good for growing crops. Understanding the movement of the Sun and the passing of the year, people knew when the river would flood, when to sow crops and when to reap the harvest.

At first they sowed and reaped by hand, but once the Egyptians started using a strangely shaped bit of wood called a plough they suddenly produced far more food than they needed. That meant they didn't have to spend every day worrying about where their next meal would come from. They had time to think, experiment and invent things that improved their lives.

The food they grew had to be stored so it wouldn't go bad, so they invented some of the first clay pots. They made lots of pots and had to know what was in them and who they belonged to, which meant inventing some of the first kind of writing. Keeping track of how much food there was and how to divide it needed mathematics. When the Nile flooded, it could wash away the markers that said who owned which bits of land, so people needed ways of recording those spaces and marking them out again. That needed more complicated maths. Irrigation systems and building projects needed more complex skills – and tools. Weapons were needed to stop anyone stealing the food. Extra food and inventions could be swapped with other peoples – so trade was invented. People could even earn food by doing things that weren't directly useful: making up stories and songs to entertain everyone else.

This sequence of major inventions took time. There was about 1,500 years between people settling by the Nile and them building what we think was the world's first large stone building – the step pyramid of Djoser at Saqqara (which you can glimpse in the opening moments of Fourth Doctor story *Pyramids of Mars* (1975)). But what's important is that these developments – what we now think of as the beginning of civilisation – were only made possible by first understanding the movement of the Sun.

'I'm the Doctor. Who are you?'

'Organon, sir … Astrologer extraordinary. Seer to princes and emperors. The future foretold, the past explained, the present apologised for.'

The Fourth Doctor and Organon, *The Creature from the Pit* (1979)

People studied the movements of the other 'planets', too. For example, it was handy to know how the Moon behaved in the days before electric lights. If you were planning a party, you'd want it on a night when there would be a full Moon so your guests could see their way home safely. Understanding the Moon also helped keep track of the passing of time on a scale longer than a day but shorter than a year. If you lived by the sea, understanding the Moon helped you predict the tides.

Some people also thought that events in the sky were connected to events on Earth. If so, knowing how the planets moved and where they'd be in future meant you could predict what was going to happen here. Today, we call that astrology, and it's different from the science of astronomy. In ancient times, astrology and astronomy were mixed up together.

We know ancient people kept careful note of the movements of the planets. In Room 55 of the British Museum in London, there's a clay tablet covered in small, triangular marks. This cuneiform writing details sightings of Venus over 21 years between 724 and 704 BC. (Some archaeologists think the tablet is a copy of sightings recorded 1,000 years before that!)

These sightings showed that the planets moved slowly through the sky in curved paths – just as you'd expect if they were attached to crystal spheres we couldn't otherwise see. But there was something odd when you examined the records, too. Every so often, the outer planets – Mars, Jupiter and Saturn – seemed to double back on themselves in little loops. Why?

Sometime around 250 BC, the ancient Greek astronomer Aristarchus came up with an explanation for this strange movement. He said that if the Sun was at the centre of the cosmos and the Earth circled round it we would go round the Sun faster than the outer planets. The 'loops' were the effect of us overtaking them. Aristarchus was right, but at the time people didn't think so – for sensible, logical reasons. After all, if the Earth is moving, why don't we feel it? (We now understand that we don't feel motion but *changes* in motion – what's called inertia.) Why isn't there a constant wind as we move through space, so that birds can't fly in a straight line? (We know now that space is empty, and the atmosphere moves with the Earth.) If we're moving round the Sun, why don't the other stars get bigger as we get closer to them and smaller as we move away? (We now know they do, but the difference is tiny because the stars are a very, very long way from us – as we'll see in Chapter 2.) What's more, Aristarchus couldn't demonstrate his idea to people using computer graphics. To even understand the problem of the loops in the first place, you had to know some tricky maths.

When a Polish astronomer, Nicholas Copernicus, suggested in AD 1543 that the Earth moved round the Sun, plenty of people still did not believe it – or understand the maths. But by now the printing press had been invented, and books could get to those people who could follow the argument. Argument is probably the right word. It didn't help that political and religious leaders had for centuries told their people that the Sun circled round the Earth. Questioning that system seemed like questioning *them* – which meant you were guilty of treason or heresy. For exactly that reason, Copernicus didn't share his ideas until he was on his deathbed, but a monk called Giordano Bruno was burnt at the stake in 1600 for agreeing with Copernicus and even suggesting that there might be planets circling other stars.

(The *Doctor Who* story *The Ribos Operation* (1978) touches on this period of history when Unstoffe meets Binro the Heretic, a poor man tortured for suggesting that his planet circles its Sun and that the points of light in the sky are not ice crystals but other, distant suns.)

In 1609, German astronomer Johannes Kepler published *New Astronomy*. This book agreed with Copernicus about the planets circling round the Sun, but Kepler went even further. He used very accurate recordings of the movements of the planets going back many years to show that planets didn't go round the Sun in a perfect circle but in an oval shape called an ellipse. He spotted, too, that a planet's speed also varied as it went round.

Again, what we now call Kepler's laws of planetary motion involve some complicated maths and not everyone could follow them. But the same year his book was published, an Italian astronomer, Galileo Galilei, pointed a new invention called a telescope up towards the sky.

A telescope uses curved glass to bend light so that things seen through it appear bigger than they are. Looking through a telescope on 7 January 1610, Galileo spotted small stars beside Jupiter. Over the next few nights, these stars still looked close to Jupiter but were in different positions. He soon realised that these four small 'stars' were circling round Jupiter – they were Jupiter's moons, and proof that not everything in space circled round the Earth.

Galileo was also the first to see the rings of Saturn (though only dimly; he didn't know what they were) and found that Venus had 'phases' like the waxing and waning of the Moon. That matched something Copernicus had said: in an Earth-centred system, Venus could only show two phases; in a Sun-centred one, it would be like the Moon.

The people in charge at the time didn't like Galileo's ideas: he was arrested and they stopped his book being published – at least in countries they controlled. But despite their best efforts, his ideas quickly spread. For the first time, people who couldn't understand the complex maths started to follow the argument, for one important reason. The telescope was a simple enough device that they could copy the experiments Galileo set out in his book. They could see for themselves.

'My dear chap, I'm a scientist, not a politician.'
The Third Doctor, *Day of the Daleks* (1972)

That's an important principle of science as we understand it today: we should be able to repeat experiments and see the proof for ourselves. Just like the Doctor, scientists don't believe something just because they're told to, even if the person telling them is very clever or important. They insist on seeing evidence.

From that, we get a system for carefully testing new ideas, called the scientific method:

- » First we gather good **evidence**.
- » Using that evidence, we come up with an idea – called a **model** – of what is going on.
- » We use the model to make **predictions**, and see – with more evidence – if we've got it right.
- » We might have to **modify** our model, or throw it out and start again. Or we might just have got it right.
- » We **share** our model with other scientists, who – often in a process called **peer review** – try and find problems with it. Sometimes it takes years to find a problem with a model, which then turns out to be completely wrong.

One *Doctor Who* writer, Douglas Adams, explained it like this: the scientific method 'rests on the premise that any idea is there to be attacked. If it withstands the attack then it lives to fight another day and if it doesn't withstand the attack then down it goes.'

After Galileo's discovery – and people being able to check it for themselves – science became a fashionable hobby. In some countries, there were clubs where you could go for a night out to watch the latest experiments be performed. One such club, the Royal Society, was founded in 1660. A few years later, a debate among its members about the movements of the planets prompted Isaac Newton to write up his own ideas.

Newton was a genius, but he's been described as a sorcerer as much as a scientist. It's thought that it was his interest in magic – and the ability to apply force from a distance – that led him to come up with the theory of gravity. But, in the scientific method, it doesn't matter where his ideas came from, only that they fitted the evidence. And gravity more or less did.

Very simply, Newton worked out that bodies in the universe – for example, planets – are drawn towards each other, and the strength of the attraction is related to both their combined mass and how far they are apart. His explanation was complex, but he supplied a simple mathematical formula that allowed people to test if he was right.

Science was still fashionable a century later when the musician William Herschel caught the bug for astronomy. In 1781, from his garden in Bath, he spotted through his telescope a star that didn't behave like the others. At first, he thought it was a comet, but then realised he'd discovered an entirely new planet – Uranus.

But the movement of Uranus didn't quite match Newton's simple formula. Which meant either Newton was wrong or that *another* large object was out there in space, and the effect of its gravitational pull on Uranus was the reason its orbit was odd. Sure enough, in 1846 another new planet was discovered – Neptune. It's orbit was odd, too, so astronomers searched for *another* planet, even further out in space. Pluto was discovered in 1930 – and was still too small to explain the odd orbit. It was discovered in the 1990s that we had overestimated Neptune's mass; the correct numbers matched the oddness of the orbit.

There were problems with the theory of gravity closer to home, too. Mercury – the closest planet to the Sun – was never quite where Newton's formula said it should be. Then in 1916 Albert Einstein suggested that the Sun was so big it warped space and time, bending it like a lens in a telescope bends light. In 1919, new observations of Mercury showed it exactly where Einstein – not Newton – said it would be, proving Einstein's theory of relativity.

When *Doctor Who* landed on its first alien world in December 1963 (Skaro, home planet of the Daleks), we knew in reality of nine planets, all of them in orbit round our Sun. Pluto was a planet – the Doctor even calls it one when he visits in *The Sun Makers* (1977). But we still didn't know what a planet was. So, what changed?

In November 2003, astronomers spotted what was reported in the press as the tenth planet – Sedna. More discoveries soon followed: Haumea in 2004, Eris and Makemake in 2005. Were these all planets, too? Eris seemed to be larger than Pluto, but if we made the decision based on size then surely Ceres counted, too. Ceres, discovered in 1801, is the largest rock in the asteroid belt between Mars and Jupiter – and had originally been thought to be a planet before more of the asteroid belt was discovered.

So, after much debate, in 2006 the International Astronomical Union passed Resolution 5A, setting out three things that define a planet. A planet:

» Is in orbit round the Sun
» Is big enough that its own gravity makes it (nearly) spherical
» Doesn't share its orbital path with other objects.

The Tenth Planet and Vulcan

Before Einstein came up with relativity, there were other theories about why Mercury didn't move exactly as Newton's formula said it should. As with the odd orbits of Uranus and Neptune, it was suggested that there might be another, as yet undiscovered planet affecting its gravity. But why hadn't we seen this other planet?

One explanation was that this planet was so close to the Sun that it was hidden by its glare . That's why the theoretical planet was named Vulcan after the Roman god of fires and forges (as we learnt in *The Fires of Pompeii* (2008), Vulcan is also where we get the word 'volcano'). Another explanation was that Vulcan was always on the far side of the Sun from us, moving round it at the same speed that we were. The only way that could happen was if it shared our orbit – a twin planet, just like Earth, always hidden from view.

Though Vulcan turned out not to exist, it influenced two *Doctor Who* stories in 1966. In *The Tenth Planet*, Earth's long-lost twin, Mondas, is home to the Cybermen. The very next story, *The Power of the Daleks*, is set on a planet called Vulcan. By coincidence, that same year a new science fiction series began on American television. *Star Trek*'s Mr Spock was also from a planet called Vulcan.

Ceres, Pluto, Haumea, Makemake and Eris were recognised as 'dwarf planets' – though the IAU was clear that that meant they are *not* planets.

At the same time we were losing one planet, we were discovering thousands more.

In 1992, astronomers announced the discovery of two planets round a star called PSR 1257+12. As of February 2015, we've discovered 1,523 planets, while the space observatory named after Kepler has found a further 3,303 that await confirmation by more tests. We found these planets by measuring tiny but regular wobbles in the light from distant stars. Using Kepler and Newton's laws, we can use these wobbles to work out the size of the planets and how far they are from their suns.

That means we also know a little about what some of these planets might be like. There are 'hot Jupiters' – huge planets that orbit very close to their stars. It's thought there could be planets made of carbon – perhaps like the diamond planet in *Midnight* (2008). And there seem to be planets like Earth.

> 'The Doctor won't tolerate anyone deliberately playing havoc with his favourite planet.'
> The Master (about the Sixth Doctor), *The Mark of the Rani* (1985)

As we've learnt about other planets, we've also learnt about our own. We've not (yet) found life anywhere else in the universe, so what makes Earth so special?

The Earth has lots of features that make it good for life. It has had a stable orbit for billions of years, which the Moon – proportionately large compared to other planets' moons – helps regulate. We have a ready supply of energy from the Sun. Our magnetic field protects the planet from high energy particles that can be harmful to life. Earth is rich in carbon – as the Doctor tells Sarah in *The Hand of Fear* (1976), we are carbon-based life forms. The planet is big enough that its gravity keeps hold of its atmosphere, which keeps Earth nicely warm and allows us to breathe.

With all these things going for it, it's no wonder so many alien races (in *Doctor Who*) want to conquer Earth. But there's something else, too.

We know that oxygen *isn't* essential for life as we've found micro-organisms living on Earth that don't need it. But there's one thing all life we know of depends on: liquid water. Oceans make up seventy per cent of the Earth's surface.

For water to be in liquid form, a planet needs to be just the right distance from its sun. Too close and the water evaporates, while too far away and the water freezes. We call the right distance the 'habitable zone'. About one in five of the planets Kepler has found fit this category. Kepler has only looked in a small region of space but, from what it has found, scientists think there might be as many as 40 billion Earth-like planets in just our galaxy. These planets could have liquid water on them, and that means they could have life.

Is there life on these planets? Venus is in the habitable zone around our Sun, but its thick clouds of carbon dioxide make it extremely hot. Could life still exist there anyway? At the moment, we simply don't know. As yet, we haven't found any.

What might alien life be like? In *Doctor Who*, we've met all kinds of strange life forms – fish people, butterfly people, slug people, rock people, gas people, water people, even viruses that can talk and people who exist in only two dimensions. In reality, life on Earth is extremely varied and diverse. Anything seems possible. In fact, the chances are that alien life will turn out to be something we haven't even thought of.

Think about that. Discovering the first alien life would mean we're not alone in the universe. But it could also mean we have to redefine what life actually is.

All we have to do is find it. And that means us getting out into space…

The Solar System according to Doctor Who

- The Sun
- Mercury
- Venus – has metal seas (*Marco Polo* (1964)), flowers (*The Wheel in Space* (1968)), spearmint (*The Shakespeare Code* (2007)) and a creature called a Shanghorn (*The Green Death* (1973)). The Doctor is skilled in Venusian aikido, first seen in *Inferno* (1970).
- Earth – the Doctor's favourite planet.
- Mars – the Doctor visits in *The Waters of Mars* (2009). Indigenous species include the Ice Warriors and the Flood. The Osirans also built at least one pyramid on Mars in the time of the ancient Egyptians (*Pyramids of Mars* (1975)).
- Unnamed 'fifth' planet – the home planet of the alien Fendahl was time-looped by the Time Lords, possibly creating the asteroid belt. The Doctor says it was 107 million miles out (from Earth?) and broke up 12 million years ago (*Image of the Fendahl* (1978)).
- Jupiter – British astronaut Guy Crayford is rescued by the Kraals while trapped in orbit around Jupiter (*The Android Invasion* (1975)). At some point in the future, the 'planet' of gold, Neo Phobos, moves into orbit around Jupiter as one of its moons and is renamed 'Voga' (*Revenge of the Cybermen* (1975)).
- Saturn – the Doctor is infected by a talking virus while on Saturn's moon, Titan (*The Invisible Enemy* (1977). It seems Titan is destroyed at the end of the story.
- Uranus – the only source of the rare mineral taranium, used to build a time destructor (*The Daleks' Master Plan* (1965–1966).
- Neptune

- Pluto – the Doctor calls it a planet when he visits in *The Sun Makers* (1977). One of its inhabitants, Mandrell, doesn't believe there is life on any other planets.
- Mondas – Earth's long-lost twin planet drifted 'to the edge of space' before returning in 1986 – and exploding (*The Tenth Planet* (1966)).
- Planet 14 – used as a base by the Cybermen in *The Invasion* (1968) – it's not stated that Planet 14 is in the Solar System, but since the Cybermen come from the tenth planet (Mondas), it is possible they've colonised other, outer worlds.
- Cassius – according to K-9 in *The Sun Makers*, Pluto was thought to be the 'outermost body' of the Solar System until the discovery of Cassius.

THE LOST GENERATION
GEORGE MANN

It was like this every time they landed recently: the Doctor, whizzing his scarf around his neck and jamming his hat atop his curly mop of hair, would throw caution to the wind, fling open the doors and charge out into the sunlight like an excited child.

It was almost inevitable, really, that he'd sniff out the first sign of trouble, and then mire them both in it. Sarah had come to expect nothing less. This, she realised, was his *modus operandi*, his idea of having fun. She, on the other hand, wasn't quite so convinced.

There was no discussing it, though. Each time she'd tried to raise the issue, suggesting even a preparatory glance at the scanner before hurtling headlong into... *whatever*, he would just nod sagely and say, 'Yes, I see precisely what you mean. Terrible business. You'd better have another jelly baby,' before handing her the paper bag and carrying on as if the conversation was over.

This time had been no exception. He'd bustled them out of the TARDIS in an unnecessary hurry, urged her on into the strange wooded glade, and marched them straight into oncoming danger.

Still, Sarah had to admit – even she hadn't been expecting a rabid, mutant sheep.

Presently, they were crouched behind a bush while the Doctor tried to keep the thing distracted with the trailing end of his scarf. Sarah peered at it through the foliage. It was the strangest sheep she had ever seen – if it could even be *called* a sheep. It was overgrown (at least twice the size of a normal sheep) and clearly carnivorous (she could tell this from the way it had tried to bite her calves as they ran). It had wild, flitting eyes, and elongated canines that protruded over its bottom lip. Its wool coat was wiry and matted with dried blood that Sarah suspected wasn't the sheep's. It snorted in frustration and made another lunge for the Doctor's scarf.

'Remember I told you that, besides Earth, oak trees didn't grow anywhere else in the galaxy?' Tentatively, so as not to attract the attention of the sheep, the Doctor patted the bough of a nearby tree. It was barely broader than his hand, yet still towered far above their heads, its uppermost branches disappearing into a canopy of green.

Sarah, exasperated, nodded in the affirmative. 'Yes. This was just before we were shot at by a gang of homicidal androids, if I remember correctly.'

He seemed to ignore her qualification. 'Well, I was wrong.' He beamed at her encouragingly. 'They grow here, too. Wherever *here* is.' He tugged absentmindedly on his scarf, and the sheep gave a ferocious growl. 'Watch out, I think he's grumpy with us.'

'These are *not* oak trees,' said Sarah. 'Look at them. They're all tall and spindly.'

'Ah, but then, so would you be if you'd spent your formative years in a place like this. It's all about gravity, you see. Don't you feel a little lighter?'

Sarah thought about this for a moment. 'Well, yes, I suppose I do. But what's that got to do wi—' she stopped abruptly at the sight of the sheep, which had followed the Doctor's scarf around to their side of the bush and was now preparing to launch another attack. Ribbons of saliva dripped from its open jaws. It looked positively monstrous. 'Um... Doctor...'

A horn blared suddenly, somewhere in the near vicinity, and the wooden shaft of a spear came whistling through the air and struck the earth a few inches from the Doctor's left boot, burying its tip in the loam. Sarah stifled a scream.

The sheep, terrified by this sudden incursion, dropped the end of the Doctor's scarf, turned about, and fled into the trees.

'Well, that's a bit of a ewe-turn,' said the Doctor, winding in the end of his scarf and looking forlornly at the macerated end. He flicked it resignedly over his shoulder.

By now, Sarah could hear the thunder of approaching footsteps. She parted the bush and peered through. Around thirty men and women dressed in rags and carrying primitive-looking weapons were forming a wide semi-circle around them. They were humanoid, but looked… odd. Like the trees, they were tall and willowy, at least eight feet tall, with thin, gangly limbs. Their skin tones were pale and washed out, like they hadn't seen enough sunlight, and their noses were almost flat upon their faces, little more than wrinkles of flesh protecting tiny vents.

The Doctor stood, coming out from behind the bush with his hand extended. 'How very nice to meet you. I'm the Doctor. This is Sarah. We're new around these parts.' He grinned, flashing his teeth.

The tribes people glared at him, still brandishing their motley assortment of weapons.

'No?' said the Doctor. He shrugged and lowered his proffered hand. 'I should work a little on your hospitality, if I were you. All those spears, you'll scare off the tourists.'

A tribesman in a bright headdress stepped forward, jabbing his weapon in the Doctor's direction. Sarah, who had now come around the bush to join the Doctor, could see that it resembled a garden spade.

'Oh, now that's very interesting,' said the Doctor. 'Very interesting indeed. A spade, a hoe, a laser cutter… What fascinating weapons you all have, Mr…?'

'Euripides,' said the man. His voice was guttural and deep, and, although the accent was thick and unfamiliar, he spoke clearly in a form they could understand. 'I am Euripides, and you, Doctor and Sarah, are our prisoners.'

'Oh, why aren't I surprised?' muttered Sarah. 'It would be nice if, just once, we were greeted by people who wanted to give us tea.'

The Doctor laughed. 'Let me guess, Euripides. You're going to take us to your leader. Good.'

Euripides jabbed his spade at them. 'You will come with us to the Temple of Life,' he said.

'Oh, if you insist,' said the Doctor, tipping the brim of his hat. 'Lead on, lead on!'

The Doctor and Sarah were led at spear point through the flora, following trails that felt more like the claustrophobic tunnels of a military bunker than any natural environment. They walked in single file, with little conversation, and although they must have trudged through the undergrowth for over a mile, the going wasn't too tiresome, given the reduced gravity.

After being poked, prodded and ignored by their captors, Sarah was close to boiling point by the time they reached the place Euripides called the 'Temple of Life'.

It was, in fact, a large clearing in the heart of the forest, a nexus point for the paths through the trees. Here, the tribe had erected makeshift shelters from sheets of corrugated plastic and tempered steel. Sarah was surprised to see winking diodes and other signs of electrical power nestled amongst the foliage. Children gambolled around them, playing games of chase, and men were distributing food amongst themselves on tarnished metal dishes. Clearly, these tribes people weren't as primitive as she'd first imagined.

'In here,' said Euripides, gesturing to one of the huts. 'You shall face the judgement of the Elders.'

'How delightful,' said the Doctor. 'I do enjoy a good chinwag with an enlightened one,' he added, quietly.

'You're incorrigible,' said Sarah, unable to contain a laugh. She followed him into the hut, closely followed by Euripides, still wielding his spade.

Inside, two figures sat cross-legged on wooden plinths, at either side of another open doorway. One, on the left, was male. The other, on the right, was female. Both had their eyes closed, in meditative trance. They were similar in appearance to the rest of the tribes people, save for the fact they weren't carrying weapons.

Euripides gestured to a woven mat in the centre of the floor, and, with some reluctance, Sarah lowered herself onto it beside the Doctor.

'I am the left-tenant,' said the man, after a moment.

'And I am the right-tenant,' said the woman.

'You come before us as strangers,' went on the left-tenant, 'but I see you are not of the other tribe.'

'I'm Sarah Jane Smith, from Earth,' said Sarah.

'And I'm the Doctor.' He raised his hat in genial fashion, and then replaced it. 'I suppose you could say I'm a citizen of the galaxy.'

The right-tenant arched an eyebrow. 'You trespass within our borders. Were you sent by the pilot?'

'The pilot?' said the Doctor, his tone thoughtful. 'No, no. Not the pilot. We've only just arrived, you see.'

'Then you have come to plunder the crucible,' said the left-tenant, his voice growing in ire.

'No!' said Sarah. 'It's not like that at all. We're explorers. We're here to help.'

'To help?' said the right-tenant. She looked from Sarah to the Doctor. 'Then you come to protect us from the other tribe?'

'Yes, if you like,' said the Doctor. 'Tell us about them.'

'They hunger for the crucible,' said the left-tenant. 'Once, we were many, and our borders ranged for quadrants. Food was bountiful, and the wild beasts did not trouble us. Now, we have been forced to withdraw to protect the crucible. The other tribe grows strong, while we grow weak. Our people are diminished. The sheep and rats hunt us for food. The Temple of Life is our last remaining stronghold.'

'What do they hope to achieve, this other tribe, by capturing the crucible?' said the Doctor.

There was a collective intake of breath from the two Elders. They glanced at one another. 'They are heathens,' said the right-tenant. 'Unschooled in the Manual.'

'As surely as the pilot guides our way,' agreed the left-tenant.

'We told you, we've only just arrived,' said Sarah. She could hear the impatience in her own voice.

'The crucible is the source of all life,' said the left-tenant. 'The origin of the Uman species.'

'The well-spring from which we all flow,' added the right-tenant. 'When we reach Fall, the avatars will live anew.'

'And this other tribe want the glory for themselves,' said the Doctor. 'They want to be there when the avatars awaken. Oh, I've heard it all before. Usual story. And here I was hoping for something new.'

Sarah heard footsteps entering the hut behind her. She looked round. One of the tribes people was silhouetted in the doorway, but she could tell from the ragged breath and a glimpse of his troubled expression that something was wrong. 'They're here!' he said. 'They've come for the cruc—'

He broke off abruptly as the tip of a spear buried itself in his back, and he toppled forward, gasping for breath. Outside, Sarah could hear shouting. 'Doctor?' she said, panic rising.

The Doctor was already on his feet. He grabbed her hand and pulled her up beside him. 'In there,' he said, nodding toward the other doorway.

'You cannot enter the crucible,' said Euripides, raising his spade to block their path. 'No one but the Elders are permitted.'

Sarah watched as the two figures relinquished their positions on the pedestals and walked – with some dignity – into the adjoining chamber.

The Doctor, of course, was having none of it. He grabbed at the spade, wrenching it from Euripides' grasp and tossing it angrily to the floor. 'I told you we'd help, didn't I?'

Euripides hesitated and, with a quick 'Come on,' the Doctor led Sarah into the crucible.

It was not what she'd been expecting. Hearing the Elders go on about the place, Sarah had envisioned a grand temple, an ornate religious structure, but in the event the room was relatively small and underwhelming.

The floor was formed from a series of interlocking metal grids, while the walls and ceiling were bland metal plating, now tarnished and worn. Around the room were arranged a dozen lozenge-shaped pods, standing upright against the walls, each of them protected by a shattered glass dome. There were no plants in the room, save for the questing vines spilling from the front of the broken pods.

'It reminds me of Space Station Nerva,' said Sarah.

'Stasis pods,' said the Doctor as he circled the room, taking it in. 'They've all failed.'

'Then the people in them...' began Sarah. But it was quite clear. The people inside the pods had long ago decomposed, and now they were reduced to nothing but compost, giving sustenance to the plants.

'We must protect the crucible at all costs,' said the left-tenant. Sarah had almost forgotten he was there.

'Oh, I think we're long past that,' said the Doctor. He was pacing back and forth, a crooked finger held to his chin, looking thoughtful. 'The crucible... the pilot... the Fall...Yes, of course!' he exclaimed, evidently pleased with himself.

'They're colonists from Earth,' said Sarah. 'They've just forgotten they came here by spaceship.'

'What?' said the Doctor, in astonishment. 'No, of course not. We're still on the spaceship.'

'But...we *can't* be!' said Sarah. 'Wooded glades, oak trees, tribes of indigenous people...'

'Ah!' said the Doctor.

'Now what?'

'So you admit they're oak trees?'

Sarah harrumphed.

'Think about it, Sarah,' said the Doctor. 'Trails through the woods that seem like corridors. Blinking diodes in the walls. Farm animals that have evolved into killers. Stasis chambers that have given up the ghost. Then there's the devolution of language – "left-tenants", the "Uman" race.' The Doctor glanced at the Elders, who were regarding him placidly. 'These people have been on this ship for a very long time. Or rather, their forefathers have. Long enough for their physiology to adapt. It's a generation ark ship, heading out to the stars. You see? The technology is the same as on the Ark.'

'But what about the plants?' said Sarah.

'Brought on board to generate oxygen,' said the Doctor. 'At some point they must have spread from their biodomes, slowly taking over. Behind all of that forest is a gleaming spaceship interior.'

'And the people?' said Sarah.

'What remains of the colonists,' said the Doctor. 'And the original crew.' He glanced at the failed stasis pods to underline his point.

'Those are dangerous truths, Doctor,' said a woman's voice from the doorway. It was crisp and clear, and somewhat bizarrely, had an East European accent.

Sarah saw the Elders freeze. She turned to watch the Doctor approaching the doorway, just as a gleaming figure emerged into the dim light. It was humanoid, but made no pretence at replicating human form. It was smaller than the tribes people, about the height and build of Sarah herself, and appeared to be made from the same base metal as the walls. It was sexless, with a moulded human face, eyes that shone a brilliant, electric blue, and an open slit where its mouth should have been. It was carrying a gun in both hands.

'The pilot, I presume?' said the Doctor.

'In a manner of speaking,' said the woman's voice. 'I'm operating this drone, along with a handful of others, which are currently pacifying the colonists.'

'How very timely,' said the Doctor. 'May I assume that we are cordially invited to the bridge?'

'Too right,' said the woman. 'You're going to explain exactly how you came to be walking about my ship.' The drone hefted its gun, and indicated for them to follow.

'Tally-ho!' said the Doctor.

The bridge, the pilot explained as they walked, was on an upper deck, accessible via a lift shaft that bisected the vessel through its midsection.

The Doctor walked ahead of her, deep in conversation with the drone that had found them in the crucible – or rather, with the female pilot controlling it. Sarah couldn't make out much of what was being said, but she gathered the Doctor was explaining about the TARDIS and how he and Sarah came to be on the vessel in the first place, while no doubt doing his best to charm any relevant information from her.

After a while the forest began to thin, and the canopy gave way to brightly lit corridors, of a kind so familiar to Sarah. They were functional and clean, with luminous panels, sliding metal doors and ancient, dusty computer terminals installed at regular intervals. The place felt deserted, as if it hadn't seen life in decades. The drone guided them along, until, after what seemed like hours, they finally arrived at the lift shaft.

'After you,' said the Doctor, waving her through the portal and into the small metal box that would transport them up to the bridge. She noted the drone wasn't joining them, instead retreating to an alcove in the opposite wall, watching them with its eerie, expressionless face.

'Are you sure you know what you're doing?' said Sarah.

'*Sarah*,' said the Doctor, with mock chiding. 'Don't I always?'

'Now I know we're in trouble,' she muttered.

The lift shot up like a bullet in the barrel of a gun, almost knocking the Doctor sideways and forcing him to grab Sarah's arm for support. He grinned that ridiculous grin.

Moments later, the doors opened onto a small antechamber, devoid of any furniture or other signs of life. Stencilled on the wall, in bright red, foot-high letters, was the word 'PROSPERITY'.

'Of course,' said the Doctor. 'Now everything makes sense.'

'Care to enlighten me?' prompted Sarah.

'All in good time,' he said. He waved quiet any further protest as he crossed the room, heading for the hatchway that, she presumed, led through to the bridge.

The pilot must have been aware of them, as Sarah heard her voice, booming out from the console. 'Come in. And please accept my apologies. The place must be a state.'

Sarah ducked her head and stepped through the hatchway onto the bridge.

The first thing that hit her was the thick, cloying odour of decay. The second was the sight of the corpse in the pilot's chair. It was partially skeletal, but dry, leathery flesh still clung to the bones, encasing much of the chest and skull. The eyes had dried and shrivelled away, and the lips had curled back, exposing a gap-toothed smile. Wires erupted from the back of the skull, snaking away into a hatch in the ground. Sarah could see fluids bubbling in them.

'Oh… goodness…' she said, trying not to balk at the sight.

'Please don't be alarmed,' said the voice from the console. 'I may look half-decomposed, but I'm still in there. The machines are keeping me alive. They won't allow me to die until my mission is complete.' She paused. 'The name's Ana, by the way.'

'How long…?' started Sarah, but found she couldn't finish the question.

'Three and a half thousand years,' said Ana, 'give or take a few.' She laughed. 'It's been a long shift.'

'Does it hurt?'

The laughter stopped abruptly. 'That doesn't matter,' said Ana. 'I have a job to do. I promised I'd get *Prosperity* to landfall, and that's precisely what I'll do.'

'*Prosperity*,' said the Doctor. 'The first of the great Ark ships to leave the Earth. You were declared lost after only three hundred years, a triumphant failure. The transmissions stopped. People mourned for you.'

'We were never lost,' said Ana. 'Our mission continues to this day. Things might have gone a little awry…'

'A devolved population who've forgotten the purpose of their mission, and live out their days according to complex superstitions derived from it. A crew that's been dead for centuries. Farm animals grown into monstrous predators.' The Doctor sighed. 'Awry might be something of an understatement.'

'But they're still *people*,' said Ana, 'and they deserve to be saved. There's a colony waiting for them. The first of its kind.'

'Things have changed, Ana, while you've been navigating a path through the stars,' said the Doctor. 'Relatively speaking, millennia have passed on Earth. The human race has developed faster-than-light technology. They've populated the stars, forged immense empires, and encountered other sentient species. People pass unhindered between populated worlds. It's really quite wonderful.'

'Then it's all been for nothing,' said Ana. 'The mission has failed.'

'*Oh no*,' said the Doctor. 'Where would the universe be without pioneers to blaze a trail? Your mission inspired thousands of people to build more and better. It's because of you that they succeeded. Don't you see? It was a marvellous success.'

'And yet those people down there in the lower levels – I've failed them,' said Ana. 'Their antecedents gave their lives to the stars. I owe it to them all to continue.'

The Doctor crossed to the console. His fingers danced over the controls. 'I could end it, Ana, if you asked me to,' he said. 'I could override the engines, boost them to unimaginable speeds. You'd reach landfall in a day or two. You could complete your mission, give those people a new world, where they can prosper.' He turned to look at her. 'But you know what that would mean.'

There was a moment's pause. 'Yes, Doctor.'

'What?' said Sarah. 'What is it?'

The Doctor turned to her. 'I'm sorry, Sarah. There'd be no going back. The engines will be destroyed in the process.'

'And she'll *die*,' said Sarah. 'That's the choice you're giving her.'

The Doctor nodded. 'That's the choice I'm giving her.'

'But there has to be a way!'

'Will they be all right?' asked Ana gently. 'I mean, the planet you've chosen. Will they prosper there?'

The Doctor turned his head away from her, closing his eyes – as if in sorrow, thought Sarah. No, as if he was listening to something, tuning in to infinity…

Then he opened his eyes. 'I don't know,' he said at last. 'I hope so.'

'Well then,' said Ana. 'A leap into the dark. But that's all this ever was anyway…'

From the safety of the TARDIS, they watched *Prosperity* breach the atmosphere of the unnamed planet, lighting up like a silent firework with the heat of entry. Sarah studied the scanner until it was gone. She felt maudlin.

'She was a brave woman,' said the Doctor. 'She gave her life for those people, in more ways than one.'

'But it could all be for nothing.'

The Doctor didn't say anything. Then he gave her a broad, impish grin. 'Let's say we nip forward a few thousand years to find out.' His hands moved swiftly over the TARDIS console and the engines gave a desperate, wracking wheeze. He pressed a button and the doors burred open. 'Come along, Sarah. Chop, chop. No time to lose.' He was out the door before she'd had chance to protest.

Sarah expelled a long, heartfelt sigh. '*Doctor…*'

TWO

SPACE TRAVEL

'There are worlds out there where the sky is burning, where the sea's asleep, and the rivers dream. People made of smoke and cities made of song. Somewhere there's danger, somewhere there's injustice – and somewhere else the tea's getting cold. Come on, Ace, we've got work to do!'

The Seventh Doctor, *Survival* (1989)

On 21 June 1969, in Episode Ten of *The War Games*, the Time Lords found the Second Doctor guilty of interfering in the affairs of other people. As punishment, the Doctor was exiled to Earth, without the use of his TARDIS, just as the planet faced a series of new perils. He was furious at the idea. Like us, he'd be trapped on a single world.

Except that a month later, on 20 July, a small box touched down on the Moon.

'That's one small step for [a] man,' said Neil Armstrong as he ventured out of it, 'one giant leap for mankind.' An estimated 600 million people back on Earth watched this first human footstep on another world as it was broadcast live – thanks to new communications satellites, one of many technologies advanced by the race to the Moon.

According to the *Doctor Who* story *Day of the Moon* (2011), the clip of Armstrong's first moonwalk will become the most watched piece of footage in human history.

'The human race will spread out among the stars. You just watch them fly. Billions and billions of them, for billions and billions of years, and every single one of them at some point in their lives, will look back at this man, taking that very first step, and they will never, ever forget it.'

The Eleventh Doctor, *Day of the Moon* (2011)

But that giant leap didn't last long: just three and a half years later, on 14 December 1972, another small box blasted off from the Moon's surface carrying astronauts Harrison Schmitt and Eugene Cernan back towards the Earth. No one has been back to the Moon since. (Sixteen days later on 30 December, BBC One broadcast Episode One of *The Three Doctors* – the story that ended the Doctor's exile. By strange coincidence, he was trapped on a single world for almost exactly the period we weren't.)

At the time of writing, we are only in the early stages of plans to send people out beyond Earth orbit again – but that won't happen until the 2020s, some fifty years after we last stood on the Moon. Why did we stop going into outer space?

First, getting into space is expensive. The Apollo programme that first got man to the Moon cost $24 billion at the time – or $395 billion if we were to undertake the same project today. There are plenty of other worthy causes that need that kind of money. On the day of the Moon landing, protesters outside Mission Control on Earth demanded that the money spent on space exploration should be used to help the poor.

Of course, that first Moon landing had to invent all the technology that got us to the Moon in the first place but, even with modern technology, space travel is still not cheap. To escape the strong pull of Earth's gravity, you need a lot of thrust and that takes a lot of fuel. The more you send up into space, the more fuel you need to get it there, so the amount of stuff – or people – you can take up is very strictly limited. One NASA estimate is that it costs about £14,000 for every kilogram sent into space. Virgin Galactic offers members of the public the chance to fly, for a few minutes, more than 100 kilometres above the Earth – the official definition of the height at which space begins. Tickets are on sale for $250,000 each.

Besides the cost, space is dangerous. *The Ambassadors of Death* (1970) saw the Doctor on the trail of a missing space capsule. Between the broadcast of its fourth and fifth episodes, events on screen were mirrored in real life as an oxygen tank ruptured on Apollo 13 on its journey to the Moon. With limited power, loss of heat and little water, the crew just got back to Earth – but missed their chance to walk on the Moon. In fact, two days before Neil Armstrong took his first steps on the lunar surface, US President Nixon pre-recorded a TV address, in case something went wrong and the astronauts were stranded on the Moon, where they would have died. Luckily, the message wasn't needed and Armstrong and his crew got home safely.

Others were not so lucky. The following year, the three-man crew of Soyuz 11 were found dead when their capsule arrived back on Earth, due to a mechanical error. The space shuttle Challenger exploded in 1986, as did Columbia in 2003 – in each case killing the whole crew. Just training to get into space could be dangerous: a sudden fire in 1967 killed the crew of Apollo 1 as they practised their launch sequence, their space capsule still on the launch pad. The following year, Yuri Gagarin – who, in 1961, became the first man to go into space – was killed in a plane crash while training for a space mission. People working on space rockets have been killed in explosions, as have people living nearby when rockets have gone off course.

Astronauts go into space well aware of the risks. In fact, in 2004 (after the Columbia accident) NASA thought it was too dangerous to send astronauts on a repair mission to the Hubble Space Telescope – but the astronauts lobbied to be allowed to go, and NASA ultimately let them. In 2014, one of Virgin Galactic's spacecraft crashed during a test flight, killing one pilot and injuring another – but the company vowed to learn any lessons and continue with its programme to get members of the public into space.

Once you are up there, space presents lots of problems for the human body. Being weightless weakens your bones and tissues because they don't need to work as hard in the low gravity. The circulation of your blood and lymphatic fluid can also be affected. Gravity helps food pass through our bodies, so digestion is more difficult in space. Weightlessness causes problems when you go to the toilet or if anyone is sick – astronauts have had to deal with stinking matter floating round their spacecraft.

It's a three-day trip to the Moon, so with a day on the Moon's surface you need a week's food for each astronaut – all of it packed into your spacecraft when you launch (because you can't just nip out to the shops if you run out of anything). You also need oxygen, spacesuits, washing things, changes of clothes... To get to Mars takes at least 150 days. Think of all the food and equipment you'd need to take, even for a small crew – and Mars is the second closest planet to us.

There's more. Astronaut James Irwin was the eighth person to walk on the Moon. While there he suffered something like a heart attack. The stress of the mission might have worsened a pre-existing condition, but other astronauts have shown disturbances in the rhythm of their heartbeats while in space. They also suffer sickness from decompression, the effects of pressure in the body's tissues, weakened immune systems, and there are effects on sleep, balance and eyesight, to name but a few. Astronauts might be exposed to dangerous radiation in space – or even from the ultrasound imaging tools they use on their spacecraft.

There are psychological effects, too. It's not only the stress of going into space and facing those dangers. Returning to Earth, some astronauts have struggled to fit back into everyday life – it just seems boring after you've been in space.

'You took me to the furthest reaches of the galaxy, you showed me supernovas, intergalactic battles, and then you just dropped me back on Earth. How could anything compare to that?'
Sarah Jane Smith, to the Tenth Doctor, *School Reunion* (2006)

If it's extremely expensive and very dangerous, is it worthwhile going into space? What do we get in return? The answer to that question says a lot about our relationship with space since we first walked on the Moon.

We learnt a lot by going to the Moon. For example, Neil Armstrong and Buzz Aldrin set up a series of mirrors on the lunar surface. Scientists on Earth then fired a laser – a very accurate beam of light – at these mirrors, and measured the precise time it took for the laser to bounce back to them: it took 2.4 seconds. A laser beam moves at the speed of light (299,972,458 metres per second). Halve the time it takes to get to the Moon and back, and multiply that time by 299,972,458 and you have a very accurate measurement of the distance from the Earth to the Moon: 359,966,949.6 metres. Repeating the experiment over many years, we now know the Moon is getting further away from us, by about 3 cm every year (the opposite of what happens in the year 2049, during *Kill the Moon!*).

Other lunar experiments included studies of moonquakes, the composition of solar wind and the lunar atmosphere, the strength of the Moon's magnetic field, heat flow from and electrical currents through the lunar crust, the properties of the regolith (the loose dust and rock covering the Moon's surface), variations in surface gravity and levels of cosmic rays. Some 385 kg of moonrock was returned to Earth for further tests. All this study has given us new ideas about the formation of the Moon – and Earth – and the history of the Solar System.

But we didn't just go to the Moon for the science. Only one of the twelve people to walk on the Moon was actually a scientist (Harrison Schmitt, the second-last person there, was a geologist). The race to the Moon between the USA and the then USSR was as much about politics as science – and once one side had won that race, it was much harder for any country to justify the expense. Ten more flights had been planned to the Moon after Apollo 11; only six were launched (one, Apollo 13, didn't get there).

Yet the effort of going to the Moon benefited us closer to home. The technology invented to get there led to improvements in everything from computers to non-stick saucepans. As we saw, communications satellites allowed those 600 million people around the world to watch the Moon landing live on TV. Satellite pictures improved weather forecasts, and assessments of erosion and irrigation. We now have maps on our mobile phones that use live connections to satellites to tell us exactly where we are. (Our new reliance on satellite navigation systems was used against us in *The Sontaran Stratagem / The Poison Sky* (2008)). For the time being, we can justify the cost and risks of going into orbit to launch and service satellites, and even have an international space station circling the Earth. We just don't go any further.

That may change – as we can see in *Doctor Who*. In *Colony in Space* (1971), Jo Grant is told why humans have settled on the bleak planet Uxarieus in the year 2471. On Earth, there is apparently, 'No room to move, polluted air, not a blade of grass left on the planet and a government that locks you up if you think for yourself.' (We'll return to Jo and her feelings about space travel in Chapter 5.)

If it's currently difficult to justify sending people further than a near-Earth orbit, computers and robots don't need the same volumes of food and water, and don't have the same risks of disease or injury. An unmanned rocket or craft still costs a lot, but nowhere near as much as sending people. And something going wrong isn't quite so disastrous as when there's a loss of life.

We've sent robots and probes to all the planets in our Solar System. The failure of Beagle 2 to land on Mars on Christmas Day 2003 inspired the loss of Guinevere One at the start of the *Doctor Who* story *The Christmas Invasion* (2005). Gadget, the friendly robot in *The Waters of Mars* seems influenced by exploration rover Opportunity, which landed on Mars in 2003 and is still sending us back data from the Martian surface. (Opportunity has since been joined by another rover, Curiosity, and both are now searching for evidence of life on Mars. So far they've not found any, meaning the known population of Mars consists entirely of robots.)

Even the look of outer space in *Doctor Who* – all brightly coloured nebulae and star systems – is the result of unmanned technology we've sent into space. The Hubble telescope's view of outer space isn't distorted by Earth's atmosphere, so it's captured the brightest, most detailed images ever seen using visible light (rather than ultraviolet or other spectra).

These probes and spacecraft have taught us lots about other planets, space and even the origins of the universe. As we'll see in Chapter 5, they've taught us a lot about our own planet, too. They've even shown that *Doctor Who* gets its science right – if entirely by accident. In *Planet of the Daleks* (1973), the Doctor stops an army of Daleks by detonating a kind of volcano. On this particular planet, volcanoes don't burst with hot lava but with molten ice.

In 1973, that was a fun idea dreamt up by writer Terry Nation. But on 25 August 1989, space probe Voyager 2 flew by Triton, largest moon of Neptune, and spotted real ice-canos. It's now thought there is cryovolcanic activity – the scientific name for ice-canos – on several other moons in the Solar System.

Triton was Voyager 2's last meeting with one of the planets – and their moons – orbiting our Sun. Launched on 20 August 1977, it sent us back data from Jupiter, Saturn, Uranus and Neptune before venturing on to study the edge of the Solar System – there's some debate among scientists about whether it's got there yet. That gives us some idea of the vast size of the Solar System: Voyager 2 is moving at 15.5 kilometres per second – 55,800 kilometres or 33,673 miles per hour. Even so, it took it 12 years to reach Neptune and it's only just escaping the furthest reach of our Sun's gravity after 38 years. (That's more than seven whole lifetimes for the Doctor – when Voyager 2 was launched, the Fourth Doctor was about to face the *Horror of Fang Rock*).

Voyager 2 – and its sister craft, Voyager 1 – are journeying out of the Solar System with a message to the stars. Each carries a record of sounds and images from Earth. It's a sign of how long ago these craft were built that the sounds and images are contained on phonograph records – what we now think of as old technology. These records are a greeting to any alien life that the Voyager craft might encounter, the sounds and images chosen to represent the diversity of Earth, with greetings in 55 languages. The idea was that part of us – part of everyone – would travel with these spacecraft out into deep space.

It's a nice idea, but Voyager 2's 38-year journey to the edge of the Solar System is almost nothing compared to the distance to the nearest star to our Sun. Proxima Centauri is 4.2 light years away – that is, it would take 4.2 years to get there travelling at the speed of light, 299,792,458 metres per second (or 1,079,253,000 kilometres or 670,616,600 miles per hour). Voyager 2 isn't going anything like that fast: even at 15.5 kilometres per second, it would take 81,236 years for it to reach Proxima – and that's our nearest neighbour!

Space is enormous. It's hard for us to get our heads round just how vast it is. So how can we possibly get out there to explore it?

One solution might be spaceships that can travel close to or faster than the speed of light. There are several examples of craft that can apparently do this in *Doctor Who*, but it still comes at a cost. A ship would take hundreds of years of Earth time to cross hundreds of light years, though due to relativistic time dilation (which we'll talk about more in Chapter 6), people on board would experience only a few weeks or years of travel time. However, if they returned to Earth they would discover that hundreds of years – even millennia – had passed, and everyone they'd left behind at home would be long dead.

Alternatively, people might journey to other stars in ships that take thousands of years – just like in the story that preceded this chapter. Astronauts setting off from Earth would never see their final destination, and neither would generation after generation of their descendants. Civilisations might rise and fall on those spacecraft – as they do in the *Doctor Who* story *The Ark* (1966). Over 80,000 years, it's possible that gradual evolution would mean that by the time people arrived at Proxima Centauri, they'd be a different species from the people back on Earth. (For more on evolution, see Chapter 11.) Or perhaps they'd arrive to find people already there – supposing that new, faster spacecraft had been invented on Earth in the millennia since they left. In fact, it's possible they'd arrive at Proxima Centauri to find the *ruins* of a civilisation that left Earth long after they did.

There are still two ways we can reach the stars. First, we can use ever better telescopes and technology to explore space in greater detail – we stay on Earth but let information about the distant universe come to us in the form of light and other kinds of radiation. As we saw in Chapter 1, in just the last twenty years we've discovered thousands of planets orbiting other suns. We might yet find life on one of these worlds, even if we can't physically get there. And it's just possible that that alien life will already know all about us because of the other way we can reach the stars.

In 1888, Heinrich Hertz sent a pulse of electromagnetic radiation to a receiver: the first undisputed man-made radio signal. Radio waves travel at the speed of light. In about a second, a radio transmission spans the gap between the Earth and the Moon. In less than five minutes it passes the orbital path of the planet Mars. As we know, in 4.2 years it reaches Proxima Centauri – the nearest star to the Sun. In less than ten years, it passes Sirius – the bright Dog Star binary system, which the Doctor points out to Captain Avery in *The Curse of the Black Spot* (2011).

Our broadcast radio signals are not particularly powerful by cosmic standards and their strength decreases still further as they pass through Earth's atmosphere and then spread out across the vastness of space. But over the past century, the sheer number of radio signals that we produce has increased enormously as we've invented things like radar systems and television. For around a hundred years, a bubble of radio noise has been expanding around our Solar System, spreading out across space at the speed of light.

On 23 November 1963, the first episode of *Doctor Who* was broadcast from transmitters in the UK. The signals would have reached into space. It's possible they kept going, and in early 1968 – 4.2 years later

The Need for Speed

Doctor Who has suggested lots of ways to cut down travel times in space – though they don't always conform to the laws of physics as we currently understand them.

Sleep through it – *The Ark* (1966)

The Earth's population is miniaturised and stored in trays, 1 million people to a cabinet, to be returned to normal size on arrival hundreds of years later. It's not said on screen, but presumably they're unconscious for that time.

Skip it – *Frontier in Space* (1973)

Earth ships 'jump' into hyperspace as a shortcut and almost collide with the TARDIS – suggesting it travels through hyperspace, too. Yet in *The Stones of Blood* (1978), the Doctor says hyperspace is a 'theoretical absurdity' (though a theory can be both absurd and true). He also calls it a different dimension – another *kind* of space.

Bend it – *Nightmare of Eden* (1979)

The interstellar cruise liner Empress and other ships can 'warp' across long distances, presumably bending space to make the journey quicker. In *Planet of the Spiders* (1974), a starship travels by 'time jump' which suggests space is being warped, too.

Surf it – *Boom Town* (2005)

A tribophysical waveform macro-kinetic extrapolator allows the user to 'surf' across space and time.

Go faster – *The Waters of Mars* (2009)

The Doctor says Susie Fontana-Brooke will pilot the first lightspeed ship to Proxima Centauri in about 2089.

Make a hole

Quantum tunnels in *School Reunion* (2006) are used to join distant bits of space. Matter transmission (or 'transmat') technology can also move people quickly – though in *Doctor Who* it's usually for relatively small distances such as the Travel-Mat or T-Mat system from the Earth to the Moon (*The Seeds of Death* (1969)). The Time Lords have 'open-ended' transmats (*The Five Doctors* (1983)), but we don't know what range that might mean.

Go backwards

With time travel, you can arrive on a far distant planet before you set off – but it gets complicated (as we'll see in Chapters 6 to 10).

— they passed Proxima Centauri. As *Doctor Who* celebrated its tenth anniversary on Earth, that first episode had reached Sirius. As the Ninth Doctor made his debut in *Rose* (2005), the first episode reached the stars Rho Cancri (which we know to have four planets) and HR3259 (which we know to have three planets). As *The Day of the Doctor* was broadcast on 23 November 2013, the show's first episode had covered 473,026,420,000,000 kilometres or 293,924,990,500,000 miles.

There are at least 2,000 stars within fifty light years of Earth and the majority of them almost certainly have planets. If alien creatures live on any of them, they could – just could – be watching *Doctor Who*. We might be stuck – for the moment – on a single world, but not the Doctor. He might be a fictional character, but he really is travelling on our behalf, far out into space.

The vast scale of outer space is boggling. But at the very small scale, space is even weirder…

THE ROOM WITH ALL THE DOORS

JAMES GOSS

'Oh, I wouldn't open that door,' said the man.

Carefully not showing my surprise, I reached instead for the door on the right. He tutted.

'And not that one either.'

My hand froze on the plain white handle. I turned to the little man who'd come from nowhere. He really was remarkably odd, with his mop of untidy black hair and crumpled suit. A cloud of anxiety hovered around him, as though he'd borrowed someone else's clothes and now found himself expected to make their decisions. It probably wasn't helping that I was shouting at him.

'But there are no other doors!'

His drooping face managed to be both supercilious and nervous. 'Ah, well, are you quite sure?'

Ludicrous! We were in a large white room. It had two doors at the end and that was it. No windows. No furniture. Just a huge whiteness that gave nothing away.

Yet, somehow, at the far end, was now a third door.

I marched towards it, but the man scurried in front of me with a funny little run.

'Please don't,' he begged. 'It may no longer be safe.'

'Safe? What do you mean?' I growled.

'It could be dangerous. It may not have been a moment ago. But now you've observed it, its behaviour may have changed. Perhaps one of the other two may be safe to open now. What about the one on the left?'

With skipping strides he rushed up to the door I'd originally chosen. Screwing his eyes shut he twisted the handle, throwing it open with a flourish. His face split with delight. 'Aha! I was right – look, another room!' He danced through, the door slamming closed behind him.

For a moment, I was alone again in that vast white room. Then the door opened just a crack. 'I forgot all about you, I'm afraid,' the man murmured dolorously. 'Come on in. The water's lovely. Only there is, sadly, no water.'

I stood in another large white room, the little man dancing at my side.

'Who are you?' I demanded.

'Me?' the man blinked with sad surprise. 'I'm the Doctor. At least I think I am. But that may not count here.'

'Where is here?' I was suspicious.

He threw his arms up. 'This? This is The Multivarium. And, anticipating your next question, no one quite knows what one of those is. A lesson. Or a prison.'

'Are you my jailer?'

'Are *you* my jailer?' the Doctor snapped back, with cunning but no malice. He rubbed his hands together with the most ill-placed glee. 'Oh, don't answer. I can tell you don't know. Doesn't matter. We stand on a precipice of uncertainty.'

'Huh?'

'Didn't I just tell you? The Multivarium was created at an intersection between parallel universes. Literally anything is possible here… anything and nothing. If you see what I mean.'

'Frankly, no I don't.' I wasn't sure I liked or trusted this Doctor. He seemed to just expect people to put up with him.

He edged nervously towards a wall. 'I swear there was a door here earlier. Ah well, there'll be another one along in a minute. Or a year. Or at some point. Eventually. Probability, you see.'

He settled down cross-legged on the floor and breathed horridly into a musical instrument.

A long time passed. Or no time at all.

A door was there. It didn't flicker into existence. It simply stopped not being there. The Doctor seized the handle excitedly.

'Is it safe?' I asked.

'Only one way to find out.' He stepped through. 'I've got a good feeling about this one.' He vanished with a wail.

There was a long, tense silence. And then a tiny cough.

I leaned over the lintel. Tumbling down into a vast white nothing was the Doctor's recorder. He was dangling over the abyss, clinging on to the door frame. 'It, ah, seems I was wrong.' He dangled there. I said nothing.

'I say,' the Doctor called. 'Can you help me up?'

The room had somehow stretched while we'd not been looking.

'Almost a corridor now,' remarked the Doctor. 'How many doors would you say there were? No, it's all right, don't bother to count. I think the number is close to infinity.'

'Don't be absurd. It's a hundred. Maybe two.'

'You think so, eh? I've always thought the human mind had trouble with anything above seven, but there we go. Two hundred doors. Maybe.' He rubbed his hands together happily. 'Which one shall we choose?'

'We don't have to choose any of them.'

'Aha! You've hit upon the heart of the Multivarium.' The Doctor settled himself down on the floor, stretching his legs out. 'All right then. Let's choose nothing.'

He lay down, and contemplated the ceiling.

🜨

'Could you stop that?' I asked exasperated.

'Stop what?'

'The humming.'

'Oh, I am sorry!' The Doctor sat up. 'Just slipped into it. How much time do you think has passed?'

'I don't know,' I snapped.

'Neither do I.' The Doctor frowned. He sucked a finger and held it up to the air. 'No air flow. What a pity. Would have been rather helpful.' He stood and dusted himself theatrically down. There was no dust here. 'Maybe we should choose a door. Might break things up a little…' He threw himself at a door handle before I could stop him. He pushed it down, letting it linger there a moment. 'After all, what's the harm?'

He opened the door. Huge flames poured out.

The Doctor slammed the door shut.

'I knew that was going to happen,' he pronounced, sucking his burnt fingers.

🜨

'Why should we open any of the doors?' I pressed him again on this.

We were walking the length of the room. There were a lot more than two hundred doors.

'Don't you want to get out?' The Doctor sounded petulant. I didn't reply. I wasn't sure any more. 'One of these doors, just one of them, holds the possibility of escape. But even then that's not a fixed probability. Merely looking at one door for a moment too long might allow the exit to sidle away elsewhere. Escapes are crafty things,' he chuckled.

He was infuriating. Like a child who'd never grown up. A wise old man pretending to be a clown. I wanted the Doctor to go away. I also knew he was the only company I'd find here.

🜨

'The world in a door,' he mused, leaning his face against one. He beckoned me over. 'Can you hear anything?' he whispered. 'Something scratching?'

'No.'

'What's behind this door?' He stepped back, forlorn. '"Shall I walk along the beach, Do I dare to eat a peach?"' He turned on his heel and went away with his little waddling walk.

I'd had enough of him. I opened a door and stepped through.

The room was small and peaceful. It felt very calm in here, the air unnaturally still.

A worrying thought fluttered up. Why was I here?

It didn't matter. Not now I'd found this room.

I closed my eyes.

I woke to find the Doctor leaning over me, patting my cheeks.

'There you are! Oh, thank heavens.'

I was in a different room. Bigger. Six doors.

'You are very lucky I saw where you'd gone and followed. Had to think on my feet. Air's a potent mixture of oxygen and nitrous oxide. Most soporific. I hadn't considered that. But of course, an infinite variety of atmospheres is possible. And, of course, radiation... imagine that. A room that looks and feels normal but contains a minute particle of uranium. We could have been exposed to that already and now it's too late. Oh dear.'

He stopped talking and looked gloomily around. He mopped his brow with a spotted handkerchief.

'I wonder what happens...' The words were pouring out of him now. '... when two atmospheres meet? Under the right conditions you could open a door, the elements would mix and BOOM!'

Before I could stop him, he flung open another door.

There was no explosion.

Dust was drifting down through it.

'I wonder how long that's been happening.' He didn't notice my fury.

We edged through, our feet leaving prints in the dust. 'Try not to breathe too much of it. Just in case.'

We reached a door at the far end and he looked back. 'Footprints!' he exclaimed. 'Kilroy was here.'

We went into the next chamber. When I looked back, our footprints had gone.

'How did we get here?' I asked.

The Doctor contemplated the ceiling.

'Well, that's the thing about the Multivarium. Just as it's almost impossible to leave it, it's utterly possible to enter it. I was on the Moon. Zoe and Jamie and I were dealing with the Ice Warriors. I opened a door...' He wrinkled his nose. 'Or did I? I'd like to get back. Dread to think how they're getting on without me. Perhaps this is an Ice Warrior trap... Seems a bit subtle for them. What about you?'

'I really don't know,' I said. 'I have a memory of falling.'

'Not very helpful.' The Doctor was accusing. 'Perhaps you've been here no time at all? Or a very long time. My jailer, watching my every move. Subtly influencing my behaviour.'

I couldn't remember. I panicked at that, answering him hotly.

'I can assure you I'm not. It's far more likely to be you. You're the one who keeps putting us in danger.'

'Well, there is that,' he conceded. 'Perhaps we are each other's keeper. That's a thought. Unless you suddenly remember you're an ancient entity that likes to imprison people,' he wrinkled his brow. 'You're not are you?'

'No,' I said, firmly.

We walked on.

We walked on some more.

We did not get hungry.

We did not sleep.

We just kept walking.

We stopped walking.

We sat down.

We waited.

We waited until we got bored of waiting.

'A chair,' sighed the Doctor.

Neither of us had spoken for some years.

'I do rather fancy a chair,' he repeated. 'Never really cared for them before. They just happened. But in all the rooms we've seen, no chairs. Somewhere in this infinity there must be a chair. A room that is just chairs. A room of chairs that are too small to sit on. A room where you need a Sherpa just to climb onto the seat. All chairs are out there somewhere –' he chewed his lip – 'and yet we've not seen any of them.'

'Now that you've mentioned it,' I smiled, 'perhaps the next door we open will have a chair.'

'Maybe you're right,' the Doctor agreed.

We had a week of opening doors. We'd suddenly taken to it again.

Many of the rooms had been identical, but the Doctor had assured me that, like snowflakes, no two rooms were quite alike. One room had been so short we'd had to crawl through it. Another had clouds. We liked that one.

Our present room was unremarkable.

We had opened the doors. The rooms beyond were the same again.

As we had closed each door, the Doctor had marked it with a stick of chalk. He had developed this habit recently. It did not matter as, once through a door, we never encountered the markings again. You could open a door one moment and it would show a huge space with six doors. You could open it again and there would be nothing but a cupboard soaked with fresh rain.

'Why do you bother?'

'Force of habit,' he said, and then stopped, repeating the phrase as though it was important. He stopped making his marks shortly after that.

We stepped through a doorway.

Suddenly I was pulled back, the Doctor grabbing hold of me.

We were crammed in the doorway.

'Mrph?' I said. My voice seemed odd.

'Gravity differential,' he said. 'That room has too much of it. You could see the door slow as it opened. We'd have been crushed. We have to stay here.' He was gripping the frame tightly. 'Go forward and we'll die. Let go and we'll be swept up.'

'By what?' I was finding it hard to hold on to the Doctor.

'The pressure between the two rooms is evening out. Like a tide. For a room to have its own gravity is nonsense, of course. But...' He gingerly let go with one hand and pushed it into the room. 'Ah yes... heavy, but not too bad.'

He let go of me, and we edged into the room. It was like wading through a bog.

'We should hurry,' he said as we slumped forward. 'It's tidal, which means the force will return and squash us like pancakes.'

We noticed the same patterns of rooms repeating, becoming more frequent. Closing in.

For a while that became a game. Could we predict correctly whether the room beyond would be some variation of fire, rain or gravity?

That amused us for a time. Until the mere act of opening a door became a chore.

🔲

'Are you all right?' I asked the Doctor.

He was lying on the floor again. These days he no longer bothered even leaning against the wall.

'Perhaps,' he murmured, 'you are the Doctor.'

'Me?' I was annoyed. Did that mean he expected me to do something? I just wanted to lie here for ever.

'Maybe I'm keeping you here. You should be out there...' The little man raised his hands. Once that gesture would have taken in the universe. Now it just stroked the wall gently. 'Doing things. Struggling against impossible odds. Instead of which... I'm keeping you trapped in this small room.'

'It's not that small,' I began.

'They're all small!' The Doctor scrambled unsteadily to his feet and stood there, shaking. His clothes were little more than rags, his hair long and matted. He flung open a door and marched through. I could hear his voice echoing from the room beyond. Wearily I traipsed after him.

'It's not so small,' I said of the echoing space.

He did not reply. He simply padded through the room, opening doors and letting them fall shut.

He reached a wall and sank against it.

'There may as well not be any doors.'

🔲

'Long ago...' began the Doctor.

He had not spoken for a long time and his voice was a croak. He cleared his throat.

'Long ago, I said this may be a prison. Or a lesson.' The Doctor was lying on the floor, his foot kicking out lazily against a door. Tap. Tap. Tap.

'I think I've finally learned the lesson.'

Tap. Tap. Tap.

The Doctor said nothing.

Tap. Tap. Tap.

If he was waiting for me to speak, I didn't care. I didn't care about anything any more.

Tap. Tap. Tap.

The Doctor kept on with his futile kicking against the door. One door. One door in a room with all the doors. A door that would not give way. No matter how many times he kicked it.

'Stop that,' I snapped eventually, after a day or two had passed.

'Shan't,' the Doctor was truculent. He carried on kicking the door.

'What are you hoping to achieve?' I asked.

The Doctor just laughed, a sad and weary chuckle.

His shoe, scuffed now, carried on tapping.

'We are in a room. A room full of doors. Beyond each door is another room. Universes and universes of possibilities. It's a perfect, infinite trap. And yet… The doors are gateways. I am hoping to wear one down. To make a mark. Then the system will be, just a little less perfect. That's all.'

'That's all?'

The Doctor finally, wearily stopped tapping the door and gazed up at the empty ceiling.

'The lesson of the Multivarium is this: it shows you how pointless any action is. Whatever we do, whatever door we open, it is just one choice in an infinity of possibilities. Somewhere else, someone else does the opposite.' The Doctor stood up and looked around himself as though seeing the room for the first time. 'I am here to be humbled. To learn my lesson. To do nothing. To not interfere. But…' He indicated the door. A tiny amount of shoe-leather remained against the edge of it. 'Some of us just can't help leaving our mark.'

This should have been the saddest moment in our lives. Caught in an eternal prison, unable to do more than scuff a door.

Instead, I felt a surge of hope. The Doctor seemed to gather strength. I've no idea where he got it from, but he chuckled. He winked at the doors as though to say, 'I know what you're up to, my friends, and it won't work.'

The Doctor rubbed his hands together.

'Come on,' he said, wrapping an arm around my shoulder. 'We've got work to do. My friend Zoe would love this. We need a system – a methodology. She'd approve. She loves science.'

We examined the doors. The handles were uniform and grew out of the doors themselves. There were no screws. Similarly the hinges joined to the frame with impossible smoothness.

'Too easy.' The Doctor shook his head, ruefully awarding someone else the points.

We carried on walking. We negotiated the familiar rooms like old friends. The cold room. The oxygen room. The room with no floor. The room with heavy gravity. The room of clouds. The room that smelt of flowers. The rooms that had many doors. The rooms that had only one. The room where thinking changed the colour of the walls. The rooms where speaking hurt.

As we went, the Doctor started marking the doors again.

'Oh, I know,' he chided me. 'But previously, ah, that was meddling. Now I have a system!'

He carried on. A little mark for fire. Another mark for rain and so on.

Soon the symbols began to reproduce themselves on the doors. Not all the time. But sometimes.

'We're changing things,' I remarked, astonished.

'I rather think it's meant to mock us. But we are simply breaking the rules through playing by them.' The Doctor winked as though he'd made a little joke.

The room had four doors. We reached it by walking through a room where the air was argon. The Doctor looked around and smiled.

'This will do splendidly,' he grinned. 'A final lesson for you.'

'A final lesson?'

'Indeed.' A birdlike nod. 'The theory of multiple universes is smug. I don't care for smug things.' He looked more than a little smug himself. 'Suppose you say, "I don't believe in multiple universes." Well, "Aha!" someone snaps back. "That's all very well. But even if, in this universe, multiple universes don't exist, then in another one they do!" And then comes the nodding. I do hate the nodding.' He nodded.

He turned to each of the doors. 'The Multivarium puts you firmly in your place. Teaches you not to interfere because it is an exercise in futility. But if you never try then no one ever wins. There is no way out of the Multivarium. Except that, if there is no way out of the Multivarium, then, obviously, in another room there must be a way out.'

It was nonsense. All that excitement and now he was just babbling. He'd gone mad. I was stuck here for ever with a madman.

Then I noticed the doors around us. All of them were labelled with the familiar signs. Except for one. I stared at it. Amazed.

'What now?' I asked the Doctor. 'Are you going to clap your hands and go home?'

'I could,' he conceded. 'But where's the fun in that? I do rather prefer a decisive victory.'

I tried not to stare again at the new door. Scuffed and a slight shade of blue. He indicated that I should try the handle. I did.

'Locked.' My voice was a whisper.

'Splendid.' He beamed. 'I hope you don't mind a show-off.'

'Not at all.'

The Doctor indicated the door we'd come through. Argon, an inert gas. Which he'd closed hastily.

He'd left ajar a door marked with his sign for 'heavy gravity'. It was steadily, wrongly, creeping into the room. I lifted my foot. It left the floor grudgingly.

'Would you care to open the door marked "Oxygen"?' He offered it to me like an ice cream at the seaside. The seaside! I could remember that. And ice cream. Food. How long since I'd eaten?

My heart beating faster, I opened the door.

'We'll have a little longer to wait because the heavier gravity impedes the Brownian motion of the molecules, but it'll be worthwhile in the end, you'll see.' He no longer cared that I didn't understand. He was just so very pleased with himself. 'We're waiting around for our probabilities to meet. We're creating an oxygen-rich environment.'

We waited.

Then the Doctor indicated I should take a deep breath and stand in the room full of argon.

'A little aside from the door. Just in case I've made a mistake.'

I did so.

I saw him scamper over to the room marked with the sign for fire and fling it open.

Then I saw him running towards me.

Then there was an enormous explosion.

The Doctor was lying on the floor of the inert room. He stood up, clearly desperate to breathe. I'd not had time to close the door as he'd flown through. The ball of fire had ballooned in, almost reaching him, but had then washed out again like a tide.

Equilibrium ruled in the room with all the doors.

We stepped back out into the chamber. It was a burnt-out wreck, the doors that led to gravity, oxygen and fire swinging limply from their hinges. They didn't matter any more.

We just stared at the blue door. It had gone. Blown away. Beyond it lay darkness.

'I think I've made my point,' the Doctor said slowly. 'There's always a way.'

He led me to the doorway. To the darkness which seemed suddenly so uncertain.

'I've no idea who you are. I've no idea who I am really,' he said, his hands in his pockets. 'Maybe you're the Doctor, maybe I am.'

'I think you are,' I smiled. 'What's out there? Is it the way out?'

We stared through the exit into the blackness beyond.

'I have absolutely no idea,' the Doctor grinned. 'Shall we go and see?'

THREE

THE MULTIVERSE

The TARDIS can travel anywhere in space and time – and even to other universes, of several distinct kinds...

When *Doctor Who* began in 1963, the intention was to have three kinds of stories. The first two are obvious: historical stories in which the TARDIS travels back in time through Earth's history, and science fiction stories in which the TARDIS travels forwards into the future or away to alien worlds. The first season more or less alternates between these two types: historical (the caveman bits of *An Unearthly Child*, then *Marco Polo*, *The Aztecs*, *The Reign of Terror*) and science fiction (*The Daleks*, *The Keys of Marinus*, *The Sensorites*).

The third type of story would have seen the TARDIS travel 'sideways' in time. An early example is *The Edge of Destruction* (1964), but the sideways kind of story was pretty much abandoned as a result of the huge success of the Daleks. Gradually, the show became more about battling monsters. By 1967, even stories set in Earth's history had sci-fi monsters lurking in them.

There's another example of a sideways story from the first twelve months of the series. In *Planet of Giants* (1964), the TARDIS doors open just as it is landing and – because of what the Doctor calls 'space pressure' – he and his friends are miniaturised. They've landed in a garden in England, apparently in the (then) present day.

Planet of Giants is not the last time the Doctor is miniaturised. It happens again in *The Invisible Enemy* (1977), *The Armageddon Factor* (1979), *Let's Kill Hitler* and *The Wedding of River Song* (2011), and *Into the Dalek* (2014). In each story, things that are normally harmless – such as a cat, a virus or antibodies – suddenly become dangerous because our heroes are so much smaller. The process was even used as a weapon. Between *Terror of the Autons* (1971) and *Planet of Fire* (1984), the Master frequently killed people by miniaturising them – though when he accidentally miniaturised himself, it didn't kill him.

If we really could miniaturise ourselves – and survive – we'd find the micro-world very strange indeed. For one thing, the molecules of the air around us would be proportionately larger, so we would feel the air as thicker, warmer and more viscous. It would be a little like walking through a heated swimming pool. Just as humans can float in water, small creatures find it easier to fly because the syrupy air helps to support them. Just as we can dive safely from a diving board into deep water, small creatures can safely tumble from great heights because the air cushions their fall. Maybe next time the Doctor and his friends are miniaturised they could have a go at flying.*

When we've seen the Doctor miniaturised, he and his friends can still recognise and interact with the world around them: in *Planet of Giants*s, they mountaineer into a kitchen sink, light a match the size of a battering ram and help to catch a full-sized murderer. But go smaller, and the world is unrecognisable – and very strange indeed.

---

* In *The Armageddon Factor*, Drax suggests that the miniaturised Doctor should 'fly over' and close the TARDIS door. This Time Lord ability to fly is only mentioned once again in the series – in *City of Death* (1979). Perhaps Drax is only joking – there are lots of occasions when being able to fly would have got the Doctor out of difficulty, such as when he's hanging from a radio telescope at the end of *Logopolis* (1981), so it seems odd that he doesn't use this ability more often.

At our normal scale, we can use everyday laws of physics to work out how things relate to one another. For example, if someone throws a ball, we can work out how to catch it from the amount of force used to throw it, its speed and the direction it's going in. We often work all that out in our heads without even realising: when a ball is thrown to us, we catch it. A skilled cricketer (such as the Fifth Doctor) can do more, judging the movement of the ball just right to hit it with a bat and send it to a good spot on the cricket pitch.

But at a much smaller scale, things don't move like a cricket ball. Take light, for example. As we saw in Chapter 2, light moves at 299,792,458 metres per second, but to understand *how* it moves – and predict its movements like we can with a cricket ball – we need to know what it's made of and how that stuff behaves.

What is light made of? The smallest possible amount of any physical entity is called a quantum (from the Greek word for 'how much'). Quantum mechanics is the science of working out how quanta behave. It usually comes into effect on a very small scale of less than 100 nanometres – a nanometre is one billionth of a metre; there are a million nanometres in a millimetre – and is extremely strange. It doesn't help that light sometimes behaves like a particle (that is, like a very, very small cricket ball) – called a photon – and sometimes it behaves like a wave of energy. But is it a particle or a wave? Oddly, it can be either – or both at the same time. Scientists call this strange property of quantum mechanics 'wave-particle duality'. Sometimes, quantum particles are even able to pass through solid barriers in a process called 'tunnelling' (which doesn't actually involve tunnelling at all). The weird behaviour of matter and energy at quantum scales is so far removed from everyday experience that it is very hard to visualise – even for physicists. Richard Feynman, who won the Nobel Prize for his work in physics, once said: 'I can safely say that nobody understands quantum mechanics.'

In this chapter, we're interested in just one small part of quantum mechanics: the so-called uncertainty principle. Objects on the quantum scale are so small that we can't measure them without affecting them, which in turn affects the measurement that we're trying to make. In 1927 German physicist Werner Heisenberg explained that the more precisely we know where a particle is, the less precisely we can know how fast it is moving – and vice versa. We can never be entirely certain about every single detail of a particle or a system of particles and there's no such thing as an independent observer – the observer is always inextricably involved in the process that he or she is trying to observe.

However, although we can never have precise knowledge about the exact state of every particle in a system, we can still work out the probability of how the system will behave. In 1926, Austrian physicist Erwin Schrödinger came up with an equation that can be used to predict the behaviour of particles in terms of probabilities.

An odd consequence of Schrödinger's equation is that, although it describes the behaviour of particles, it treats them as though they are waves – the same wave-particle duality that we saw with photons of light. In our everyday experience, a particle can only be in one place at once, while a wave can be spread out over a wider area – more strongly present in some places than others, but not confined to a single position. If we fire a particle such as an electron at a sheet of metal that has two holes in it, we might expect the electron to pass through one hole or the other, but not through both. But in Schrödinger's treatment the wave-like electron has a particular probability of passing through each of the holes and its behaviour on the far side of the metal sheet is a combination of these probabilities – as if it had passed through both. This might seem like a very odd way for a particle to behave, but experiments have shown time and time again that this is exactly what particles like electrons, protons and neutrons really do in real life.

Wave-particle duality is a very strange thing to imagine but it is the basis of technologies such as the laser, the atom bomb and the DVD player – so every time you watch an episode of *Doctor Who* on DVD you're demonstrating that the weird behaviour of the quantum realm is real. We might be happy to accept that a DVD player relies on the weirdness of subatomic particles, but wave-particle duality on the

Particles and waves behave in a characteristic manner ...

Particles that pass through the slits build up a pattern of impacts that matches the two slits.

As waves that pass through the slits radiate outwards, they overlap. Where a crest of one meets a trough of the other, they cancel out. Where a crest meets a crest, they amplify each other. We detect a distinctive, stripy interference pattern.

... But experiments show that light (made of photons) and subatomic particles such as electrons and protons can show properties of both

When we fire individual electrons at the slits, they build up a stripy pattern, just like that created by the interference of waves.

But if we try to observe the same electrons passing through one or other of the slits, they change their behaviour and behave like particles – as if caused by the act of observation itself!

quantum scale also has some rather disturbing implications for objects in the everyday world – implications which have troubled physicists for almost a hundred years.

Schrödinger himself was very worried about this. In a series of letters to Albert Einstein, he described an imaginary 'thought experiment' which showed how the weirdness of tiny quantum particles might translate into weirdness on a larger, everyday scale. Schrödinger's equation treats quantum particles as if they exist in a mixture of all their possible states, right up until the particle's state is measured. So a radioactive atomic nucleus, which has a particular probability of decaying over time, will exist in both a 'decayed' and an 'undecayed' state until an observation is made – at which point it will settle into either one state or the other.

In Schrödinger's thought experiment, a cat is placed in a box along with a bottle of poison gas. The bottle is connected to an atom of a radioactive element that – using Schrödinger's equation – has a fifty per cent chance of decaying in one hour. If it decays, the bottle will open, the poison gas will escape and the imaginary cat will die. If it doesn't decay, the imaginary cat will be fine.

Of course, once the hour has passed and the lid is opened, we'll know whether the cat has survived. But, according to quantum mechanics, until the box is opened the atom is both undecayed and decayed, the bottle is both closed and open, and Schrödinger's imaginary cat is both alive and dead.

The idea of a cat being both alive and dead at the same time might be hard to swallow, but physicists have come up with several different ways of explaining what this might actually mean – some of which are rather strange themselves.

In 1957, American physicist Hugh Everett III suggested that every time a quantum system is observed, forcing it to choose one state out of many possibilities, different universes split off – one for each of the possible outcomes of the observation. In the case of the cat, two almost identical universes would be created: one where the cat is dead and the other where it's alive. All we do in opening the box is discover which of those two universes is the one we exist in. Physicists disagree on whether this idea is realistic but it certainly seems to have influenced the *Doctor Who* story *Inferno* (1970).

In many ways, the other Earth seen in *Inferno* is very similar to our own, but there are also some startling differences. Britain is ruled by a dictator, the royal family have been executed, and a mining project is run by nightmare versions of the Doctor's friends in UNIT. For example, 'Brigade Leader' (rather than Brigadier) Lethbridge-Stewart is a coward who tries more than once to kill the Doctor. Presumably (though not stated in the story), at some point in history this world diverged from our own – perhaps when Britain chose whether to fight the Nazis in the Second World War. Later *Doctor Who* stories explored more 'similar-but-different' versions of the Earth: in *Battlefield* (1989), there's an Earth where King Arthur is real and the Doctor is Merlin, and in *Rise of the Cybermen* (2006), there's an Earth where the Doctor's friend Rose Tyler never existed – except as a dog.

If this 'many worlds' interpretation of quantum mechanics is correct, there must be an infinite number of universes, each with its own version of Earth. In this 'multiverse', there's a universe for every possible outcome of every possible choice. As we'll see in Chapter 6, the multiverse might explain how time travel and changing history are possible. But at present we can't really test the idea of the multiverse scientifically, which has led some physicists to argue that it isn't a scientific idea at all – since science is all about testing our ideas against evidence.

However, a related idea does make predictions that might one day be tested. String theory argues that all of the particles which make up the universe are really the result of the vibration of extremely tiny one-dimensional objects called 'strings'. Atomic physics takes place on scales of about 1 nanometre – that is, a millimetre divided by 1,000,000. The strings in string theory are a lot smaller than that. They're thought to exist at the scale of a millimetre divided by 62,500,000,000,000,000, 000,000,000,000,000 – what's called the Planck length, named after physicist Max Planck.

If string theory is right, it should be possible to detect 'string harmonics', with a tell-tale distribution of heavy copies of the sub-atomic particles with which we're familiar. But to do so, we'd need a particle accelerator machine many times more powerful than the Large Hadron Collider at CERN – which, at about £2.8 billion, is one of the most expensive scientific instruments ever built. It seems unlikely that such a machine will be built any time soon.

A more practical test may be the way the behaviour of these tiny strings (if they exist) has affected the structure of the universe on much larger scales. Some physicists have suggested that strings might sometimes get stretched to sizes big enough to be detected using telescopes. So far, no evidence has been found to either support or disprove string theory, but particle physicists and cosmologists are still actively searching.

But why is string theory related to the idea of other universes? To make the equations of string theory work, it needs more than the four dimensions we're used to – the three dimensions of height, width and depth plus the dimension of time. Different ideas about string theory suggest different numbers of dimensions: M-theory (physicists can't agree whether the 'M' stands for magic, mystery or matrix) requires eleven dimensions while bosonic string theory requires twenty-six.

So why don't we see these extra dimensions? It's possible that they are 'rolled up' very tightly so that they're invisible to objects on the scale of human beings. Depending on how tightly the dimensions are coiled, it might still be possible for smaller objects like atoms to be 'pushed' into them – in which case they would seem to disappear from our familiar three-dimensional world, though they would still exist. In *The Stones of Blood* (1978), the Doctor discovers a spaceship hovering above a stone circle but hidden from view because it's in 'hyperspace' (which the Doctor and his companion Romana both describe as 'a theoretical absurdity'). Could hyperspace in *Doctor Who* simply be a way of shunting large objects sideways into string theory's extra dimensions?

Other types of universe in *Doctor Who* seem to be more self-contained. In *Full Circle* (1980), the TARDIS ends up in E-Space, a space-time continuum separate from our own universe but with planets and star systems of its own. In the following story, *State of Decay*, we're told E-Space is smaller than our own N-Space – a 'pocket universe'. In *The Doctor's Wife* (2011), the TARDIS leaves our universe to reach the world called House. Again, that might be in a separate, smaller pocket universe, though the Doctor suggests it's more complicated than that:

'So we're in a tiny bubble universe, sticking to the side of the bigger bubble universe?'

'Yeah. No. But if it helps, yes… Not a bubble, a plughole. The universe has a plughole and we've just fallen down it.'

Amy Pond and the Eleventh Doctor, *The Doctor's Wife* (2011)

It seems that in *Doctor Who* the physics of these other universes can be different to ours. On the TARDIS scanner, E-Space seems to have a greenish tinge compared to the blackness of our own N-Space, and – according to K-9 – its smallness makes it easier for the TARDIS to move a short distance within it. In *The Three Doctors* (1972–1973), the Doctor and Jo travel through a black hole to a universe of antimatter 'where all the known physical laws cease to exist'. This is rather different from current ideas of what might really happen inside a black hole, but we'll find out more about these strange objects in Chapter 4.

Conditions in our universe could present physical problems to creatures from anywhere else. In *Flatline* (2014), the Doctor says that the Boneless are 'from a universe with only two dimensions' and must learn to move about in three. Einstein's General Theory of Relativity tells us that in a universe with fewer than three space dimensions the force of gravity would not be able to operate, which might explain why the 2D Boneless initially find our own universe so challenging to get around in.

Like the Boneless struggling with our universe, we, too, struggle to understand how the universe might exist with more than the four dimensions that we're used to. Again, General Relativity hints at how weird things might get: in a universe with more than three space dimensions, gravity would be weaker, stars would not be able to hold on to their planets and life as we know it might be impossible.

The very first episode of *Doctor Who* suggests that if we don't understand how other dimensions operate, we can barely understand the universe at all. In *An Unearthly Child* (1963), the Doctor's granddaughter, Susan Foreman, is a pupil at Coal Hill School. Her science teacher sets her what he thinks is a simple problem using three dimensions – A, B, C. But Susan gets upset, arguing that it's impossible to solve the problem without using the dimensions D and E as well. 'You can't simply work on three of the dimensions,' she insists, claiming that the additional dimensions required are 'time' and 'space'. By 'space' perhaps she means the extra space dimensions predicted by string theory? If so, young

Gallifreyans clearly like to make their maths problems as complicated as possible.

However, the way different universes are described in *Doctor Who* is not always very consistent. In *Flatline*, the Doctor describes the Boneless as 'creatures from another dimension'. In this sense the world we know is an intersection of four different dimensions: one of width, one of depth, one of height and one of time. However, in *Battlefield*, too, the Doctor says the knights are from 'another dimension' and 'another universe'. Does he mean that 'dimension' in *Doctor Who* is another word for 'universe'?

The initials 'TARDIS' come from Time And Relative Dimension In Space, and the Doctor claims that 'dimensional engineering' is the reason the TARDIS is bigger on the inside than on the outside. In *The Robots of Death* (1977), he explains to Leela that its 'insides and outsides are not in the same dimension'. In *Frontios* (1984) and *Father's Day* (2005), the exterior of the TARDIS is separated from the interior – as if they're two different realms, connected by a door.

Or perhaps 'dimension' and 'universe' have subtly different meanings in *Doctor Who*. In *Hide* (2013), the Doctor refers to the alien world as both a 'pocket universe' (like E-Space) and 'another dimension', but corrects Clara when she calls it a 'parallel universe'. In geometry, lines are parallel if they do not touch or intersect, so perhaps in *Doctor Who* a parallel universe is one that doesn't branch off from ours but simply exists alongside it – something we'll discuss more in Chapter 6.

In 2003, physicist Max Tegmark suggested that there might be four different types of multiverse. The first, a Level I Multiverse, is anywhere in our universe further than 46 billion light years from Earth. That distance is the furthest that we can see into the universe, so anything beyond it is effectively cut off from us.

In Level II, our entire universe is just one of a number of distinct bubbles inside a greater whole – like E-Space and N-Space in *Doctor Who*. In Level III, there are universes for 'every conceivable way that the world could be' – universes branching out from each other as choices lead to different outcomes, such as Schrödinger's dead and alive cats or the consequences of Donna's choice to turn left or right in *Turn Left* (2008), which we'll discuss more in Chapter 6.

Lastly, in Level IV universes, even the laws of physics can be different and anything might happen. In *Battlefield* (1989), the Doctor says the Arthurian knights come from 'another dimension' and 'sideways in time from another universe' – one where magic seems to be real. That suggests the other Earth where King Arthur is real has its own laws of physics, different to our own. If all possibilities are played out somewhere, then there's a universe where *Doctor Who* is real – all of it, even the bits that are contradictory or silly – and another universe where *you* are the Doctor, and another where you're a Dalek.

Perhaps there are even more than these four levels of universe. In 2011, physicist Brian Greene suggested nine different types. There might be many more. It's ironic, isn't it? Trying to understand the very smallest size of matter has led to fundamental questions about how the universe works at the very biggest scale.

Double trouble

In 2003, physicist Max Tegmark argued that even in our universe there's a good chance that physical circumstances repeat themselves, so that there are distant worlds where copies of you and me live copies of our lives. He called this a Level I Multiverse. In *Doctor Who*, we've seen several people who look just like Doctors or companions. (This list does not include robots or creatures who disguise themselves as Doctors or companions.)

- Steven Taylor looks just like tourist Morton Dill – seen in *The Chase* (1965)
- The Brigadier looks just like Space Security Service agent Bret Vyon – seen in *The Daleks' Master Plan* (1965–1966)

- The First Doctor looks just like the sixteenth-century Abbot of Amboise – seen in *The Massacre of St Bartholomew's Eve* (1966)
- The Second Doctor looks just like dictator Ramón Salamander – seen in *The Enemy of the World* (1968)
- Harry Sullivan looks just like Lieutenant John Andrews – seen in *Carnival of Monsters* (1973)
- The first Romana looks just like Princess Strella of Tara – seen in *The Androids of Tara* (1978)
- The second Romana chooses to look just like Princess Astra of Atrios in *Destiny of the Daleks* (1979)
- Nyssa looks just like a woman from 1925, Ann Talbot – seen in *Black Orchid* (1982)
- The Sixth Doctor looks just like Maxil, Commander of the Chancellery Guard on Gallifrey – seen in *Arc of Infinity* (1983)
- Torchwood's Gwen Cooper looks just like Victorian servant Gwyneth – seen in *The Unquiet Dead* (2005)
- Martha Jones looks just like her cousin Adeola Oshodi – seen in *Army of Ghosts* (2006)
- Amelia Pond looks just like the Soothsayer – seen in *The Fires of Pompeii* (2008)
- The Twelfth Doctor looks just like marble merchant Lobus Caecilius – seen in *The Fires of Pompeii* (2008), and that might be on purpose (as we'll discuss in Chapter 15)
- The Tenth Doctor looks just like a human copy of himself created by regeneration energy – seen in *Journey's End* (2008)
- Clara Oswald looks just like a number of people the Doctor has met throughout his life, including space traveller Oswin Oswald – seen in *Asylum of the Daleks* (2012)
- Danny Pink looks just like time traveller (and Danny's relation) Orson Pink – seen in *Listen* (2014), which we'll discuss more in Chapter 11.

THE HUNGRY NIGHT

JONATHAN MORRIS

'It's time to leave the airlock, if you dare.' The snatch of tune went around Tobbs's head, just as it did whenever he entered the airlock, turned the dog lever and opened the exterior hatch. It was a tune from the olden days, hundreds of years old, and those probably weren't even the right words. And now he'd have it looping around in his head for the rest of the EVA. If only he knew what the next line was.

He reached outside, gripped a handrail in his thickly padded gloved hand and swung through the hatchway. Ahead of him stretched a horizontal ladder of more handrails, leading across the rust-red panelling. Above him lay a night sky of infinite blackness, speckled with a billion points of unwavering light. Although, of course, out in space, concepts like up and down were a matter of personal choice. Tobbs made a conscious effort to think of the star-dotted firmament as 'up' and began to float along the ladder, one handrail at a time.

'Nearly there,' crackled Locklear's voice in his helmet. 'Outage in aft hull, section twelve. Spreading to sections ten to fourteen.' That was unusual. A localised power failure was a familiar occurrence in interstellar space, hence why a lowly third-class engineer had been assigned to investigate. The assumption was that it was the result of the ship being struck by a piece of debris and only warranted direct observation because the failure had also blacked out the exterior cameras and the sensor array. For a power failure to *expand* was seriously out of the ordinary.

Tobbs felt a flutter of excitement in his stomach, thinking of congratulatory handshakes and well-earned bonuses. Maybe, when he was hero of the hour, he'd even get up the courage to ask Thelesa out to dinner. He maintained a steady speed, grasping each rung and propelling himself forward. According to extra-vehicular protocol, he should've been tethering and decoupling a safety line to each rail, but this was an emergency and, besides, he could always use his jet if needed.

The line of the song kept going round his head as he reached the end of the ladder. The aft section was hidden out of sight below the side of the hull. Tobbs hauled himself over the edge, and the sloping aft hull rose into view. He held his breath, the only noise the hiss of static.

The hull was in absolute blackness. His headlamp lit up a number of plates scattered over its surface. The plates were dome-shaped, like flattened cones, as white as bone and covered in ridges.

'What can you see?' said Locklear. 'Tobbs. Report.'

Tobbs realised he'd been holding his breath. 'It's not an impact. It looks like, mad as this sounds, organic material.'

'Organic? Specify.'

Tobbs drifted closer. The plates were *shells*. This was an undiscovered life form. They'd probably be named after him.

'I'm not sure,' said Tobbs. 'They look like sea life. Barnacles. Space barnacles.'

Something moved. Tobbs leaned forward, his nose almost touching the glass of his helmet. One of the shells ejected a cloud of dust. Then, as it was caught in the glow of his headlamp, it detached itself from the hull and floated silently upwards. Tobbs could make out glittering, gossamer tentacles undulating beneath its shell.

'They seem to respond to light,' said Tobbs. Hearing his own words back through his earphones, his voice sounded full of wonder. 'Like it's waking them up.'

'Report on hull damage,' said Locklear. 'Outage in sector eleven.'

'Can't see any damage, but there's too many of them, they must be covering the cameras.' Tobbs swung his headlamp back and forth. Was it his imagination or was the light fading?

'Return to airlock,' said Locklear.

'What?' said Tobbs. One of the barnacles rose up before him, so close he could reach out and touch it.

'We're picking up a power loss on your life support—' Locklear's voice was buried in static, then the radio fell silent.

Tobbs checked his life support. The row of indicator lights just below his eye line flashed. He switched to back-up, and the lights lit up, then began flashing again.

Tobbs looked up, just in time to see the underside of one of the barnacles as it rushed towards him, its tentacles twirling, lights pulsing up and down the glass-like filaments. It hit the front of his helmet, clasping onto the glass. Tobbs could see its squashed, fleshy innards.

He reached up to pull it away. His heavily padded fingers could barely grip and he couldn't wrench it off; the angle was wrong and it had excreted some form of glue.

'Request assistance,' said Tobbs, forgetting that his radio had stopped working. 'Request assist—'

Something hard and hefty slammed into his back. Then something hit his left arm, sticking fast. Then more and more of the barnacles smacked into him until he was encrusted in a ball of the creatures. He couldn't see anything through his helmet. All he could see were the indicator lights going out one by one.

Then he heard a terrible, high-pitched squeaking. Cracking. The sound of breaking glass.

His last thought was that he would never find out the next line of the song.

'Tobbs, respond! Respond!'

The only answer was the hiss of static.

'Life support's out,' reported Thelesa, her questioning tone betraying her shock and grief. 'He's... gone.'

Locklear turned away from the communication desk. The flight deck of the *Godspeed* was in near-darkness, the faces of the crew lit by flashing viewscreens.

'What's our power situation?' she asked Keinholz.

Keinholz tugged at the collar on his uniform, as he always did when it was bad news, and indicated the schematic diagram on his viewscreen. 'Down to thirty-five per cent. Never seen anything like it.'

'Still no idea of the cause?'

'Something in section twelve. That's the centre of the energy drain, where it started.'

'Whatever it was that Tobbs found,' said Thelesa, brushing away something in the corner of her eye. 'He said there were "barnacles".'

'You heard of anything like that, Professor?' said Locklear, turning to the ship's xenobiologist.

Ferrier frowned. 'No, Captain, but I suppose a space-borne creature is theoretically possible. Several extremophiles have been known to survive in a vacuum.'

Any excuse for a biology lecture, thought Locklear.

'Power reserves down to thirty per cent,' said Keinholz with all the gravity of a tolling bell.

Locklear turned back to Thelesa. 'Looks like we have no choice,' she said, trying to sound confident despite her stomach tightening with dread. 'Send out a distress call.'

Thelesa nodded, swallowed, and pressed the activation sequence. The mayday signal sounded, a succession of urgent bleeps. Then it faded away to silence.

'What is it?' said Locklear. 'What's happening?'

Thelesa's fingers ran over the controls of her workstation, to no effect. She shook her head. 'The power-drain, it's affecting the comms.'

'Of course,' said Keinholz resignedly. 'The transceiver is based in section ten.'

'We might've got a message out for a few seconds, but that's it,' said Thelesa, her voice filled with fear. 'There's not enough power left to broadcast a distress signal.'

Locklear stared at the main viewscreen, blacked out due to the power shortage. Every instinct made her want to scream, but she had to do her duty, she had to remain calm. 'So we're stuck in a dying ship, with no means of calling for help, and nobody to come to our rescue.'

'What you talking about?' said a brazen male voice. 'I'm here, aren't I?'

Locklear turned – to see a tall man standing in the middle of the flight deck with his arms folded and his chin raised.

'Who are you?' said Locklear indignantly. 'What are you doing here?'

It was difficult to see in the gloom, but Locklear thought she could see his lips curl into a mocking smirk. 'I got your message,' he said matter-of-factly. 'I'm the guy who's gonna save your lives. But that's a bit of a mouthful, so you can call me "the Doctor".'

Locklear stared at him. The rest of the crew were also staring at him. The man relished being the centre of attention, acknowledging each of them with a cheery nod. 'The Doctor?' said Locklear, looking him up and down. He appeared to be wearing a jacket made of tanned animal hide.

'That's right, don't wear it out,' he said, as he jogged across to the engineering workstation. The electric blue glow from the schematic diagram illuminated an aquiline nose, two protruding ears and a gaze of ruthless determination. 'Here's the deal. Do exactly as you're told and you might just get to live.'

'Are you threatening us?' said Locklear.

'It's not me you have to worry about.' While Keinholz stared at him in disbelief, the Doctor tapped at the workstation keypad. 'Reserves down to fifteen per cent. It's gonna start getting very dark, very cold and very hard to breathe. No, what you need to worry about are these little tykes.' The Doctor held up a pen-shaped device which buzzed and glowed blue. The main viewscreen flashed into life.

Locklear gasped. The viewscreen showed the ship's starboard hull, facing aft. The ship's surface was coated in barnacles. As she watched, more of the creatures drifted out of the blackness and adhered themselves to the hull.

'What *the hell* are they?' she said.

The Doctor shrugged. 'No idea. Never seen them before. Just picked them up on my scan when I came in.' He grinned wildly. 'A brand new form of life. Fan-tastic!'

'And they're the source of the power outage?' said Keinholz.

'Evidently,' said Ferrier, gazing at the viewscreen in awe. 'If they can eat through metal, they could've chewed through the power lines.'

'Do they look like they have teeth?' said the Doctor incredulously. 'Do you see any teeth? I don't see any teeth.'

'Whatever they are, they're attacking my ship,' Locklear snapped at him. 'If we don't deal with them, we're dead. Keinholz, use the plasma cannons.'

Keinholz began tapping at his keyboard. The Doctor turned on Locklear. 'So, what? You discover a new life form, and what do you do? Shoot at it!'

'We have to defend ourselves, Doctor,' said Locklear.

'Don't you think you should try to understand them first?'

'What is there to understand? They're not intelligent. We can hardly negotiate. Once we're finished, Professor Ferrier can dissect their remains.'

'Plasma cannons energised, Captain,' said Keinholz.

'Then destroy them,' said Locklear firmly. 'Maximum dispersal. Wipe them out!'

'Listen to me—' began the Doctor, but the howl of the cannons drowned him out. The floor shuddered as the sound was conducted through the fabric of the ship.

On the viewscreen, a shaft of plasma flashed through the darkness and one of the creatures exploded into a cloud of dust. The cannon fired again, winging another of the barnacles, causing it to spin away into the void. It fired again, and again, but each time it fired, more of the creatures appeared. They swarmed over the side of the hull, streaming towards the viewscreen like a slow-motion snowstorm.

'Keep firing!' said Locklear, and muttered, 'Where are they all coming from?'

'They can't be reproducing,' said Ferrier doubtfully. 'Can they?'

'Plasma cannons losing power,' said Keinholz. 'We can't keep this up much longer.'

'Keep firing,' repeated Locklear, even as the creatures inundated the viewscreen.

'Oh, you stupid, stupid apes,' said the Doctor. 'Work it out. Energy's their meat and drink. So firing plasma at them, you're just inviting more of them to lunch.'

'That *would* explain the power drain,' said Ferrier.

'And the life-support failure Tobbs experienced,' said Thelesa sadly.

'They're breeding,' said the Doctor. 'Converting your ship's energy to mass.'

'Captain, we're running out of power,' said Keinholz.

Locklear sighed. 'All right. Stop firing. Stop firing!'

Keinholz tapped a button and the cannons stopped.

Locklear leaned towards the Doctor, her face inches from his. 'So, Doctor. What d'you suggest?'

'Answer's obvious,' said the Doctor. 'But first, you tell me something. What are you doing out here? What's the purpose of your mission?'

None of the crew responded, so Locklear answered. 'Our mission is to seek out unregistered planets and stake claims on behalf of the parent company.'

'What sort of claims? Research? Colonisation? Mineral extraction?'

'What the company does with them is none of our business.'

'No, your job is to roam the galaxy calling dibs,' said the Doctor. 'You humans like to think you own things you had nothing to do with creating. OK. Listen. I get you out of this, you leave this system, never to return. And you tell your company there was nothing of interest here, so these barnacles can get on with their lives in peace. Agreed?'

'Very well,' said Locklear. 'There was nothing of value here anyway.'

'Doctor,' said Keinholz. 'We're down to two per cent. What is the solution?'

'Simple. Switch everything off. Put the ship on silent running. They're attracted by energy, so make them think there's no more left. Lunchtime's over.'

The crew didn't respond. Locklear nodded wearily. 'Do it.'

Keinholz pressed a sequence of switches and one by one, the work-stations around the flight deck went dark. The ever-present background hum of the ventilation system faded away and silence filled the room.

'All systems off-line,' said Keinholz. 'Including life support.'

'What?' cried Thelesa. 'But without that, we'll suffocate.'

'No you won't,' said the Doctor. 'You'll freeze to death first.'

'He's right,' said Keinholz. 'Temperature dropping below ice-point.' As he spoke, his breath clouded in the air.

'Good, good.' The Doctor checked the readouts at Keinholz's workstation. 'We have to convince them this ship is just a derelict lump of junk, floating in space.'

'And then what?' said Ferrier frostily, rubbing her arms for warmth. 'They'll just become dormant, stuck to the hull. We won't be able to turn the engines back on.;

'You will,' said the Doctor. 'Someone just has to make them a better offer.' He strolled over to the rear doors, buzzed his pen-shaped device, and they slid open.

'Where are you going?' asked Locklear.

The Doctor paused in the doorway. 'The TARDIS. My wheels. You can come along if you like.'

Locklear stood in the TARDIS control room, gazing open-mouthed at the high, curved walls pulsing with green light. She'd never seen anything like it before in her life.

The Doctor darted around the central console, flicking switches embedded in its coral-encrusted surface. As he did, jets of steam hissed out of vents in the floor. He grinned the most manic of grins. 'Nearly there!'

There was a stomach-churning rumble and the central glass pillar of the console began to rise and fall. Then the rumbling stopped with a crunch. The Doctor slammed down a lever and sprinted over to the exterior doors. He pulled them open in a grand gesture to reveal the *Godspeed* floating through space a short distance away.

Locklear approached the doorway warily. 'I'm guessing there's some sort of force field preventing us being sucked out?'

'You guess correct. I can see why they made you captain.'

Locklear nodded dumbly and peered outside. She could just about make out the barnacles covering the *Godspeed*'s hull. 'So how do we lure them away?'

The Doctor dashed back to the console. 'Power, Captain Locklear. Power!'

A few moments later, out in the darkness of space, the lamp on the top of the TARDIS started to flash. It sent out a dazzling, swirling beam of light, like a lighthouse, on and off, picking out the barnacles on the hull of the *Godspeed*.

Very gradually, a couple of the barnacles detached themselves from the hull and began to swim through the vacuum towards the TARDIS. Then a few more barnacles detached themselves and followed. Then the entire encrusted body crumbled away as the whole mass of barnacles released the ship and swarmed slowly towards the police box.

The Doctor stood in the doorway, waving the creatures towards him. 'That's it! Come to Daddy!' Then he smiled and slammed the doors shut.

The first of the barnacles settled upon the wooden panelling of the TARDIS and its slanting roof. Then more arrived, clinging to the sides, the roof and the underside, burying it in a tightly clustered mass of shells. Then more barnacles covered those barnacles, until not a glimpse of the police box remained.

In the TARDIS, a warning alarm hooted and the engines made a low grinding sound. The Doctor checked the monitor, which showed a series of revolving circles. 'Yes, I think I've got them all. They're tucking in, happy as Larry.'

'But won't that mean you'll be stuck here?' said Locklear. 'They'll be drawing power from this... ship?'

'Oh, the TARDIS has plenty of welly, don't worry about that,' said the Doctor proudly. An instant later, the lights went out.

'You were saying?' said Locklear.

The Doctor dashed around the console, adjusting switches by the light of the glowing central column. 'OK, we're gonna have to be quick, they're breeding like, well, like barnacles.' The controls didn't respond, so the Doctor pulled a hammer out from under the console and whacked it. Part of the panel exploded into sparks, but the central column started moving up and down.

The Doctor laughed. 'First we dematerialise, taking our new friends with us, then rematerialise in the inner asteroid belt, nice sunny spot, and dematerialise leaving them behind to feed!'

Out in space, the barnacles clinging to the TARDIS had multiplied until it was buried beneath a sphere of thousands of bumpy shells. The creatures ejected clouds of spores which swiftly grew into minuscule barnacles, which attached themselves to the sphere and quickly expanded to become full-size barnacles.

Then there was a wheezing, groaning sound, and the ball of blistering barnacles faded away.

In the flight deck of the *Godspeed*, the emergency lights grew brighter. Then the main viewscreen lit up, showing the hull of the ship now clean of barnacles, followed by all the workstation viewscreens.

The crew stared at each other in surprise. Keinholz checked his controls. 'Emergency generators on line. Power supply at forty per cent and rising. We're saved. We're saved!'

Thelesa, Ferrier and the rest of the flight crew cheered in relief. The ventilation hummed on and blasted the room with warm air. Then the overhead lights flickered into life and the deck was restored to its normal bright appearance.

'What happened?' said Thelesa.

'The barnacles,' said Ferrier. 'They've… gone. Completely disappeared.'

'Yes, they're all feeding in the asteroid belt,' said Locklear, standing in the doorway. She strode onto the deck as though it was just another day at work. 'Thanks to the Doctor.'

'The Doctor?' said Ferrier. 'But how?'

Locklear sighed ruefully. 'He took them out to lunch.'

FOUR

THE POWER OF THE TARDIS

'The Eye of Harmony. Exploding star in the act of becoming a black hole. Time Lord engineering. You rip the star from its orbit, suspend it in a permanent state of decay.'
The Eleventh Doctor, *Journey to the Centre of the TARDIS* **(2013)**

On 28 November 1967, as the Second Doctor battled the Ice Warriors for the first time in *Doctor Who*, two Cambridge University radio astronomers – Jocelyn Bell Burnell from Northern Ireland and Antony Hewish from Cornwall – detected something strange in space. Every 1.33 seconds there was a pulse of energy – radio waves – from the same part of the sky. Or, rather, the place it was coming from slowly moved, but perfectly in time with the movement of the stars as the Earth rotated under them (as we saw in Chapter 1). That meant it was very unlikely that the pulse had been created on Earth: it had to be coming from somewhere deep in space.

Bell Burnell and Hewish called the pulse LGM-1, short for 'little green men', because the regularity of the pulse at least suggested that it was artificial in origin, as if some kind of alien life form had engineered it. Scientists soon worked out that the pulse was a natural phenomenon, produced by a kind of star, but the explanation turned out to be just as remarkable as if it really had been some alien broadcast.

Stars like the one Bell Burnell and Hewish found are now called pulsars – short for 'pulsating radio star' – because of the regular pulses of radio waves they create. The pulses are the result of two characteristics of a pulsar. First, they have strong magnetic fields. Earth also has its own, less strong magnetic fields which can interact with particles emitted from the Sun to create dazzling displays of light in the atmosphere, usually at high latitudes near the North and South Poles. These displays are called aurora, or the Northern and Southern Lights. Jupiter, Saturn, Uranus and Neptune also have magnetic fields that create aurorae.

The Earth's relatively weak magnetic field is able to funnel electrically charged particles from the Sun down over our planet's poles, where they collide with molecules of air high above the ground and cause them to glow. But the magnetic field of a pulsar is around a trillion times stronger than the Earth's, blasting charged particles *away* from its magnetic poles and out into space. As they accelerate, these particles emit radio waves along their direction of travel, creating a narrow beam of electromagnetic energy that shines out from each of the star's two magnetic poles. But the magnetic poles are not precisely lined up with the star's axis of spin (this is also true on Earth, which is why the magnetic north indicated by a compass needle is a few degrees different from the true, geographical north shown on maps). As the pulsar spins, these beams of radiation sweep around the sky, and each time one passes over the Earth we detect a pulse of radio waves. Imagine a lighthouse with a revolving lantern at the top, casting out a beam of light. The beam sweeps round and round in the darkness but if you were out at sea, too far away to see the lighthouse, you'd see a regular flashing on and off of light. (With the pulsar, only one beam hits the Earth; the other is facing in the wrong direction.)

Of course, the speed of the pulse that Bell Burnell and Hewish found showed that the pulsar had to be revolving very quickly – every 1.33 seconds. This is dizzyingly faster than the rotation period of an ordinary star like our Sun, which spins once every 24.47 days (measured at its equator). Even the Earth's 24-hour rotation seems leisurely by comparison. But this incredible speed wasn't the strangest thing about the discovery of the first pulsar.

Astronomers knew that when a very large star reaches the end of its life, it explodes – in what's called a supernova – leaving behind a huge cloud, or nebula, of gas called a supernova remnant. The gas ejected in these violent stellar death throes can eventually condense and collapse to form a new generation of stars and planets but some physicists wondered whether supernova explosions might also leave something else behind. They calculated that, as the outer layers of the dying star were blasted into space, the star's core would suffer the opposite fate, being crushed and squeezed by gravity into a tiny remnant made almost entirely of neutrons. They called this theoretical remnant a neutron star. It would contain almost as much matter as our Sun, but squeezed into a compact ball just ten kilometres across. A teaspoon full of this incredibly dense material would weigh as much as a thousand Egyptian pyramids. That might come in useful: a spaceship made of such material would have so much mass it could warp space, allowing it to cross long distances more quickly. That's what happens in the *Doctor Who* story *Warriors' Gate* (1981), with the ship made of 'dwarf star alloy'.

The pulsar discovered in 1967 was spinning so rapidly that astronomers knew it must also be very small – just a few kilometres across. Yet its intense magnetic field implied that it contained a mass similar to that of the Sun. The pulsar was clearly a neutron star – the first one ever found.

However, by the same calculations with which physicists had predicted the existence of neutron stars before finding one, some had suggested that the explosion of an even more enormous star would create a sort of funnel of increasing density which would have extraordinary properties. In 1964, an American science journalist, Ann E. Ewing, came up with a name for this amazing (and, some thought, ridiculous) idea: she called the funnel a black hole.

> 'A black hole's a dead star. It collapses in on itself, in and in and in until the matter's so dense and tight it starts to pull everything else in, too. Nothing in the universe can escape it. Light, gravity, time. Everything just gets pulled inside and crushed.'
>
> **The Tenth Doctor, *The Impossible Planet* (2006)**

The gravity of an object depends on how much matter it contains, and the more densely its matter is squeezed together the more intense its gravity becomes. This gravity warps the space-time around the object, causing nearby objects to fall towards it. We discussed in Chapter 1 how a very massive object such as our Sun warps its surrounding space-time so much that the planet Mercury doesn't appear where it ought to according to Newton's laws of gravity.

A black hole contains at least four times as much material as our Sun, but squeezed into a region far smaller than a neutron star. As we see in the *Doctor Who* episodes *The Impossible Planet* and *The Satan Pit* (2006), it's very difficult for anything – such as a planet or spaceship – to escape the enormous gravitational pull close to a black hole. But the closer you get, the stronger the gravitational pull becomes. At a certain distance – called the event horizon – the pull is so strong that you would need to be moving faster than the speed of light to escape it. According to Einstein, nothing can move faster than the speed of light, which means that nothing – not even light itself – can escape the gravitational pull at this point. (According to *Doctor Who*, the TARDIS can, which is why it can rescue spaceships from inside a black hole, as it does in *The Satan Pit*.) Once inside the spherical boundary of the event horizon your fate is sealed. All possible trajectories lead only to the centre of the black hole – a point of zero size and infinite density which physicists call a singularity.

If light cannot escape from a black hole, we'll never be able to see one directly – which is why they were given that name. But the discovery of a neutron star proved the theory that had predicted them, and suggested

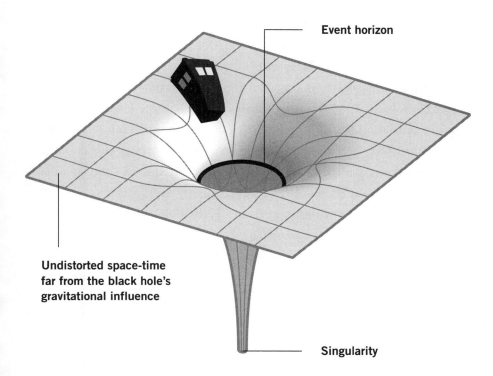

Event horizon

Undistorted space-time
far from the black hole's
gravitational influence

Singularity

that black holes might really exist, too. That encouraged more physicists to puzzle out what they would be like and to look for them.

How can you find something that's effectively invisible – because light can't escape from it? There are ways of detecting things that are otherwise invisible, by looking for the effects that they have on their surroundings. For example, in the *Doctor Who* story *The Daleks' Master Plan* (1965–1966), the Doctor, Steven and Sara are transported to another planet, but don't know where they are. We see they are not alone: an invisible something leaves a trail of footprints as it follows the Doctor. Later, when the invisible creature makes a noise and moves the branches of the foliage, the Doctor strikes out with his walking stick – and makes contact with something he cannot see. He strikes again, confirming his suspicion that it's an invisible creature and forcing it to retreat. From this encounter, he deduces that he has just been attacked by a Visian, which means he's on the planet Mira.

In the same way, we can deduce the existence of invisible black holes from their effects on their surroundings. Rather than leaving footprints or moving foliage, material from nearby can spiral round the black hole in what's called an accretion disk. The strong gravitational field close to a black hole can pull nearby gas towards it, making it spiral inwards faster and faster and heating it to extremely high temperatures. Before it disappears for ever inside the black hole's event horizon, this doomed material emits a blaze of radiation, from infrared to X- and gamma rays, allowing our telescopes to detect it.

At slightly larger distances from a black hole, objects can – just about – orbit safely, but the hole's extreme gravity yanks them round at very high speeds. An object such as a star moving in such a tight orbit will still be visible and its rapid motion can betray the presence of an invisible companion – the black hole. Astronomers can detect this motion by studying the spectrum of light which the star gives off. In 1972, astronomers Louise Webster and Paul Murdin at the Royal Greenwich Observatory and Charles Thomas Bolton at the University of Toronto published evidence of exactly this phenomenon, suggesting they had found the first black hole: Cygnus X-1. The discovery – or all the talk about black holes generally – inspired the people making *Doctor Who* at the time.

'Singularity is a point in space-time which can exist only inside a black hole. We are in a black hole, in a world of antimatter very close to this point of singularity, where all the known physical laws cease to exist. Now, Omega has got control of singularity and has learned to use the vast forces locked up inside the black hole.'

'Now, that is how Omega is able to create the world we are now living in – by a fantastic effort of his will.'

The Second and Third Doctors, *The Three Doctors* (1972–1973)

The Three Doctors was the first *Doctor Who* story to feature a black hole, and its writers also threw in another exotic (but unrelated) prediction of theoretical physics called antimatter (see box). It's a very important black hole, created by a Time Lord engineer called Omega as the power source that originally gave the Doctor's people their mastery over time. In fact, just as we refer to 'the' Sun when it's only one of millions of similar suns out in space, the Time Lords refer to this as 'the' black hole.

In fact, we now know that at the centre of every galaxy is a 'super-massive' black hole – yes, that's what astronomers really call them. The supermassive black hole at the heart of our galaxy, the Milky Way, is estimated to have a mass four million times that of our Sun (which is itself 330,000 times the mass of Earth). That's the material of four million stars squeezed into a tiny point at the centre of the galaxy. Don't worry, though: we're at a very comfortable distance of 26,000 light years from this monster black hole: in fact our solar system, and almost everything else in the galaxy, is safely orbiting round it.

How do we know this if, again, we can't see a black hole? The deduction work goes like this. It takes our solar system over 200 million years to make one complete orbit around the galaxy, but stars in the centre of the Milky Way zip around their orbits in just a few years. Moving at such rapid speeds, these stars would be flung out of the galactic centre unless there was a very powerful source of gravity – and yet no object is visible to hold them in place. From their speeds and the size of their orbits scientists can calculate the mass of the central, invisible object. It turns out to be very small but very massive indeed – and invisible. A supermassive black hole is the only answer that makes sense.

But how could a black hole help *Doctor Who*'s Time Lords travel in time? We already know that an object with a large mass warps space-time. If you were standing on the surface of a neutron star – wearing a special spacesuit so you were not squished by the intense gravity – time would be slowed down by about thirty per cent compared to time on Earth. Time would seem to pass normally for you, but if somehow you could see the Earth from where you stood, things happening there would appear to be speeded up. Effectively, the neutron star's gravity would allow you to travel through time by fast-forwarding into the Earth's future.

Close to a black hole, the effect would be even greater. In fact, warping of space-time caused by the black hole's extreme gravity can lead to some very strange effects indeed. As you fell towards a black hole an observer watching you at a safe distance from the event horizon would see time appear to slow down for you. On reaching the event horizon itself, the observer would see you apparently frozen in time. But from your point of view time would seem to pass normally, while events in the rest of the universe appeared to run at an ever increasing rate. If you could somehow pause at the event horizon and look out at the rest of the universe, you'd see all of eternity passing. That's what seems to happen to Mother of Mine at the end of *The Family of Blood* (2007): we are told that the Tenth Doctor tricks her into the event horizon of a collapsing galaxy.

But if you journey past the event horizon, there is no force which could stop your fall – and, as you plummeted ever closer to the singularity, the distorting effects of gravity would become even more pronounced. Once inside the event horizon, the normal directions of space and time become wrenched around. The space direction which was 'down' – towards the centre of the hole – becomes the time direction 'into the future'. Effectively your destiny becomes the singularity at the centre of the black hole and the universe outside the event horizon is forever barred to you, because it's locked in your personal past. So travelling into a black hole inevitably involves travelling through time, faster and faster into the future – and to escape it you'd need to be able to travel backwards in time into the past.

In effect, whatever the size of the black hole she was imprisoned in, Mother of Mine wouldn't feel she was there for very long: time outside would whizz by in an instant as she plummeted to her doom in the singularity. It's a boggling concept and not easy to comprehend. But if a ship such as the TARDIS could somehow move freely inside the black hole's gravitational field it would inevitably also travel through time. No wonder the Time Lords are interested in black holes.

'You know why this TARDIS is always rattling about the place? ... It's designed to have six pilots, and I have to do it single-handed. ... Now we can fly this thing ... Like it's meant to be flown. We've got the Torchwood Rift looped around the TARDIS by Mr Smith, and we're going to fly Planet Earth back home.'

The Tenth Doctor, *Journey's End* (2008)

In *The Deadly Assassin* (1976), the Doctor reveals that all the power of the Time Lords devolves from the nucleus of a black hole called the Eye of Harmony – though it's not clear if this is the same black hole as the one in *The Three Doctors*. According to the Time Lords' own histories, the Eye of Harmony was created by a Time Lord called Rassilon – not Omega. That might just be the official history leaving out Omega's role, but whereas we see the black hole in *The Three Doctors* somewhere out in space, the Eye of Harmony is revealed to exist on the Time Lord home planet, Gallifrey. It's such an outlandish idea – a black hole being kept on a planet – that other Time Lords don't believe it.

Another of the Doctor's own people – his companion, Romana – is surprised when the Doctor suggests in *The Horns of Nimon* (1979–1980) that a black hole can be created artificially using a gravity beam to track matter to one point in space, until there's enough mass pressed together that it collapses to a singularity. It turns out that two artificial black holes have been created, with a hyperspatial tunnel between them. The fact that this is a surprise in the story is important: it suggests that the Doctor and his people don't fully understand the physics of black holes.

Yet in the television movie *Doctor Who* (1996), we learn that the Doctor's TARDIS is powered by something also called the Eye of Harmony. When opened, this power source has the ability to warp matter so that the Doctor can step through a pane of glass, while later it endangers the whole planet. It's not stated in the TV movie that this Eye of Harmony is a black hole, but the Eleventh Doctor confirms that in *Journey to the Centre of the TARDIS* (2013).

We're not told if the Eye of Harmony in the Doctor's TARDIS is the same Eye of Harmony that was on Gallifrey in *The Deadly Assassin*. Perhaps every TARDIS was somehow linked to the same, single Eye of Harmony, which is still on Gallifrey. However, Gallifrey has been lost since the last day of the Time War (which we'll discuss more in Chapter 9) – the Doctor thought his home planet had been destroyed before discovering in *The Day of the Doctor* (2013) that he himself had moved it into a pocket universe. If there was a continuing link between his TARDIS and Gallifrey, surely he would never have believed the planet had been destroyed, and he might even have been able to use that link to make contact again with his people. There would also be no reason for him to refuel the TARDIS with rift energy, as he does in *Boom Town* (2005).

So it might be that every TARDIS contains its own unique black hole, each one called an Eye of Harmony. But other Time Lords in *The Deadly Assassin* and *The Horns of Nimon* don't seem to know much about black holes. It would be like people driving cars but not knowing about them having engines or needing petrol.

That suggests another possibility: some time between *The Deadly Assassin* and the TV movie, did the Doctor take the one and only Eye of Harmony from where it was kept on Gallifrey and use it as a new power source for his TARDIS? The Doctor tells Rose in *The Satan Pit* that his people 'practically invented black holes … Well, in fact, they did.' But it seems that he's one of the few Time Lords to know that.

At least, that's one theory, deduced from the available evidence. We might learn in a future episode that it's not right at all – that all TARDISes have black holes for engines, and there's nothing special about the one in the Doctor's TARDIS. But that's the point: we need more and better evidence before we can be sure.

Science is a series of statements that are revised and sometimes completely overturned when new evidence comes along. As we saw in

Chapter 1, the progress of science has often been the result of people puzzling over the bits of evidence that don't fit the accepted rule: that the position of Mercury doesn't fit what Newton predicted, for example. Our knowledge is provisional rather than certain.

We're still not absolutely certain that Cygnus X-1 *is* a black hole – it's just that the evidence available to us so far seems overwhelmingly to fit that idea. But it's possible that it might turn out to be something else entirely, or that we have to completely revise our ideas about black holes. Time, and better evidence, will tell.

In fact, a vast amount of the universe remains a complete mystery to us. Just four per cent of the universe is made up of baryonic matter – the atoms that make up galaxies, stars, planets and people, and that we can detect directly. We can deduce that *something* else is out there: something that does not absorb or emit light (meaning we can't see it) but that generates enough gravity to affect things around it – just like the footprints of the invisible Visians. This mysterious stuff affects the speed that stars orbit in galaxies and the way galaxies cluster together. We can even deduce that this stuff exists in the halo of our own Milky Way galaxy, and that it makes up twenty-three per cent of everything in the universe. But we currently don't know exactly what it's made of – scientists simply refer to it as 'dark matter'.

It gets stranger still. Our observations of distant galaxies tell us that the universe is expanding – getting bigger and bigger. This is what we would expect for a universe which began in the tremendous explosion of the Big Bang. But over time we would expect the gravity of the galaxies to act as a brake, pulling against the expansion and slowing it down. Instead astronomers have discovered the opposite – rather than gradually slowing down, the expansion of the universe is actually getting faster and faster as time goes by. So there must be something else in the universe, some kind of invisible force or energy which acts against gravity. Scientists have named this mysterious quantity 'dark energy' – and we can deduce that it makes up the remaining seventy-three per cent of the universe – almost three quarters of everything out there. Together, dark matter and dark energy make up a whopping ninety-six per cent of everything in the universe – almost all of it! These invisible components help to explain the large-scale structure of the universe we *can* see, but they also remind us just how little of what's out there we currently understand.

In spite of these mysteries – or because of them – we continue to explore the universe with our telescopes and spacecraft, looking for answers, slowly deducing the strange and incredible nature of reality.

In fact, that's what really drives the TARDIS – not the black hole it has as an engine, but the attitude of its pilot. Other Time Lords have TARDISes, but the Doctor uses his to explore time and space in search of the weird and wonderful, the stuff he doesn't already know. It's this unknown wonder that he offers each of his companions – and so each of us watching his adventures on TV, as well. And that's why *Doctor Who* remains so successful even after fifty years: it is powered by curiosity.

Antimatter

In *The Three Doctors*, the black hole is the source of an energy beam reaching to the Earth, a bit like the beams of electromagnetic radiation generated by a pulsar. (In fact, scientists think that black holes can also generate jets of matter and energy which are blasted into space.) Journeying along the beam and through the black hole, the Doctors discover a universe composed entirely of antimatter.

Although scientists don't know exactly what happens to material once it reaches the singularity inside a black hole, it's unlikely to be a gateway to a universe of antimatter. But antimatter does exist and is made of particles that have the same mass as ordinary matter but with the opposite electrical charge. For example, normal matter contains electrons which have a negative charge, but in antimatter the role of electrons is taken by similar particles with a positive charge – called 'positrons'. When matter and antimatter come into contact they destroy each other completely in a tremendous blast of energy – a process known as 'annihilation'. This process is important to the ending of both *The Three Doctors* and *Arc of Infinity* (1983).

As far as we can tell, our universe is made almost entirely of normal matter. It's still a bit of a mystery why the universe wasn't created with equal amounts of matter and antimatter, but perhaps it's just as well, because it wouldn't have lasted very long if it had been. However, it's possible to imagine universes like the ones in *The Three Doctors* or *Planet of Evil* (1975), where antimatter dominates over matter.

Despite its extreme rarity, antimatter is found in our universe, and tiny amounts can even be made artificially in particle accelerators like the Large Hadron Collider at CERN in Geneva. Antimatter particles are also created by natural processes such as lightning strikes and radioactive decay, although with so much normal matter around they don't usually last long. The extreme physical environments around neutron stars and black holes are also good places to look for antimatter particles and astronomers have detected the characteristic bursts of energy as they annihilate with particles of normal matter. Scientists have speculated that combining matter and antimatter could be a very efficient way of producing large amounts of energy, but the main problem would be collecting enough antimatter to be useful in the first place. So we're still a long way from understanding antimatter well enough to use it to power spacecraft, as they do in *Earthshock* (1982).

ALL THE EMPTY TOWERS

JENNY T. COLGAN

'"Kiss-me-quick-squeeze-me-slowly"?'

'Yes! Hilarious. See?'

'"Kiss. Me. Quick… Squeeze. Me. Slowly." Nope. Still nothing.'

'It's just a joke.'

'Is speed of central importance in these actions?'

Clara fixed the Doctor with a look, which he ignored as he placed the pink shiny metallic hat back down on the TARDIS console without trying it on.

'Fine, change the subject,' she said with a sigh.

'Shouldn't it be quick*ly*? Kiss me quick*ly*? Is it funny now?'

'Never mind.'

'*Kick* me quick. Now I can see how that might work. Kick me quick… appease me slowly.'

Clara marched across the console room, doing her best to keep calm.

'I just thought you might like to see where I'm from. That's all. My home. I thought you might like to visit it.'

Once upon a time, she thought bleakly, you would have. And we'd have had such a wonderful time. And you'd have loved that damn hat.

'A "black pool". Right. Good things very seldom come out of black pools in my experience. Oozing things do. Scuttling beastie type things.'

'Well, *I* did.'

'That's why you scuttle so much.'

'I do not *scuttle*! I...'

'Flounce?'

'*Glide!*' Clara tried again. 'We'll go up the tower! See the ballroom! And the illuminations! And I'll make you eat candyfloss!'

There was a very long pause. The Doctor's face was stern. Then he turned round, slowly.

'I love candyfloss.'

The TARDIS wheezed to a halt. Dressed in a black top and mini-skirt, Clara ran delightedly to the door.

'Home!' Then she turned round and regarded the Doctor. 'You'll have to take that coat off.'

The Doctor looked up, surprised. 'Well, I don't think so.'

'It's Blackpool. Nobody ever wears a coat.'

'Oh dear. A deal breaker.' He turned back towards the console display.

'You always get like this when you're doing something nice,' shouted Clara cheerily as she headed for the door. 'I just ignore it. Mind you,' she went on, almost to herself, 'Blackpool in November... maybe we can let you off just this once.'

Then she stepped out of the TARDIS into a steaming hot jungle.

The vines hung heavy in the trees, which were weighed down with strange brightly coloured fruits. The air was damp and sweet with the scent of rotting vegetation. Underfoot were fallen fronds and burst pomegranates, decaying where they lay.

'Oh no,' said Clara, looking round, her hands on her hips. 'This isn't Blackpool. Stupid TARDIS.'

The Doctor popped his head out of the door, then glanced back at the console readout. 'It most certainly is,' he said as he stepped out into the lush green landscape. 'Oh, it's lovely! You should have said!'

'No!' said Clara. 'This is a jungle! Blackpool has a Ferris wheel. And a beach! And...' She looked up. Overhead, the great wrought iron structure of the Blackpool Tower was slightly tilted. It had oxidised, and great vines twisted their way through the gaping holes in its structure. Brightly coloured birds swooped round the top. In front of them was what remained of the Golden Mile. Smashed lightbulbs crunched underfoot from the ruined illuminations; the promenade was completely overgrown, and high black waves lapped right across the cracked tramlines. In the distance, through the broken-down struts of the Big One rollercoaster, she saw, stilting along awkwardly –

'...*giraffes?*' Clara whipped round to face the Doctor. 'Giraffes? What's happened to my hometown?'

The Doctor took out his pocket watch. 'Oh. Yeah. Bit late.'

She glanced at the writhing greenery. 'Is this the trees doing a thing again?'

The Doctor shook his head sadly. ''Fraid not. This is here to stay. It's 2089. It's climate change. The real deal. Looks like all those Bags for Life you bought didn't quite do the trick.'

Clara stepped forward, horrified. 'The Golden Mile, the sand... it was already eroding in my time, you could see it. But they built these sea defences...' She looked at them. The concrete barriers were overwhelmed with water; crumbled away.

Horrified, Clara started to run down the promenade, broken glass crunching under her feet. The pier sagged heavily into the high seas, bent and twisted into cruel shapes, dripping vines. Past the pier, a spit of black sand remained, in front of the ruins of the fish and chip shops; upturned plastic ice cream bins bobbing up and down in the water; a shipwrecked tram. She stopped and stared, mouth open.

Hurtling across the sand at full pelt, their heads and manes tossing in the warm wind, their hooves galloping in the rushing water, was a herd of wild donkeys. They looked beautiful and strange, outlined against the dark seas.

Clara's hand went to her mouth.

The Doctor came over, casually eating a handful of grapes that stained his mouth. 'This place is amazing... What?'

'The donkeys! They're running wild!'

'Beautiful...'

As they watched the animals gambolling in the surf, suddenly, as if out of nowhere, came a flashing, buzzing noise. A jagged silver disc, smaller than a frisbee, zipped through the sky, and embedded itself in the side of one of the donkeys, which immediately whinnied in distress and collapsed on the beach.

'Oh no!'

Clara darted across the sand towards it, as the herd left the creature behind. The wounded animal was tossing and writhing in pain, and she couldn't get close for the thrashing hooves.

'That projectile was about the size of a CD,' said the Doctor, coming up behind her. 'I wonder what it was. Simply Red? I mean, I can understand the urge to throw...'

The donkey was grunting and screeching as the Doctor moved closer, his face taking on an expression, Clara thought, rather gentler than the one he habitually wore when dealing with creatures on two legs.

'Sssh,' he said. He knelt down away from the animal's pistoning limbs, and put both hands either side of the donkey's head.

The flailing, terrified creature was immediately soothed at his touch, and quietened its terrible keening and thrashing.

'Sssh.'

The donkey and the Doctor regarded one another, as the Doctor very carefully and steadily, making no sudden movements, took one hand from the creature's head, and slowly pulled the jagged silver weapon from the donkey's side, hurling it away. Then, without breaking eye contact, he took out his sonic and quickly sealed and cauterised the wound.

The donkey's muzzle relaxed in the Doctor's hands, and it made a quiet braying.

'There, there.'

Clara looked around. She screwed up her eyes against the sun.

'Who did that? Who was it?'

Bang. The next silver disc missed the Doctor's boots by inches. He jumped up, patting the donkey briefly on its flank.

'Don't worry, Meghan. We'll get this sorted, OK?'

Pow!

The disc shot straight across the black sand. The sun poured through the canopy of overgrown bushes on the promenade, as Clara and the Doctor backed away rapidly towards the water.

'The donkey's called Meghan?'

'She's not called anything... Thought she might like Meghan.'

They splashed through the black water and crouched behind a twisted stanchion, as the Doctor pointed towards a distant window in an overgrown boarding house. A tumbled sign read 'The Arnold Guest House'; Clara remembered it well. It had already been nearly derelict when she was a girl.

Now, the jungle had grown straight through it. Thick vines had broken through the tiles of the roof, so it looked like the guest house had come down from the sky and landed on a tree, rather than the other way around. Every empty window frame was a mass of twisted greenery. In one of the upper windows, Clara suddenly caught sight of a flash of light; and in the next instant, a buzzing silver disc shot right over their heads.

The Doctor grabbed her by the hand and they splashed deeper backwards into the water under the eerie blackness of the skeletal pier. Clara blinked as, from the waves, a shoal of flying fish leapt up, their strange yellow webbed fins glinting in the spots of light; then they splashed back underwater.

'Whoa!'

Together they spied an abandoned pedalo; flotsam, bobbing underneath the pier. They glanced at one another.

'I don't think so,' said the Doctor.

'Pedalos are cool,' pleaded Clara. 'It'll be fun!'

The latest disc bounced off the top of the water.

'It's not a day for fun!' said the Doctor.

'Yes, well, that's becoming clear,' said Clara.

Instead, they waded across to the other side of the pier, out of range, then splashed full pelt over the esplanade wall that was covered in broken glass from the shattered lights. They ducked across the tramlines, faded and dull underwater. Then they circled round and backed up Pleasant Street, looking out for the sniper. Clara noticed in passing her old favourite chippie, but all she could smell now was thick green vegetation, heavy and exotic fruit.

The Doctor opened the rotting wooden back door of the Arnold with a swift kick.

'Hey!' he shouted loudly. 'Sniper boy! We're completely unarmed and you're playing "Now That's What I Call Chopping Up a Donkey Volume 1", so how about you come down and we have a wee chat about that?'

There was silence. The ancient carpet beneath their feet was brown and moist, but in here, amongst the damp creepers, Clara could still sense something of the many, many old breakfasts, the bacon and the sausage and over-stewed tea and HP sauce. She found it comforting.

There was no noise. The building was large, with many creaking, chipped old doors opening off a long corridor, covered in peeling fire exit signs.

'Third floor, fourth window from the left,' whispered the Doctor. They stopped and listened.

Suddenly, overhead, there came a footstep – steady, heavy in tread – then another.

'Come out, you big feartie!' shouted the Doctor

'What if he comes down and shoots us with his silver frisbee thing?'

'I'll talk him out of it with my friendly wit and charm.'

'So we're doomed, then.'

There was a creaking of a vine, and a large pineapple bounced down the stairs straight past them. Clara jumped, and glanced at the Doctor, whose face was impassive.

The footsteps continued slowly, and Clara found she was holding her breath.

'Hello?' she shouted. The staircase, wound around with vines, headed upwards into darkness.

The footsteps stopped over their heads. Then, very slowly, a foot appeared at the top of the twisted stairwell. It was wearing a very worn, grubby sheepskin slipper, over a pair of very baggy tan-coloured tights. The Doctor and Clara watched as another leg continued down, revealing a matching slipper: but the leg in this slipper was a skeletal steel.

'Are you going to shoot us?' said Clara, trying to sound brave.

'It's after 9 a.m.!' came a harsh metallic voice. 'No guests in the guest house after 9 a.m.!'

Clara backed away. The figure continued to descend. It was half a very old woman, swathed in layers of nighties and a huge filthy floral patterned housecoat. Ancient rollers were wrapped in thin dead wisps of hair, under a dirty headscarf. The other half of her face, where the wizened skin had been worn away, was metal.

The half-woman, half-machine brandished a large silver circular launcher at them.

'What is she?' asked Clara.

'Most horrifying creature in God's creation,' whispered the Doctor. 'A landlady!'

That got the half-woman's attention.

'No guests in the guest house after 9 a.m.!'

The Doctor moved forwards. 'I'm sorry to disturb you, madam. We were hoping to rent a room for the night?'

'Off-season! No guests in the guesthouse after 9 a.m.!'

She blinked very hard suddenly, looking slightly confused, and Clara wondered if she knew what she was.

'Where did everybody go?' asked Clara gently.

'Off-season! Off-season!' Her voice was sounding more robotic. She lifted up the blaster. 'No guests in the...'

Clara moved towards her.

'No, wait!' said the Doctor, trying to stop her. But Clara shook him off.

'Are you all right?' she asked gently. The woman's face suddenly looked more human than robot, and Clara felt very sorry for her.

The woman looked down. 'I don't like it when it gets dark,' she said. 'The animals make noises.'

'What are you doing shooting animals?' asked the Doctor in consternation.

The woman's face turned still and her voice took on a metallic tinge again. 'Got to have sausages for breakfast! Guests need sausages! Sausages and out by 9 a.m.! But you're not guests, are you? Are you sausages?'

The woman moved forward suddenly, incredibly swiftly, and opened her mouth. The scream, when it came, was horrifyingly loud.

'NO GUESTS!' she screamed, advancing with the blaster. 'NO GUESTS!!!!!'

The Doctor grabbed Clara by the hand and led her backwards towards the door.

'Wait!' wailed the half-woman.

'But she's...' said Clara, still stricken.

There was a sudden whirring noise outside.

'Clara, she's *not* a confused old lady!' said the Doctor, furiously. 'Have you seen how they make sausages?'

They ran out of the old boarding house – but it was already too late. Four spaceships were hovering above the ground, surrounding them. They were small ships, open at the top, and in each was a young man or two, staring at them, laughing, pointing their blasters in their direction.

The spaceships were silver: pointed at the front, short range, nippy-looking things, and they bobbed strangely up and down in the air. They reminded Clara of something, but she couldn't think what.

'Hands up!' came a loud, entitled voice. The Doctor let out an irritated growl.

'Nice ships,' whispered Clara, putting up her hands.

'What!? They're all round… and slick, and aerodynamic-y,' said the Doctor in disgust.

A young man in a bright red jacket popped his head out of the top of one of the ships and waved his arm crossly. 'I say, what the ruddy hell are you doing in my hunt?'

'Your *what*?'

'My hunting grounds. It's clearly marked. All of the Pleasure Beach is a hunting ground.'

'It's a *what*?' said Clara again.

The man sighed. 'Oh lord, are you frightfully dim? My friend and I have hired out the Hunt. You're trespassing on my shoot.'

'Climate change drove people out… so they turned it into a hunting zone?' said Clara, incredulously.

'Well, you would keep electing those posh boys,' murmured the Doctor.

The man's lip curled. 'Anything that comes across our path is fair game, what?'

All his fellows laughed and passed a bottle amongst themselves, and one launched a silver disc straight up into the air. It caught the sun as it fell, slicing through the air. The man took a large swig of his own hip flask, and smiled unpleasantly.

'We were hoping to bag a big one today – it's my stag night.' He glanced at his fellows. 'Shall we bag an oik, boys?'

The other men laughed unpleasantly.

'Debag the oiks, more like!' squealed one excitedly. 'Let's go, Triss!'

The Doctor stepped forward, gripping his lapels. 'I don't think so.'

'Oh, it *talks*!' said Triss. 'Calm down, dear.'

The other men guffawed.

'You probably want to think very seriously about what you're doing here,' the Doctor went on.

Triss whirled round in his silver ship, his mouth slack and wide.

'No we *don't*!' he roared suddenly. 'We have to live in a world your generation ruined. We have to live in a world nobody your age "thought seriously about" at all. You left us with black sand and black water and black pools. And all we have left is a damn rare chance to have a little sport. And this is my stag night. And I shall have my sport, old man.'

He unleashed a disc that struck the Doctor's foot, and would have made anybody else jump.

'Hang on... Who on earth would marry *you*?' said Clara, stepping forward.

'I own the very last snow-topped mountain in Switzerland,' said the man called Triss. 'They're queuing up, I assure you.'

His friends laughed again. Triss looked down on Clara and the Doctor, a dangerous look on his face, and took another swig from his flask. 'The landlady wasn't expecting you,' he said. 'Which means *nobody* knows you're here. I wonder if you'll be missed?'

The others laughed. He raised his circular blaster.

'Three... two... one – tally ho!'

And one of the others blew a hunting horn.

The Doctor and Clara pounded down the esplanade and hurled themselves into the first building they came to, a huge old crumbling edifice of brown stone. They found themselves in a large ticket office with glass windows facing inside and out.

Clara looked around. 'Oh my god,' she said. 'This is the old circus! My nan brought me here!'

'What animals did they have?' said the Doctor.

'Oh, *now* you're interested in my childhood... Are they really trying to kill us?'

'*Hunting is a savage pleasure, and we are born to it*,' quoted the Doctor, then leapt forward and pulled Clara to the ground, as a jagged silver disc shot right through the rotten wood, embedding itself where her neck had been moments before.

The Doctor got up and pulled the disc out of the wall. It was incredibly sharp. Clara looked at him from the floor, her heart thudding in her chest. She looked around the ruined palace.

'Is this what happens? Is this it? Is this what happens to the town I was born in? To my home? To the world?'

The Doctor shrugged. 'It's not a fixed point in time, if that's what you mean.'

Clara's face brightened, a little, and she straightened up. 'Then that's good enough for me.'

She crept very carefully closer to the small window, and eyed up the little silver ships, buzzing and bouncing around the sky, the men boasting and shouting to one another.

'Is it just me, or is there something odd about those ships?' said Clara. 'They don't look like they're being steered properly, they just bump all over the place.'

'You're right,' said the Doctor, joining her. 'You'd expect them to move differently depending on who was driving them. But they don't. They all look the same. Like—'

'Like dodgem cars!' burst out Clara, suddenly. 'They wobble around each other like they're being really badly steered. Like dodgems!'

'But dodgems have an overhead power source.'

'I know.'

The Doctor held up his sonic and did some fast triangulation. 'If you connect up the angle of their aerials,' he said. 'You come back to the power source...' He followed the line with a long finger. Then he stopped and stabbed at the sky. 'It stops just overhead. What's overhead?'

'The tower,' gasped Clara, suddenly realising. 'We're at the bottom of the tower.'

'Hunting ships for hire,' said the Doctor. 'But attached.'

Triss suddenly stood up out of his ship again, laughing dangerously and pointing at them.

'Why is he laughing?' said Clara nervously.

'You know how I was asking what animals they had in the circus?' said the Doctor.

There was a sudden, low growl just outside the dusty space.

Clara jumped up. She could see the lion now, through a window in the office door. It was prowling through a great cavernous dusty space, with a wooden floor and old peeling posters for long-gone attractions. It was old, shaggy of mane, thin and hungry-looking, pacing the floor as if it didn't know what else to do; occasionally raising its great mangy head to sniff the air.

'Oh, my goodness,' said Clara. 'The circus! The zoo! The donkeys!'

'The hunt,' said the Doctor, opening his hands.

Clara glanced around the office desperately. There was a large works cupboard in the corner. As she opened it, a harsh hot wind blew down into the room, and a rattling noise filled their ears. The large space was completely filled with rubble.

'What's that?'

'Lift shaft,' said the Doctor. It was full of collapsed metal equipment. 'Can you climb it?'

Outside the office on one side, the lion threw back its ancient head and roared. On the other, another disc smashed the one remaining glass window, and Clara caught a glimpse of flashing silver.

Clara glanced at the lion and back at the Doctor. 'You know, he reminds me of someone.'

'Up!' said the Doctor sharply, as Clara pulled herself onto the oily metal chain.

They managed to climb two floors up the lift shaft before it became impassably blocked by machinery.

'There must be another lift,' said the Doctor.

Clara pushed up the hatch, and they both leapt out to run across the floor.

'Careful,' shouted the Doctor. 'It might be rotten.'

But Clara had made it as far as the middle of the floor, then stopped stock still.

The red velvet curtains bloomed with flowers of rot. The famous Wurlitzer organ lay in pieces, scattered amongst the vines that trailed across the famous sprung wooden dance floor; the gilded balconies crushed and collapsed one on top of the other.

'The tower ballroom,' said Clara reverently.

The Doctor had made it to the end of the floor already, and was opening up the opposite shaft with his sonic. 'Come on Clara!'

'I always... when I was a little girl I was too shy. But I always wanted to dance on this floor. I always dreamed of it. Of coming back here one day...'

'You can't go home again,' the Doctor said. 'But you can get shot at by a bunch of overbred chin-free maniacs, if that helps.'

Clara wasn't listening; she was caught in a spell. She moved a step across the floor, then another, then looked up at him. 'Can you dance?'

The Doctor paused in exasperation. 'No, of course I can't dance! Come on, get climbing!'

'Never mind,' said Clara, sadly, as she followed him out and up.

The exterior lifts had long collapsed to the bottom, and the only thing to be done was to climb up and out, scaling the struts of the tower itself, hand over hand. It was frightening and exhausting, as they got higher and higher, and Clara looked out over the black water as far as she could see, and down, over her ruined town; and across, to where she saw great tall electrified fences, wild animals roaming the abandoned streets, the endless jungle and great lakes beyond, and above, a thick blanket of cloud, keeping in the oppressive heat, the sun blazing just beyond.

A hot wind swayed the tower, and the Doctor's foot slipped, but he managed to grab back on. The noise, however, startled a great company of parrots, who rose in the air, squawking wildly, and the Doctor and Clara heard the noise of the hunting horn, as the birds attracted the silver ships, which came rushing up towards them, bumping each other in their hurry. They felled a couple of the beautiful birds, but their real target was the Doctor and Clara themselves, who ducked underneath to attempt the far more difficult job of climbing up the inside. After two agonising floors of this, they reached a small platform with a service ladder, and started to move at full tilt, as the noise of connecting discs jarred their way up the metal structure.

They reached the trap door to the top viewing platform just in time, as one disc sliced through a cable, and an entire section of the ladder peeled off the side of the building and clanged its way a hundred metres below, smashing through the ballroom roof.

They found themselves in a high room lined with heavy glass that hadn't yet cracked: for the first time since they'd landed, Clara realised, there was power on. The room hummed with it. There was a central console with a large connecting wire that shot straight through the ceiling – the aerial.

The Doctor ran to the computer.

As soon as he touched the keyboard, immediately the alarm went off: 'NO GUESTS! NO GUESTS! NO GUESTS!!'

And from the dim shadows in the tiny control room at the top of the Blackpool Tower appeared another hideous half old lady, half robot; this one in a huge floral day dress covered in a stiff blue nylon tabard. Her face was more metal than the other's; the little skin left on it was dried and fraying off, like old leather.

'Sausages!' it said, starting to slowly raise its hand with the circular launcher. The silver pods surrounded the glass control room, buzzing back and forth and laughing. One was filming from a tiny device.

'Now that,' said the Doctor, typing furiously, 'would be a terrible last word to hear, wouldn't it? I mean, even "blood sausage" might have worked a bit better.'

He continued working feverishly on the console as the robot landlady advanced despite Clara's best efforts to kick at her swollen ankles in the sheepskin slippers.

'Doctor!'

Clara was back to back with the Doctor now, looking over his shoulder.

'Leave me alone,' said the Doctor, huffing in frustration. 'I need to do this... stupid computer...'

'Yeah I know,' shrieked Clara, as the hand rose higher and the scent of old breakfasts and popcorn and Rothmans filled the space. 'But you've left the Caps Lock on.'

'Oh yeah,' said the Doctor tutting. He typed some more, and suddenly the humming noise stopped, and the robot landlady abruptly powered down and collapsed onto the floor.

Clara let out a sigh of relief that turned to a yell of fright – as she saw through the glass walls the four silver pods surrounding them lurch, and then, suddenly, drop out of the sky.

'They're falling!'

The Doctor paused. For a barely an instant.

Then, with a sigh, he took out his screwdriver and planted it into the circuit, where it connected up the overhead power again.

'I think I've had a fall,' said the woman, querulously. Clara looked at the Doctor, who shook his head tersely, typing with one hand. Instead, she peered out of the windows. The silver ships had juddered to a halt, and now were descending slowly and gracefully, round and round the tower, like a fairground ride, until they gently reached the ground and came to a halt. The lion leapt out of the booking office window to have a sniff about. The men's bravado did not extend to them getting out of their pods.

The Doctor complained about his burnt-out screwdriver all the way back down the endless climb and halfway across the ballroom.

Clara took one last look around. 'So no one will ever come here again?'

'I've sealed the fences and put in a skynet,' said the Doctor. 'These hunting grounds are closed.'

'I could never come back here anyway,' said Clara with a shudder, looking at the thick dust covered in their footprints. Motes floated in the air, lit by the hole in the ceiling that let in the sunlight, the whirling ghosts of dancers forever departed.

'Things decay,' said the Doctor. 'But remember, Clara, this isn't a fixed point. It doesn't have to be like this.'

Clara nodded glumly as they crossed the once pristine floor.

The Doctor looked at her stricken face. 'So maybe I do dance,' he said quietly. 'A bit.'

She looked at him.

'Obviously,' said the Doctor. 'You don't infiltrate the deadly French court without mastery of the gavotte.'

'The gavotte?' said Clara. 'Is that the only dance you can do?'

'No,' said the Doctor. 'Also, the quadrille. Take it or leave it.'

He knocked his blackened screwdriver several times hard against his boot, until it emitted a tiny peep and beam of light, and directed it towards what was left of the organ, which started up, creakily, painfully, its old programme, a very slow, mournful version of 'We Do Like to Be Beside the Seaside' in a minor key.

Clara put on her bravest smile as he reached for her hand.

The lion had long gone by the time they got down to street level and marched the chastened men to the perimeter fence. The Doctor saw Clara desperate to ask questions, and halted her with a look.

'Don't,' he warned gently. 'And you,' he said to Triss. 'If I hear of you treating your wife with a fraction of the contempt with which you treat the rest of creation – and I hear everything – I will happily bounce you off that tower myself, do I make myself understood?'

'Yes, sir.'

'Good boy. You can go.'

They stood on the beach, throwing pebbles in the water. The Doctor looked at Clara. 'You need to work harder in your own time, don't you think? Educate all those millions of children of yours? It's not fixed… yet.'

Clara nodded. Then she looked up at him. 'You do know they're not actually my children? I just teach them?'

The Doctor ignored her, and spoke on, gazing out at the sea.

Suddenly he was almost knocked into the surf by a donkey launching itself on him, licking his face like an overgrown dog.

'Hey!' he said. 'Hey, Meghan! How are you? How are you, girl? There you are.' He scratched behind her ears and she rubbed her head against him adoringly. Then she got down on all fours.

'Oh no,' said the Doctor. 'No. No. Definitely not.'

Clara smiled. 'I think she wants to. You should roll up the bottom of your trousers so you don't get wet.'

The Doctor gave her a look.

'Ooh!' She felt into her pocket and pulled out the pink plastic hat she'd grabbed from the console. 'And here. Stick this on!'

'No hats!'

'Stick it on!' She reached up and put it on for him.

'I don't want…' Meghan had already nudged herself underneath him, and got to her feet, lifting him up. 'I don't…'

But it was too late. Donkey and Time Lord were already proceeding at a stately pace through the shallow waters against the twisted wreckage of the pier. Clara, giggling, watched them splashing away in the light of the huge pink setting sun, as the Doctor gently rubbed the donkey's ears and, when he thought he was unobserved, planted a very quick kiss on the animal's head.

FIVE

THE FUTURE OF EARTH

'Why are Earth people so parochial?'

The Fifth Doctor, *The Visitation* (1982)

Learning more about outer space has taught us a lot about the Earth and our existence here. But some of what we've learnt is pretty scary...

What do we gain from exploring outer space? As we saw in Chapter 2, it's very expensive to send spacecraft and people into orbit round the Earth, let alone to other worlds. Government-funded space programmes have to justify that expense to the taxpayer, while privately funded programmes are paid for by people who want to see a return on their investment.

On 20 July 1969, a few hours after the first two people to walk on the Moon began their journey back to Earth, the BBC's *Panorama* listed the benefits of the space programme as they were seen then. Reporter Julian Pettifer explained that 'the analysis of pictures taken hundreds of miles out in space can reveal new mineral deposits. They've already led to the discovery of new oil fields. In agriculture, satellite pictures can provide data on erosion and irrigation, and their value to the weather forecaster is already established. Soon, urban planners may be using astronauts' photographs to help them plan road systems.'

In going to space, we learnt more about the Earth, but pictures from space did more than tell us about new ways to exploit our planet's resources. One photograph in particular helped transform our ideas about our relationship with Earth.

Before Apollo 11 could put the first people on the Moon, scientists needed to test their equipment and calculations, and also know more about the lunar surface. In December 1968, Apollo 8 became the first manned mission to be sent there. It didn't land on the Moon but orbited ten times, taking pictures of potential landing sites.

Then, on Christmas Eve, Apollo 8 astronauts William Anders, Frank Borman and James Lovell saw the most incredible sight over the lunar horizon. Their voices were recorded, so we know their reactions as they struggled with a camera:

'Look at that picture over there! There's the Earth comin' up. Wow, is that pretty!'

'Hey, don't take that – it's not scheduled.'

'You got a color film, Jim? Hand me that roll of color quick.'

William Anders and Frank Borman, Apollo 8, 24 December 1968

Borman was joking, but the astronauts *hadn't* been scheduled to take pictures of the Earth from space – only of the Moon, and those in black and white. The focus of the mission was getting out into space, not to look back at where the astronauts had come from. However, Anders quickly put colour film in his camera (a reminder of how long ago this was and how basic the technology was back then!) and took pictures of that extraordinary view...

The photographs show the blue and white Earth hanging brightly in the black of space above the cratered, grey lunar surface. One of the photographs, known as 'Earthrise', became one of the most recognised and reprinted images of the twentieth century: it was soon used on the cover of the influential magazine *Time* and issued as a stamp.

Why was 'Earthrise' so effective? Satellites had been taking increasingly detailed pictures of Earth from space since 1959. What made 'Earthrise' different was that it also shows the lunar landscape in the foreground. We're used to seeing the same view the other way round: the Moon in the sky over Earth's horizon. More than that, including the lunar landscape also provides a disturbing sense of scale. The Earth looks tiny and vulnerable – and at the time, to many, it was a surprise to learn that our planet is brightly, vividly blue.

Something similar is going on at the start of *Spearhead from Space* (1970), the first adventure of the Third Doctor. The opening shot is of stars in space. The camera pans left and finds the shining, blue-white Earth, while eerie sound effects suggest an alien threat.

It's a quick and simple way of establishing the new format of the series. With this Doctor stranded on Earth without the use of his TARDIS, we would no longer travel in space and time to find monsters, so they would have to come to us. But Earth was at threat from more than just monsters. In *Spearhead from Space*, our dependency on plastic is made to work against us. In the next story, *Doctor Who and the Silurians*, a research project that aims to develop cheap atomic energy unleashes a deadly force. In the same year, *Inferno* sees a mining project unleash its own terrible threat to humanity. The characters running these projects are keen to press on, despite the warnings from the Doctor and other scientists. One politician ignores the Doctor and unwittingly spreads a killer disease across London. One scientist ignores the evidence in front of him and ends up destroying the world. (Luckily, it's a parallel world, as we discussed in Chapter 3.)

These stories seem to reflect wider concerns from the time in which they were made about the inherent dangers in the way we exploited our planet's resources. As *Inferno* was being recorded in April 1970, the first 'Earth Day' saw 20 million Americans take to the streets to call for a healthy, sustainable environment. Earth Day was directly inspired by a large oil spill in California, but it was also the result of an emerging public awareness about pollution of the water and air.

That awareness had been helped by a 1962 bestseller, *Silent Spring*, in which marine biologist Rachel Carson spelt out the damage being done to birds and the countryside by the uncontrolled use of pesticides. She also said that the makers of the pesticides lied about the effects of their chemicals, and that the government was too willing to believe whatever they said.

The evidence presented in *Silent Spring* led to the banning of the pesticide DDT in the United States of America. It also clearly influenced *Doctor Who* stories such as *Planet of Giants* (1964) – which we discussed in Chapter 3 – and *The Green Death* (1973), which we'll come on to shortly. However, it's been argued that environmental concerns remained abstract ideas to the general public until the 'Earthrise' photograph suddenly made the issues very clear. Whatever the case, going to the Moon and what we learned there taught us a lot about how our own environment can be threatened.

For example, evidence collected by going to the Moon proved what caused the lunar craters. Before that, theories had included volcanic eruptions or the movements of glaciers, but now it is known they are the result of meteorites and asteroids colliding with the Moon. Scientists wondered if Earth might also have suffered such impacts – and found evidence of that, too. Then, in 1980, physicists Luis and Walter Alvarez suggested that an asteroid hitting the Earth 65 million years ago wiped out the dinosaurs. That theory was used as the basis for the *Doctor Who* story *Earthshock* (1982) – although it wasn't until 2010 that an international panel of scientists finally favoured the Alvarez hypothesis over other theories.

We also now know that the presence of the Moon stabilises the tilt of the Earth's axis, helping to regulate the seasons, and affects the tides and movement of tectonic plates – all things that it has been suggested helped life to develop and thrive here. As *Kill the Moon* (2014) showed, changes to the Moon's orbit and gravitational influence would be disastrous for life on our planet.

It's not just the Moon we have learnt from. Venus is the nearest planet to Earth. As we saw in Chapter 1, Venus, like Earth, is just about at the right distance from the Sun for water to be in liquid form – in a region known as the 'habitable zone'. However, the atmosphere of Venus is many times thicker than Earth's and is mostly composed of carbon dioxide, with a dense layer of sulphuric acid cloud. In 1962, the Mariner 2 spacecraft orbited Venus and confirmed a theory that the carbon dioxide acts like a blanket, trapping the Sun's heat and raising the temperature of the planet. We now know that, despite being further from the Sun than Mercury, Venus actually has the highest average surface temperature of any planet in the Solar System – an incredible 462°C! Water would evaporate in that incredible heat, and tin and lead would melt!

It's thought that, until four billion years ago, conditions on Venus were more like those on Earth, with lots of liquid water. What changed is much debated among scientists, but it seems a moderate increase in temperature meant that the surface water evaporated into the atmosphere where it began to trap the Sun's heat, causing the temperature to rise still further. Without any water on the surface, carbon dioxide from volcanoes also began to build up in Venus's atmosphere leading to a runaway warming effect and creating the searing temperatures which we find there today. An Earth-like world was transformed into a planet so hot that it soon destroys any spacecraft we send there.

The climate of Mars has also been transformed. It's a cold, dry world now, but the robots currently exploring its surface – Opportunity and Curiosity – have found minerals that are formed only in water. This and studies of the networks of valleys on the Martian surface suggest that Mars was once warmer, wetter and much more like Earth. It seems that conditions changed about four billion years ago – roughly the same time that they changed on Venus, too. Here the problem was reversed: Mars's thin atmosphere is also mostly composed of carbon dioxide but there is too little of it to hold on to the Sun's warmth. As its temperatures plunged, Mars's water was frozen into the icecaps and soil, and the planet became a chilly desert with an average surface temperature of -55°C. (In *Doctor Who*, this change in climate is the reason why the Ice Warriors were forced to abandon their Martian home.)

Planetary scientists are still trying to understand the details of how Mars and Venus could start out in such a similar state to the Earth and yet end up looking so different. But the fact that conditions on the two planets closest to us transformed so dramatically is a worrying prospect – especially when we look at how conditions on Earth are currently changing.

Here on Earth, carbon dioxide and other gases in the atmosphere also act to raise the planet's average temperature. Without this 'greenhouse effect', Earth would have an average surface temperature of just -18°C rather than its current balmy value of +15°C. Our planet would be too cold for liquid water, and life could probably not exist here.

Up until very recently, Earth's natural carbon dioxide levels had a beneficial effect, helping to keep the planet warm and habitable. However, evidence is mounting from satellites and ground-based measurements that this natural thermostat is increasingly out of balance. For the past few decades, the average temperature of the world has been increasing. As the planet warms, ice sheets, snow cover, glaciers and Arctic sea ice are all rapidly declining. The melting of large areas of ice on land produces huge volumes of water that flow into the sea. This means that sea levels have risen more in the past decade than they did in the last century. The oceans are warming, too, as is the planet as a whole: ten of the warmest summers since 1880 have occurred in the past twelve years.

This rise in global temperatures affects our weather: a warmer climate can carry more water vapour in it, so we experience heavier rainfall and there's a higher likelihood of extreme weather conditions, such as major storms and tornadoes. It's highly unlikely that the Earth will ever suffer such dramatic transformations as Mars and Venus but any change in sea level or seasonal patterns of weather and temperature could make life very uncomfortable for our planet's natural ecosystems. As Clara and the Doctor found when they visited Blackpool in 2089, climate change will have serious consequences for all of us.

What could be causing this rapid rise in temperature? Unfortunately, the most likely culprit is us. Since the Industrial Revolution began in the eighteenth century, humans have been burning fossil fuels such as coal, oil and gas at ever-increasing rates. The waste product of all this energy-guzzling activity is carbon dioxide. At the same time, we've been clearing large tracts of the Earth's surface for agriculture and urban development, removing the forests and marshlands which once helped to suck additional carbon dioxide from the air. Our atmosphere's carbon dioxide level is now almost fifty per cent higher than it was before the Industrial Revolution began, just 250 years ago – and it's still going up.

If learning more about space helped reveal what we're doing to Earth, perhaps it can also help us find solutions to slow or even reverse the damage. Perhaps the *Doctor Who* story *The Green Death* might show us how.

At the beginning of *The Green Death*, the Doctor and his companion Jo Grant talk at cross purposes. He wants to show her the famous blue sapphires of the planet Metebelis 3, while Jo wants to rush to Wales to take part in a protest against pollution caused by a chemicals firm. The Doctor makes the same offer he makes all his companions – the chance to see the universe. Yet Jo turns him down.

'Jo, you've got all the time in the world,
and all the space. I'm offering them to you.'

'But, Doctor, don't you understand? I've got to go!
This Professor Jones, he's fighting for everything
that's important, everything that you've fought for.
In a funny way, he reminds me of a sort of younger you.'

The Third Doctor and Jo Grant, *The Green Death* (1973)

Note that Jo is keen to join the protest *because* of what she's learnt from the Doctor – travelling with him in space and time has made her better appreciate what needs to be done to save Earth in her own time.

In fact, Jo's reaction to travelling in the TARDIS is unlike that of any other companion. When she first meets the Doctor in *Terror of the Autons* (1971), he can't operate the TARDIS and is stuck on Earth. The Doctor and Jo both work for UNIT, their job to help keep Earth safe from alien menaces. Jo doesn't visit another world until her fifteenth episode – and she isn't impressed:

'That's an alien world out there, Jo. Think of it.'

$\partial^3 \sum x^2$ 'I don't want to think of it. I want to go back to Earth.'

The Third Doctor and Jo Grant, *Colony in Space* (1971)

It's the same a year later in *The Curse of Peladon* – Jo would much rather go on a date with Captain Mike Yates than visit another world. When the Time Lords give the Doctor control over the TARDIS again in *The Three Doctors* (1972–1973), Jo agrees to go with him on a test flight – and is then horrified to get caught up in three consecutive adventures in space and time. She leaves him in the next story.

We can understand why the people making *Doctor Who* created a companion who didn't want to travel in space and time: if she doesn't then neither do we, so we're less likely to resent the Doctor's exile to Earth. But the people making *Doctor Who* were also keen to address concerns about contemporary politics and the environment – even when the Doctor was occasionally able to take the TARDIS out into space.

As we saw in Chapter 2, in *Colony in Space* Jo is told that on the Earth of AD 2471 there is 'No room to move, polluted air, not a blade of grass left on the planet and a government that locks you up if you think for yourself.' When she visits Earth in the twenty-sixth century in *Frontier in Space* (1973), those who speak out against the government in favour of peace are sent to prison on the Moon – where corrupt officials conspire to murder them. We see more corruption in *The Mutants* (1972), when Jo visits an Earth colony in the thirtieth century. We see the Earth Empire's brutal exploitation of the planet Solos with little thought for the Solonians – who are kept in segregated communities and murdered by the authorities. War, pollution and corruption are all too familiar aspects of recent history, and *Doctor Who* seems to be warning us that – just as in the past – the biggest risk to human health and happiness in the future might be our own greed and violence.

Of course, human activity isn't the only danger threatening our planet's future. As we've seen, it's thought that the dinosaurs were wiped out after a large object collided with the Earth. How likely is another such collision – one that could wipe out humanity? A smaller asteroid exploded above the Tunguska region of Siberia in 1908, destroying thousands of square kilometres of forest, while in 2013 a 20-metre-wide asteroid blew up over the Russian city of Chelyabinsk, shattering windows and injuring more than a thousand people. Astronomers know that larger asteroids are out there and eventually one of these will inevitably strike our planet again.

Even if Earth survives the threat of impact, there is one fate our planet can't avoid. A star like our Sun has a lifespan of about ten billion years. For most of this time it will remain stable and well-behaved. At around 4.5 billion years old, our Sun is currently middle-aged, and will continue to shine reliably for billions of years to come. But as it nears the end of its life it will slowly become hotter and brighter. The 'habitable zone' will gradually migrate outwards, eventually leaving the Earth behind so that our planet begins to follow the path taken by Venus billions of years before, losing its oceans to evaporation and entering a period of runaway greenhouse heating. As if this wasn't enough, as the Sun uses up the last of its fuel it will begin to swell up, cooling and reddening as it does so, until it becomes a Red Giant – a bloated, dying star around a hundred times its current size. Mercury, Venus and quite probably the Earth will all be swallowed up and incinerated – and life on Earth will finally be over. In *Doctor Who*, the Doctor takes Rose to see this happen in *The End of the World* (2005).

There isn't much we can do about this destruction of the Earth except find ourselves a new place to live. But until that happens many of the dangers threatening the Earth could still be avoided – if only we set our minds to it.

Perhaps the most influential of Jo's journeys in time and space is her trip in *Day of the Daleks* (1972) to a version of the Earth in the twenty-second century. It's 'a version' of the Earth because, having seen a terrifying future in which humanity is enslaved by the Daleks, the Doctor is able to return to the present day and stop the event that creates that future. The lesson for Jo – and us – from exploring space and time is that we *can* save the Earth, if only we act now.

Day of the Daleks is just one example in *Doctor Who* where history – in this case future history – can be changed. But there are consequences to making those changes, and the Doctor's own people have very strict rules about interfering in time…

The Destructions of Earth

Each incarnation of the Doctor has seen life on Earth threatened in inventive ways. Here are some examples…

1. Plague and motor – *The Dalek Invasion of Earth* (1964)

The Daleks were the first of many aliens to invade Earth in *Doctor Who*. Their plague bombs wiped out whole continents of people and they enslaved the rest to help mine out the planet's core and replace it with a power system so that they could pilot the Earth anywhere in the universe.

2. From the depths – *The Underwater Menace* (1967)

Professor Zaroff's plan to raise the sunken island of Atlantis involved draining the sea into the centre of the Earth – but the Doctor pointed out that the heat of the planet's core would turn the water to steam and crack the Earth's crust, destroying all life.

3. Roll back the clock – *Invasion of the Dinosaurs* (1974)

The appearance of dinosaurs in modern-day London was actually a diversion, not an invasion. A misguided group of scientists and politicians were so horrified by man-made pollution that they tried to use time-travel technology to rewind history returning the Earth to a 'Golden Age' before people came along.

4. Swallowed whole – *The Pirate Planet* (1978)

The hollow planet Zanak was made to materialise around other, smaller planets and then mine out their precious minerals. The Doctor stopped the pirates in charge from doing this to Earth.

5. Crash course – *Earthshock* (1982)

The Cybermen tried to wipe out humanity by crashing a spaceship powered by antimatter into it. But the ship accidentally travelled back in time 65 million years – and wiped out the dinosaurs instead.

6. Moving places – *The Trial of a Time Lord* (1986)

At some point in the future, the Time Lords moved Earth and its 'entire constellation' by a couple of light years. The effect was like that of a solar firestorm. Some humans survived in the London Underground system.

7. Industrial progress – *The Curse of Fenric* (1989)

The Doctor describes a dying Earth some thousands of years in the future, the surface just a chemical slime as a result of pollution. However, his actions seem to stop this future happening.

8. Inside out – *Doctor Who* (1996)

When the Master opens the Eye of Harmony that powers the Doctor's TARDIS, the effect is to warp reality and threaten to suck the Earth inside out.

9. Here comes the sun – *The End of the World* (2005)

The Doctor takes Rose some five billion years into the future to watch the Earth destroyed by the expanding Sun.

10. Reality Bomb – *The Stolen Earth / Journey's End* (2008)

Davros and the Daleks move the Earth across space to join other planets and a moon as the power source of a Reality Bomb that can destroy all life in the universe.

11. Crash course 2 – *Dinosaurs on a Spaceship* (2012)

A large spacecraft threatens to crash into the Earth in 2367 – just like the one that wiped out the dinosaurs in *Earthshock*. Except, the Doctor discovers, this spacecraft is itself full of dinosaurs.

12. Wood you believe it? – *In the Forest of the Night* (2014)

The Earth is engulfed by forest overnight, but the Doctor discovers that the trees are not invading: instead, they act as a shield from solar flares that would otherwise destroy life on Earth.

regen = 12

PART 2
TIME

$$\partial^3 \sum x^2$$

Fig 19

Flight

Diameter
4-8

Hayon

$$XII \geq \textcircled{M} \text{ or } \textcircled{2} ??$$

FULL
LOADING

REWRITING HISTORY

JAMES SWALLOW

'This is a very important thing,' said the Doctor, thrusting the small plastic container into Martha Jones's hands. A skinny fellow in hi-tops, a pinstripe suit and a long brown coat, he gave her an intense stare that made it hard to look away. 'I need you to keep this safe,' he went on, 'for about the next five minutes or so.' A thunderous crash of noise sounded off the black stone walls and the network of waterlogged caverns around them. The Doctor shot a worried glance over his shoulder. 'Maybe ten minutes,' he corrected.

The brackish, alien seawater of the planet Karadax was sloshing over Martha's shoes, getting her feet soaked and making her jeans damp. And somewhere nearby, something very large and very angry was moving through the caves on hissing mechanical piston-legs, getting closer. It wasn't an optimal situation.

'OK.' She held the box gingerly.

'Good!' The Doctor fished in his pocket for his sonic screwdriver. 'What's in there is vital! The fate of hundreds of worlds turns on you making sure nothing happens to it.'

'You're overselling it,' she told him.

'Little bit,' he admitted. The sonic's tip flashed as he activated it. 'Here we go, then! Stay out of sight till I come back.' And with that, he dashed away through a gap in the rock, his coat flapping open behind him.

The unseen big and noisy thing reacted a second later, with a hooting, robotic snarl that made Martha cringe. She retreated into a corner, and decided not to look out into the tunnels beyond. Martha climbed up a hump of damp volcanic sand where the seawater didn't reach and clutched the box to her.

Distantly, she heard the Doctor yell out '*Ha-hah!*', followed by another echoing crash. And before she was even aware of it, Martha was flipping the latches on the plastic box – it was like the ones you'd use to keep leftovers in – and lifting the lid. *What exactly was so vital that it couldn't...*

Martha's shoulders sank. Inside the box was a limp object, curled up in a rough knot. She poked it with a finger and realised her first impression was correct: that the Doctor's important item was, in fact, a sock.

'Are you making fun of me?' she snapped, but the Time Lord couldn't hear her, not with the crashing and banging going on outside the cave. 'This is just a—'

'Yeah,' said a voice behind her. 'It is.' Martha felt the hairs on the back of her neck stand up, and she spun around as a shadowy figure stepped through a shimmering tear in the rock wall. But not a tear, not really. More like some kind of portal, that snapped shut the moment she was through.

Because the person the voice belonged to was a she; and while this person didn't have Martha's red leather jacket and Martha's spiked hair, what she did have was Martha's face and voice.

'Hello, you,' said the new arrival. 'This might take some explaining...'

Martha looked at the other woman, at a face that was a bit more drawn than hers, a hairdo a bit more serious and mumsy. 'You're me,' she said, 'but... older?'

'Oh,' said the second Martha. 'Maybe it won't.'

The clawed tentacles of the Karadax drone slammed down into the ankle-deep water with a crash, narrowly missing the Doctor as he twisted away. A second slower, and the sleek, deadly war machine would have turned him into Time Lord confetti. He ducked low, calling on moves he'd learned in dance lessons with a Spanish Contessa, and deftly sidestepped to avoid another pair of weapon-limbs. Each was festooned with clacking, buzzing, stabbing implements that he really did not want to go anywhere near.

'Could we just chat about this?' he called, as the machine gave a juddering growl. 'I know you think you'd like to destroy me, but you're making a big mistake. Stop for a second, take a moment. It's not the best idea.'

As he spoke, the drone pulled away. The Doctor guessed the artificial intelligence core inside its body was processing new methods to separate bits of him from other bits of him in the most unpleasant manner possible. The machine the Karadax had created to take over the universe vaguely resembled an Earth octopus, with a roughly ovoid body and eight long, flexible tentacles. But there the comparison ended, as it was made of polymorphic phase-metal, capable of fabricating dozens of different weapon templates on the fly and was the size of a battle tank.

That the Karadax – a race of bad-tempered shark-people – had built such an ingenious weapon did not surprise the Doctor. He'd met plenty of people who thought the way to get ahead was to make everyone else's lives miserable. But that they'd decided to test their prototype on him… Well, that had come as a bit of a shock.

'I should be flattered!' he told it, as the drone turned a glowing blue sensor grid on him. 'But seriously. There are better ways to get on my good side…'

He trailed off as the machine gave a shiver and rose up. Panels snapped open and produced the maws of lethal energy cannons, all turning to train on him.

'Ah,' he said, as the cave lit up with flashes of atomic lightning.

'You're handling this well,' said the other Martha, brushing a strand of hair out of her eyes.

Martha's hand was halfway raised, about to do the same thing, and she suddenly felt self-conscious. 'Um. I suppose. But I've seen a lot of strange stuff lately. Judoon, Plasmavore, Carrionites… Travel in space and time, yeah? So the idea of meeting an older me isn't that weird.' She paused; it was *very weird*, to be honest. 'Hello.'

'Hi.' Her elder self gave a sad smile. Martha could see her better now; a fair bit older, with wrinkles at the corners of her eyes, a bit of grey in her hair, and the way she moved spoke of someone who had seen a lot, done a lot. 'Look, I'm really sorry to do this,' she said, 'but this is the only place where you're not with him, and we can talk. He'd be furious if he saw us together.'

'The Doctor?' In the distance, there was a crash of steel on rock.

Older Martha nodded. 'It's because of him I came back in time to talk to you. Because of what happens in the future.' A melancholy look crossed the other woman's face. 'If you stay with him, you're going to see a lot of amazing things… But he'll break your heart.'

Martha stiffened. 'I don't know what you're on about. It's not like that.'

'Yes it is. Remember who you're talking to?' said the other woman, in a tone like the one Martha's mother used. 'But it's more than that. Terrible things will happen if you travel with the Doctor. People will get hurt, people you love. You'll see stuff that will change you for ever, and not for the better. Right now, you're free of all that. You haven't been… tainted.'

'What are you saying?' Martha gave her future self a hard look.

'Go back to the TARDIS, right now. It can take you home. Forget you ever met the Doctor, or saw any of this.' The older woman gestured around her. 'It's for the best. Please, you must believe me!'

'You want me to change my future,' said Martha. 'Your past?'

'That's right. Make sure it never comes to be. The Doctor will go on and do what he does, but you'll be safe. You and everyone you care about.'

Martha shook her head, her thoughts reeling. *Could it be true,* she wondered? *So I've seen some scary monsters... But what if there's worse to come?* 'If I do what you say,' she said haltingly, 'won't that mess up history? I mean, for me what you say hasn't happened yet, but for you it *has*. Isn't that a, what's it called? A *paradox?*'

Another thunderous crash echoed down the stony tunnels. 'That doesn't matter. I know what I'm doing. If you can't trust me,' said the other Martha, 'who can you trust? I don't want you to have the terrible life I had! To end up alone, on a devastated Earth...'

Martha's blood ran cold. 'What about my family?'

'You can make sure they're safe. Mum and Dad, Leo and Letitia...'

'What did you say?' Suddenly, something very unpleasant occurred to Martha Jones.

'I get why you're doing this,' said the Doctor, skipping from stone to stone across a pool of oily water. He ducked a laser bolt that chopped off a dangling stalactite. 'You want to be important!'

The octopoid drone drew back its weapon-arms and stalked around the edge of the cave, scanners humming as it considered its next attack.

The Doctor guessed that whatever nasty sort had set this thing running was probably watching him through its sensor eyes, so when he talked, that was who he was addressing. 'Because you don't want to go on being second-banana scourges of the galaxy, do you?' He gave a shrug. 'I mean, when they're handing out the Cosmic Menace of the Year Awards, you don't want to be sitting in the audience. Again.' The Doctor made a mock-sad face. '*Who wins this year? Oh, the Daleks, what a surprise.* Runners-up? Those silver fellas, always the CyberBridesmaid, never the CyberBride. Even the Draconians get a look in, but not you, eh? I bet that stings.' He puffed himself up. 'You want the Karadax to be *feared*. For the very stars themselves to quake at the sound of your name!'

And then he opened his hands, and gave a compassionate look. 'Why have you got to be like that? It never turns out well. Why can't we all just get along?'

For long seconds, the drone paused, and the Doctor started to entertain the idea that it might actually be considering his words; but then it leapt at him with a snarl, extruding blades like spreading flower petals.

'How do I know you're *really* me?' Martha jabbed a finger at her older self. 'You could be some kind of shape-changer or something!'

'That's ridiculous,' said the older woman, tapping her chest. 'It's *me*. I mean, *you*. I mean, *us*.'

'But you would say that, wouldn't you?' Martha shook her head. 'When the Doctor comes back—'

'You can't wait for him,' she insisted. 'You've got to decide. Him or your family. His future or yours.'

Martha took a step closer, her eyes narrowing. 'My sister's name is Tish. Never Letitia. She can't stand being called that. Too posh, she always says.' She glared at her other self. 'If you were me you'd know that.'

'I did. I do. But she… Got used to it.' The older woman blinked, her tone becoming evasive. 'You know Tish. So changeable!'

'Who was the first boy we ever kissed?' Martha said, in a low voice.

'You're testing me? You don't trust yourself?'

'What was his name?' she demanded.

The older woman blinked, as if she was going to cry. 'I'm sorry. I don't remember that, it was a long time ago. At my age, you forget some things… But you have to listen to me, Martha. It's important! You have to do what I say! We don't have any choice. You have to abandon the Doctor, and you have to do it right now!'

'Why are you so determined to make me leave?' Martha reached out to grab the older woman, and her other self shrank backward. 'Tell me—'

She grabbed Older Martha's wrist, and something strange happened. Instead of encountering warm skin, her hand sank *through* the flesh like it was smoke and grasped a thin, cold rod concealed beneath.

A flicker ran through the other woman, as if she were an image on a TV screen pixelated by interference. 'Visitors must not touch the exhibits,' said Older Martha, and her words had a metallic echo to them.

'What... are you?' Martha gasped, snatching back her hand.

'I'm sorry,' said her duplicate, her face shimmering. 'I didn't want to do this. And now I've failed, they're going to come here.'

***

'OK,' said the Doctor, between panting breaths. 'I'm getting peeved now.' He kicked aside the slushy ice the drone had made, using a cryotherm cannon in an attempt to flash-freeze him. 'Stop trying to kill me. We hardly know each other. It's rude!'

He worked the tiny, complex controls on his sonic screwdriver, eyeing the octopoid as it went through yet another reconfiguration cycle. What was it going to produce this time? An electro-charged restraint web? Photonic lance? Bio-shredder? The machine had the templates of millions of different weapons in its memory, and the will to use them.

'I know why you're doing this,' he told it. 'My reputation precedes me, doesn't it? I've beaten pretty much every big bad in the universe at one time or another, if I do say so myself. And you think if you can take down the Doctor, everything else will be child's play.' He raised the sonic. 'Fair enough. Bring it on.'

***

For a second, Older Martha's body flashed and then it was gone. Revealed beneath was a skinny, shop-window dummy made of coppery metal, covered in glowing, gem-like projector lenses. 'This is really me,' she said, still speaking with Martha's voice. 'I am exhibitoid UF-032, an artificial simulacrum from the Museum of the Doctor on planet Reldeen, chrono-location forty-fifth century by your measurement system.'

THE SCIENTIFIC SECRETS OF DOCTOR WHO

'The Doctor has his own museum?' Martha blinked at that idea.

'A monument to his adventures and accomplishments,' said the android. 'Built by the grateful Reldeenii people after he saved them from a neuro-parasite invasion.' The lenses shimmered and the robot projected a holographic 'skin' over its metal form, and Martha found herself looking at a mirror image. Then it juddered and changed into various different versions of her. There she was in the lab coat she wore as a medical student. In some kind of all-black military outfit, with short hair. Dressed like a Victorian housemaid. In a spacesuit. 'Stop!' she shouted, and the image flicked back to its earlier setting. 'Why do you look like me?'

'I am an exhibit. I represent Martha Jones.' She cocked her head. 'I'm sorry. They made me come here. I was stolen from the museum. They reprogrammed me. I didn't have a choice but to tell you all those things.'

Martha struggled to hold all the questions she had in her thoughts, and went for the most important. 'Who did this?'

'If you won't go of your own accord, they'll have to take steps,' said the android. 'A more permanent solution. They didn't want to do that, in case it disrupted the timeline even more. But now they have no choice!' Her duplicate grabbed her hand. 'I didn't want this to happen, Martha! I'm programmed to be just like you. I didn't want you to get hurt...'

The dark stone wall behind the android rippled, and it began to peel back as forces from across time pushed their way into the damp cavern.

'You have to run!' cried the android.

'That time has passed,' said a hissing, breathy voice, from a mouth with far too many teeth. A hulking, muscular figure came into existence, a monster with blue-grey flesh and a huge head that was sharp like the prow of a ship. It had dead eyes, doll-like black marbles that radiated malice. All over its body were cybernetic implants and embedded armour plates, and a long, finned tail trailed lazily behind it. If a shark could walk and talk, this was how it would look. 'You would not delete yourself from the Doctor's timeline willingly,' it gurgled, flexing clawed hands. 'So you will be undone here instead.'

The sonic screwdriver didn't work. *It usually works*, the Doctor said to himself. He could do so many clever things with the tool, and he was sure he'd got it right this time. *Use the sonic to project solid-wave sound echoes off the basalt rock walls, confuse the targeting system of the drone, make it stumble, cause a cave-in and bury it.* Good plan. Great plan. *Brilliant* plan.

If it had worked, of course. But instead, the machine saw right through the sonic illusions he created and came smashing its way toward him, and this time it had plasmatic flame-throwers and bone-seeker microdarts with his name on them.

'Time for Plan B!' he shouted, and ran away in big splashy steps with an angry robot octopus on his heels.

'Get lost, mackerel-face!' Martha shouted.

The shark-man was fast, and it was all she could do to keep out of the reach of the glistening talons on the end of its fingers.

'You merely prolong the inevitable,' it hissed. 'The Karadax will see victory at your end, human. Your absence is the key-point. Without you, the Doctor fails.'

'Stop—' began the android, but the Karadax warrior shoved it away.

'We calculated for centuries,' said the creature. 'Found the exact moment. Laid our plans.'

'Why?' Martha shot back.

'The Doctor!' roared the Karadax. 'Again and again, the Time Lord has thwarted our plans for conquest! So we drilled into the deep past, searching for the perfect time to strike. Through *you*, human. We will change our own defeats into victories. We rewrite history!'

Martha saw an opening and broke into a run – but the warrior slapped her back with a heavy blow that shocked the air from her lungs. She landed hard on the sandbank, groaning in pain.

As Martha looked up, the shark-man loomed over her, his too-wide mouth yawning open to reveal row after row of dagger-tip teeth. 'The journey from the future was long,' he said. 'It made me hungry.'

'No!' Martha heard the shout in her own voice, and suddenly she was watching herself attack the Karadax, a different Martha Jones grabbing the alien's dorsal fin and punching him in his gill-slits. The warrior spun around, and the museum android's holographic skin winked out, but the Karadax could not dislodge the machine's implacable grip. 'Overloading holo-matrix!' she cried.

Martha had to cover her eyes as a powerful electrostatic charge blazed out of the robot's core and shocked through the Karadax's twitching body. She smelled cooked fish and the shark-man released a bellow of agony as sparks collected around the implants fixed to his flesh.

Finally, the android dropped, but the Karadax was still wailing, beating at itself as it were trying to put out flames. Then at once, the ground beneath the alien's feet rippled and he fell into nothingness with a tortured screech, disappearing from sight.

'What… just happened?' Martha staggered to the exhibit-droid's side.

'I short-circuited his temporal recall module,' explained the machine. 'Sent him back to his origin point in the far future.' Her voice was slurred and full of static. 'At considerable cost to myself. Power levels dropping. Shutdown imminent. I am sorry, Martha Jones. I am programmed to be like you. I wanted to be… You.'

'You think I'm that brave?' said Martha, in a small voice.

'I-I know it,' the android stuttered. 'What I said before. S-some of it was not true, some of it was. I must tell you what's to come.'

'No!' Martha shook her head firmly. 'Don't. That would be rewriting history, wouldn't it? And we shouldn't mess with that.' She paused, thinking. 'I don't need to know my future, I trust the Doctor. That's enough for me.'

'Yes,' said the android, the light in her eyes fading. 'You are going to be... Brilliant...'

And then Martha was alone.

The Doctor burst into the cavern where he had left Martha, with the octopoid a heartbeat behind him, and he instantly had the sense that he was missing something. For starters, there was a robot of some kind lying on the rocks, that he was sure hadn't been there when he'd left, and Martha looked like she was fit to burst into tears.

'You all right?' he offered.

But before she could answer, the war machine crashed into the gap in the rocks and gave a furious howl. The cavern entrance was too narrow for it to fit through, and it began clawing at the sides, breaking off bits of black rock, trying to widen the gap. Its oval body squeezed forward, the bright blue sensor grid flashing cold light across the chamber.

'Tell me later!' the Doctor said. 'The box! I need it right now, tell me you've still got it!'

Martha blinked like she was shaking off a trance and then looked around. 'I had it... I must have dropped it when... I mean...' Something caught her eye and she dashed across the cavern. 'Here it is!'

He watched her snatch up the little plastic box floating atop the sloshing water and his hearts sank, both at once. 'Please do not say you got the contents wet! If you got it wet, we are in a lot of trouble!' He ducked as the octopoid managed to get a single tentacle into the cavern and whip it around.

She fished out the old sock and held it like it was a dead rat. 'Why did you give me this?'

The Doctor grabbed it, a grin blooming on his face. 'You trust me, don't you?'

'Yes,' she said, a little warily.

He bounded away toward the drone. 'Karadax technology is very good stuff, but it does have a weak point. It doesn't react well to certain kinds of dry, organic, non-conductive materials…' He got to the 'head' of the oval body and stared right at it. 'Like, for example, if you stuff a smelly old sock into one of their very delicate sensor grids.' The Doctor did exactly that, and the octopoid let out a howl of distorted sound that was almost a cry of pain.

It staggered backwards, tentacles reaching up to pluck at the grid and failing to dislodge the errant footwear. Something important deep inside the machine sizzled unpleasantly and all life fled from the drone. The machine skidded into a deep pool and sank silently beneath the surface.

'Done,' he said, with a smirk, brushing imaginary dust from his fingers. 'Hmm. That was a bit harder than I thought it would be, actually. From now on, I'll keep a closer eye on the Karadax. Come back every hundred years in case they're trying anything else unpleasant, and put a stop to it.' The Doctor turned around and fell into a hug as Martha grabbed him. 'Oh. Um. OK.'

She gave him a squeeze, then let go. 'Glad I could help.'

He looked around, frowning. 'Did, uh, something happen while I was gone?'

A smile crossed Martha's face. 'Nothing you need to worry about. Just you and me, being brilliant.'

That made him grin again. 'Yeah, I suppose we were!' he said. 'Come on, then. Back to the TARDIS. Stuff to do. Things to see.'

'History to make,' she added.

He offered her his hand. 'You got that right, Martha Jones.'

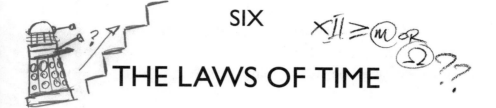
'I have seen you change time, I have seen
you break any rule you want.'

'I know when I can; I know when I can't.'

Clara Oswald and the Twelfth Doctor, *Dark Water* (2014)

Even as you read this sentence, you are travelling in time. We're all time travellers, moving at a constant rate of one second per second, each of us growing steadily older. The trick would be to move at a different speed from everybody else – either faster into the future or back into the past.

Surprisingly, we can already travel into the future to a small degree. Einstein's Special and General Theories of relativity predicted that relative velocity and gravity can both alter the rate at which we experience the passage of time compared to observers moving at different speeds or experiencing a different gravitational field from us. This process is called 'time dilation'. In Chapter 1, we saw proof of Einstein's theory, in which he correctly predicted the position of the planet Mercury given the warping of space-time by the Sun. Today, modern technology gives us many examples of relativistic time dilation in action.

When we send craft into space, differences in gravity and velocity affect the amount of time which passes for them, relative to us back here on Earth. The clocks on spacecraft travelling to low Earth orbit have been shown to run very slightly slower than clocks on the planet's surface. Clocks on satellites circling Earth run very slightly faster than clocks on the ground. The differences are only fractions of a second, but if the navigation systems in our cars and mobile phones – which use satellites as a reference – are to work properly, this difference in time must be taken into account. Because that means keeping track of very slight variations, satellite navigation systems usually keep correct time to about a 10,000,000th of a second.

We would see a greater effect of time dilation on longer and faster journeys into space. The closer to the speed of light a spacecraft travelled, the more time would dilate. For example, imagine a very fast spacecraft is sent out to explore space travelling at ninety-nine per cent of the speed of light. The astronauts would return to Earth after experiencing the passing of ten years on board the ship – but they would discover that on Earth one hundred years had passed. (In the *Doctor Who* story *Aliens of London* (2005), the Doctor thinks he and Rose have been away for twelve hours, but they discover that for people on Earth it has been twelve months. However, this isn't the result of time dilation but of the Doctor making a mistake.)

The astronauts on their spacecraft and the people on Earth wouldn't feel time passing any quicker or slower. Their local experience of time would remain the same. This is because, as Einstein said, time is relative: you only notice the difference when you compare different clocks moving at different speeds. (This seems to be fundamental to the TARDIS, the initials of which stand for Time And Relative Dimension In Space.)

The astronauts in our example would effectively be travelling a hundred years into the Earth's future while using up only ten years of their own lives – effectively jumping ninety years ahead of where they'd be if they'd stayed at home. The faster their spacecraft could fly, the further into the future it could take them. In Chapter 4, we saw how the extreme gravity close to a black hole has a similar effect, slowing the local passage of time while time outside passes at its usual rate, potentially allowing an astronaut to fast-forward into the future.

So travelling forwards in time is certainly possible – if somewhat risky. But is it possible to travel in the opposite direction, backwards into the past? After all, if you can only go forwards into the future then time travel is a one-way trip and you could never return to your own time. But if we *can* go back in time, that begs an intriguing question: is it possible to change history?

When *Doctor Who* began, the Doctor was quite clear that we couldn't change history. As he told his companion, Barbara:

> 'But you can't rewrite history! Not one line! ... What you are trying to do is utterly impossible. I know, believe me, I know.'
> **The First Doctor, *The Aztecs* (1964)**

That might be interpreted as the Doctor saying that we can, technically, change history but we ought not to. However, later the same year the point was made more explicitly. In *The Reign of Terror* (1964), Barbara and Ian see Napoleon years before he becomes emperor of France. Ian wonders what would have been the result had they written Napoleon a letter telling him some the things due to happen to him. The Doctor's granddaughter Susan explains that, 'It wouldn't have made any difference, Ian. He'd have forgotten it, or lost it, or thought it was written by a maniac.'

The implication is that they physically cannot change history. If they try to, circumstance will conspire to stop them. As Barbara says, 'I suppose if we'd tried to kill him with a gun, the bullet would have missed him.'

Some physicists agree that circumstance or some force of nature would stop you changing history. One argument given for why we can't change history is the so-called 'grandfather paradox'. The idea is that you go back in time to a point before your grandfather had children. You shoot and kill your grandfather, so he *never* has children – which means one of your parents now never existed. That means you never

157

existed, either. However, if you never existed, you can't have gone back in time to kill your grandfather – so he was never shot. But if he was never shot, he had children and grandchildren, and that includes you. Which means you're able to go back in time and shoot him... We go round and round in a loop.

A paradox isn't only created by killing someone. In *Dark Water* (2014), Clara asks the Doctor to change history and save the life of Danny Pink. The Doctor has to say no.

'If I change the events that brought you here, you will never come here and ask me to change those events. Paradox loop. The timeline disintegrates. Your timeline.'

The Twelfth Doctor, *Dark Water* (2014).

Note that he doesn't just say no because a paradox would be created, but because that paradox would destroy Clara. So in *Doctor Who*, it is possible to create paradoxes, but they have deadly consequences – which we'll discuss more in Chapter 9.

It's thought that paradoxes might even be created by tiny changes to history. In 1961, the American meteorologist Edward Lorenz used a computer programme to predict the weather. This involved entering a series of numbers describing the initial conditions, then letting the computer work out what those initial conditions would lead to. One of the numbers to be entered was 0.506127 but to save time Lorenz rounded it up to 0.506. He was then amazed to discover that this small change in just one of the initial conditions produced a radically different prediction of the weather.

This phenomenon became known as the 'butterfly effect' – named after the idea that a butterfly flapping its wings could eventually trigger the circumstances which lead to a hurricane on the other side of the world. It's not that the butterfly causes the hurricane, but without the butterfly, the initial conditions are different so the complex chain of events leads to something else – perhaps a nice sunny day.

The weather is just one of a number of systems that can be massively affected by small changes in initial conditions. Since these systems can be so complex that they appear chaotic, attempts to understand them better are known as 'chaos theory'. Chaos theory suggests that even a tiny change in history could be catastrophic for the world as we know it.

In *Doctor Who*, the Doctor doesn't seem too worried about this. When he takes Martha Jones back in time to meet Shakespeare, Martha asks about changing history.

'It's like in the films. You step on a butterfly, you change the future of the human race.'

'Tell you what, then, don't step on any butterflies. What have butterflies ever done to you?'

'What if, I don't know, what if I kill my grandfather?'

'Are you planning to?'

'No.'

'Well, then.'

$$\partial^3 \sum_i x^2$$

Martha Jones and the Tenth Doctor, *The Shakespeare Code* (2007)

In fact, the Doctor *does* change history. He frequently claims that time can be rewritten. When he visits the past, the future – that is, the time we live in now – is always at risk. In *Pyramids of Mars* (1975), the Doctor and Sarah battle the alien Sutekh who wants to kill all life on Earth in the year 1911. Sarah says that they already know Sutekh will lose because she is from 1980. The Doctor sets the controls of the TARDIS for 1980, which they find a desolate, ravaged world – because they've not yet defeated Sutekh. Sarah agrees that they have to go back and finish the fight.

Does the Doctor cause paradoxes? We saw in Chapter 5 that in *Day of the Daleks* (1972) he changes an event in the present day to stop the Daleks conquering Earth in the future. He only changed history because people from the future told him what to do. Surely if he changes things, they never existed to be able to come back and tell him?

One possibility to explain what happens is that the new future the Doctor creates is something like the alternative worlds we talked about in Chapter 3. Imagine time as the letter I. The future is at the top, the past at the bottom. The TARDIS travels back in time from the future to halfway down the I. There, the Doctor makes a change and creates an alternative world: turning the I into a Y. He doesn't stop the original future existing altogether, he branches off from it. Some physicists argue that this might get around there being a paradox.

Doctor Who stories such as *Father's Day* (2005) or *Turn Left* (2009) show us other Earths, but make a point that these are branches created by the Doctor's companions (Rose saves her dad's life; Donna doesn't turn right on a particular day). In both stories, history must be put back on course, the alternative branch destroyed.

The trouble with branching history is that such an idea is very hard for us to test scientifically. Does it at least match the evidence in *Doctor Who*? The problem is that the Doctor never tells us exactly how time travel works. We know from River Song that he lies, but he's also vague on detail. He gives a good explanation in *The Waters of Mars* (2009), but begins by telling us that he's not sure if it's right.

> 'I mean, it's only a theory, what do I know, but I think certain moments in time are fixed. Tiny, precious moments. Everything else is in flux, anything can happen, but those certain moments, they have to stand. This base on Mars with you, Adelaide Brooke, this is one vital moment. What happens here must always happen.'
>
> **The Tenth Doctor, *The Waters of Mars* (2009)**

In *Kill the Moon* (2014), the Doctor seems able to see how the future changes just by closing his eyes. He never needs to look up what counts as a fixed moment and what doesn't – he seems somehow to feel it. In

City of Death (1979), he and the Time Lady Romana are able to feel changes made to time, while in the 1996 television movie *Doctor Who* (1996), the Eighth Doctor can glimpse people's future just by having a good look at them. But perhaps his understanding is based less on the physics of whether it's actually possible to change history or not, and more on the moral case for whether or not it is right.

'You have heard the charge against you, that you have repeatedly broken our most important law of non-interference in the affairs of other planets. What have you to say? Do you admit these actions?'

$$\partial^3 \sum \chi^2$$ 'I not only admit them, I am proud of them.'

A Time Lord and the Second Doctor, *The War Games* (1969)

The Time Lords put the Doctor on trial twice – in *The War Games* (1969) and *The Trial of a Time Lord* (1986). On both occasions, evidence is presented on screens – as if the jurors are watching TV.

We're told in *The Trial of a Time Lord* that this evidence was recorded by the TARDIS. That's interesting because it implies how the TARDIS *ought* to be used. We know TARDISes are designed to disguise themselves, blending in with their surroundings. (The Doctor's TARDIS is stuck in the shape of a police box, but if its Chameleon Circuit was working properly, it would change its shape wherever it landed.) If Time Lords can blend in with their surroundings unobtrusively, it suggests they can visit other worlds and times without making any change. They never risk stepping on butterflies and thus changing the whole of the future.

The charge against the Doctor is that he's been irresponsible. If it's all right for Time Lords to travel through time and space and observe what's going on, the problem with what the Doctor does must be that he's not content to merely watch. He steps out of the TARDIS – the implication being that even just doing that changes the initial conditions of wherever he turns up, and so changes history to at least some degree.

In both trials, the Doctor's defence rests on the fact that he battles evil, defeats monsters and improves the lot of the people he meets. He is changing things – implicitly, he is changing history – for the better.

Both times the Time Lords concede the point and allow the Doctor to continue his adventures. After *The War Games*, they exile him to Earth – but at a time when Earth will need his help, and even then they send the Doctor on specific missions to alien worlds, too. In *Genesis of the Daleks* (1975), the mission they send him on is explicitly to change history: they want the Doctor to stop the Daleks ever being created. (We'll discuss this, and time travel being used as a weapon, in Chapter 9.)

The issue – in *Genesis of the Daleks* and more broadly in *Doctor Who* – is not whether history *can* be changed but whether it should be. That seems to match another important law of the Time Lords:

> 'The First Law of Time expressly forbids him to meet his other selves.'
>
> Time Lord Chancellor, *The Three Doctors* (1972–1973)

This First Law of Time is presumably to prevent earlier incarnations of the Doctor learning information from or about their future selves that would create a paradox. Yet exceptions can be made: in *The Three Doctors*, the Chancellor is overruled and the Time Lords themselves send the First and Second Doctors to assist the Third. In fact, when the Doctor meets his other selves in *The Three Doctors*, *The Five Doctors* (1983) and *The Day of the Doctor* (2013), it's because Gallifrey itself is in danger. The Time Lords might have laws about changing history, but the only way the Doctor can save his own people is to ignore their rules. (In *The Day of the Doctor*, it seems the Doctor forgets his encounters with his future selves, which solves the problems of paradox.)

Despite all these potential problems some scientists think that there might just be a way of travelling into the past, but this involves one of the strangest ideas in physics: a wormhole.

Wormholes are effectively a 'shortcut' in space-time, linking two otherwise distant parts of the universe. Although they are predicted by some branches of theoretical physics, no one knows if they actually exist – certainly scientists have yet to find any convincing evidence for them. If wormholes do occur in nature they're likely to be extremely small and only last for a tiny fraction of a second, but some physicists have speculated that it might just be possible to stabilise one and expand it to a size that a person or even a spaceship might fit through. As well as providing a shortcut through space, such a wormhole might also provide a means of travelling back and forth through time.

The wormhole creates a shortcut between two parts of space-time, A and B, linking them in both space and time. An object travelling through the wormhole from A would arrive at B much more quickly than if it had travelled through conventional space.

Travelling through conventional space

A

B

Shortcut travelling through wormhole

Imagine that two physicists manage to create a useable wormhole in their laboratory. By stepping into one end of the wormhole, they can emerge instantaneously at the other end, which is on the far side of the lab. This is fun, but not particularly useful. Now the first physicist takes one end of the wormhole and places it inside a spaceship, leaving the wormhole's other end in the laboratory. Bidding farewell to her colleague she pilots the spaceship out into the depths of the cosmos, travelling at ninety-nine per cent of the speed of light.

Back in the lab, her colleague tracks the spacecraft through a powerful telescope. After watching for a hundred years, this physicist is now very old. But on the spacecraft, ninety-nine light years from Earth, things look rather different. Travelling at such a colossal speed, time on board has been passing at a vastly different rate and, while one hundred years have passed on Earth, only ten years have elapsed on the spacecraft. The first physicist is just ten years older than when she left home – and so is the end of the wormhole which she has carried with her.

This is where the strange properties of wormholes could become useful for time travel. The two ends of the wormhole remain directly linked to each other in space, forming a shortcut between the laboratory and the spaceship. But they are also linked to each other in time. The end of the wormhole on board the spacecraft is now ten years old, and is connected to the end of the wormhole back in the lab *when it was also just ten years old*. By stepping into the wormhole on board the ship, the first physicist will emerge back in the lab, but only ten years after she left it. She has effectively travelled ninety years into her past. She could even join her colleague – who would also only be ten years older – at his telescope and see her spaceship, still only partway through its journey. The two physicists could then step back through the wormhole and emerge instantaneously on the distant spacecraft, just moments after the first physicist left it, ninety years in the future.

If a wormhole used in this way can allow travel both backwards and forwards through time, what about the grandfather paradox? Could the first physicist travel back to the lab and prevent the wormhole from ever being created, thus preventing her from travelling back in the first place, thus preventing her from preventing the wormhole and so on into an infinite paradoxical loop?

Luckily, time travel by wormhole seems to come with its own in-built paradox prevention mechanism. Because the two ends of the wormhole are always linked to each other in time, you could never enter one end to emerge from the other before the wormhole itself was created. The physics of the wormhole would also stop you from meeting past and future versions of yourself. Because the physicist has to move her end of the wormhole through space before she can use it to travel back in time, when she gets round to making her trip back in time to the lab, her past self has already left on the spaceship.

Perhaps something like that is happening in *Doctor Who*. We know that the Doctor's people, the Time Lords, are one of the oldest civilisations in the universe. They invented time travel long before everyone else – as we've already seen, the Doctor claims in *The Satan Pit* (2006) that his people 'practically invented black holes'. Perhaps the first black hole is like the end of the wormhole fixed in the lab. When the Doctor visits us in what we think of as the present day, to him it is the far future – like the wormhole on the spacecraft. He can still head back through the tunnel to his own time, but his own time is slowly moving forward in time.

That might explain why the Doctor's encounters with his own people occur in the same order for both him and them. It doesn't even need to be encounters on Gallifrey itself. The Master is, like the Doctor, a time traveller, and yet usually when they meet they refer to the events of their previous meeting – and it's the same previous meeting for both of them. For example, in *The King's Demons* (1983), the Doctor says that he last saw the Master trapped on the planet Xeriphas in *Time-Flight* (1982). The Master explains that he found the robot Kamelion on Xeriphas and used it to escape.

Compare that to the Doctor's meetings with River Song, which don't happen in the same order for both of them. Whenever they meet, they need to work out where in each other's timelines they are.

'Right then, where are we? Have we done Easter Island yet?'

'Er, yes! I've got Easter Island.'

$\partial^3 \sum x^2$ 'They worshipped you there. Have you seen the statues?'

River Song and the Eleventh Doctor, *The Impossible Astronaut* (2011)

If there was any chance that the Master in *The King's Demons* had not yet experienced the events of *Time Flight* – because they remained in his future – surely the Doctor would not dare to mention Xeriphas, for fear of giving the Master an advantage when he eventually gets there. Instead, the Doctor takes it for granted that he and the Master experience events in the same order.

If that's generally what happens, there are exceptions. In *The Five Doctors* – the story immediately following *The King's Demons* – the Master meets four incarnations of the Doctor all at once. The first three Doctors are all meeting him out of sequence.

There's also evidence that the Doctor can sometimes travel back into Gallifrey's past or to before the Time Lords invented time travel. In *Listen* (2014), the TARDIS lands in a shack where Clara meets the Doctor when he was a child. This moment is clearly way back in the Doctor's past, long before any previous story set on Gallifrey. We may also have seen time travel capable of reaching back to the very start of the universe. In *Terminus* (1983), fuel from a time-travelling space station is jettisoned and explodes, and the Doctor concludes that it might have caused the Big Bang – the beginning of time and space as we know it.

In *Doctor Who,* it therefore seems possible to travel back to a time before the first time machine or wormhole is invented. Maybe, one day in the future, we will understand how.

SILVER MOSQUITOES

L.M. MYLES

The Doctor, all silver hair and belligerent eyebrows, had promised Clara Rome; so far, he'd given her several miles of uninhabited Germanic forest, which he'd irritably pointed out was still a part of the Roman Empire so, broadly speaking, was more or less what she'd asked for.

Clara had disagreed, but as she looked down into a valley cut in half by a vast, winding river, she was glad she had the chance to see her world like this. Like the forest behind her, it felt so much wilder, grander, than the Earth she knew. Even the air seemed to taste different.

'Aurochs,' said the Doctor, pointing at a great herd of animals grazing by the river. 'Extinct hundreds of years before your century, but you can find them all over Europe just now.'

'They look like really big cows,' Clara said.

'They are.'

'Are they dangerous?' she asked. Their horns were over two feet long, and she really didn't fancy being on the wrong end of a charge.

'Not unless you're a patch of nice tasty grass,' he said, 'or you're planning on having one for dinner. They get a bit tetchy about that.'

'And what's that?' She indicated further down the valley, where the river disappeared behind a forested ridge of hill. All she could make out was a flicker of colour, and sunlight glinting sharply off a reflective surface.

The Doctor frowned, and, with a faint sense of satisfaction, Clara realised that he hadn't noticed it until she'd pointed it out. 'Romans,' he said at last. 'A military camp.'

'A Roman encampment,' said a voice behind them. 'And we don't take kindly to spies.'

Clara and the Doctor turned to see two gleaming short-swords held by two grim-faced men wearing chainmail and legionary helmets.

She raised her hands and attempted a friendly smile. 'Don't worry,' she said, 'we won't hurt you.'

'So much for Roman law and order,' muttered Clara. 'Are you going to kill us just for walking around a forest?'

The soldiers said nothing as they marched the Doctor and Clara through the fortified army camp. From their vantage point on the hill, she had seen only the very tip of it but, past the walls and ditch, the full camp held dozens of rows of tents, thousands of soldiers. As their little party moved along the painstakingly straight dirt roads, soldiers paused in their duties to watch the new arrivals.

In the centre of the camp, they were ordered to stop before a large wooden building and were left with a single guard for a few minutes, before being escorted inside.

They were brought to a richly furnished room where two men and a woman looked over a large, finely detailed map. The woman straightened as they entered, her dark brown eyes inscrutable as she looked them over. 'Ah, our spies. What have you to say for yourselves?'

'How about we're not spies?' said the Doctor.

'Well, of course,' said the woman, with a slight nod of her head. 'Who are you, then?'

'I'm the Doctor, and this is Clara Oswald.'

'Doctor?' She glanced to one of the men beside her and raised an eyebrow. 'Senator?'

The man shook his head. 'Foolish,' he said. 'Be rid of them and let us return to the matter at hand.'

'And who, exactly, are you?' the Doctor asked her.

The woman took a step towards him, moving with an imperious grace. 'I am Ulpia Severina, Caesar and First Citizen of the Senate and People of Rome, wife of the Restorer of the World.'

'You're Caesar?' said Clara, unable to hide her surprise.

'Yes,' she said sharply. 'My husband is dead, murdered by traitors. I rule now, in my own name.' She turned her attention back to the senator. 'Well, I doubt they're Germanic spies: this one sounds as though she's from Britannia, and his voice has the barbaric pitch of some Scotti tribe.'

'You want to say that again?' said the Doctor.

Ulpia gave him an assessing gaze. 'Or perhaps the Picts,' she said. 'It makes little difference.' She tapped her fingers on the table, considering. 'Perhaps you can be of some use; we're short of doctors, and many of my soldiers are injured. I need—'

Ulpia's head snapped up, and Clara became aware of a buzzing noise, like a thousand tiny insects, coming from outside. Ulpia strode out of the tent followed by her guards and the senator. The Doctor and Clara exchanged an uneasy glance and followed.

Outside, the legionnaires were in a flurry of activity as orders were shouted, and archers and slingers lined up.

'Perhaps it would be better if you were to stay inside,' the senator said to Ulpia.

'I won't cower like some frightened child,' she told him, her eyes scanning the camp. 'Where are those wretched things?'

As she spoke, Clara saw a shining mass fly steadily down the road towards them. As someone shouted an order to fire, Clara's eyes began to make sense of what she was looking at, and she realised it wasn't some strange silvery cloud but a vast swarm of insects. It swept through the gathered soldiers, unaffected by their missiles and arrows, and moved towards the central square.

'Caesar, please,' the senator said, backing into the building behind him.

'What are they?' asked Clara.

'A curse,' said Ulpia. 'You may run too, if you like. To be bitten by one is to invite death.'

'They look like mosquitoes,' said the Doctor.

'They're silver,' Clara pointed out.

'Robot mosquitoes?' the Doctor suggested as the insects entered the square.

He took out his sonic screwdriver and ran towards the swarm. As he activated the sonic there was a sudden change in the swarm's buzzing, and it became more high-pitched and tinny. They paused in their flight – and then scattered, fleeing from the Doctor's sonic signal.

Ulpia stared at him in surprise. 'You're a doctor of magic.' A statement, not a question – like magic was something ordinary and everyday.

'Hardly – just insect repellent,' said the Doctor off-handedly. 'How long's this been going on?'

'They've been attacking for five days, spreading disease amongst my soldiers, killing dozens. I cannot risk contact with any of my other legions.' Her eyes moved to the darkening horizon, and her voice grew harder. 'My husband defeated the Alamanni, the Vandals, the Gallic Empire and countless others. He restored Rome to greatness, and yet I am paralysed by mere insects. I don't know how to save my people.' She turned her attention to the Doctor. 'Can you help me?'

Clara glanced at the Doctor. 'Of course we can,' she said.

'We can try,' said the Doctor. 'Where are the patients?'

Before they'd even set foot inside the medical tent, the stench of rotting meat assaulted Clara. Her eyes stung and her throat burned as she and the Doctor stepped inside. She covered her mouth with her hand and took shallow breaths, but it was still overpowering. 'I'm not sure I can stay in here.'

'You think it's any better where you're from?' he asked, approaching the nearest patient. He looked him over with an impersonal precision, checking his eyes and his pulse before moving on.

'Yes!' said Clara.

The Doctor looked at her as though she'd just grown a second head. 'You still cut people open and poke around inside. You dose patients with radiation hoping that it does more damage to the cancer than the cancer does to the patient. You haven't the first clue how to tackle hundreds of diseases.' He moved to the next bed, offered a few calming words to the wounded soldier as he examined the dark patches of mottled skin on his face and neck.

Clara glared at him. 'Antibiotics, anaesthesia, X-rays.'

'They've got anaesthetic here,' said the Doctor, as he moved on to an unconscious patient and quickly examined the injuries beneath his bandages. 'These symptoms are very odd; very *different*.'

'Insulin,' said Clara. 'Vaccinations, knowing what the heart actually does. We've made progress!'

'All right, fine, there may have been one or two slight improvements,' conceded the Doctor, 'but on the grand scale of things—'

'On the grand scale of things, I'm right, and you'd rather be a patient in twenty-first-century Britain than here.'

'That would depend on what was wrong with me,' said the Doctor.

'You know, Doctor, it's healthy to admit when you're wrong.'

He pretended not to hear, caught up in his examination of the sick young man in front of them.

'Doctor?'

'Would you let me concentrate? And if you are going to throw up, please do it outside.' He moved on to another patient, and walked straight into a Roman clothed in a long tunic and fresh bloodstains.

The Roman looked into the Doctor's eyes and frowned. 'You're new,' he said.

'Yes,' agreed the Doctor. 'Just recruited by her Royal Highness to help with your little medical problem.'

The Roman's frown deepened. 'I'll assume you're referring to the Empress. I'm Vettius Falco, commander of the camp physicians. How do you think you can help?'

'Treatment hasn't been going very well so far, has it?' said the Doctor.

'Hardly. The best news we have is that it isn't a contagion. Only those bitten directly by the mosquitoes have been infected, but there've been dramatic differences in their symptoms. No herbal remedies have aided them, and when infected limbs have been removed, the infection has resurfaced in other parts of the body.'

'So what have you been doing for them?'

'Praying,' said Vettius.

'Don't you dare,' said Clara to the Doctor as he opened his mouth to respond.

He raised his eyebrows. 'You've no idea what I was going to say.'

'I can guess, and it wasn't anything helpful.'

The Doctor turned back to the row of patients he'd just examined. 'They've all been bitten by these mosquitoes, but are exhibiting reactions diverse enough to suggest they've not all been infected by the same illness. The mosquitoes themselves are artificial, and that attack didn't look random. It all feels to me like someone is using your army as laboratory specimens.' He paused, then spoke in a low voice: 'Clara, I hope you're paying attention and have noticed the noise outside.'

The buzzing noise was faint but steady – and getting closer. 'They're coming back,' she said.

'I guess I'll have to be more convincing this time.' The Doctor took out his sonic screwdriver. Clara looked out of the open tent flap to see the approaching swarm heading straight towards her. The Doctor pulled Vettius down behind a table of gleaming surgical tools.

'Do they know we're here?' asked Clara, ducking back inside and joining the other two behind cover.

'I don't think it's us they're after,' the Doctor told her.

Vettius' eyes widened with realisation. 'The patients.' He tried to stand but the Doctor pulled him back down.

'There's nothing you can do. No point in making yourself a target.'

'Isn't there?' snapped Clara. 'We're not the ones who're defenceless.'

'I have a duty,' said Vettius.

'Stay. Here. Both of you.'

As the shimmering swarm swept into the tent, the Doctor stood and activated his sonic screwdriver, sweeping it round in a wide arc. The swarm reacted with a shudder and sudden swerve before dozens veered away in random directions. A handful fell to the ground, but the rest were unimpeded as they swept down on the first patient.

'Can't you just get rid of them again?'

'I could, but then they'd just come back. I'm trying to deactivate a few. We need to get a closer look at them.'

Clara rolled her eyes, ducked up to grab a basket from the table, and tipped all the tools out.

She edged round the swarm, closer to the bed they were focused on, upturned basket in hand. She moved closer, focusing on several mosquitoes close to the ground.

In one swift, smooth movement, she leapt forward and slammed the basket down over them.

The Doctor adjusted his sonic and tried again. The swarm seemed confused, as though they'd lost their sense of direction, before they flew out of the tent and up into the air, climbing higher and higher until they'd vanished from sight.

'Well,' said the Doctor, 'I don't think we'll be seeing those ones again.' He crouched down next to Clara's basket. 'They don't sound happy.'

'What are they?' asked Clara. 'Some sort of alien robot mosquitoes are invading the planet?' She gave the basket a speculative look. 'Should we squash them?'

'Let's try for a more subtle approach. I should be able to deplete their power, then we can take a closer look.'

Vettius hurried over to the patient who'd been the swarm's target. 'He's dead.'

The Doctor stared over the corpse as he thought. 'Terminating the specimen after they collect the results.'

'That's horrible,' said Clara.

The Doctor nodded. 'That's why we're going to put a stop to it.'

He waved his sonic screwdriver over the basket and, when the trapped insects ceased their buzzing, he gingerly flipped the basket over. Three of the mosquitoes lay beneath it, inert.

Clara crouched down and picked up one of the fallen insects. It was exquisite. Beautiful. Less than two centimetres long, but she could make out the delicately constructed legs, the antennae, the diamond sheen of the compound metal eyes. 'Are these safe now?'

'Safer,' the Doctor told her. 'I'd avoid the mouth if I were you; it may still bite.'

He carefully plucked another of the fallen mosquitoes from the floor. 'All right, you wee beastie, let's take a good look at you.'

Ulpia Severina paced the room, her hands clasped behind her back as she considered what the Doctor had told her.

'Then this is an attack?'

'Possibly. Or someone's made a terrible mistake. Either way, those mosquitoes don't belong here. You've nothing like the technology needed and the component alloys don't even come from this planet.'

'Someone sent them here?' asked Clara. 'Why?'

'I don't know, but if we can find where they're coming from, we might be able to stop them. They need an energy field to recharge their power, so their range is limited.'

'Energy field?' asked Ulpia.

'They need to rest before they come and attack you again,' said Clara.

'And when you find their resting place, you intend to destroy it, alone?' said Ulpia.

'I think it'll be rather a delicate operation,' the Doctor told her. 'A lot of soldiers trampling around the place would only attract unwanted attention, and might prompt another attack.'

Ulpia was silent for a few moments as she held the Doctor's gaze. 'Why are you helping me?' she asked.

He gave her a slight smile. 'I like helping people. My generous nature.'

'I want your word that you will do everything in your power to destroy these creatures.'

'I'll try.'

'I'm not inclined to make threats—'

'So don't.' He moved fractionally towards her. 'Trust me.'

She nodded. 'I suppose that'll have to be enough. Very well, you may go. Succeed and I'll grant you any reward it's in my power to give, within reason. Fail...' She shrugged. 'Fail, and I suppose you'll be dead, too.'

The Doctor asked for the times and locations of the attacks and stood over the Empress's map, his eyes half-closed, as he began his calculations to triangulate the most likely location for where the mosquito swarms were recharging.

After tripping over another exposed root on the forest floor, Clara stopped and folded her arms. 'How long are we going to have to walk around in circles before you admit we're in the wrong place?' she asked.

'All right, all right,' said the Doctor, 'we'll try the second most likely location.'

They moved through the trees as though they were tracking a wary fawn. From some distance away, Clara had spotted the clearing in the forest and its tiny silver occupants. Her heart was beating fast as they made their way forward. Her footsteps through the undergrowth sounded horribly loud. But the mosquitoes didn't seem to hear.

In the midst of the clearing stood a tall, twisted tower, soaring into the sky. Around it, there were thousands of shining mosquitoes, hanging in the air. Still and silent, as though they were captured in invisible amber.

'How do we get through?' asked Clara in a low voice.

The Doctor took out his sonic screwdriver and adjusted the settings. When he activated it, nearby mosquitoes began to buzz faintly and move away from them, slowly clearing a path to the centre of the clearing. 'Come on,' said the Doctor quietly, 'quick as you can.'

Clara followed the Doctor through the swarm. There were so many of them, and they were so close. Any moment, surely one would reach out and sting her... When they reached the central tower, she allowed herself a sigh of relief. There was a good clear gap of a metre or more between the swarm and the tower. She noticed the tower itself was emitting a low hum, like the sound of high-voltage electricity pylons.

'Interesting,' said the Doctor. 'This thing isn't just recharging, it's transmitting too.' He pocketed his sonic and pressed his palm against the tower. Instantly, the structure shifted, the silver metal reshaping itself into a control panel. As he tapped at the controls, the tower's hum changed pitch.

'Tell me that's a good sound,' said Clara.

'It's the sound of me trying to disconnect this tower from wherever the data's going, since that's also where the instructions for the mosquitoes are coming from.'

'Right. Good.'

'Ah,' said the Doctor.

'Ah? Good ah?'

'Bad ah. They're sending something back down the datastream.'

'Please don't let it be orders for all of these mosquitoes to eat us.'

The Doctor hesitated, then said, 'No, it's a message.'

'Oh.'

'They'd like to know who we are and why we're interfering with their scientific research,' he said, before he began tapping away again.

Clara was appalled. 'Then they *are* using the poor people! I hope you're giving them a suitably angry reply.'

'I am.'

'Is there swearing? Angry swearing?'

'There may be one or two pointed comments on their lack of ethical standards,' said the Doctor. The panel bleeped. 'It seems that their exploratory probe found no sentient life forms on the planet, and so they felt able to begin experimentation to search for a cure.'

'A cure for what?'

'A plague ravaging their own worlds.'

'So they decide to infect another planet? Brilliant plan.'

'Desperate people do desperate things,' said the Doctor. 'And a little compassion wouldn't go amiss.'

'It's not your planet they're sending alien diseases to.'

The Doctor shot her a look, then read on: 'However, since we're communicating with them, they accept there may have been an error and are prepared to terminate.'

'No sentient life?' said Clara. 'Seriously? Did they not notice all the people?'

'I think they did.'

She stared at him. 'You mean humans don't count as sentient?'

'Apparently not, not by their standards anyway.'

Clara narrowed her eyes. 'I don't like these aliens.'

'Well, they've seen reason so I—' The panel beeped again. 'Stand well back,' read the Doctor. The ground began to tremble, while the tower folded the communications panel back into itself and began to shake in an alarming way.

'Yeah,' said Clara, pulling on the Doctor's arm. 'I think that might be a hint to get out of here.'

Clara wasn't quite sure if the tower had taken off or exploded but, either way, it and the mosquitoes had gone, leaving a charred and smoking clearing in their wake.

'Well, all done here,' said the Doctor, sticking his hands in his coat pockets. 'How about we take another try at the Eternal City, hmm?'

'Hang on, what about all those sick patients?' He didn't answer. 'What? Doctor – what?'

'No one else is going to get sick, not because of this. I did as much as I can.'

She held his gaze. 'They'll die.'

'Everyone dies. When you go back home, everyone here will've been dead over a thousand years. We helped, Clara, but I'm not your planet's medical service: I can't cure everything.'

'And we're not going back to tell Ulpia what's happened? She did promise you a reward; you could get your own villa.'

'The problem with despots, Clara, is that when they find someone useful, they tend to want to keep them. I'm sure she'll figure it out soon enough.'

'Right, I'll keep that in mind. So which direction is it back to the TARDIS?'

The Doctor spun around, and then pointed off into one patch of trees that looked much the same as all the others. 'Forwards, of course.'

SEVEN

THE PRACTICALITIES OF TIME TRAVEL

'Have you ever thought what it's like to
be wanderers in the fourth dimension?'

The First Doctor, *An Unearthly Child* (1963)

We've discussed different ideas about how time travel might be possible, but if we could really travel through time, what skills and knowledge should we take with us?

It's not easy becoming an astronaut. First, it's not often that a job comes up in space. Since the European Space Agency was founded in 1975, it has recruited new astronauts on just three occasions: in 1978–1979, 1991–1992 and 2008–2009.

There was a lot of competition for those jobs when they came up. On the last occasion, there were 8,413 applications from people who could meet all the initial requirements, which included supplying a JAR-FCL 3 Class 2 certificate – the same kind of medical certificate you need when applying for a private pilot's licence. Further medical, psychological and cognitive tests, plus interviews, helped ESA narrow the 8,413 applicants down to just six people, who then began their astronaut training. The rejected 8,407 candidates could try applying to the limited number of other space agencies round the world, or give up on their dreams of going into space.

For the six candidates who made it, basic training at ESA takes about sixteen months. There are lessons in the practical skills needed to live and work in space: engineering, orbital mechanics, propulsion, human physiology, biology, astronomy and ways to study the Earth. Scuba-diving lessons help prepare astronauts as much as possible for being – and working while – weightless. They are taught how to operate the systems on the International Space Station where they will work, plus all the different spacecraft that dock with it. There is focused tuition on operating robotic systems, and rendezvous and docking in orbit.

Trainee astronauts at ESA also study psychology and human behaviour to help them deal with the stress and weirdness of being out in space. One training programme includes living underground in a system of caves for a week to better understand human behaviour and performance in extreme conditions. They are taught about national and international laws and policies that affect space, and learn about all current and planned space missions planned by different countries and organisations. They even learn to speak Russian, since ESA often launches and lands its astronauts from Russia.

That's just the basic training. There is then a year's advanced training on technical skills needed to live and work on the International Space Station, including being able to run science experiments there. After that, the candidate astronauts are assigned to a flight into space – and have eighteen months of training specific to their particular role and mission. In total, astronaut training takes about four years – and many astronauts are selected because they already have skills and experience they can bring to the job. For example, one of the six astronauts recruited by ESA in 2009 was Major Timothy Peake, who was already a graduate of both the British Army Air Corps and Empire Test Pilots' School, and had a degree in flight dynamics and evaluation – all good preparation for becoming, in 2015, the first British ESA astronaut to visit the International Space Station.

All this effort is to equip astronauts for the difficulties of work in space and to prepare them for the various hazards they might face there. As we discussed in Chapter 2, missions can go wrong. In 1970, when an oxygen tank exploded on the Apollo 13 spacecraft while on its way to the Moon, the crew and their team back on Earth knew their equipment and the science so well that they were able to improvise a number of brilliant fixes that got the astronauts back to Earth alive.

In *Doctor Who*, the Doctor's companions – who face the same hazards plus monsters and explosions – have to develop their skills and state of mind as they go. The Doctor doesn't expect his companions to provide a JAR-FCL 3 Class 2 certificate, but he clearly has criteria for what makes a good companion. Even when he's not travelling alone, he's on the lookout for people with the 'right stuff' to join him on his travels – he offers 'all of time and space' to Rita in *The God Complex* (2011) and Osgood in *Death in Heaven* (2014). He's also been known to dump would-be companions after one trip if they don't measure up – as he does with Adam in *The Long Game* (2005).

So what makes the 'right stuff'? Quite often, the Doctor's companions are scientists of different kinds (there are many different ways to pursue a career in science). One of the first companions in *Doctor Who*, Ian Chesterton, teaches science at Coal Hill School. The Second Doctor's companion Zoe Heriot is an astrophysicist with a pure mathematics major – useful for her work on a space station. The Third Doctor's companion Liz Shaw, we're told, has 'degrees in medicine, physics and a dozen other subjects'. Later companions Romana and Nyssa, being aliens, don't hold qualifications from Earth but they're clearly both scientists: in *The Pirate Planet* (1978), we learn that Romana studied the life cycle of the Gallifreyan Flutterwing; in *Terminus* (1983), Nyssa synthesises an enzyme on the table in her bedroom. Adric, another alien, wears a gold star for mathematical excellence. In *Planet of Fire* (1984), Peri is meant to be working on an ecology project; we learn later that she is a botanist. Harry Sullivan, Grace Holloway and Martha Jones are all medical doctors. Ace failed her chemistry exams at school but the Seventh Doctor calls her an 'expert' in explosives.

Other companions are from the future, which means they understand science and technology we have not yet developed.

River Song is – depending when we meet her – a student, doctor and then professor of archaeology. We'll talk more in Chapter 10 about whether history and archaeology count as 'science' as we understand the term, though the word derives from the Latin word 'scientia' – knowledge. But is a knowledge of history any use to the Doctor? Another of the first companions in *Doctor Who*, Barbara Wright, teaches history in the same school as Ian. But few companions since Barbara have had particular qualifications in history. Sarah Jane Smith was a journalist, another job that involves researching, analysing and organising information. She knows a surprising amount about ancient Egyptian mythology in *Pyramids of Mars* – recalling the number of gods listed in the tomb of Thutmoses III – but generally it's the Doctor who provides any historical detail that a story requires.

For all the Twelfth Doctor says he doesn't like soldiers, many of his companions have had military experience. Harry Sullivan was on active service when he joined the Doctor. Steven Taylor, Jamie Macrimmon and Vislor Turlough had all fought in wars. Leela is a warrior of the Sevateem. Ian Chesterton would presumably have done National Service. Rose, Mickey, Martha, Amy and Rory all learn to become soldiers, using guns to battle Daleks, Cybermen, Sontarans and the Silence.

A general level of fitness is also important to being a good companion: as Donna complains in *The Doctor's Daughter* (2008), 'Seriously, there's an outrageous amount of running involved.' The Doctor doesn't need to travel with athletes, but Rose's bronze in gymnastics is crucial to her helping him in her first story.

Knowing about science and history, and being able to fight monsters and run are all useful skills in a series that travels in time with plots involving monsters and chases. (We could think of it another way: it's useful for the writers of *Doctor Who* if the companions are able to help explain and drive the plot.)

Yet some of the most successful of the companions in *Doctor Who* are not scientists or soldiers. The Doctor doesn't offer trips in the TARDIS to Rose Tyler, Donna Noble, Amelia Pond and Clara Oswald – to name just a few of them – because they have particular skills or qualifications (though Donna's ability to type a hundred words a minute comes in handy in *Journey's End* (2008)). So what do they offer that makes them the 'right stuff' for being a companion?

Before we try to answer that question, it might help to think about the sorts of problems and hazards we would face if we could travel in time. The crew of Apollo 13 had to deal with an oxygen cylinder exploding. We've seen the TARDIS get into difficulties, such as when the police box exterior shrinks in *Flatline* (2014) or collides with a salvage ship in *Journey to the Centre of the TARDIS* (2013). Just as the crew of Apollo 13 improvised a solution, Clara and the Doctor are able to work out how to save the TARDIS – by giving it an energy source or sending a message back in time.

In *Journey to the Centre of the TARDIS*, it's the Doctor who works out the solution. Clara works out the solution in *Flatline* – but several times in the story we're told she has started to think like the Doctor and in *Death in Heaven* (2014) she fools the Cybermen into thinking she *is* him. The implication is that it's his influence – what she's learnt while she's been travelling with him – that helps her solve the problem. Just as some companions learn to operate at least some of the TARDIS controls, these are skills learnt on the job – not something the companions arrive with.

A more common problem in travelling in the TARDIS is not knowing where or when you've arrived. The Doctor might aim for London but end up in Glasgow – as he did at the end of *Deep Breath* (2014). Being able to work out your location would be a useful skill.

In fact, for centuries before global positioning satellites allowed us to work out our position on the Earth's surface with a high degree of accuracy, people used the stars. In the northern hemisphere, we can use Polaris, also known as the Pole Star because it appears in the sky almost directly over the North Pole.

To find Polaris, you first need to look for a distinctive group of seven stars called the Plough (it's also known in America as the Big Dipper, among other names). Imagine a line between the two stars at the right end of the Plough – they're called Merak and Dubhe. Extend that line up away from the 'rectangle' of the Plough, going five times the distance of the gap between Merak and Dubhe. The bright star you come to is Polaris.

Point with your finger to where Polaris is lowest in the sky and you are pointing north. That's useful for navigation, but you can also use Polaris to work out your latitude. Latitude is a measure of how far north or south you are on the Earth's surface: at 0° you are on the Equator, an imaginary line running round the Earth's middle, exactly

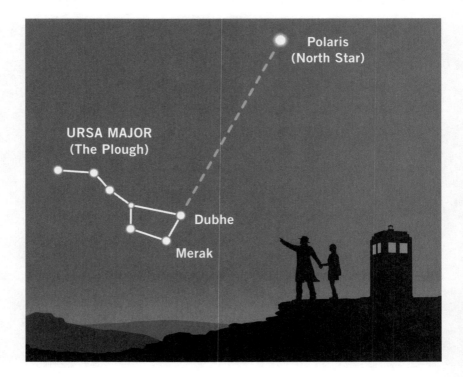

halfway between the South Pole and the North Pole, and running through countries such as Brazil, Kenya and Indonesia.

Every 111.2 km (or 69 miles) north or south of the Equator, there's another imaginary line of latitude, measured in degrees either plus or minus, depending if you're heading north or south. The North Pole is at +90° (sometimes called 90° north), and the South Pole is at -90° (sometimes 90° south). On a map with north at the top, the lines of latitude run horizontally.

The Western Rocks on the Isles of Sicily are the most southerly part of the United Kingdom and are at +49°51' (like hours, degrees divide up into 60 'minutes' – indicated by the inverted comma symbol). The southernmost part of the British mainland is Lizard Point in Cornwall, at a latitude of +49°57'. Southampton is more or less at +51° and London at +51°30'. Milton Keynes is roughly at +52°, Stoke-on-Trent, Derby and Nottingham are all close to +53°. York is close to +54°, Newcastle upon Tyne and North Shields close to +55°, Edinburgh close to +56° and Aberdeen a little above +57°. The northernmost part of Britain, Dunnet Head in Scotland, is at +58°40'. Out Stack in the Shetland Islands – the northernmost part of the United Kingdom – is at +60°51'.

Here's the clever bit. You used the Plough to find Polaris, and by pointing to Polaris you are now pointing north. But the angle your arm is making to the ground will give you your degree of latitude, too. If you're pointing straight up at Polaris, then you must be directly underneath it which means you're at +90° – that is, the North Pole. If you're pointing directly ahead, Polaris is on the horizon which means you're at a latitude of 0°C and standing on the Equator. Anywhere in between those two reference points (which should make a right angle), the angle of your arm will match your degree of latitude.

This was extremely useful in navigation, but knowing how far north or south you are is only half the problem. To fix your location on the Earth's surface you also need to know how far east or west you are – and this is much harder to do. Again, a solution lies in the stars. For more than 200 years, the annual *Nautical Almanac* has provided navigational tables and charts of the Sun and Moon along with 58 of approximately 6,000 stars that are visible to the naked eye, with details for another 115 stars. These tables can be used to calculate your position not just in terms of north and south, but also east and west and they have enabled sailors and other travellers to make their journeys safely and quickly, while also allowing cartographers to greatly improve their maps of the Earth.

However, pinpointing your position by the stars like this is tricky. Britain's Royal Observatory was founded in Greenwich in 1675 to find a way to do it, and astronomers there took almost a century to solve the problem and produce the first *Nautical Almanac*. Making north-south measurements is the easy part: Polaris is unique among celestial objects because it is almost directly above the Earth's North Pole, which is the axis on which the planet rotates. That means that as the Earth turns, Polaris appears to stay in the same place in the sky, hovering always above the pole. But, as we saw in Chapter 1, all other stars appear to move through the sky as if fixed to a wheel – though in fact it's we who are turning.

For example, take the brightest star in the sky – the Sun. As we also saw in Chapter 1, the Sun is at its highest position in the sky at midday. But because the Earth is turning, 'midday' is different in different places round the Earth. While it's midday in the United Kingdom, it's the middle of the night in Australia. But we also know that the Sun and other stars move through the sky in a regular cycle – which we can use to fix our east-west position – or 'longitude'.

Longitude, like latitude, is a series of imaginary lines measured in degrees. Whereas lines of latitude run parallel to one another (and so never touch), lines of longitude all run between the two poles – dividing up the Earth like the segments of an orange. Because of its long history of using astronomy to perfect the art of navigation, the line of longitude that runs through the Royal Observatory Greenwich in London is designated as 0°. This is known as the Prime Meridian and it is the reference line from which all other longitudes are measured.

Because there are 360 degrees in a full circle we divide up the Earth into 360 lines of longitude: 180 heading east of Greenwich and 180 heading west. On the opposite side of the Earth from Greenwich is the antimeridian, a line of longitude that is 180° both east and west of the prime meridian. It cuts through parts of eastern Russia, the Fiji Islands and the middle of the Pacific Ocean.

Since we know the Earth rotates every 24 hours, we can work out that midday on the antimeridian will be 12 hours different to midday in Greenwich, halfway round the world. In fact, if we divide the 360° of longitude by 24 hours, we see that every 15° of longitude means an hour's difference in time. That calculation has been used as the basis for the different time zones on Earth – with some variation for political and historical reasons.

For most of us, this difference in time only affects us when we try to call someone in another country and must factor in that our mid-afternoon is their middle of the night, and so on. When we travel to other countries in another time zone, we must change the time on our watches to give local time.

Knowing the difference between the local time – that is, the apparent position of the Sun and other stars in the sky from where we are – and the time back in Greenwich means we can calculate our longitude east or west of Greenwich. For example, if the Sun has just reached its highest position in the sky at our location but a watch set to Greenwich time is reading 1 p.m., we must be 15° west of Greenwich. It sounds simple in principle, but before it could be used in practice astronomers had to map the positions and motions of the Sun, Moon and stars with extreme precision, and clockmakers had to design and build clocks which would accurately keep Greenwich time – even on long and arduous sea voyages lasting many months.

It still takes training and practice to make the necessary measurements, but knowing where on Earth you are is such a useful – even lifesaving – piece of information that for centuries people were willing to make the effort. Today, of course, anyone with a smartphone can use the satellites of the Global Positioning System to tell them their location. But this technology is in many ways a development of those early measurements of longitude using clocks and stars: the GPS satellites form an artificial constellation and computer software does all the difficult calculations for us, but the basic principles remain the same.

Being able to find out where you are – your position in space – is something that we all find useful, but for time travellers like the Doctor and his companions finding out *when* you are – your position in time – is also a skill that can come in very handy. Surprisingly the stars could also prove very useful here, too. As the Earth spins on its axis, everything in the sky appears to move around us once every twenty-four hours – and in particular the position of the Sun relative to the horizon is what tells us whether it's morning or afternoon, day or night. As the Moon orbits round the Earth, we see different portions of it lit up by the Sun. This 29.5-day cycle of lunar phases – new Moon, waxing crescent, Full Moon, waning crescent, and then back to new Moon – is the origin of our calendar system of months. The Earth also orbits the Sun, so that throughout the year the Sun appears to move once around the sky, relative to the background groupings – or 'constellations' – of stars. Days, months and years are therefore all astronomical measurements, marked out by the motions of the Earth and the apparent movements of the Moon and Sun in the sky. By understanding how their positions change, we can use the heavens as a giant clock, telling us hours, days and months.

One thing that doesn't seem to change is the constellations of stars. Night after night they appear to rise, move across the sky and set, but their familiar shapes – the Plough, Orion the Hunter, Taurus the Bull and dozens of others – are reassuringly constant. However this constancy is an illusion and if we compared their positions after fifty or a hundred years, we would see small changes as each individual star slowly shifted its position in the sky. This is because the Sun, along with every other star we can see, is orbiting round the centre of the Milky Way galaxy. It takes our Sun, and the entire Solar System with it, between 225 and 250 million years to travel once around the galaxy. The last time we were in this part of the Milky Way we're in now, the dinosaurs had just evolved and the Earth had only one continent. The Sun has made this epic journey about eighteen times since it formed 4.5 billion years ago and will probably make another twenty orbits before it finally dies.

Our galaxy is vast and, even moving at typical speeds of about 230 kilometres per second, the changes in the positions of the stars are barely noticeable in a human lifetime – at least to human eyes. But with instruments like the European Space Agency's Gaia space telescope, astronomers are beginning to measure and track the motions of around a billion stars in the Milky Way. Using computer simulations we can fast-forward these motions millions of years into the future or rewind them into the past, making the night sky seethe and swirl like a swarm of bees as each star follows its own unique path through the spiral arms, clouds of gas and billions of other stars which make up our galaxy.

The constellations which hung above Tyrannosaurus Rex and Velociraptor were not Orion or the Plough, and our own descendants will need to invent new names and stories to describe the patterns that the stars make in the unfamiliar skies of the distant future. Perhaps a time traveller with enough knowledge of galactic dynamics would be able to take one look up and know exactly when they had arrived in the Earth's long journey through the Milky Way.

We'll talk about other ways we might work out the year in which we'd arrived in Earth's history in Chapter 10, which would be useful for a time traveller. But in *Doctor Who*, the Doctor rarely needs his companions to deduce where and when the TARDIS lands. He can do that himself. For example, in *The Time of Angels* (2010), River checks the TARDIS controls for information while the Doctor just pokes his head out the door.

'We're somewhere in the Garn Belt.
There's an atmosphere. Early indications suggest that—'

'We're on Alfava Metraxis, the seventh planet of the
Dundra System. Oxygen-rich atmosphere, all toxins in the
soft band, eleven hour day and chances of rain later.'

River Song and the Eleventh Doctor, *The Time of Angels* **(2010)**

In fact, a companion's skills and experience are unlikely ever to match the Doctor's. We can leave flying the TARDIS – and fixing it when it goes wrong – largely to him. Instead, the biggest risk of travelling with the Doctor is what to do if we get separated from him – which happens a lot in the series. So the 'right stuff' required to be a companion means practical things like self-reliance, bravery, the ability to adapt quickly and improvise.

But there's more than that, too. Time travel may be commonplace in the universe of *Doctor Who*, but its consequences can still be very hard for his companions to deal with. When the Doctor first takes Rose Tyler into the future in *The End of the World* (2005), she finds all the aliens – and being able to understand their languages – a bit overwhelming. To help, the Doctor fixes Rose's mobile phone so that she can call her mum, back in the distant past. For a moment, Rose is happy just to hear Jackie's voice. But the moment the call is over, the truth hits her hard:

'That was five billion years ago – so she's dead now.
Five billion years later, my mum's dead.'
Rose Tyler, *The End of the World* **(2005)**

We're repeatedly shown in *Doctor Who* the odd side effects of travelling in time. Rose doesn't just travel to the future where her mum is dead but also – in *Father's Day* (2005) – goes to her parents' wedding in the 1980s and meets herself as a baby.

In *The Power of Three* (2012), Amy and Rory know that the amount of time they've been travelling with the Doctor for doesn't match the amount of time that has passed for their friends and family on Earth. Their friends don't know that Amy and Rory travel in time, but we see that it still affects their relationships: Amy's friend Laura isn't sure about asking her to be a bridesmaid because Amy's not always around. We don't know if Amy makes Laura's wedding, but we do know Amy and Rory end up back in time at the end of *The Angels Take Manhattan* (2012), separated from their friends and family for ever. How companions survive after they've travelled with the Doctor – how they return to ordinary life after all of time and space – is a worry, too.

Companions have to be tough psychologically. To travel with the Doctor, they must ask questions and solve problems, but they have to be ready for answers that can be surprising and unsettling. They are often threatened with death and they often see people die. There are times when they can stop and help and save people, and there are times when they must walk away. It's OK to be scared, it's OK to make mistakes, and it's OK to be ordinary. What gives a companion the 'right stuff' is an open mind, being willing – even eager – to explore all the strangeness of time and space, to puzzle out how it works and fits together, to face the consequences of discovery.

But that, after all, is what scientists do every day. Rather than a collection of facts, science is really an attitude – a way of looking and thinking about the world. It's a quest for knowledge, no matter how counterintuitive or strange, with a readiness to accept – in the face of new evidence – that everything you thought you knew is wrong. That's what makes science such a powerful tool for understanding the universe around us.

In *Battlefield* (1989), the Seventh Doctor takes Ace with him when he visits UNIT, handing her an old security pass so she can get past the soldiers on guard. The pass is for Liz Shaw, the companion of the Third Doctor with degrees in physics and medicine. Ace – who we later learn couldn't pass her school chemistry exams – is worried. But the Doctor reassures her: it's not qualifications that matter but attitude.

'Who's Elizabeth Shaw? I don't even look like her.'

'Oh, never mind. Just think like a physicist.'

Ace and the Seventh Doctor, *Battlefield* **(1989)**

IN SEARCH OF LOST TIME
UNA MCCORMACK

Here we are now, in the park. With the pram beside her and the little one asleep, Tilly Pilgrim is watching a father pushing a child on a swing. *Up* curves the swing, and then, because this is how swings work, *down* comes the swing, and then it comes *back*, then *down*, then *up* and the child opens his mouth to laugh...

And then Tilly comes unstuck in time...

A cold red Sun curves across a darkening sky in a great arc – rising, peaking, and plunging down again behind the horizon. A bare Moon rises and speeds on its path. Then the Sun again, and the Moon, and the Sun, and the Moon – never-ending, and all the time Tilly can hear the cries of the damned trapped in this hell-time. Months, it seems, pass – years, and the chorus of screaming is ceaseless.

And then a single voice comes, rising steadily above the rest, breaking through...

'Can you hear us? You must hear us! We are coming! Coming through...'

And *down* comes the swing. And back and down and up and down and back and –

'Hello,' says the man now sitting beside her. 'Your daydreams. They're very disruptive. There should be a warning sign. Something of a nuisance for you, too, I should think.'

The man is funny-looking, limbs awkward like a baby giraffe. Tilly owns a lot of giraffes these days – or, rather, the little one does – but the point is Tilly knows what giraffes look like when she sees one. And this man looks like one – a baby giraffe that is – or he would, if baby giraffes wore bow ties.

'And tweed,' Tilly says, and giggles.

'Tweed?'

'My daydreams.'

'Your daydreams are tweed?'

'Don't be silly,' says Tilly, and giggles again. Then the man looks at her with such compassion that she thinks she might start crying. 'How do you know about my daydreams?'

'Well, I could hardly miss them, could I? They almost knocked me off course!'

'Off course? Well, of course!' Tilly says gaily. Very little about her life makes sense at the moment – what with the daydreams that seem more real than everyday life, and the thinking that the world is ending, and the being unstuck in time – so why not something else? Why not a tweedy baby giraffe with a bow tie?

He is looking at her now, intensely, and the urge to weep is very strong again. This man, she thinks, has seen whole worlds become unstuck. He has seen monstrosities, and he has judged, and – sometimes – he has forgiven. And Tilly – who doesn't know what is to be done, but knows that something must be done and quickly – makes a decision.

'Let's go for a coffee,' she says.

The man with the bow tie stares at her in horror. 'A *coffee*?'

'A coffee!' He looks around, enchanted, and his hands flap about, like a dodo's wings might have done when failing to fly. 'Me! Going for a *coffee*! In a *café*! Me!'

'It's nowhere special,' Tilly says apologetically. 'Just one of those chain ones.' But the staff are nice and they don't hurry her out, and the mums in the indie cafés are slim and blonde and judge.

'Can I have one of those giant chocolate biscuits?' says her companion.

'You can have whatever you like. Your dollar—'

'Ah.' He fidgets. 'Yes. You see, I don't have any money.'

Tilly sighs. 'Two double espressos and a big bourbon biscuit, please,' she says to the nice young woman at the counter. Bow-tie man, happy again, capers off to find a seat, and she adds, 'Could you make one of those espressos decaffeinated?'

'So,' says the man-boy, after she's wheeled the pram round and sat down opposite him, 'These dreams.' He's not flapping or fidgeting now. 'Serious business, dreams. Particularly ones that can knock a time machine off course.'

The baby stirs, but rolls her head to the other side and goes back to sleep. 'Time machine,' Tilly says, meditatively.

'Don't worry about it,' he urges. 'Tell me about the dreams.'

She ponders how to explain. 'Have you ever read the Narnia books?'

'Read them? I built the wardrobe!'

'It's a made-up wardrobe—'

'Believe that, by all means, if it helps.'

Tilly decides, sensibly, that this is the least of her worries. 'The Pevensie children. They went into the wardrobe, and became kings and queens of Narnia, and reigned for years. Then they went on a hunt, and they chased the white hart through a waste land—'

He is nodding. He knows the story. 'And they fell out of the wardrobe no older than they were when they went in.' He picks up a little packet of brown sugar from the table and twists it around between thumb and forefinger. All this nervous energy, Tilly thinks, could make you feel really rather tired, if you weren't very tired already from the sleepless nights and the dream-filled days. 'Is that what happens, Tilly? Do you fall into the wardrobe and become a queen of Narnia, and then fall out again no older than you were when you went in?'

'I didn't tell you my name.'

'No, you didn't. I'm the Doctor. There – equal footing. Is that what happens?'

'Yes,' Tilly says, with great relief. 'That's how it happens. How it's always happened.'

He's very intent now. 'They've not just started, then?'

'No, I got them as a child…'

The Most Beautiful Place in the World

Here she is now, in her home away from home, back again in the magic land, the daydream land, the garden, the place where a child can roam safe and free. This is Middle-earth, this is Narnia, this is where the wild things are and the white flowers bloom at night. This is where colours are brighter, sounds sharper, and she is still young enough that she misses nothing, records all, remembers all.

Here she quests, and explores, and wanders, and sometimes just sits by running water and watches it ripple over her toes. Here she becomes a hero, a captain, a navigator, a gardener, a king and a queen. Here she leads many long lives of adventure, and peace – and, later, love. But when she returns home, she is still on the bed, and the clock still shows the same time.

And the places she visits are always various and new, and the people are generous and kind, and the summers are warm but not unbearable, and the winters are beautiful but not cruel, and spring is full of life, and autumn full of promise, and time, relentless time, is passing – and then, and then, and then…

'And then?'

'And then it… *stopped.*'

'Why?' says the Doctor, urgently. 'What happened?'

Tilly sighs. 'I guess I fell out of the wardrobe,' she says with regret.

'So the dreams?'

'Went away.'

'Where did they go?'

'Where did they *go*?' Where *do* dreams go? 'They were childhood stories,' she says, as if that should be enough explanation. 'Things I told myself to help me fall asleep.'

Softly, the Doctor says, 'I think we both know that they were something more than that. And still are.'

Tilly thinks of the voice – the latest voice. *We're coming. Coming through...* She drinks her coffee in one quick gulp. He has made short work of the big biscuit, she notices. 'I grew up. There were exams, university...'

The Doctor nods sagely. 'Lipstick. Parties. Girls. And boys.'

Tilly can't help laughing. 'Something like that, yes.'

'So you became less open to the messages. You didn't have the bandwidth. Busy time, being a teenager. Brain expanding. Going supernova. Learning about cause and effect and life and death and getting the first tiniest inkling that you're not, in fact, going to live for ever.' He's getting excited now, and he wags his hands about, sending biscuit crumbs everywhere. 'Big issues. Big deal. Needs a bigger brain. But even that bigger brain – it's so *full*, all the time, *too* full, not enough room for *everything* any more—'

Tilly holds up a hand to stop the flood. 'Whoa there, mister!'

'Doctor.'

'Doctor-mister. Hold on a minute. Did you say *bandwidth*? Like some kind of receiver?'

'Yes, yes, a receiver!'

'You make me sound like a telephone! I'm not a *receiver*!'

'No?'

'No! I was the kind of child that had an overactive imagination. Daydreamed a lot. Probably read too much—'

'There's science to prove that's not possible,' the Doctor says, earnestly. 'Real science, of the best and most authoritative kind. And if there isn't then I'll do some. So there will be.'

'There'll be what?'

'Science. And proof.'

This has all, Tilly thinks, got quite out of hand. It's time to stop dreaming and time to stop making up stories. She is a grown-up now with grown-up responsibilities. There is a pram, with a baby asleep in it, and a landlord who likes regular rent, and on top of everything the washing machine has been making a funny noise the past few days and she simply can't manage without the washing machine. 'These are not messages,' she says firmly.

'Yes, they are. They always were. And now they've come back. But they're not how they used to be.'

Tilly shudders.

'Yes, back with a vengeance. Look at it this way,' he says. 'Either you're receiving messages from somewhere, or you're hearing voices inside your head. I know which I'd rather.' He leans towards her. Suddenly, the clatter and chatter of the café seem to recede, leaving them in their own quiet bubble of space and time. 'I can help. I'm the Doctor. But you need to tell me about it. Tell me what you can see.'

Tilly puts her hands to her forehead to block him out. She shakes her head. She doesn't want to go back to that place.

'Have some big biscuit,' says the Doctor. 'It helps.'

The Scariest Place in the Universe

As a child, she walked along these streets a hundred thousand times. She knew them when they were beautiful — broad avenues lined with great trees, full of laughter and song. She watched the trees grow and age, and saw new ones planted and flourish. She heard the music swell and fall away and rise again. She watched fashions change — in clothes, in buildings, in ideas — and come round again. She saw growth, and decay, and new growth.

But now it is all the hell times, all at once. It is the Book of Revelation.

It is Dante's Inferno and dying Charn. It is the Waste Land, with red rock and without relief. Where once there was sweet music, now there is only mourning — but not the order and transcendence of a requiem. There is no logic, no order to pain. There is only the present moment, an endless moment of agony...

'They're hurting each other,' Tilly whispers. Tears are sliding down her face. 'They were so wise, so *kind*. And now all they do is hurt each other. Why are they doing it? Why don't they *stop?*'

The Doctor doesn't answer (perhaps, Tilly thinks, there is no answer to those questions), but on the table between them something is going *beep*. Quietly, as if it doesn't want to make a fuss, but insistently, as if it knows its business is important. Tilly reaches out a finger to touch it, like a shipwrecked sailor bobbing in the ocean, grabbing something to stay afloat. 'What is this?' she whispers.

'I'm trying to track the source of these messages. Find out who's sending them, and why...' *Beep beep beep*. 'Could be an invasion, you see.'

'An invasion?'

'Could be. World ending. Looking for someone else to move. What's the word for that? Lebkuchen?'

'Lebensraum,' says Tilly. (Her degree happened a while ago now but had covered that kind of thing thoroughly.) 'Lebkuchen's a sort of biscuit.' Her hand reaches for the pram. 'Do you really think this is an invasion?'

'I don't know. But have to do something about it, if that's the case. Make a plan. Or eat a biscuit. Probably go with the plan plan first. Eat the biscuit after. If I can just work out where they're coming from...'

Beep beep beep.

For a minute or two he becomes so focused on his little machine that he seems oblivious to everything around him: the muzak, the chatter, the scared woman sitting opposite him. He is in his own world and she has the faintest impression that he has forgotten about her, and that her troubles have turned into a puzzle to be solved, with quick thinking and clever widgets.

'I'm frightened, Doctor,' she says.

He looks up at her. He reaches out and, tentatively, pats the hood of the pram, and clears his throat. 'Well, yes, of course you are,' he says. 'You're carrying the whole history of a civilisation in your head, and that history is ending. Coming all in a rush. Burning into your brain—'

'That's where you've stopped helping.'

'Have I? Sorry.' The beeping gets suddenly louder. A man with a suitcase at the next table looks at them curiously. 'Hush,' the Doctor says to the widget, and turns it off. He peers at it. 'Yes,' he says. 'There they are.' He looks at Tilly. A kindly, almost tender, smile spreads across his funny mismatched face. 'Do you want to meet the people who've been talking to you?'

'Shouldn't they be talking to someone else? Someone proper? A world leader, or something?'

'A world *leader*?' He looks at her in bafflement. 'I want us to be *friends*.'

'Fair enough. Will it be dangerous?'

'I don't think so. But I can't *see* the future. Only travel there.'

Tilly stands up. 'How do we get there? Through the wardrobe?'

'Near enough,' says the Doctor, and offers her his hand.

Tilly takes the measure of the blue box. 'What about the pram?'

'It'll fit,' he says, and opens the door to eternity.

The Most Beautiful Place in the Universe

Here they are. Here they really are. And this world no longer has the translucence of dream, or the rounded edges of memory, but all the roughness of a real world.

'It's all true,' says the Doctor. 'You didn't make it up.'

'But how?' says Tilly. She touches the walls. They are as solid as the pram. 'How could that happen?'

'They were clever, once upon a time, the people that lived here,' the Doctor tells her. 'They loved their beautiful world, and their wise ways, and they wanted people to know about them. So they transmitted images from their lives – sent them out to anyone who might listen and understand.'

'And I heard them.'

'Yes, you heard them, Tilly. Not daydreams. Memories.'

On the walls are pictures of a world that was lost; a world that Tilly once knew as well her own. 'What happened?' Tilly asks. 'What made them cruel instead of kind?'

'Who knows? We can guess, I suppose. Conjecture. Perhaps their sun began to die. Perhaps the water or the soil became poisoned. Perhaps they simply became too proud and forgot what had made them great.' His eyes are dark and limitless. 'That happens sometimes.'

They walk along the corridor. Their footsteps echo. This is a stark place, sterile and lonely. Outside the world is ending. But here, inside the bunker, someone is still working.

A woman sits behind a desk. Her hair falls in rats' tails about her face. She is thin and tired, but she is carrying on.

Tilly peers through the glass that separates them. 'Who is she? What is she doing?'

'I think,' says the Doctor, 'that she's been trying to tell you something.'

Tilly watches for a while and then, very gently, taps on the glass that separates them.

The woman looks up.

Tilly raises her hand and presses it against the glass. Slowly, the woman raises her own hand. In greeting.

'I hear you,' Tilly says, and although the other woman cannot hear, she smiles. She understands. 'I have always heard you.'

Here we are now, in the park. Here is the pram and here is the little one, still asleep. Over there, a father is pushing a child on a swing – a smooth arc that goes up and down and back – and the child is laughing.

'I wish we could have saved them,' Tilly says.

'So do I,' says the Doctor, after a pause. 'But sometimes I'm too late.'

There's a time machine, Tilly thinks, but even so there would have to be constants. It is not possible always to live in the present, not even as a trick of the mind. There must be change and growth – and ending. That is the way the universe works.

'I don't want to forget them,' she says.

'You won't forget them. How could you forget them?'

'I don't want them to be forgotten.'

'Ah,' the Doctor says. 'Now that's something different.' He looks at her, curiously. 'So what will you do?'

She could tell people, she thinks. Tell them what she has seen and what she knows. And they'd laugh and tell her she's talking rubbish, or else look away awkwardly and start talking about house prices instead. There is a lot to discuss when it comes to house prices.

'You could tell *her*,' says the Doctor, and taps the pram. 'I bet she'd like to hear.'

And she could – and she will. She'll tell the little girl, and maybe together they will write it down, and that way somebody will remember those wise people who lost their way. *Once upon a time some people lived, and sometimes they were happy.* That is all we know, she thinks, and all we need to know.

EIGHT

TIME AND MEMORY

'A man is the sum of his memories, you know
– a Time Lord even more so.'

The Fifth Doctor, *The Five Doctors* (1983)

Moondust is clingy. Because there's no atmosphere on the Moon, the dust isn't weathered and smoothed as it is on Earth. Instead, the dust – about half of it fragments of silicon dioxide glass created by meteor impacts – remain sharp, just right for sticking to spacesuits.

The astronauts who walked on the Moon between 1969 and 1972 brushed down their spacesuits before returning to their spacecraft, but some of the dust stuck fast and was carried inside. As a result, when the astronauts removed their space helmets inside their ship, they got a whiff of the Moon. It smelt, they said, like gunpowder. Apollo 17 astronaut Jack Schmitt even had an allergic reaction to it a bit like hay fever.

It's odd learning what the Moon smells like – that detail brings it vividly to life. Smells can often bring on sudden, strong memories and even change our moods. We understand the reason for this: the olfactory bulb (at the front of the brain, responsible for our sense of smell) is connected to the brain's limbic system. This limbic system includes the amygdala (which processes emotion) and the hippocampus (which learns associations between things).

The ability of certain smells to bring back rich recollection is just one of the quirks of memory that psychology and neuroscience are beginning to explain. The things we've learned so far are often surprising and counterintuitive. For a start, it might not be accurate to think about so-called memory as a single entity at all. It actually describes a diverse set of processes that help us to navigate our day to day world and – literally – make sense of our lives.

We can, however, make some broad generalisations to help us to think about memory. Information from the outside world needs to be encoded; it needs to be stored somewhere; and it needs to be retrieved when you need it. Disrupting any of these activities will interfere with memory, both in the real world of physical and mental health, and in the world of *Doctor Who*.

Encoding is the first stage of any memory formation process. We're constantly receiving information from our five senses – our sight, hearing, smell, taste and touch – and our brains seem to store these perceptions in detail for about half a second. Through a process called 'attention', our brains select parts of this sensory information over others to create our short-term memory.

You're using your short-term memory as you read these words. To understand this very sentence, you need to keep in your head the words at the beginning of the sentence while reading the rest of it. Our short-term memory seems able to hold about seven items of information in our heads for up to about fifteen seconds, allowing us to process information and make sense of the world around us. So you'll soon forget the first words of this sentence – unless your brain thinks they will be useful to you in future, and stores them in your long-term memory.

What we remember is therefore not a video recording of the world, but a selection decided by conscious and unconscious processes. In his 1932 book *Remembering*, British psychologist Frederic Bartlett conducted an experiment where people were asked to read a story from traditions of the native people of Canada, called the 'War of Ghosts'. When Bartlett asked people to retell the story they'd read, he found that they omitted or reshaped elements they were less familiar with, changing the story to better mirror their own culture.

In *Remembrance of the Daleks* (1988), the Seventh Doctor and Ace battle Daleks in London in 1963. Ace, who is from London twenty-five years in the future, wonders why she hasn't heard of this battle as part of the history she grew up with. The Doctor asks her about other alien invasions of London featured in the series – and she's not heard of those either. 'Your species has the most amazing capacity for self-deception,' he concludes – as if people have simply *chosen* not to remember.

The Day of the Doctor (2013) suggests that the Doctor's friends at UNIT are actively involved in helping in this process. We learn that they tell the public that the arrival of the TARDIS in Trafalgar Square is a stunt by TV magician Derren Brown – a cover story that will work because it better fits people's experience than an alien in a time-travelling police box.

The hippocampus seems to sort new information by comparing it with memories already recorded. We know this from studying people who have suffered damage to the hippocampus and have trouble creating new long-term memories. For example, in 1953, an American man called Henry Molaison who suffered from epilepsy and seizures underwent brain surgery which removed much of his hippocampus in an attempt to improve his condition. Afterwards, Molaison could no longer create new long-term memories. Until he died in 2008, Molaison enjoyed doing crosswords – but his general knowledge was limited to things he'd learnt before he'd had the operation in 1953.

We can use the associative nature of memory to our advantage when it comes to recalling facts and figures. We can remember complicated information by associating it with something much simpler, using a device called a 'mnemonic' (from the Greek word for memory). For example, we might struggle to remember the order of the colours in a spectrum, such as a rainbow – red, orange, yellow, green, blue, indigo and violet. But it's much easier to recall that sequence using a simple mnemonic sentence using the same initial letters – 'Richard of York gave battle in vain.'

But, as we've already mentioned, our brains don't only encode and store those memories that we consciously want to remember. Imagine you're a child taking part in a school sports day. You're out on the playing field which has been newly mown and the air has a tangy stink of cut grass. (We think plants such as grass release strongly smelling chemicals when they're attacked as a defence mechanism against insects – and that they can't tell the difference between an insect and a lawnmower.) Your brain remembers this sports day. Because of the way the limbic system is connected, the hippocampus links the memory to the smell that the olfactory bulb detects – the cut grass – and to how the amygdala says you're feeling.

Years later, you're out for a walk on a nice, sunny day and catch a whiff of cut grass. In an instant, your brain connects that smell to the memory and emotion it has stored away. Perhaps you immediately recall standing on the playing field that particular sports day. Or perhaps it's just the emotion that hits you: it's a lovely day where you are now but you suddenly feel sad – because all those years ago you didn't win your race. Sensations like this are called 'involuntary memory', named by the French novelist Marcel Proust in his famous book, *In Search of Lost Time* (first published between 1913 and 1927).

The people making *Doctor Who* sometimes use this quality of smell for dramatic effect. In *The Doctor's Wife* (2011), Amy must think of the smell of dust after the rain to open a locked door on the TARDIS. In *The Krotons* (1968–1969), the arrival of the TARDIS on an alien world was recorded in a quarry in Malvern – one that looks little different from the many other quarries used as planets in the show. However, without expensive special effects, the writer of *The Krotons* – Robert Holmes – makes this planet seem more interesting by giving us two contradictory responses to it.

'Lovely, lovely, lovely.'

'Pwaw, bad eggs! Let's try somewhere else.'

The Second Doctor and Jamie Macrimmon, *The Krotons* (1968–1969)

The contrast makes us laugh. If we've ever experienced the stench of bad eggs, our memory will remind us how horrible it was. Even if we don't have that direct experience, Jamie's horrified reaction will make us think, 'Yuck!' – an emotional response because our sense of smell is linked to our emotions. But this is a trick: television can only convey sound and images, not smells. We react emotionally to something we're not actually sensing, which makes this alien planet seem more vibrant and real.

The End of the World (2005) does something similar with smell, but the other way round. At the end of the episode, the Doctor reveals his great secret to Rose – and to us watching at home: his planet has been destroyed and he is the sole survivor of his people. It's a big moment whether or not we have memories of the Doctor's home planet from previous adventures.

But the Doctor shares his secret on an ordinary street on Earth in the present day. We don't *see* anything of the great Time War that destroyed the Doctor's planet until *The End of Time* (2010) – and then only briefly. We'll discuss the Time War in more detail in Chapter 9, but the name suggests something epic and complex – which might have been difficult for the people making *Doctor Who* to convey on screen. Yet the first time we hear of the Time War, it's made to seem vibrant and real – using the same trick as in *The Krotons*.

'I'm a Time Lord. I'm the last of the Time Lords.
They're all gone. I'm the only survivor, I'm left travelling
on my own, cos there's no one else.'

'There's me.'

'You've seen how dangerous it is. D'you want to go home?'

'I don't know. I want… Can you smell chips?'

'Yeah.'

'I want chips.'

'Me, too.'

The Ninth Doctor and Rose Tyler, *The End of the World* (2005)

Watching at home, we can't smell those chips, but it's a recognisable smell and one likely to spark warm, happy memories of times when we've had chips. Again, our memory evokes an emotional reaction. More than that, because chips seem normal and real, so does all this talk of the Time War, even though we don't see it.

We've talked in previous chapters about the different ways scientists can measure and test things, using ever more sophisticated technologies to make more accurate measurements. But there's a basic problem: human beings don't experience the universe directly. As we've already discussed, our brains are supplied with data by our five senses. We then process that data into something we think of as meaningful.

That means our perception can be subjective – and our senses can be fooled. Television is a series of still images like photographs, run together at speed to make your brain think that it's watching movement. Look closely at the TV screen and you'll see the picture is made up of tiny blobs of just three colours: specific combinations of blue, green and red. At a distance, our brains can't differentiate these separate blobs, so we see a seamless picture.

Another good example is our sense of time passing. Explaining his theory of relativity, Einstein is said to have used the analogy that a minute spent doing something we don't enjoy can feel like an hour, while an hour spent with someone we really like can feel like only a minute has passed. Of course, this has nothing to do with the physics of relativity, but Einstein was making the point that our experience of time is a slippery thing and one we shouldn't take for granted. There's a related phenomenon, where people who've been in accidents or faced great danger speak of time seeming to slow down.

> 'Let me tell you about scared. Your heart is beating so
> hard, I can feel it through your hands. There's so much
> blood and oxygen pumping through your brain, it's like rocket
> fuel. Right now, you could run faster and you could fight
> harder, you could jump higher than ever in your life.
> And you are so alert, it's like you can slow down time.
> What's wrong with scared? Scared is a superpower.'
> **The Twelfth Doctor,** *Listen* **(2014)**

Is it true that when we're stressed our brains work faster, effectively meaning that we experience everything else around us passing more slowly? To find out, in 2007, the American neuroscientist David Eagleman conducted an experiment that was as brilliant and ridiculous as anything the Doctor might think of: he dropped people – including himself – off the top of a very tall building.

The falling people were caught by a net, but the fall itself was still scary. Did that fear make people's brains work faster? While they were falling, the people in the experiment had to look at a special wristwatch they'd been given to wear, on which two numbers were displayed. The numbers alternated very quickly – faster than could be read in normal conditions. The question was whether people could read the numbers clearly while they were falling and scared.

The experiment showed that they couldn't, which proved that stress doesn't make the brain work more quickly – and doesn't slow down time. But Eagleman had a second experiment, and after people had fallen and been caught in the net, he gave them a stopwatch. They were asked to let the stopwatch run for the same amount of time that they had fallen for. People who had watched the fall but not fallen themselves were also given stopwatches and asked to estimate the length in time of the fall. The results showed that people who had fallen thought about a third more time had passed than those who didn't fall. The fallen people felt that time had passed more slowly as they fell, even though their brains hadn't been working any more quickly.

There are different theories about why that might be. In a stressful situation, our perception seems to focus on ways to escape or solve the problem facing us. We stop taking in everything else around us – so the world seems less busy and complex. That might affect our sense of time.

Another idea – which might happen in tandem with the first – is that there's a difference between how we experience time as it's happening and how we look back at time that has passed. As we've seen, our emotions and sense of smell are linked to the way we make memories. Strong emotions seem to etch memories more strongly into our minds. A key way in which, looking back, we feel how much time has passed is through the number of new memories made in that period. Say we usually create a strong new memory once a day. In a stressful situation, we create several strong memories in a few hours. Looking back, it will feel like several days' worth of time happened in those hours.

If that is right, it explains why, as we get older, time seems to pass more quickly. Individual days still feel the same length, but it seems as if Christmas comes round faster than it used to. The reason would be that as we get older we experience fewer new things, we get into routines and maybe have better control of our emotions. All that means that we lay down fewer strong new memories, so when Christmas arrives we look back to the last one and feel little time has passed.

The Doctor and his companions are constantly having new experiences and dangerous adventures – so perhaps they wouldn't feel Christmas coming round any more quickly. More than that, they might be healthier, because our subjective sense of time has been linked to various diseases such as depression and dementia. There's good evidence that having lots of new experiences and laying down new memories helps with 'cognitive reserve' – that is, the way the brain resists damage and these kinds of diseases.

Our bodies also keep time in another way, called the circadian clock. We seem to unconsciously keep track of levels of daylight all the time. The suprachiasmatic nucleus of the brain uses this information to control a number of things, such as production of melatonin – a hormone that makes us sleepy. The hormone cortisol, which affects levels of blood sugar and so affects whether we feel hungry, also seems to be governed by this internal clock, as are body temperature and women's menstrual hormones. In animals, hibernation seems to be controlled by the same inner clocks.

Our inner clocks also synchronise our senses. If someone touches your foot and your shoulder at the same time, you feel both sensations at once – but the sensation in your foot has much further to travel to your brain than the sensation in your shoulder. It's thought that your brain leaves a tiny amount of time between what's happening and your perception of it, effectively a buffer that allows the sensation from your foot to catch up with the sensation from your shoulder. That buffer means the world as we experience it is always slightly behind the world as it is happening – so we are always living slightly in the past. It's even thought that the taller you are – and the further sensations have to travel to reach your brain – the longer the delay you experience, so the more in the past you are living.

It also seems that we continually use our senses to check our inner clocks are in sync with the world around us. There's an experiment that gets you to press a button which turns on a light. You keep pressing the button, but the light starts coming on fractionally later – say by 200 milliseconds. You continue pressing the button long enough that your brain puts the two things in sync, then we stop the delay. Now you press the button again and the light comes on immediately – but your brain, synchronised to the tiny delay – makes you think the light came on before you pressed the button. It feels as if the light turning on has travelled backwards in time.

Because our bodies depend on the workings of this inner clock, when that clock gets out of sync it can make us feel very peculiar. If we travel a long distance round the Earth, we cross many time zones. If we travel relatively slowly – say, on a ship – our bodies can keep in sync with the changing time. But if we cross time zones more quickly – such as by flying in a jet plane – it can make us ill, with a condition called desynchronosis or 'jet lag'.

The Doctor's companions don't seem to experience jet lag when they travel in the TARDIS. In *The Bells of Saint John* (2013), the Doctor and Clara jump ahead a few hours as a weapon against their enemies.

'Why did we travel to the morning? What's the point in that?'

'Whoever's after us spent the whole night looking for us. Are you tired?'

'Yes.'

'What? Then imagine how they feel. They came the long way round.'

Clara Oswald and the Eleventh Doctor, *The Bells of Saint John* **(2013)**

Clara's not tired because they're jumped forward from night to day, but because she's already had quite an adventure. If the jump in time caused jet lag, she'd be feeling sick. Perhaps the TARDIS compensates for jet lag somehow.

We can get over jet lag in a few days as our inner clocks adjust to the time zone we've moved to. But people who regularly work or party into the night can be at risk of more serious harm. They might sleep longer into the next day, but their bodies' sense of time will still be out of sync. It's been shown that shift workers have a greater chance of heart disease, stomach illness and problems sleeping. What's more, our inner clocks seem to explain seasonal affective disorder – a kind of depression that usually strikes in winter, when there is less daylight – and may be related to diseases including type 2 diabetes, obesity and cancer. It's even thought that our inner clocks decide how long human beings can live for – as we'll see in Chapter 14.

How do you know what happened to you in the past? And how do you *know* that you know it? In *Listen*, the Doctor and Clara meet a small boy called Rupert Pink – who will grow up to be Clara's boyfriend, Danny. Clara is worried about the consequences of the encounter.

'Will he remember any of that?'

'Scrambled his memory. Gave him a big old dream about being Dan the soldier man.'

$\partial^3 \sum_i x^2$

Clara Oswald and the Twelfth Doctor, *Listen* (2014)

The suggestion is that Rupert won't remember Clara and the Doctor explicitly, but something of their adventure together will remain with him – and shape his personality.

There seem to be two kinds of long-term memory: explicit and implicit. Explicit memory is conscious and intentional: we remember that a new episode of *Doctor Who* will be on at a specific hour, and we remember to watch it. Implicit memory is different: we're not conscious of the way that past experience affects our behaviour. When you tie your shoes or ride a bike, you do it without (consciously) thinking.

In young children, the ability to make implicit memories develops before the explicit memory. Babies recognise things that make them feel safe or scared and develop responses when those things happen again.

The possibility that memories that aren't part of our conscious thoughts might still affect our behaviour has long intrigued doctors and scientists. In the late nineteenth century, Austrian neurologist Sigmund Freud proposed that shameful or traumatic memories that people hid from themselves might be the reason that they experienced mental health problems and unexplained physical symptoms. He argued that this process of repression made people unwell, and bringing such things to light through a new kind of treatment – psychoanalysis – could be helpful. Psychologists and neuroscientists have moved on from Freud's theories, but they are still influential in clinical practice and in the way writers think about personality and memory, as we shall see shortly.

A number of conditions can affect our memories. The general term for memory loss is 'amnesia'. Memory loss is not uncommon clinically. It might be a short-lived process (for example, following mild brain injury), permanent as in the case of Henry Molaison, or progressive, in which case patients are said to have dementia. In many cases we can find anatomical damage that explains the memory loss, but sometimes there seems to be a psychological explanation.

Some treatments for these conditions use the associative nature of memory. For example, Henry Molaison was able to modify some of the long-term memories he retained from before his operation to include new information – less creating new memories than adapting old ones.

Something similar might be happening in *The End of Time* (2009–2010). In *Journey's End* (2008), the Doctor saves the life of his companion Donna by removing her memories of him. But those memories are not destroyed – it seems he only removes her ability to access them. In *The End of Time*, when she sees people around her turning into copies

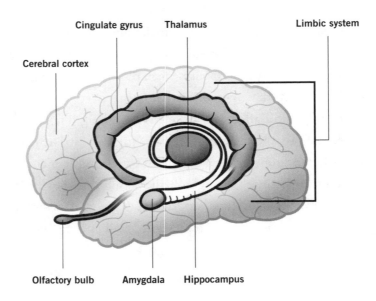

of the Master, it reminds her of things she's seen before. Her brain processes the new experience by comparing it to previous memories – and that need to associate new memories to old ones is strong enough to bring everything back.

Importantly, our memories – what we learn and experience – make us who we are. In Chapter 7, we saw what the Doctor looks for in potential companions: they need to have the right attitude. As they travel in the TARDIS, he provides them with skills and experience, and makes them better people.

Heartbreakingly, Wilfrid Mott says just that to the Doctor in *Journey's End*, when Donna has lost all her memories.

'I had to wipe her mind completely. Every trace of me – or the TARDIS, anything we did together, anywhere we went – had to go.'

'All those wonderful things she did ...
But she was better with you.'

The Tenth Doctor and Wilfrid Mott, *Journey's End* **(2008)**

In fact, the suggestion is that memories can be used to change how we behave in the future.

Recent research has revealed some interesting quirks about implicit memory. So-called 'priming' involves tinkering with implicit memory in ways that will subsequently affect behaviour. For example, in the early 1970s, American psychologists David E. Meyer and Roger W. Schvaneveldt conducted an experiment where people were shown a series of groups of letters – some of the groups with letters in a random order, and others where the letters spelled out an everyday word. The speed at which people recognised the everyday words was recorded.

It was found that people were faster at recognising the word 'nurse' if they had seen the word 'doctor' earlier in the series. This suggested that the word 'doctor' prepared or primed them to recognise associated words.

Although the science of priming is still contested, the idea seems to have influenced *Doctor Who*. At the end of *Listen*, Clara meets and reassures a scared child who will apparently grow up to be the Doctor. She holds his ankle and talks to him soothingly, creating a memory – and entirely changing his life to come.

'Fear is like a companion. A constant companion, always there. But that's OK, because fear can bring us together. Fear can bring you home. I'm going to leave you something, just so you'll always remember, fear makes companions of us all.'

Clara Oswald, *Listen* (2014)

The First Doctor will later (for him) quote the words 'Fear makes companions of all of us' to his new companions in the very first *Doctor Who* story, *An Unearthly Child* (1963) – and goes on to say that fear lives with another sensation: hope. Hope despite fear seems key to the Doctor's character – and it might come from one brief childhood experience.

Memory is not just something we have but something we do: encoding memories, storing them, recalling them and acting on them. Remove our memories and we become different people. In *Into the Dalek* (2014), we learn that Daleks shut off certain memories to extinguish any glimmer of kindness or compassion, making themselves more ruthless. The Doctor gives the Dalek back one of its memories – of a star being born – and the Dalek feels a strong emotion, speaking of the star's 'beauty'.

At the end of the story, the Dalek rejoins the other Daleks – but with 'unfinished work' to do. Because the Doctor changing its memory has changed this Dalek's whole personality. It has switched sides, and we are left to wonder what damage it will wreak among the rest of the Dalek race. The Doctor has used memory and emotion as weapons against his worst enemies.

But once, he and his people fought the Daleks using time…

NATURAL REGRESSION

JUSTIN RICHARDS

The universe convulsed. For a moment, time itself held its breath. Then it let it out again in a chaotic amalgam of past, present and future. Might-have-been and could-have-done crashed into what-if and never-was.

Caught at the edge of the temporal wave, the TARDIS rode out the storm. The first the Doctor knew of it was when the ground dropped from under his feet and his head cracked into the console. When he woke a few moments later, he was lying on the floor. Until recently he'd had a mass of dark curly hair that might perhaps have cushioned the blow. But now his hair was cut short – like the soldier he resolutely refused to be in this most catastrophic of wars. The lights fizzed and flickered like an electric storm. The Cloister Bell sounded cracked and melancholy. He dragged himself back to his feet and surveyed the panels in front of him. Every warning light was blinking at him. Even several he was sure he'd never seen before.

High above his head, the roof of the TARDIS had faded into a view of the contorted star systems as they folded in on themselves. Stars went nova; black holes collapsed; planets collided and spun away into oblivion. Several whole galaxies vanished from history – never having existed. The view and the readings from the instruments that were still working told him everything he needed to know.

'The Time Destructor,' he murmured, the words lost in the alarms. So the Daleks had finally got it working, finally deployed it in this seemingly endless war against his own people, the Time Lords. Even here at the edge of the blast sphere it was impossible to predict the effects of such a device. But one very obvious effect was that the TARDIS was out of control. Crashing.

Desperately, the Doctor scanned the immediate area. He was in real space at least. It would take a while for the Vortex to settle down again, Until it did, he was safer here. Wherever 'here' was. The instruments tried to match the alignment of stars to known constellations. Finally it settled on a probable location. But there were gaps. The Nestene Homeworld was gone, wiped away in the blink of an eye. Temporal shockwaves rippled out through systems from Grantaginus to Mellandrova, from the Farflung Rift to the Wolf's Heart Nebula.

Finally, he saw it. A tiny planet on the edge of the nearest system. It was impossible to know if it had been affected, but it seemed stable. For the moment. It would only take the merest hint of the ripple to turn the planet's sun into a supernova or a black hole, or an empty space where no star had yet formed. But he needed to wait out the worst of it, and give the TARDIS time to recover.

Only as the materialisation circuits cut in, wheezing and complaining, did the Doctor realise that he needed something else. 'K7,' he read on the fault locator screen. The fluid links had ruptured. Wherever he was landing, he hoped he could find some mercury to replenish them. Another screen gave the name of the planet: Rontan 9. For the first time since the floor disappeared from beneath him, the Doctor smiled. It seemed he'd landed on his feet – figuratively if not literally. He patted the console and reached for the door control.

It had taken Professor Targus Kornick years to develop the technology behind the Nihilism Chamber. It had taken him almost as long to book space at the Rontan 9 facility and persuade the university to give him the time off. But now, at last, his dreams were coming to fruition.

'Is the field holding?' he asked.

Lizbet Harkening, Kornick's deputy nodded. 'One hundred per cent.'

'We have total isolation,' Dalla Fronstat, one of the students, confirmed.

The other student, Archan Noon, was drumming his fingers in an annoying rhythm on the workbench.

Kornick adjusted his spectacles, an anachronistic affectation which he believed imbued him with authority. He cleared his throat. 'Then for the next three months,' he announced proudly, 'we are completely shielded from any external interference or influence. Our experiments will be the first – the very first ever, anywhere – to be conducted in an environment devoid of cosmic ray activity, electromagnetic radiation, stellar neutrinos, gravitational waves, or any other transmissions or incursions. Nothing, absolutely nothing, can get inside this Nihilism Chamber.'

If he said anything else, his words were drowned out by the ear-rending scrape of noise that announced the arrival of a large, blue box in front of him.

If the Doctor was disappointed by the reception he received, he contrived not to show it. He grinned and waved, he buttoned and then unbuttoned his velvet jacket and ran a hand through his hair as if it was still as long and curly as it had once been.

'How the hell did you get in here?' an elderly man with grey hair and spectacles demanded.

'I came out of that box,' the Doctor told him. 'You saw me, just now, remember? Now then, I wonder if you have any mercury I could beg off you?'

'Mercury?' The man's voice rose an octave.

'This is Rontan 9, right?' the Doctor said. 'The facility where scientists from all over the system can rent laboratory space to conduct their experiments away from the prying eyes and ears and wallets of large corporations, the press, and disappointed husbands and wives waiting at lonely dinner tables, yes?'

'Yes,' the middle-aged woman standing beside the man agreed. 'But we don't have any mercury, Not in here.'

'Out there, then?' the Doctor suggested, gesturing towards a heavy airlock-style door at the back of the room.

'We're not allowed out there.' It was one of the youngsters who spoke. Well, the Doctor thought, she was probably in her early twenties. A student, he guessed – as was the young man sitting on a metal stool beside her.

'Not for months,' the young man added. 'Because this whole laboratory is a Nihilism Chamber so nothing at all can get in or out.' He glanced at the elderly scientist and stifled a smile. 'Except mercury hunters in big blue boxes, apparently.'

'Ah.' Well, that explained why he wasn't being welcomed effusively. 'Sorry about that. But the good news is that you're probably shielded from the temporal effects in here, even if you're not immune to the incursion of a relative continuum stabiliser in materialisation mode.'

The older scientist's anger seemed to have become a grudging acceptance. His eyes narrowed behind the lenses of his spectacles. 'What temporal effects?'

'Oh sorry, getting ahead of myself. The Daleks have deployed a Time Destructor.' He regarded their blank expressions. 'Great Time War, no? Passed you by? OK then, maybe I've dropped back a few centuries in the blast wave, no problem. But I still need mercury.'

'And we still don't have any,' the woman told him. 'Not in here.'

'We'll have to start again,' the scientist said with a frustrated sigh. 'We can't conduct non-interference experiments with dirty great boxes and grinning maniacs just appearing out of thin air all the time. Who are you, anyway?' he demanded.

'I'm the Doctor,' the Doctor told him. 'And I don't want to alarm you, but we really should check that the world outside this laboratory still exists.'

The scientists introduced themselves to the Doctor while they shut down the various isolation field generators and withdrew the energy shutters. Finally, Professor Kornick unlocked and opened the main doors.

The world outside the chamber did still exist. But it had changed.

They picked their way through the debris, the two older scientists confused and the younger students pale with shock. The door from the chamber opened into a corridor, which led to a reception area. The receptionist was sprawled across her desk, uniform and flesh ripped open. The chairs were overturned, deep gouges scratched down the walls.

There were more bodies in the adjoining areas. The lights that were still working flickered erratically.

'What could have done this?' Kornick asked.

'Some savage animal?' Lizbet Harkening suggested, her voice hoarse with nerves. 'Loose within the facility?'

'Let's hope so,' the Doctor murmured. The alternatives were even more frightening.

'What's that?' Dalla was staring at an open doorway. 'Can you hear that?'

'I can,' Archan said. He put an arm round Dalla, pulling her gently back.

The Doctor could hear it too. A low rumbling sound like an approaching storm. Or an animal. He took a step towards the doorway, watching as the shadows beyond coalesced into a shape – huge, hairy, savage.

The rumble became a roar as the creature appeared in the doorway, like an upright wolf. The face was a snarling mass of hair and teeth punctuated by deep-set eyes and a dark snout. Claws ripped through the air as the beast bounded towards them.

Kornick backed away, white-faced. Lizbet grabbed him, and pulled him clear as the creature leaped. The students, Dalla and Archan ducked behind an overturned table. Only the Doctor stood his ground, staring in horrified recognition at the matted fur bursting through the remains of a white lab coat. The deep red eyes fixed on him, and the beast charged forward.

He grabbed a chair, its metal legs twisted and rusty. He swung it in front of him, like a lion tamer. The creature ignored it, kept coming – leaped towards the Doctor, who tried to parry it swinging like a cricketer. Chair and fur collided and both hurtled off at a tangent, crashed into the wall, and slid down in a crumpled heap. The beast's claws scrabbled for a moment on the floor, then were still.

'I think it's out cold,' Kornick said, pushing his glasses up his nose so as to see better.

The Doctor caught his arm. 'I know you're curious, but it might wake up again.'

'I just want to know what it is. How could it have got in here? There are no animals like that on Rontan.'

'There are now,' the Doctor told him. 'Come on.'

A glassed-in walkway led to the next building. The glass was warped and discoloured. The Doctor paused to examine the metal struts that held the structure together. It was corroded, dull with age.

'How old is this facility?' he asked.

'They had their tenth anniversary last year,' Lizbet told him. 'But this looks… ancient.'

Before the Doctor could reply, Archan called back from further along the walkway. 'Come and look at this. It's…' His voice tailed off, as he failed to find the words to describe it.

The young student was peering through the discoloured glass. The landscape beyond appeared and vanished with the flickering light above them – their own reflected faces staring back at them intermittently.

'It ought to be daylight out there,' Dalla said. 'We should be able to see the accommodation block.'

'So where is it?' Kornick said.

'I think that is the accommodation block,' the Doctor told them. They stared out at the flickering view of the crumpled steel supports and the rubble strewn across the landscape.

The walkway gradually became darker as more lights failed. The Doctor's sonic screwdriver cast a pale blue glow ahead of them, enough to see that the structure ended as if it had been bitten off. Their feet crunched on old, brittle glass as they walked slowly onwards.

'Time distortion,' the Doctor told them.

'You mean, this area has grown old and decayed?' Kornick said. He stared into the gloom, his expression a mixture of scientific curiosity and horror.

'We should head back,' Archan said. 'There's nothing out there, except maybe more of the creatures that killed those people.'

'Certainly no mercury,' the Doctor murmured.

They retraced their steps to the reception area. The wolf-like creature was still unconscious, drawing rasping ragged breaths. They picked their way warily around it.

'We should try B Block,' Kornick decided. 'That's where Malatan Benervan and her team are working. If they don't already know about these animals, we need to warn them.'

He led the way through the wreckage to another door. The electronics had failed completely, so they had to prise the door open with their hands. The lights in the corridor beyond were on. It would have seemed perfectly normal were it not for the viscous grey-green liquid that stained one wall. It dripped from the ceiling, pooling in the middle of the corridor.

'It's leaking through,' the Doctor realised. 'What's above here? Some sort of storage tank?'

'Just another lab,' Lizbet told him. 'Where Malatan and her team are working.'

'Maybe something they were working on has spilled,' Archan suggested.

'We should check they're all right.' Kornick didn't sound optimistic.

'What's that?' Dalla said, pointing down the corridor ahead of them.

It was like smoke, drifting slowly towards them. Thin and pale, almost ethereal, coiling and extending.

'Escaping gas of some sort?' Archan wondered.

'Don't breathe it in,' the Doctor warned. 'Just in case.'

They held their breath, and hurried through. From somewhere nearby a voice called out, the words indistinct as if lost on the breeze.

'What was that?' Lizbet said, turning.

'Must have come from the lab above us,' Kornick said. 'We should get up there.'

The lifts weren't working, and they had to force open the door to the emergency stairs. The Doctor held the doors open while the others squeezed through the gap. He eased himself after them, and the doors clanged shut again behind him. Kornick was looking pale, leaning forward with his hands on his knees and breathing heavily.

'Are you all right?' the Doctor asked.

Kornick straightened up, his face drawn. 'Of course I'm all right. We need to find Malatan.' His eyes were ringed with red, as if he'd been rubbing them. Maybe they'd been irritated by the smoke, or whatever it was.

The lighting fizzed and flickered as they made their way up the stairs. Sections of the handrail were rusted almost through, yet next to them were sections of untarnished steel. The stairs too were a juxtaposition of polished elegance and fractured, crumbling stone.

The doors were gone, along with a large part of the lab. No rubble or debris, just nothing. Like those sections had never been built. Wind scattered papers and raked through broken glass as the Doctor and the others picked their way through the mess. Double doors at the other end of the room stood in the middle of an incongruous section of wall.

There were pools of the grey-green sludge on the floor. One metal stool was covered with it. The Doctor dipped the end of a rusty stylus into the slime, sniffed at it, and grimaced as he realised what it must be. He dropped the stylus into the viscous liquid and straightened up.

As he did, he spotted a store cupboard, standing alone against a wall that was no longer there. The doors opened easily, but the contents were a mess of smashed jars and broken test tubes. Sand that used to be glass was scattered across one shelf. A viscous silver stream ran fluid along another. Mercury. He didn't need a lot – and there was just about enough. The Doctor pulled an old, battered toffee tin from his pocket and coaxed the mercury to flow and drip into it.

'What happened here?' Dalla asked, her voice barely more than a whisper and almost lost in the sound of the wind.

'Time distortion on a massive scale,' the Doctor began as he pressed the lid tightly back on the tin full of mercury. But he got no further.

The doors opposite them burst open. The wail of the wind became the roar of the creatures charging towards them. This time, no one hesitated. For once the Doctor didn't need to shout 'Run!' because they were already running.

They clattered down the stairs, growls and roars echoing down after them. Back to the corridor below, desperately wrenching open the doors again, and squeezing through the narrow gap.

'Give me a hand,' the Doctor gasped.

Lizbet and Kornick were already off down the corridor. But the two students stopped to help the Doctor force the doors shut again. A hairy arm rammed through the gap, claws scratching for them as the creature tried to force its way through. Dalla took her shoe off and hammered at the arm with the heel until the creature drew back. Then the Doctor and Archan slid the door fully closed. The Doctor's sonic screwdriver fused the lock. But there were already dents appearing in the metal as they hurried after Kornick and Lizbet.

Lizbet was standing just inside the reception area, hand to her mouth, staring ahead wide-eyed.

'What is it?' the Doctor demanded. 'Has the creature woken?'

She shook her head, unable to speak, just pointing. Her hand seemed insubstantial, strangely translucent. A trick of the flickering light, perhaps.

But what she pointed at was no trick. Kornick was in the middle of the room, tearing at his lab coat with clawed hands. His face was a mass of matted hair, eyes receding and features blurring.

'Help...' he pleaded, 'Help me.' But the words became a guttural roar of sound.

'What's happening to him?' Dalla gasped.

'Regression,' the Doctor replied quickly. 'Let's get past him before the process is complete,'

'But – we have to help him,' Archan said.

'Too late,' the Doctor told him. 'He's been caught in a residual time distortion. It'll happen to us all if we hang around. I thought the effects had dissipated, but I was wrong.' He sighed. 'Sorry.' Then he led them at a run across the room, keeping clear of Kornick. The scientist watched them through rheumy eyes. A trail of saliva trickled down his inhuman chin.

'We're going back to the Nihilism Chamber?' Dalla asked as the Doctor led them down the corridor.

'The only place that's safe.'

From behind them came a roar of anguish and rage.

'And probably not for long,' the Doctor added.

They quickened their pace. The door behind them crashed open, and they broke into a run. None of them turned. They could all hear the growling anger, the claws scratching on the floor as the creature that had been Kornick bounded towards them

'Hang on,' Archan said, breathless. He risked a look over his shoulder. 'Where's Lizbet?'

The Doctor looked back too. A thin mist, like smoke drifted down the corridor after them, blurring their view of the slavering creature as it approached. 'So, not a trick of the light after all,' he murmured.

The smoky cloud caught up with them, keeping pace. The voice was faint, as if it came from another room. 'What's happening to me?'

'I'm sorry,' the Doctor said. He passed his hand slowly through the misty air as he ran. 'I am so very sorry.'

'You can't help me?' The voice was fainter.

'It's too late.'

'Then help the students. Get them to safety.' The last words were all but drowned out by the roar of the approaching creature.

The smoke thickened, coalescing as if gathering itself in a misty curtain across the corridor. Through it, the Doctor could see the dark shape of the Kornick-creature bounding towards them. He stood transfixed, the two students either side of him.

'We'll never outrun that thing,' Dalla said, her voice trembling.

'I'm hoping we won't have to.'

'What do you mean?' Archan asked.

The Doctor didn't need to answer. The creature hurled itself at the wall of hazy smoke, claws ripping down through and scattering it. Suddenly the air was alive with light and sparks. Illuminated in the middle of it all was Lizbet – an image of light picked out in points of fire. Then the air cleared, and she vanished with the last residue of smoke.

The creature too was on fire – glowing with an inner light that ripped out through it. With a howl of anger and pain, it shimmered and faded. For a moment, Professor Kornick was there again, staring back at them, then he was gone.

'Forget the Nihilism Chamber,' the Doctor said. 'Back to the TARDIS.'

He grabbed Dalla's hand, and she grabbed Archan's. Together they hurried down the corridor.

'What happened?' Dalla demanded. 'That smoke?'

'It was Lizbet, wasn't it?' Archan said. 'She's changed. Like Professor Kornick. But then she came back – they both did.'

'And now they're gone,' the Doctor said. 'I'm sorry. One regressed, the other advanced.' His words were breathless and urgent as they ran. 'Like Malatan and the scientists in the lab upstairs, regressed through time to primordial sludge. Like this whole facility – parts of it aged to ruin, others not yet built.'

'But, Kornick and those creatures?' Dalla gasped.

'An evolutionary blind alley. What humanity never became.'

He bundled them through the door to the Chamber.

'And Lizbet?'

'What the human race may one day evolve into. Ethereal beings, all mind and no substance. When they met, they cancelled each other out. Two might-have-beens that ultimately never existed.'

'Will it happen to us, too?' Archan asked, ashen-faced as he took deep breaths.

The Doctor unlocked the TARDIS and shoved the two students inside. 'Not if I can help it,' he told them.

They stood inside the doors, looking round in amazement. But the Doctor's attention was drawn to the roof, the view depicting the sky above them. The sun, darkened and blotched slowly shimmering as if with suppressed energy.

'Just in time.' He ran to the console, closed the doors and fumbled in his pocket for the tin full of precious mercury.

Moments later, a door burst open and creatures that evolution never created stumbled into a corridor. Intelligent smoke drifted away towards the reception area. A wheezing, rasping sound split the air as the TARDIS dematerialised. And high above all that, the sun of Rontan 9 exploded into a supernova, millions of years ahead of schedule.

'What happens now?' Dalla asked as they watched the spectacle unfold on the TARDIS scanners. Crimson, orange and yellow stained across the darkness of space.

'"Now" no longer has any meaning here,' the Doctor told her. 'But now I'm going to take you home. Or at least, somewhere stable and safe.' He glanced up at the roof, burning with a stellar explosion. His expression was grim. 'And then I have work to do.'

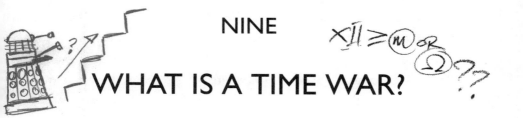

NINE

WHAT IS A TIME WAR?

> 'There was a war – a Time War. The last great
> Time War. My people fought a race called the
> Daleks for the sake of all creation. And they lost.'
>
> **The Tenth Doctor,** *Gridlock* **(2007)**

On television, *Doctor Who* has only given us glimpses of the Time War fought between the Time Lords and the Daleks. In different stories, we've learnt that the home worlds of the Autons, Gelth and Zygons were among those planets lost in the conflict. In *The End of Time* (2009–2010), we see smashed up Dalek spacecraft littering the Time Lord home planet, Gallifrey.

We finally witness some of the actual fighting in *The Day of the Doctor* (2013), with Daleks moving through the Time Lord city of Arcadia. But the focus of that episode is well away from the conflict, based in the shack where the War Doctor faces a terrible dilemma. Because of the war, he says, 'Every moment in time and space is burning.' He alone can end the conflict by using a special Time Lord super-weapon called the Moment – but if he does so, he'll destroy all the Daleks and Time Lords, too, including the 2.47 billion Time Lord children on Gallifrey.

Now, that's a lot of Time Lords and Daleks to destroy in an instant, an act of appalling double genocide. But when the choice is between them and all the rest of the life in the universe, what the Doctor must do is clear – isn't it?

The decision he makes at the end of the Time War haunts each of his subsequent incarnations, perhaps most notably in *The Parting of the Ways* (2005) when the Ninth Doctor is offered a similar choice again. But the choice the War Doctor is offered, his response to it and the decision he finally makes are all indicative of a broader question: the relationship between science and war.

$\partial^3 \sum \chi^2$ 'That's typical of the military mind, isn't it? Present them with a new problem, and they start shooting at it.'
The Third Doctor, *Doctor Who and the Silurians* (1970)

In *The Day of the Doctor*, and in *Doctor Who* more generally, there often seems to be a distinction drawn between two kinds of mindset: that of peaceful exploration, inquiring into the secrets of the universe, and that of violent conquest and destruction.

There's little doubt which of these two sides the Doctor is on. 'I want to see the universe, not rule it,' he tells the Master in *Colony in Space* (1971). This might explain what the Twelfth Doctor has against soldiers. In *Into the Dalek* (2014), he won't allow a soldier to join him in the TARDIS:

$\partial^3 \sum \chi^2$ 'I think you're probably nice. Underneath it all, I think you're kind and you're definitely brave. I just wish you hadn't been a soldier.'
The Twelfth Doctor, *Into the Dalek*

In *The Caretaker* (also 2014), the Doctor is rude to schoolteacher Danny Pink because Danny used to be a soldier. In fact, the Doctor seems unwilling to grasp that Danny might be intelligent or know anything about maths – let alone that that is the subject he teaches – because of the job he used to do.

It doesn't help that Danny – with the best of intentions – upsets the Doctor's plan to rid the Earth of a deadly Skovox Blitzer. When Danny suggests they should call the army in to help fight the creature, it seems to confirm the Doctor's worst suspicions that Danny is exactly the sort who, presented with a new problem, starts shooting at it. It's as if the Doctor thinks that there can be no overlap between the two mindsets, that you can't be a soldier and also have an inquiring mind.

This might seem odd because – as we saw in Chapter 7 – many of the previous Doctors' companions have had military experience of one sort or another. In *Mawdryn Undead* (1983), we even discover that the Doctor's great friend Brigadier Lethbridge-Stewart retired from UNIT to teach A level maths. On learning this, the Fifth Doctor doesn't comment, but his expression suggests he doesn't think much of the idea. Even so, it's nothing like the contemptuous way that his later incarnation treats poor Danny.

His treatment of Danny might also seem odd because maths and soldiering have long gone hand in hand. The many achievements of the ancient Greek mathematician Archimedes include designing a huge warship, the *Syracusia*. The Greeks had such a reputation for military technology that it was later claimed Archimedes had invented a 'heat ray' that set fire to invading vessels by using special lenses to focus sunlight on them – though modern tests suggest that that is unlikely.

In the Second World War, the efforts of British mathematicians including Alan Turing to break coded German messages led to the invention of the first programmable computer – Colossus, designed by engineer Tommy Flowers in 1943. As we'll see in Chapter 13, Turing went on to use what he learnt from codebreaking in the war to transform our ideas about artificial intelligence.

History has shown time and time again that the pressures of war can actually prompt huge leaps in scientific knowledge and technological ability as each side seeks a new advantage – or tries not to lose ground to the enemy. We'll discuss shortly how that is directly relevant to the creation of the Daleks in *Doctor Who*, but how real scientists approach that war work can be revealing.

On 2 August 1939 – before the start of the Second World War, though with conflict looking inevitable – physicist Albert Einstein sent a letter to US President Roosevelt about some recent scientific discoveries. Although Einstein signed the letter, it had been written for him by Hungarian physicist Leó Szilárd, who had been part of the team that made the discoveries. Szilárd – with Einstein's permission – used Einstein's fame and reputation to get the President's attention.

The letter explained that it was now thought that the element uranium 'may be turned into a new and important source of energy in the immediate future.' It went on that it was also 'conceivable – though much less certain – that extremely powerful bombs of a new type' might be made using uranium, too. Such a bomb, it said, might be 'carried by boat and exploded in a port [and] destroy the whole port together with some of the surrounding territory.' The letter suggested that the US government might 'find it desirable to' take more active interest in this new area of research and 'to speed up the experimental work' on it.

Up to this point, the letter reads as little more than an outline of facts: this has happened, these might be the consequences, you might like to watch for developments. For all the 'conceivable' possibility of a new kind of bomb, it doesn't seem terribly serious.

But the letter concluded, almost casually, that Germany had stopped sales of uranium from mines it had taken over, and that this could have been related to the fact that the son of a minister in the German government might have known about the scientific discovery, too. The letter didn't spell out what these details about Germany meant but the implication is surely obvious: the fear that the German government might already be developing these new extremely powerful bombs, which would make a sizeable difference in any coming war.

Why didn't Szilárd and Einstein spell out this warning in the letter? Perhaps they were being polite in not telling the US President what to do. Or perhaps this was a more effective way to get him to do what they wanted: presenting the facts to him in such a way that he would come to the desired conclusion himself. The way it was worded, with the polite suggestion that the US government might 'find it desirable' to look into this matter, the President could be forgiven for thinking that its author, the world-famous physicist Einstein, was not influenced by personal feelings. His reputation as a scientist and the 'scientifically' objective way he stated only the facts without offering an opinion helped make the letter much more persuasive.

Whatever the case, Roosevelt eventually heeded the warning and the US government devoted large resources to ensuring that the USA developed the new kind of bomb before Germany could. It took several years, but the Americans succeeded in building the first 'atomic bomb'. The atomic bomb gave them an extraordinary advantage over their enemies in the Second World War. By that point, Germany had surrendered but Japan was still fighting. In August 1945, US planes dropped two atomic bombs on cities in Japan and, just as the letter had predicted, the bombs were extremely powerful – it's thought 129,000 Japanese people were killed. With no weapons of equivalent power with which to fight back, Japan had little option but to surrender and the Second World War came to an end.

Historians are still divided over whether it was morally right to use such a devastating weapon against civilians, even though less powerful bombs had been dropped on civilian populations throughout the war, and the use of the atomic bomb may have helped to bring the war to a close and thus saved a greater number of other lives. (This is also the dilemma faced by the Doctor in *The Day of the Doctor*.)

But after the Second World War it became known that the 'race' between the USA and Germany to invent the atomic bomb had been nothing of the sort. The Germans had largely given up on the idea, focusing instead on finding new ways to drop conventional, non-atomic bombs on their enemies. Britain and her allies had developed a new technology called radar that could detect incoming German bomber planes from a distance, allowing them to be intercepted and shot down before they reached their targets. The Germans' solution to this problem was to develop long-range and guided rocket systems that were often too fast for their enemies to stop.

That might suggest that the letter sent to the US President, 'object-ively' laying out only the scientific facts, had been wrong. Einstein later said that signing the letter was the 'one great mistake' in his life. Szilárd, with a number of other scientists, later helped found the Council for Abolishing War (today the Council for a Liveable World), with the aim of getting rid of the USA's nuclear weapons – that is, more powerful versions of the atomic bomb developed after 1945.

Because, though atomic bombs ended the Second World War, their very existence created a new kind of conflict. Now countries in possess-ion of atomic and nuclear weapons had the power to entirely annihilate their enemies – but, because their enemies also had the same weapons, they faced the same threat of annihilation themselves. For most of the second half of the twentieth century, the world was caught up in a 'cold' war, a stalemate in which actual fighting rarely occurred but in which there was the constant threat that the tension would ignite into fully heated conflict and mutually assured destruction.

We can see something of the impact of this constant threat in the *Doctor Who* made in the 1960s, 1970s and 1980s, while the cold war was going on. Several stories express the fears and anxieties of their time. For example, *The Daleks* (1963–1964) is about the survivors of a nuclear war that has ravaged a whole planet; in *The Mind of Evil* (1971) and *Day of the Daleks* (1972), Earth in the present day teeters on the brink of global war; in *Warriors of the Deep* (1984) it seems the cold war will still be being fought in the year 2084. Yet by *Cold War* (2013), the conflict has become part of history, perhaps as strange and ancient to us now as the cassette tapes that store Grisenko's pop music in the story.

Just as the Second World War encouraged the invention of the computer and the atomic bomb, the cold war also acted as a spur for scientific advances. For one thing, the countries in possession of atomic and other nuclear weapons now needed ways to drop them on their enemies – that is, other countries, often in other continents. As a result, the German scientists who had developed long-range and guided missiles in the Second World War were recruited by their former enemies. Of the more than 1,500 German scientists who went to work in the USA in this way, one is particularly famous.

During the Second World War, German engineer Wernher von Braun developed the V-2 rocket used by the Germans to bomb Britain and its Allies with devastating effect. Not only did V-2 attacks kill some 9,000 people, but it's thought the number of prisoners and slave labourers killed building the rockets might have been even higher. There is still much debate about how much von Braun was involved or could have changed any of this, but the US government seems to have taken the view that the value of his scientific knowledge and experience was of more importance than his role in the war. They put him to work designing new and better rockets, the results of which were used in long-range nuclear missiles. But there was another practical use for von Braun's research: he developed the huge Saturn V rocket that helped land people on the Moon. It has been argued that the race between the USA and USSR to get into Earth orbit and then to the Moon – which we discussed in Chapter 2 – was as much about developing technologies and bases for long-range missiles as it was about the 'pure' science of exploring space.

The point is that we cannot easily separate the two mindsets of scientific inquiry and soldiering – however much the Doctor might want to. In fact, his greatest enemies, the Daleks, are warmongering scientists, constantly devising new technologies with which to destroy people. In *Genesis of the Daleks* (1975), we see how the Daleks were created by the scientist Davros during a terrible war. Davros claims that in creating the Daleks he is only trying to save his own people, the Kaleds, from defeat and extinction. However, in the course of the story we see that he is willing to sacrifice anything – even his own people – to achieve his goals. His elite team of scientists, working in an underground bunker to develop new technologies for the war effort, are

THE SCIENTIFIC SECRETS OF DOCTOR WHO

a clear reference to the secret research groups set up by the Nazis during the Second World War. For some of the story, Davros's subordinate, Nyder, even wears a medal associated with the Nazis – the Iron Cross.

At the end of *The Day of the Doctor*, the War Doctor decides that, yes, he will use the Moment to end the Time War, even though it means the destruction of his own people and all those billions of children. The Tenth and Eleventh Doctors arrive at the last minute – not to stop him, but to ensure that he doesn't have to go through with his terrible decision alone. They know exactly what the consequences of using the Moment will be – because they have already lived through it. So their endorsement suggests that the War Doctor is making the rational, logical choice, however awful it might be.

It's Clara who makes them pause, and she does so by making a distinction between two kinds of mindset: a soldier and something else.

'We've got enough warriors. Any old idiot can be a hero.'

'Then what do I do?'

'What you've always done. Be a doctor. You told me the name you chose was a promise. What was the promise?'

'Never cruel or cowardly.'

'Never give up. Never give in.'

Clara Oswald, the Eleventh Doctor, the War Doctor
and the Tenth Doctor, *The Day of the Doctor*

The Doctor chooses not to be a soldier: faced with this impossible problem, he doesn't shoot it, but uses his intelligence to find an ingenious solution. Yet for all this moment of genius saves his people, the Twelfth Doctor still seems haunted by that choice – by what he *might* have done.

That's why this Doctor doesn't like soldiers – not because the mindset of the scientist and the soldier are so radically opposed, but because he knows they can overlap, and how easy it was to convince himself 'objectively' that he should wipe out his own people. It's not Danny the ex-soldier that the Doctor is horrified by, but the soldier in himself. Hence him asking Clara in *Into the Dalek*: 'Am I good man?'

One further question: how did the Time War begin? Russell T Davies, the writer who came up with the idea of the Time War, has suggested that it was the Time Lords who started it when they sent the Doctor back in time to stop the Daleks ever being created in *Genesis of the Daleks*.

The Time Lord who gives the Doctor this mission says there are good reasons for doing so:

'We foresee a time when they will have destroyed all other life forms and become the dominant creature in the universe … We'd like you to return to Skaro at a point in time before the Daleks evolved.'

'Do you mean avert their creation?'

'Or affect their genetic development so that they evolve into less aggressive creatures … Alternatively, if you learn enough about their very beginnings, you might discover some inherent weakness.'

A Time Lord and the Fourth Doctor, *Genesis of the Daleks*

Although the Doctor agrees to undertake the mission, when it comes to the crucial moment of actually destroying the Daleks for ever, he is unsure he has the moral right to do so. Some things, he says, could be better with the Daleks, arguing, 'Many future worlds will become allies just because of their fear of the Daleks.'

In fact, Davros argues something similar – when the Daleks have conquered everyone, he says, then there will be peace. If the Doctor doesn't agree with that line of reasoning, he is at least unsure about wiping out an entire intelligent life form. After all, he says, wouldn't that make him as bad as the Daleks?

We'll talk more about the morality of this moment in Chapter 13, but ultimately the Daleks survive at the end of the story – though the Doctor denies that he has failed in his assignment. He admits that the Daleks 'will create havoc and destruction for millions of years', but says that he also knows that 'out of their evil must come something good.'

But is that correct? In Chapter 5, we talked about *Day of the Daleks*, in which a group of humans travel back from the future to the present day to kill a politician. They think that by doing so they'll change future events and prevent the Daleks conquering Earth in the future. But the Doctor realises that it's the death of the politician that *leads* to the Dalek conquest.

Isn't that what happens in *Genesis of the Daleks*, too? Early in the story, we're told that the Daleks' creator, the brilliant scientist Davros, does not believe that there is intelligent life on other planets. No one dares to disagree with Davros about anything, so his seems to be the prevailing view of the people of ancient Skaro. He's created the Daleks to win a war on Skaro, not to go into space.

But just by meeting Davros, the Doctor and his friends prove to him that there *is* intelligent life on other worlds. Worse, Davros learns that his Daleks will conquer these alien worlds in the future. Then, at the end of the story, the Daleks make a sinister pledge.

'This is only the beginning. We will prepare. We will grow stronger. When the time is right, we will emerge and take our rightful place as the supreme power of the universe!'

A Dalek, *Genesis of the Daleks*

If it wasn't for the Doctor, would the Daleks have had that ambition to conquer the universe, rather than just their own world? The Time Lords gave the Doctor his mission because they foresaw the Daleks destroying all other life forms. The paradox is that in trying to stop such a future from happening, it seems the Time Lords inadvertently start the Daleks on that very path.

Perhaps things would have worked out better if the Time Lords, before sending the Doctor on his mission, had known more about the state of scientific knowledge on ancient Skaro. But then our understanding of history can be problematic, too...

Battles in Time

It's not just the Time War in which time — and the ability to time travel — is used as a terrible weapon. Here are some examples...

The War Games (1969)

Using technology purloined from the Time Lords, an alien race kidnaps soldiers from different wars in Earth's history as part of a scheme to build an army for conquering the galaxy.

Pyramids of Mars (1975)

The Doctor moves the threshold of an Osiran time-space tunnel into the far future to age the evil 'god' Sutekh, caught inside it, to death.

City of Death (1979)

Having accidentally been splintered in time throughout Earth's history, Scaroth of the Jagaroth devotes himself to advancing human civilisation to a point where he can build a time machine and go back and stop that accident — but that would stop life on Earth from ever having existed.

Mawdryn Undead (1983)

Contaminated by the sickly alien Mawdryn, the Doctor's companions Nyssa and Tegan can't travel through time in the TARDIS without making their condition worse.

Timelash (1985)

Rebels on the planet Karfel are thrown into the Timelash – a kind of wormhole that dumps them in twelfth-century Scotland. (Is that really a punishment?)

Father's Day (2005)

Rose changes history and exposes Earth to an attack by Reapers – who are drawn to accidents in time like bacteria to a wound.

Blink (2007)

The Weeping Angels feed off lost futures, sending you into the past and then consuming the potential of all the days you might have had.

POTENTIAL ENERGY

JACQUELINE RAYNER

'I'm not saying folk round here are suggestible,' said Miss Perpugilliam Brown, the American with the extremely large dowry, to her aristocratic English fiancé, Lord Roderick Pottinger, 'but in the park I saw eight men with orange spats, three with polka-dot cravats, and one poor man had even gone to the trouble of putting teddy bear buttons on his waistcoat, even though teddy bears won't be invented for another hundred years.'

Lord Roderick guffawed (there was really no other word for the sounds coming out of his mouth). Peri tried not to wince. 'Dem it, could listen to you babbling nonsense all day, gel,' the man boomed before leaving the room, probably to go and hunt a fox or shoot a pheasant.

'If I get married,' Peri said to the painting above the mantel-piece, 'it's gonna be to someone *quiet*. Someone who never shouts or shoots or hunts or fights.' She sighed. 'I think maybe I'll just not get married. Ever.'

'The ingratitude!' That was the Doctor, the other shouty man in her life and the originator of the suddenly fashionable spats-cravat-waistcoat look (at least he – tall, imposing, curly and blond of hair and determined of expression – had the figure to carry it off, unlike most of the Regency spindleshanks). He had entered the room as she spoke and now stood beside her, also gazing up at the painting. 'After all the work it took to get Lord Roderick to propose to an elderly spinster such as yourself.'

'Yeah, thanks for that,' said Peri.

'Well, 21 is practically decrepit in the Regency marriage market.'

'I think I could've been 91 and it wouldn't have bothered him, with all the stuff you were spreading around about my dowry of millions.' She shook her head. 'No, I'm being unfair. He's OK. Better than his sister, anyway. It's just he's so... loud.'

They stood together for a few moments, Peri enjoying the blissful silence. But in the end, it was she who broke it. 'It's hard to believe such a beautiful picture came from something so evil,' she said.

If she hadn't known its background, the painting would have made her feel happy. Calm. Peaceful. It was a full-length study of a ballerina, something in the manner of Degas ('Edgar Degas, born in Paris, 1834, a founder of the Impressionist movement although he had little time for his fellow Impressionists and preferred to call himself a "Realist",' said the Doctor. 'That's not really relevant, though, is it?' said Peri. 'You're just showing off.'), its colours muted but perfect, the grace of the dancer singing from every brushstroke.

'Painted by an "Old Master" who at one point could barely manage a potato print,' said the Doctor.

'Do they have potatoes here yet?' Peri wondered, temporarily side-tracked.

The Doctor held up a hand and left the room. A few seconds later he reappeared and tutted. 'And you a botanist! Potatoes were brought to Europe from Peru by Spanish Conquistadors in the 1530s. Sir Walter Raleigh introduced them to Ireland fifty years later, and by the end of the sixteenth century they had spread throughout Europe, including England. So yes, by 1812 potatoes have been here for over a hundred years.'

'How come you know so much *trivia?*'

'Advantages of a large brain, Peri!'

'Which explains why you've got such a big head...' But she mumbled that one under her breath, and even though she was fairly sure the Doctor heard it he pretended not to. She decided it'd be best to go back to the subject of the painting. 'I wonder how Lord Roderick would react if he knew the person ultimately responsible for that picture is also responsible for his sister dying.'

'She's not dead yet,' the Doctor pointed out.

'But she will be,' said Peri. 'Unless we get our act together, she'll be dead in days.'

A breathless maid hurried into the room. 'Please, miss, Miss Jane is asking for you.'

Peri sighed. 'Just going away and letting the thing kill her would be wrong, right?'

'Yes,' said the Doctor sternly. 'It would.'

Peri read a novel to Jane until the sunlight faded. It was not the sort of novel she favoured, being full of women with heaving bosoms sighing heavily over men whose cold hearts would eventually be melted, probably by all those heavy sighs. 'Don't stop!' screeched Jane as Peri marked her place and shut the book.

'It's too dark to read any more, even with a candle,' Peri pointed out. 'And you said a brighter light would hurt your eyes.'

Jane put a hand on her forehead and sighed – a piteous rather than a heavy sigh, although just as fictional. 'How I do suffer,' she said (also piteously). 'I fear I will not live long enough to be able to call you sister.'

'Don't say that!' said Peri, meaning it literally. The thing was that Jane would be either saved or dead before the wedding and either circumstance meant that Peri would definitely not be turning up at St George's Hanover Square in a bridal gown on the appointed day.

The next morning, Peri was grabbing a few quiet moments in the morning room when she heard a knock at the door. She sighed at the thought of having something else to deal with. Already that day she'd had to supervise the cooking of dainty dishes to tempt an invalid's palate (as ordered – and she did mean *ordered* – by Jane; read yet more of that tiresome novel to Jane (Miss Hyde the governess had been supposed to take a turn but had mysteriously disappeared just when she was needed), and listened as Jane outlined all the beauty treatments she was undertaking to look her best for the wedding (if she lived that long). Jane was so living up to the role of a self-absorbed delusional malingerer that Peri had to keep reminding herself that an evil alien was actually draining the girl's life force. Jane was actually dying.

Now, finally, thankfully, Peri was getting a break from her sister-in-law elect while lady's maid Yvette applied those beautifying unguents and powders and creams. A maid showed a thin, scholarly-looking man into the room and announced that he was Mr Peppercorn.

'I'm afraid you've had a wasted journey, sir,' Peri said, rising to greet him. 'Unfortunately Miss Pottinger is too unwell to attend her studies. Please accept my apologies for neglecting to send word to you.' It was deliberate neglect, of course. The alien they were hunting had to be someone who visited Jane regularly (utilising a very useful ability to blend in as though he or she'd always been there, of course) and her music master was on that list. 'But perhaps I could beg a favour while you are here.'

'Anything, anything!' gushed the man, who seemed incredibly relieved that he wouldn't be spending an hour alone with Jane Pottinger.

Peri gestured towards the piano. 'Play for me? It would be such a treat. We don't have pianos back home in America.' That was a test. The Doctor had discoursed for some minutes on the history of the piano. If Mr Peppercorn didn't contradict her mistake…

… which he didn't…

… then it probably meant that he either wasn't that interested in transatlantic instruments or he was being polite in not contradicting her. So it signified nothing. It certainly didn't mean he was an alien villain masquerading as a tutor to drain the life force of an irritating girl.

'Oh, charmed,' said Mr Peppercorn. 'Delighted!' He crossed to the piano and began to play.

Or maybe it did mean he was an alien villain masquerading, etc., etc.! Because that man sure could play.

'Don't stop!' Peri told him. 'Back in a minute!'

She was back well before the minute was up, dragging the Doctor with her. 'Isn't Mr Peppercorn *good*, Doctor!' she cried. 'So good it scarcely seems *human*.'

'A masterly performance,' said the Doctor as the music master finished with a flourish. 'And not a piece I recognise. Your own composition?'

Peppercorn nodded. 'Indeed. A humble offering of my own. Not quite in the class of Herr Bach or Herr Mozart...'

The Doctor popped out of the room for a second then came back in. 'You're too hard on yourself! Of course, few can compete with Johann Sebastian Bach, born Eisenach, Germany in 1685, best known for his Brandenburg Concertos, or Wolfgang Amadeus Mozart, born 1756 in Salzburg, best known as a cheese made from buffalo milk commonly used on pizzas.' He frowned and popped out of the room again, returning swiftly. 'That is to say, best known for operas such as *The Marriage of Figaro* and *The Magic Flute* – but really, sir, you are approaching them in skill.'

The music master flushed so hard it could be seen even through the thick white make-up he was wearing. 'I am covered in confusion, sir,' he said to the Doctor as he left the room, bowing and scraping. 'Thank you for such kind words.'

'So? Is he our guy? He's a musical genius!'

The Doctor wrinkled his nose. 'Perhaps a genuine one. After all, we've found no evidence so far that our foe utilises the stolen gifts himself. And Jane has gone rapidly downhill since we arrived yet Mr Peppercorn only visits her weekly. I don't think he's our man.'

'Please, miss, the mistress is asking for you,' said the maid who'd just come in.

'Oh. Great,' said Peri.

Yvette's lotions and potions definitely hadn't done the trick. Jane was looking really ill, much more so than previously.

'My body aches from the soles of my feet to the roots of my hair!' she cried. 'Brambles are clawing their way through my throat!'

She'd been sick too, Peri noted. 'Who's been in to see you this morning apart from me and Yvette?' she asked.

'No one,' Jane moaned.

No one. So if the culprit wasn't Peri (and obviously it wasn't)...

'Doctor, I need to know the French for "So, are you a genuine lady's maid or are you an evil alien?" Hey, come back! I asked you a question!'

(Pause.)

'Oh, Peri, did you say something? I popped out to check on the weather.'

'I asked—'

'Yes, yes, yes. C'est: *Alors, vous êtes la femme de chamelle d'un véritable dame ou êtes-vous un étranger mal?*'

'Thanks.'

'Yvette! *Alors, vous êtes la femme de chamelle d'un véritable dame ou êtes-vous un étranger mal?* Why are you laughing? Er, I mean, er, *pourquoi*... Hang on, what's laugh? *Ri*-something, I think.'

'I think you mean *femme de chambre*, mademoiselle. Instead you have enquired if I am a camel woman.'

'Oh. Well, are you?'

'No, mademoiselle. I am not a ruminant quadruped of any kind.'

Peri gloomily turned away – then turned back with an 'Aha!' and a 'J'accuse!' 'That's pretty fancy language for a lady's maid!' she continued. 'Suspiciously so.'

Yvette shrugged. 'Once upon a time I was educated, mademoiselle.

The Reign of Terror made it necessary for me to change both my country of residence and my station in life.'

'Oh,' said Peri. 'Sorry.'

Peri rejoined the Doctor. 'I thought I was on to something. No good, though.' She sighed (yes, again). 'I just keep thinking of all the ones we didn't save. That Stone Age computer pioneer. Or that little chimney-sweep mathematician.'

'The galley slave who could have been an astronaut… The crossing sweeper who should have been a surgeon…'

'And now Jane. An admittedly annoying Regency miss who could be a great – what was it again?'

'An anpholier.'

'Yeah. One of those. An admittedly annoying anpholier. Whatever that is.'

The Doctor sighed. 'I can't explain it to you.'

'Because I'm too dumb?'

'No. Because you don't have the vocabulary.' He sighed again. (Everyone was sighing a lot. It seemed to be the done thing in Regency times). 'Maybe you could just download the app onto your smartphone.'

Peri blinked.

'See?' said the Doctor. 'Thirty years after you left Earth, that sentence would be understood by every man, woman and child. But it means nothing to you. The Human Genome Project! The World Wide Web! Texting! DVDs! The Large Hadron Collider! Dolly the Sheep!'

'Pardon?'

'Exactly! All scientific advances only a decade or three from 1984.' The Doctor was throwing his arms wide now, a Shakespearean actor writing his own lines. 'How much more difficult do you think it would be to explain something a century or more in your future? All you need to know is that an expert anpholier would have a rare skill. And, incidentally, one that could save lives. A lot of lives.'

'But only if Jane dies. Hmm. One really irritating life against maybe hundreds…'

The Doctor gave her a stern look.

'I didn't mean it,' she muttered. 'You know I didn't. Even if you offered me a million pounds…'

'A million pounds is probably small change to the Potentialiser.'

'The Potentialiser'. That was the name they'd given the monster they were pursuing.

Peri had known talented kids back home. There was Sadie Turtle, who won every tennis championship going. Randall Schuyler, who skipped so many grades he was practically still in diapers when he sat his SATs. Then there were also kids who didn't shine, but whose parents made them try everything – piano lessons, swimming lessons, karate lessons, art classes, chess, baseball, football, hockey, ice-skating, *everything* – in the hope of finding that one thing that would make their child rise above all the rest. Those were the ones who'd pay for the Potentialiser's services.

Because what the Potentialiser did was this: he or she detected the potential for a talent, a talent that by way of circumstance would never come to fruition, because its owner was born in the wrong place or the wrong time or the wrong social stratum or with deficiencies in health or wealth that meant the genius wouldn't or couldn't be realised. And when the Potentialiser had tracked down the would-be ballerina or artist or scientist, he or she would extract that potential and give it to someone who could use it. Which would be fine. If only the original subject didn't die during the extraction.

The Doctor had worked out a way of tracking the Potentialiser's victims, but until now they'd arrived too late to either save the victim or catch the Potentialiser. This time, however, he'd done some clever thing or other to the TARDIS and had bought them a few days' grace. Hence Miss Perpugilliam Brown's lightning betrothal to Lord Roderick Pottinger following his rescue of her from a vile gang of attackers (attackers who had to attack four times before Lord Roderick got the message, not that they minded, being handsomely paid for their banditry). And here they were, with unfettered access to Roderick's sister, the intended victim, over the course of several days, and no more clue as to how to save her than when they first arrived.

'I thought it might be Yvette,' Peri said. 'But it looks like she's genuinely French. She definitely speaks the language.'

The Doctor raised an eyebrow. 'Far be it from me to cast aspersions on your reasoning, but not only is it likely the Potentialiser can be understood in any language, so can we. TARDIS gift. Doesn't prove a thing.'

'You still managed to get the translation wrong, though, TARDIS gift or no TARDIS gift,' grumbled Peri. 'Turns out I asked her if she was a camel. Hey! Do Regency people know about camels?'

'Just a second,' said the Doctor, jumping up and exiting the room.

Peri was getting just a little bit fed up of this. She crept across the room and quietly opened the door a crack.

'Zoe!' she heard the Doctor say under his breath. 'I need to know about camels.'

'Caramels: chewy candy made of sugar, butter and milk.'

'Not caramels, camels.'

'Canals: manmade waterways—'

'Not canals, I said tell me about camels!'

'Doctor,' Peri said sweetly, 'who are you talking to?'

He started guiltily, hurriedly hiding something behind his back, and a look Peri had never seen before crossed his face. After a second she realised that the Doctor was actually looking sheepish. Well, she guessed there had to be a first time for everything.

'It's Zoe,' he said.

'What, as in Jamie and Zoe?' (The Doctor had given her a crash course on all his former friends. It had saved her life once on Karfel.)

'No – Zoe as in personal assistant and knowledge interface. Although I did name it after Zoe as in Jamie and Zoe. Zoe knew about everything, you see. Well, except candles.' He drew his hands from behind his back and Peri saw he was holding a flat rectangular device. 'This is called a tablet. No, not like Tylenol, as I'm sure you were about to say.' (She hadn't been. She might not be that up on future stuff but she was pretty sure you wouldn't try to swallow an electrical device for a headache.)

'And it's some amazing Time Lord gadget?'

'Not exactly. I bought it on the net in 2015.'

'What, like a fishing net?'

The Doctor was just about to answer when a cry reached them.

'Quick, upstairs!' yelled Peri. She hitched up her skirts and ran up the stairs in a way that would have shocked London to its core if anyone but a very rich person had done it. The Doctor followed. They burst into Jane's room…

… and saw Miss Hyde the governess standing over the unconscious girl, capturing in a vial the purple ribbons of light emanating from her mouth.

'So, we meet at last, Potentialiser!' declared the Doctor.

'Pot-what-now?' said the Potentialiser.

'It's our name for you,' Peri explained.

'Mm, I quite like it,' said the Potentialiser. 'Do you spell it with an "s" or a "z"?'

The Doctor ignored that. 'I am going to stop you, Potentialiser,' he said. 'No more poor souls will fall victim to your evil machinations!'

'What's a machination?' asked the Potentialiser.

'Machination: a crafty scheme or plot for sinister ends,' said Zoe.

'I don't have any sinister ends!' said the Potentialiser.

'You murder people!' said the Doctor.

'I do not!' said the Potentialiser.

'Shall we all sit down and talk about this like sensible people,' said Peri.

Luckily, everyone agreed.

'So draining people's potential doesn't actually kill them, then?' said Peri, pouring the Potentialiser a cup of tea.

'Of course not!' she replied indignantly. 'What do you think I am?'

'And you're not doing this for money? You're not selling skills to the highest bidder?'

'Of course not!' she repeated, still indignantly. 'After extracting the unused – the un*usable* – potential energy, I spend a lot of time finding a suitable vessel for it. You see,' she said, helping herself to a Bath bun ('a sweet roll made with yeast and topped with sugar, sometimes containing dried fruit,' pointed out Zoe), 'I just couldn't stand the waste. All that potential for the benefit of mankind, left to wither in infertile soil.'

'But you kill people!' Peri insisted. 'The little chimney sweep – the caveman…'

The Potentialiser raised an eyebrow. 'I do not! Do you know the morbidity rates for chimney sweeps and cavemen?' ('Searching: morbidity rates for chim—' began Zoe. 'Shut up!' shouted everyone else.) 'Look, I don't kill people. But sometimes, I'm afraid, they die. That's what history's like. Death taking place after I've visited is just a coincidence.'

'I don't believe you,' said Peri. 'Look at Jane. Since we arrived she's got really ill. Vomiting. Sore throat. Aches and pains…'

'Symptom checker: consistent with influenza, food poising, arsenical poisoning…' came the tinny voice from the Doctor's tablet.

Arsenic! There was something at the back of Peri's mind…

'Zoe, can you tell me about uses of arsenic in the Regency period?'

'Uses of arsenic: rat poison, wallpaper dye, facial creams…'

Face cream! Jane had been using face cream to make herself look good for Peri's wedding. She was only dying because Peri had infiltrated her house in order to save her life. That was a bit awkward.

They were back at the TARDIS. Yvette the aristocratic lady's maid had been given a lecture on how not to kill people with beauty aids and Jane was quite recovered. Peri had broken the news to Lord Roderick that she couldn't marry him because their respective countries were about to go to war (Zoe helped with that titbit), and he was quite sad about it until she told him she'd also lost all her money, and then he went off happily to do something loud with dogs or possibly horses. The Potentialiser had tried to explain to Peri what an anpholier was and how she'd make sure Jane's gift made life infinitely better for a lot of future people, but, even with the aid of Zoe, Peri failed to understand the explanation. And as for Zoe...

'Look, I don't think the TARDIS is big enough for two know-it-alls,' she told the Doctor.

'Oh, I'd hardly call you a—'

'I meant you, and you know it. Look, it's Zoe or me. And the answer had better be me.'

The Doctor had that sheepish expression on his face again. Twice in one day! Peri would have noted it in her diary, if it wasn't that time travel made keeping a diary a sort of chronological Russian Roulette. 'The trouble is, it had become expected of me that I know everything,' he said. 'And it turns out that actually, I only know *nearly* everything. Zoe helped me have the facts at my fingertips, so to speak.'

'Yeah, but half the time she got it wrong. Mozarella? Camels?'

'She just misheard me, that's all. Or I misheard her.'

'Look, it's the computer or me.'

'What do you think, Zoe? Her or you?'

'I'd keep her, Doctor,' said Zoe. 'She's much prettier than a computer.'

'All right,' said the Doctor.

TEN

THE HISTORY
OF EARTH

'Earth. England. Sherwood Forest. 1190 AD – ish.
But you'll only be disappointed. No damsels in distress,
no pretty castles, no such thing as Robin Hood.'

The Twelfth Doctor, *Robot of Sherwood* (2014)

Is history a science? That is something that's long been argued about. The word history comes from the ancient Greek 'historia', meaning inquiry or knowledge acquired by investigation. Just like science, history depends on building up theories from evidence. But there are different kinds of evidence. It's an important principle of our legal system that everyone is innocent until their guilt is proven beyond reasonable doubt by the weight of carefully scrutinised evidence. Forensic science may be used to gather that evidence, but we don't usually think of law more generally as a type of science.

Historical evidence can take different forms. In fact, the past is all around us: we remember things from the past, while people older than us can remember bits of the past from before we were even born. Our language, culture and knowledge, even the landscape where we live, have all been shaped by people now long dead. But we can use what survives from the past in our attempts to understand history.

For example, think of the people in charge of the costumes and sets for making the *Doctor Who* story *Robot of Sherwood*, who needed to know about life in the year 1190. The evidence for that might include physical remains that have survived into the present day. They could study the ruin of a castle from the time and deduce from that how its inhabitants lived. Archaeology in the castle grounds might have found artefacts such as the remains of weapons, tools or jewellery that give additional glimpses into what daily life might have been like – exactly the sort of thing that could be reproduced as props in the *Doctor Who* story. Scientific tests on even fragments of skeletal remains found in the castle might reveal medical information such as the person's age, sex, level of fitness, diet and even how they died. Again, these scientifically gathered details can help build up a vivid picture.

But, broadly speaking, evidence in history usually means written accounts by people who lived at the time. Written evidence is so central to our idea of what history is that the word 'prehistoric' is used for that period of time before the invention of writing. And written texts present a number of problems as evidence.

For example, to know about 1190, we could refer to the five-volume *History of English Affairs* by William of Newburgh, which details life in England between 1066 and 1198. It is thought that William wrote the book in the 1190s, so may have been a first-hand witness to at least some of the later events he describes. Historians particularly value his book because of its detailed account of the crisis that followed the death in 1135 of King Henry I without having a legitimate son to take the throne after him. William gives a good sense of the political intrigues and battles as Henry's daughter Matilda fought her cousin Stephen for the crown.

But how reliable is the evidence presented in this history? We don't know how much William of Newburgh himself witnessed the things he described, though it's generally thought he copied much of his information from a number of other accounts that have since been lost. That makes it difficult to know how accurately he described what happened – or whether it happened at all. We know very little about William of Newburgh himself – we're not even sure that that was his name. A copy of William's *History of English Affairs* now in the British Library contains corrections in William's own hand, so we at least know that the history we can read today is as he wrote it at the time (and hasn't been amended by later writers, as has happened with other old texts). But we don't know if he or his sources of information were biased in favour of one side in the crisis or other – which might mean exaggerating or making up stories. Some of the other things in the history are certainly so extraordinary we might question whether they're true: the strange green children from 'St Martin's Land' who appeared in the Suffolk village of Woolpit; the bishop, Wimund, who became a pirate; or what the book describes in Latin as 'Sanguisuga' – blood-sucking creatures that might be some kind of vampire.

We can only judge the quality of the evidence presented in William's history by comparing it with other evidence from the time – without knowing if they are any more or less reliable than his. In fact, one reason he's often thought to be a good historical source is that he simply tells us that he is, while pointing out errors and fabrications in the works of other writers. But he would say that, wouldn't he?

As a result, some people argue that history isn't really a science because it's all about forming an opinion on the relative value of different sources, which is too dependent on personal interpretation to be called truly scientific (although even evidence that is gathered scientifically needs interpretation). Just as in the story that preceded this chapter, history is about more than a statement of simple facts – the years a person lived, a one-line summary of their life. It's about understanding that life in context, and about how the past affects us today.

'Doctor, will he [Richard the Lionheart] really see Jerusalem?'

'Only from afar. He won't be able to capture it. Even now his armies are marching on a campaign that he can never win.'

'That's terrible. Can't we tell him?'

'I'm afraid not, my dear. No, history must take its course.'

Vicki and the First Doctor, *The Crusade* (1965)

THE SCIENTIFIC SECRETS OF DOCTOR WHO

We saw in Chapter 6 that, despite what the First Doctor tells Vicki, history *can* be changed in *Doctor Who*. But *Doctor Who* stories can also show us some of the different ways that we interpret history – and how our sense of history changes. We're told in *Robot of Sherwood* that 'King Richard is away on crusade'. In fact, the series had already shown us King Richard – the First Doctor meets him in Palestine in *The Crusade*. The script for that story doesn't give us the precise date this meeting takes place, but tells us that it is some time between the Battle of Arsuf (7 September 1191) and Richard seeing the city of Jerusalem (in June 1192).

Though *The Crusade* and *Robot of Sherwood* are set in roughly the same year, they present the past very differently. *The Crusade* is in black and white, the pace is much slower and we can see that it's been recorded in a television studio – the forest in which the TARDIS lands is clearly indoors, on an artificial set. *The Crusade* feels like a televised play, where *Robot of Sherwood* is more like a movie.

These things are obviously because *The Crusade* was made fifty years ago, when technology was less advanced. But something that isn't down to technology is the way King Richard is played. For example, when he first meets the Doctor, Richard refers to the situation back in England – but note the style of language he uses:

'And now I learn my brother John thirsts after power, drinking great draughts of it though it's not his to take. He's planning to usurp my crown, and trade with my enemy, Philip of France. Trade! A tragedy of fortunes and I am too much beset by them. A curse on this! A thousand curses!'

Richard the Lionheart, *The Crusade*

It's an old-fashioned way of speaking, very different from the way people speak in *Robot of Sherwood*. From what we've learnt in other episodes, we could perhaps argue that that's the way the TARDIS is translating Richard's words – since, as with all English aristocrats of the time, the real Richard would actually have spoken a form of French. But perhaps David Whitaker, the writer of *The Crusade*, is doing something else: the way Richard speaks sounds almost Shakespearean.

That seems intentional: at different times in the story, the Doctor's companion Ian quotes dialogue from Shakespeare's plays *King Lear* and *The Merchant of Venice*, while among the famous stories that another companion, Barbara, intends to share with Saladin is *Romeo and Juliet*.

Shakespeare – who lived 400 years after Richard the Lionheart – didn't write a play about Richard, so why would the makers of *Doctor Who* want to link Richard to Shakespeare?

It might help to compare *The Crusade* to *An Age of Kings*, a highly ambitious BBC series from 1960 that adapted eight of Shakespeare's plays to tell, in fifteen feature-length instalments, the story of successive English Kings, starting with *Richard II* and ending with *Richard III*. As the British Film Institute has said, it was 'effectively presenting a chronological history of British royalty from 1377 to 1485'.

The Crusade has something of the look and feel of *An Age of Kings* – not least because Richard the Lionheart is played by Julian Glover, who also appeared in *An Age of Kings* in several prominent roles, including as Edward IV. Perhaps the makers of *The Crusade* weren't consciously aping that particular production, but the fact that they made Richard sound Shakespearean tells us something about their depiction of history. *The Crusade* is, consciously or not, part of a fashion in television drama in the 1960s.

Shakespeare's version of history was often inaccurate and, in some cases, wholly untrue. Yet his skills as a dramatist are highly respected – something we can tell was true in the early 1960s by that fact that *An Age of Kings* was such a big-budget, prestigious series. By making Richard the Lionheart sound Shakespearean, *The Crusade* is tapping into the viewers' association of Shakespeare with quality. It's probably not how Richard would really have spoken, yet it makes him seem more authentic.

'The King takes the oath today ... to take the
cross as a Crusader. But he did that in London.'

'Who says?'

'Your history books.'

'Perhaps they got that bit wrong.'

$\partial^3 \sum_i x^2$

'No, no – too well documented.'

The Fifth Doctor and Tegan Jovanka, *The King's Demons* (1983)

The King's Demons (1983) is set in the reign of Richard's successor (and brother), King John. The story takes place in 1215, just 24 years after the events of *The Crusade* – but *Doctor Who* has a completely different look and feel. Most obviously, *The King's Demons* is in colour and the exterior scenes were recorded on location, in the atmospheric grounds of Bodiam Castle in Sussex. The interior scenes were recorded in a television studio, but they feel very different to those in *The Crusade*: there is faster cutting between individual shots and use of different angles – such as when we look down on the swordfight between the Doctor and Sir Gilles Estram.

These technological innovations – and changing fashions in the style of television production – help *The King's Demons* feel less like a televised play than *The Crusade*. Yet in other ways the historical setting of *The King's Demons* is less convincing. The iron maiden torture device that is central to the plot is completely out of place: the earliest known reference to such an instrument is from 1793. Perhaps, since the iron maiden turns out to be the Master's TARDIS, it's him who has got the history wrong.

Other things are less easy to explain away. The hair and clothes of the thirteenth-century people all seem much too clean, especially in the brightly lit interior scenes. Bodiam Castle might look atmospheric but its square shape, with a central courtyard enclosed by structures built into the surrounding curtain wall, are typical of when it was built

– which was in 1385, more than 150 years after *The King's Demons* is set. To the people of 1215, a castle like the one shown in *Doctor Who* would have seemed futuristic!

What's more, although an appropriate castle, costumes and props can make a medieval setting seem authentic – at least to a non-expert eye – it's much more difficult to get the plants and trees just right. Many species now common to the UK were only introduced in the last 300 years – and we often know exactly when particular plants first arrived. Disease, such as the outbreak of Dutch Elm Disease in the 1960s, can also drastically change the make-up of plant life in the countryside – so that it's even less likely that what we see in a TV story set in the past will be accurate.

It might be ironic for a story about the Doctor's efforts to ensure that history is not altered, but *The King's Demons* isn't aiming for a perfect recreation of the year 1215. Rather, it's conjuring a myth, one based on a popular, twentieth-century idea of the Middle Ages instead of the historical evidence.

Something similar is happening in *Robot of Sherwood*, but here the distinction between the popular, modern idea of history and what the period was really like is the whole point of the story. As the Doctor says, the real 1190 should have 'No damsels in distress, no pretty castles, no such thing as Robin Hood.' Like the Doctor, we don't expect Robin Hood to be real – or at least to be anything like the heroic character we've seen in the movies.

It's striking how very different *The Crusade*, *The King's Demons* and *Robot of Sherwood* all look, despite showing the same character (the Doctor) in the same kind of adventure story full of action and ingenuity, and set in roughly the same period of history. The fact that over time the telling of this same kind of story becomes faster paced and more complicated is not just the result of developments in the technology used to make television: it's because we as the audience have kept up with those innovations. We can follow faster, more complex stories – in fact, we demand them from the people who make TV.

Watching old *Doctor Who* stories and finding them stilted or slow is a sign of how much we take developments in technology for granted in our daily lives.

Watching old *Doctor Who* can reveal to us changes in lots of things we take for granted, the 'norms' or informal, unspoken ways we understand that we should all behave. *Doctor Who* is made for a broad, family audience. It might sometimes push the boundaries, but the people making the series always have that broad audience in mind. They might edit a scene to make it less violent or, as in the case of *Bad Wolf* (2005), to remove a glimpse of Captain Jack's bare bottom which was not considered suitable for the audience.

What is deemed suitable for a family audience can also change over time. Shortly before the transmission of *Robot of Sherwood*, a real-life incident prompted the people in charge of the programme to remove part of a scene in which a character was beheaded. As recorded, Robin lops off the head of the Sheriff of Nottingham in their duel but, since the Sheriff is a robot, he picks his head up and puts it back on before continuing with the fight. That joke didn't seem so funny in the context of real events at the time of broadcast.

Other changes in what is considered suitable happen more gradually – but we can spot them by comparing old and new *Doctor Who*. In this way, the series can act as a historical document, giving us evidence of sociological developments over time.

For example, in *The Parting of the Ways* (2005), as Captain Jack prepares to battle the Daleks – and knowing he's likely to die – he kisses Rose Tyler and then kisses the Doctor. This onscreen kiss between two men caused a moderate stir in the media, as did the fact that the character of Captain Jack was openly bisexual. Some argued that such things weren't suitable in a TV show intended for a broad, family audience. Others disagreed – as clearly did the makers of *Doctor Who*, since they put it in the programme. Gay and bisexual characters have continued to appear in the series ever since.

But a kiss like that could never have happened in *Doctor Who* when it began in 1963 – not least because homosexuality was against the law in the United Kingdom until 1967. By the same token, in *Doctor Who* of the 1960s there are plenty of things that were taken for granted as being suitable for a family audience – or at least relatively uncontentious – that would never make it into the modern programme. In the very first episode, *An Unearthly Child* (1963), the Doctor refers to a 'Red Indian' with a 'savage mind' – language that is now considered culturally insensitive and very unlikely to be used in the series today.

If, like the Doctor, we could travel back in time to see those old stories when they were first broadcast, plenty of other things would make us realise how much the world has changed over time. For one thing, we would notice the smell.

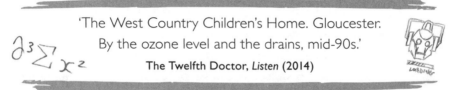

'The West Country Children's Home. Gloucester.
By the ozone level and the drains, mid-90s.'
The Twelfth Doctor, *Listen* (2014)

In Chapter 8, we talked about the relationship between time, memory and our sense of smell. If we could travel in time, our sense of smell would perhaps give us a vivid sense of scientific and technological change. Journeying back into Earth's history, we might, as the Doctor does in *Listen*, use our sense of smell to tell the time period we'd arrived in.

For example, on 1 July 2007 – the day after the broadcast of *The Last of the Time Lords* – a law made it illegal to smoke in enclosed work places in England. Similar laws had recently been passed in Scotland, Wales and Northern Ireland, too – the result of ever more scientific evidence that smoking increases the likelihood of a number of fatal diseases, not only for the smoker but for those breathing in second-hand smoke.

The smoking ban is still recent history. Yet, if we could journey back less than a decade to a time before the ban, we'd be struck by the smell of smoke in public buildings. Cigarette smoke lingers, so we'd notice the smell even if no one was actually smoking there.

In fact, we can be struck by the smell of cigarettes in public places without having to travel in time; we just need to visit countries that don't have the same ban. But then, as it famously says in the opening line of L.P. Hartley's 1953 novel, *The Go-Between*, 'The past is a foreign country: they do things different there.'

The further back we went into history, the more we'd notice strange sights and sounds and smells – and the more 'alien' the world would become. Just as in Chapter 7 we could use the stars to deduce our position on the surface of the Earth, we could calculate *when* in history we were from tell-tale clues around us. For example, in the United Kingdom:

Before 2000

Relatively few people had mobile phones before 2000. Before that, mobile phones were chunky and – the further back in time we go – only owned by the richest people. We'd also notice more people hanging around apparently not doing anything. We'd find that suspicious if we saw it today, but before mobile phones, there was no way to know if friends you were meeting were running late, so you just had to wait.

Before 1980

The end date isn't exact, but we might notice more men scarred and otherwise showing signs of service in war. We still see some wounded veterans today, mainly from recent conflicts, but we'd see many more in the past because of conscription in the First and Second World Wars, which meant so many more men went to fight.

Before 1965

Few people had automatic washing machines in their homes until the mid-1960s. There were other kinds of washing machine before that, but for many people clothes were washed by hand – generally less often and less thoroughly. Many homes still had only basic washing facilities rather than fitted bathrooms. So we'd notice that people were smellier. And fluoride toothpaste – which is especially good at stopping cavities in teeth – was first sold in 1956 but only became popular in the mid-1960s. Before then, too, we'd notice people's terrible teeth.

Before 1948

Prior to the beginning of the National Health Service, we would see more sick and injured people who hadn't been treated. We'd notice poor-sighted people struggling without glasses, and people with few or no teeth who had not been given dentures.

Travel further back to when horses were a more common form of transport than the car and we'd notice another change in smell. Animals would live much closer to humans, and there would be horse dung all over the roads. We might notice there was less pollution and overcrowding, and much more green space. Or we might notice how much dirtier, bleaker and unhealthy everything looked, with fewer laws (and understanding) about even basic health and safety.

'I don't know how to tell you this, oh great genius – but your breath doesn't half stink!'
Martha Jones to William Shakespeare, *The Shakespeare Code* (2007)

But perhaps the most striking thing we'd notice if we could really travel back in time – and which comes over clearly from nearly all the historical evidence we have – is that people wouldn't change much. We would see the same human behaviour, the fears and desires, the foolishness, meanness and kindness. One reason the plays of Shakespeare remain so popular after 400 years is that the psychology of his characters rings as true to us now as it did when he wrote them.

The difference between people in history and you and me today is the context in which they lived and understood the world around them. They'd send letters not text messages to tell someone they fancied them (in the past there were more frequent postal services, so you could get a reply the same day). They'd travel by horse-drawn carriage instead of a car. They'd die young of diseases that we can cure easily. Generally, their lives would seem harder and shorter because of the advances made since their time.

We might even argue that what we see in history is the effect on human existence of developments in knowledge and technology. Which would mean, whether or not history is a science, in some ways it is the study of how science has changed humanity.

regen = 12

$$\partial^3 \sum x^2$$

PART 3
HUMANITY

$$\overline{X} || \sum \textcircled{m} \text{ or } \textcircled{Ω} ??$$

THE ARBOREALS
MARC PLATT

The Doctor pushed through the last of the undergrowth and stepped out into what amounted to a forest clearing. His long white hair was swept back, but his eyes had the sharpness of a man half his apparent age. He leant on his cane, mopping his forehead and studying the edifice that loomed over him. 'I knew it,' he muttered with a degree of satisfaction. 'Susan, I was right! It's not a building at all.'

Susan almost fell into the clearing. The long grass had somehow wound round her ankle and she had to struggle not to lose one shoe altogether. She wore the patterned top she had won at the cloud fair on the mountainous planet Orrios. It wasn't remotely practical for exploring an alien rain forest, but she liked it and was not going to change just because her Grandfather had registered his disapproval. She sat on the ground to adjust her shoe and squinted up at the object that towered above her.

'It's a spaceship, isn't it?' she said.

A dark green wave of vegetation had broken over the grounded craft. Vines traced across its hull like veins. Heavy roots like knotted fingers gripped the fuselage, trying to crush their way inside. A small tree hung with scarlet flowers had rooted in one of the engine vents.

Nothing moved. No breeze stirred the leaves, no birds sang. Only the occasional splat of water dripping from the upper canopy broke the silence.

'Obviously some expedition has come to grief here,' the Doctor declared. 'Judging from the repair work on the hull, it was an old ship, but as to what caused its demise, I have no idea.'

While he paced off around the ship's hydraulic legs, looking in vain for an entrance, Susan walked to where a line of grassy tussocks bordered the edge of the clearing. New saplings, already young trees in their own right, were taking advantage of the extra sunlight where their ancient forest forebears had been cleared. It was hot in the open, so she sat down on one of the tussocks.

The air fizzed for a moment and the row of tussocks was suddenly alive. Susan stumbled back up to her feet as a silvery face flickered through the long grass on every mound. Women and men; some smiling gently, some broadly. A couple frowned. One winked. Another (very serious) raised her hand in military salute. Another was laughing as he carried a silently barking dog.

Susan felt uncomfortable as if she had just disturbed something sacred. And then the Doctor was at her side, surveying the display with a look of grave reverence. 'Well, this answers our question. Apparently most of the people on the expedition died.'

They walked arm in arm along the row reading the little commemorative name tags that had appeared below the faces. Flight Lt. François Degrey, Captain Cornelia Parsotam, Snr Orderly Andy Bryant and Pooch. It wasn't menacing, just a little sad. And it occurred to Susan that one of the crew, the last one alive, wouldn't be able to bury himself.

The line of tussocks ended with one new grave, freshly dug, which had no holographic memorial. Out of the mound of bare earth sprouted a spherical grey space helmet with a metal name tag attached. It named the owner as *Captain Tino Driscoll KST.*

'But this is only a few days old,' said Susan. 'So there must be survivors.'

The Doctor frowned. 'Except that the other graves have been neglected for many years. That's quite a disparity, don't you think?'

A sudden wind rustled through the trees above, scattering flowers down upon them.

Susan shuddered. 'Can we go now, please? This place gives me the creeps.' She took his arm again and tried steering him back towards the path leading to the TARDIS. To her frustration, he stopped, studied the abandoned spaceship and then glanced back at the graves.

'There are twenty-three colonists buried there, yet how many people do you think that ship was built to carry? I'd say quite a few, eh? At least one hundred.'

'Well, then they must have survived. Perhaps they found a better place to set up home.' She tugged at his arm, but he pulled free.

'But that doesn't explain the new grave.'

'Oh, Grandfather,' she complained.

He pointed upwards at something catching the sunlight: a one-eyed metal insect that winked as it flew down towards them. Susan tried again to pull him away, but the Doctor stood his ground, determined to match the prying object's stare. It stopped, humming slightly, hovering a couple of feet above them. 'Can I help you?' he called and Susan saw his knuckles whiten as he gripped his cane.

The undergrowth nearby opened with a crash and a figure in a bulky grey spacesuit stumbled into view. It stopped short when it saw them and swore loudly in a woman's voice. Then it strode in their direction with ungainly steps. 'Are you crazy? Who the heck sent you?' The dark shading on her visor cleared. She was young with sandy hair drawn back tight. Her eyes were sharp with suspicion. 'You'll get yourselves killed without a suit!'

Susan gripped the Doctor's hand, but he seemed unconcerned. 'Young lady, I have no idea what you are talking about.'

'It's the zeitgeist thing again, isn't it? Who are you with? Avbigo? Or Tyzor Properties? Once one developer gets the smell of a possible killing, then you all pile in.'

'Is this your flying camera?' said the Doctor. 'Would you please call it off?'

She studied them for a moment. 'Jeeps, you two take the muffin. That's the trouble with the open market. These days, any old codger can set up a claim.'

Susan watched the Doctor's chin tighten. 'And who exactly are you calling an old codger, hmm? I am the Doctor, and this is my grand-daughter Susan. We are visiting this planet and have as much right to be here, I suspect, as you do. Perhaps you should explain yourself before you start accusing innocent bystanders!'

'Sorry. I'm forgetting the procedure. That's not really my job. Still...' The woman fumbled in a pack attached to her belt, but her big-fingered gloves were too clumsy. The card she was trying to produce fluttered out of her grasp and landed in the mud. Susan scooped it up and studied the animated announcement.

A green planet swam up to fill the card and a formal logo overlaid it.

Kresta Survey Team: Prospecting for the Future
Project Co-ordinator – Bethan Finch

'KST has legal survey rights to this planet with the first option for further development,' said Bethan.

The Doctor glanced at Susan. 'What sort of development?'

If Bethan tried to shrug, it was obscured by the rigid confines of her spacesuit. 'That depends on what we find. Mineral deposits, opportunities for agricultural or colonial development. It's all up for grabs in this sector.'

Susan shook her head. 'But what about the people who already live here?'

'Indigenous inhabitants, you mean? If there are any.' She faltered. 'You're not with a protest group, are you? Jeeps, I hope they've given you decent decontamination facilities, because tramping around like that... in all this... well, it's irresponsible.'

'We are independent travellers,' said the Doctor. 'Although I always complain if I believe an injustice is being done. So what about the native population? Have you encountered anyone yet?'

'Only you, so far.' She seemed flustered and defensive. 'It all goes in the report. But if there are natives – anyone above Class D – that's when they bring in the contact sociologists. They deal with the negotiations and compensation. Sometimes the locals get a reserve to live in or even full relocation to another planet.'

The flying camera hovered closer.

'Yes, yes, that's all very well,' said the Doctor. 'But you and your colleagues must be aware that you are not the first visitors to this world.' He stabbed a finger in the direction of the abandoned ship. 'Their expedition did not survive. Do you imagine yours will do better? And will you please call off that bug-eyed camera of yours!' He struck out at the little drone with his cane.

'Sorry,' said Bethan again. 'All encounters are recorded for evidence and training purposes.'

'What nonsense!' The Doctor ignored Susan's entreaties for him to stay calm. 'I demand to see your senior officer!'

'I'll tell him,' said Bethan, fiddling with her heavy gloves.

After a moment, the Doctor said. 'Well? Where is he? At your ship? And how far is that, hmm?'

Susan tugged at his arm. 'Grandfather, stop it. You're upsetting her.'

'I want to see him!'

'I don't know where he is!' Bethan lowered her face inside her suit to hide her tears. 'I haven't seen him for four days.'

The Doctor stepped towards her, but she stepped back, stumbled and sat down in the mud.

'My dear, I must apologise,' said the Doctor as he helped her up. 'Are you alone here?'

'It's just the two of us!' She flapped her arms in exasperation and poured out how this was their first prospecting trip, how it was meant to make their fortune. But Tino had been excited by the raw natural beauty of the planet.

'Tino?' Susan touched the Doctor's arm in recognition and he nodded grimly, but Bethan was in full flow by now: Tino had been surveying the habitat – hundreds of new species – and they were getting behind on the other elements of the survey. Then four mornings ago, he wasn't there. She thought he had wandered off on some hike of his own – he did that too often – but he'd never come back.

And all the time she waited, it felt as if the forest was watching. But she was sure Tino would be back soon. Of course he would. He had to be.

'Bethan, I fear there is something you must see.' The Doctor took her gloved hand and led her across the clearing to the line of tussocks.

'I know,' she said. 'They were the refugees. The records show that their ship went missing in this sector about fifty years ago, just after the Tarmusiac barrages went up. So no one came looking for them.' She stopped as she saw the final grave on the line – the fresh grave with the helmet. *Captain Tino Driscoll KST.*

At first she was too stunned to react. 'But it wasn't here,' she kept saying. 'He wasn't here. Not two days ago. Did you do this? Did you find him? And bury him?'

Then she sat back down in the grass in her spacesuit and cried quietly.

As the trees stirred in the wind again, it occurred to Susan that she felt no apparent breeze.

'Extraordinary,' said the Doctor. 'This place has such a sense of tranquillity. Can't you hear it?'

The trees were still again. There were no sounds of birds or insects. All Susan heard was the occasional crack of a twig or thump of falling fruit.

'It's growing, Susan. Can't you hear the forest growing?'

While he pottered off, picking up seed pods, marvelling at the delicacy of flowers that burst out between the tree roots, Susan poked at the muddy ground around the grave. There were footprints there – bare prehensile feet with opposable digits, more like hands.

And she sensed the watching forest too – as if the place was holding its breath.

They took the path Bethan indicated. It soon reached another glade where a small empty spaceship was parked. While the Doctor sat out on the steps, Susan helped Bethan inside. 'I should never have come,' she said. 'Can't you hear it? The forest? Doesn't it ever shut up?'

Susan couldn't hear anything. She thought Bethan was feverish, and refusing to take off her environment suit didn't help. It filtered the air, Bethan said, and catered for all bodily functions. She could survive in it for eight days at least. It also made lying down impossible. Instead, she sat on a chair and fell asleep almost immediately.

The ship was spartan and functional – like most spaceships Susan had seen. Outside, the Doctor was in an unusually good mood. He had removed his jacket and undone the bow of his cravat. 'Remarkable. It's a powerhouse, this place. Most invigorating.' In his hand, the pods had split open and the newly germinating seeds had released little roots. Susan grimaced as they wriggled like hungry worms, curling around his fingers.

It was getting dark, so she went back in. It was cooler, less clammy, inside. She found some dry biscuits in a tin and sat on the bed, trying not to drop crumbs, waiting for Grandfather.

She woke with a start. Green daylight filtered in through the door. She heard a movement and guessed that Bethan had woken too. But Bethan was gone. Her environment suit lay empty and a bit ripe by the door. The floor of the cabin and chair where she had slept were strewn with scarlet petals.

Something stirred again. In a shadowy corner, a pair of round, honey-brown eyes blinked at Susan. Yet there was no shape behind them. Just shadow. She didn't scream; that would have been wrong. She wanted to reach out and touch their owner, but when she leaned forward, the eyes closed and were gone.

Vines that had either pulled themselves across the doorway or grown overnight, parted to let something, a half-traced shape or trick of the morning light, push a way out. Susan followed, but no one was outside. No Bethan, no Doctor.

She called for her Grandfather, but the forest swallowed her shout. It went nowhere.

Then the noise started – a rustling in the trees, growing into a surging turmoil as branches swung to and fro in a fury. It overwhelmed her, swamped her head. She pulled back inside the ship. On a rack was another spacesuit. She scrambled to put it on. It was voluminous, warm and best of all, once she clamped the helmet on, it shut out the forest.

Then she stepped back outside. She trudged along the path, heading towards the clearing by the refugee ship and almost tripped over Bethan Finch. The woman, dressed in loose fatigues, was crouching over Tino's grave. She was digging with her hands, sending the dark soil flying.

Susan tried to drag Bethan away, but an angry snarl was the only response. Already the grey casing of her partner's spacesuit was emerging. Overhead, the trees went quiet. Through her visor, Susan saw many pairs of honey-coloured eyes gazing down. Then Bethan gave a cry of despair. She had unearthed the chrome neck of Tino's suit – it was empty.

Above them, the trees erupted in a new frenzy. Susan glimpsed shapes capering along the branches. Foliage and figures in one.

Bethan swore loudly as a tall man stepped out of the undergrowth. He was dark-haired with a scrubby beard. 'Tino Driscoll, that isn't funny!' yelled Bethan. 'Where the heck have you been? I thought you were dead!'

He grinned. 'What's the fuss? I haven't been far.' He kicked at the burial mound with his bare feet. 'I've got a new life now. This old one's dead and buried.'

'You buried it?' Bethan said as he lifted her in a bear hug. 'You idiot!' she complained and hugged him back.

The shapes in the trees whooped. Branches swayed, raining flowers and leaves down in celebration.

But Susan stood helplessly alone. Where was her Grandfather?

The creatures above fell silent. They had gathered like a troop of ghosts, on top of the overgrown refugee ship and were watching her. She turned to run away as best she could, but she tripped and tumbled headlong to the mossy forest floor. Through her smudged helmet, she saw a familiar pair of brown patent leather shoes, neatly placed at the foot of a tree.

The Doctor sat on a branch above her, ten feet up, dangling his shoeless feet over the edge. He was gazing down with a bemused look of contentment.

Around him, the foliage twitched and rustled – almost danced. Half-visible fingers reached down towards Susan. She struggled as they lifted her, suit and all, up into the tree and set her beside her Grandfather.

'Susan, really. Take that ridiculous contraption off.'

'No,' she said. 'I won't. It's not safe.'

'Oh, for goodness' sake, child! What are you scared of?' He leaned across, undid the seals on her helmet and lifted it off. 'Now look around you.'

Susan gripped his hand. Voices called from the leaves, chuckling and cooing what almost sounded like words. The forest spoke through them. She saw the half-human faces of the tree-people with their beautiful guileless eyes.

'Years ago,' the Doctor said, 'their forebears arrived here in that ramshackle transporter ship. They were fleeing from a war. And they probably planned cities and farms – a proper colony, but they soon learned better. It's this planet. It's in a state of perfectly tuned balance. Every aspect of it is so completely at one with the rest, that it's hard to tell one entity from another. Fascinating, absolutely fascinating. The people, the trees. Perfect harmony and perfect camouflage too.'

Susan thought for a moment. 'I know they've adapted to a new environment, Grandfather, because that's what people and life forms do… but surely this is devolution? And so fast! They're changing backwards!'

'Really, Susan?' He looked surprised. 'I'd have said they were much better off, wouldn't you, hmm? In many ways, I could be quite envious.'

Susan sensed the warm air, damp and rich, pressing in around her. The branches seemed to reach down to enfold her. How could she not have noticed? The spacesuit was stifling her. She tried to pull it off and nearly fell.

Gentle hands pulled her back up to her perch. This was where she belonged, where she had always longed to belong. She was enticed and entranced. How she and Grandfather had arrived here and their means of departure, were becoming irrelevant – slipping away. Was this journey's end at last?

They sat dreamlike for hours or so it seemed. Down below, the other arboreal denizens of the forest laid flowers on the line of overgrown graves and sat around watching the flickering holographic images of their ancestors.

'Delightful,' said the Doctor at last. He swung out his legs and noticed that one of his socks had a hole in its heel. So much for perfection. 'Down, please,' he said and the hands lowered them to the forest floor.

Susan knew that he would soon be bored. She took his arm and they walked back along the line of tussocks. She wanted to say goodbye to the tree creatures, but they seemed to have lost interest and had wandered away. Finally she and the Doctor strolled through the forest towards the tree-stump-shaped ship that she remembered as their real home.

'But what about the developers, Grandfather? If they arrive, they'll destroy this place.'

The Doctor nodded. 'Perhaps. Or perhaps this world has its own ways to survive.' And he fumbled through the mossy bark for the TARDIS keyhole.

Bethan Finch, former Project Co-ordinator, struggled to remember how she used to send a planetary report. She had tapped the words in on the screen and, at the third attempt managed to send the report off to New Projects Hub at Earth Central 483 light years away.

The words were DON'T BOTHER.

Then she took Tino's hand and they ran out into the forest to play.

ELEVEN

EVOLUTION

'You have a primary and secondary reproductive cycle.
It is an inefficient system, you should change it.'
Commander Linx, *The Time Warrior* (1973–1974)

We first met the potato-headed Sontarans in *The Time Warrior*, when Commander Linx crash lands on Earth in the thirteenth century and threatens to change history by giving people guns and robot soldiers. *The Time Warrior* also introduces a new companion – Sarah Jane Smith – who, at the end of the story, sees Linx killed in an explosion.

As a result, Sarah is amazed to see Linx alive and well several thousand years in the future in *The Sontaran Experiment* (1975). But this isn't Linx: it's another Sontaran who just happens to look very like him. Later in the story we glimpse a third Sontaran and he looks just the same, too.

Asked in *The Sontaran Strategem* (2008) how Sontarans tell each other apart, one replies tersely, 'We say the same of humans.' But there's another explanation for why so many Sontarans look alike. 'They're a cloned species,' explains the Fourth Doctor in *The Invasion of Time* (1978). 'They can multiply at the rate of a million every four minutes.'

Cloning is a way of reproducing living organisms, resulting in copies that are genetically identical. We'll discuss exactly what 'genetically identical' means shortly, but the word clone comes from the ancient Greek for 'twig'. It's been known for thousands of years that it's possible to take a twig or other cutting from a healthy plant and from it grow another, almost identical plant. That's useful because if we find a plant that produces food or flowers we like, we can make lots of copies of that plant and grow more of the things we want or need.

Fittingly for the potato-like Sontarans, the potato is an easy plant to clone. Take a potato and locate the small 'eyes' of new growth on it – a largish potato will have seven to 10 eyes. Cut the potato into rough cubes of 2.5 centimetres (or 1 inch) each, with one eye per cube. Leave the cubes to dry overnight – called 'chitting', which encourages growth. Then lay your cubes out on well-drained soil, some 50 centimetres (20 inches) apart, pressing each cube into the soil with the eye facing upward. Cover the cube in 15 centimetres (6 inches) of mulch and water until evenly moist. Keep the mulch moist over the coming 16 to 20 weeks as the potatoes grow.

Each cube should produce its own potato plant, and each plant ought to produce at least five potatoes. So if you begin with a potato with seven eyes, you could expect to harvest 35 potatoes. If you then cloned each of those 35 potatoes, you'd see a harvest of 1,225 potatoes – the cloned 'grandchildren' of the original.

It's not quite the astonishing rate of reproduction that the Sontarans manage, but it means we can produce large quantities of potatoes quickly, easily and cheaply. Potatoes are also tasty and can be cooked in many different ways, so we can see why they became a staple food of the fast-growing population of Europe in the eighteenth and nineteenth centuries.

But in the 1840s this essential food crop was struck by a micro-scopic organism called *Phytophthora infestans* – literally 'plant-ruining destruction' – more commonly known as 'late blight'. Potatoes infected with blight quickly rotted away to foul-smelling mush and couldn't be eaten (or cloned). Blight infection spread rapidly, the potatoes people depended on for food were lost, and there were terrible famines in Ireland, Scotland and other European countries. In Ireland alone, a million people died and another million fled the country – in total about a quarter of the whole population. It has been argued that this huge human tragedy permanently altered the county's politics and culture: a microscopic organism changed the history of an entire nation.

Why were potatoes so vulnerable to blight? In fact, it turns out that cloned plants – and animals – are more vulnerable to disease and pests. It took some years for scientists to work out why, but perhaps the most important single step in getting to the answer was made at about the same time as the potato blight was causing such devastation.

'It is the right of every creature across the universe to survive, multiply and perpetuate its species. How else does the predator exist? We are all predators, Doctor. We kill, we devour, to live. Survival is all, you agree?'

'Oh yes, I do, I do. And on your argument I have a perfect right to dispose of you.'

'Of course. The law is survival of the fittest.'

The Nucleus and the Fourth Doctor, *The Invisible Enemy* (1977)

In 1838, the English naturalist Charles Darwin happened to read *An Essay on the Principle of Population* (1798), a book by the economist Robert Malthus, who warned that, without something to stop it, the number of people alive doubled every twenty-five years, and that meant there kept being catastrophes when there wasn't enough food for everyone. Darwin realised that if the same principle applied to animals and there were often times when there wasn't enough food, there would be a constant competition going on between the animals. Having even a small advantage could make a difference between life and death.

Now, imagine a clone race such as the Sontarans facing that kind of shortage. The Sontarans are all identical, so they all stand an equal chance of getting their three-fingered hands on the small amount of food. Being Sontarans, there might be a big fight between them with plenty of explosions, but it would basically be a fair contest.

That's not what happens with animals and plants that aren't clones. Imagine a group of human beings in the same situation, fighting over food. The humans are a varied group: some old and some young; some male and some female; some tall and some short; some healthy and some not. We can see how some of these humans would have an advantage over the others: we'd expect the young and healthy ones to grab the food.

But another important factor is where the contest takes place. If the food is somewhere up high, tall people will have an advantage, while if it's somewhere down low, they won't. The phrase 'survival of the fittest' is often used to mean that the strong survive, but really it's about who happens to be best suited to the circumstances in that particular time and place.

Darwin realised what it would mean if this sort of contest happened reasonably often. While the losers of the contest would have a higher chance of dying before they had children, the winners would be more likely to live on. They would have children, who would inherit a mix of the characteristics from their parents. If the food is high up, being tall provides a survival advantage so the taller people are more likely to survive and pass on that characteristic of tallness to their children.

But these shortages are periodic. In the next contest, if the food was still high up then the tallest of those children would have the advantage – and they would be the ones to survive and have children of their own. With each generation, if height provides a key advantage in surviving and reproducing then there would be a selection bias for being tall.

In fact, the same forces are driving all living organisms: affecting not only the people doing the eating but the living things they're eating, too. That has a dramatic impact on the way subsequent generations develop. We'll use an imaginary thought experiment to explain the idea.

Imagine a whole lot of apple trees growing in the wild. The apples contain seeds to grow the next generation of apple trees. But people also like to eat the apples, and if all a tree's apples are eaten it won't produce new trees. (Actually, that's not what happens in reality – which we'll come back to in a moment.)

A tree that produces apples higher up in its branches would have an advantage over apple trees around it as people would pick more of the apples they could reach – that is, the ones from trees where the apples weren't so high. The fruits of the trees with apples higher up in their branches would be more likely to survive – and they'd pass on to the next generation of apple trees the characteristic of producing apples high up in their branches.

If there weren't enough apples for all the people, we'd see two things happen over time. First, trees with apples low in their branches would be less likely to produce offspring, so we would expect there to be more trees that grew apples higher up in their branches. Secondly, people who couldn't reach the branches of the apple trees would be less likely to produce offspring. Over time, the average height of people taking part would be taller, and only the tallest of *them* would have the advantage, and be the ones more likely to survive and have children. Likewise, of the surviving apple trees with apples high up in their branches, only the ones with the apples most high up would produce more apple trees. And so on: with each generation, it would be the tallest people and the trees with apples in their highest branches that survived. Over many generations, there would be a gradual tendency towards taller humans and taller trees. It would be like an 'arms race', both sides unwittingly pushing the other to get taller.

Of course, this is just a simplified example, and there are many other factors to consider – which is why people and apple trees haven't got infinitely taller over the years. In real life, an apple tree doesn't die if we eat its apples. In fact, apple trees might even have an advantage if their apples get eaten. While we can digest the soft fruit of the apple, the small, hard seeds pass through our bodies and emerge in our faeces. It takes about four hours for food to pass through our bodies, so it would be likely that by the time the seeds emerged, the person would have moved some distance from the apple tree. That means an apple tree whose apples are eaten can disperse seeds over a wide area – and the faeces provides those seeds with fertiliser, too, giving them another head start in life. Over many generations, there would be a general tendency for apple trees to produce tastier apples, because they're the ones more likely to get eaten and so have that advantage.

We can see examples of how particular advantages have, over millions of years, shaped all the species on our planet in all manner of different ways. Giraffes have especially long necks to reach the food in the branches of especially tall trees. The cheetah is the fastest animal on land, able to run at up to 120 kilometres (75 miles) per hour in short bursts – and that speed has developed because it eats antelope and hares, which can run quickly, too.

Darwin didn't discover evolution – which is the name we give to descent with modification over successive generations. It was already well known that people could selectively breed plants and animals for particular, favoured traits. For example, a farmer with lots of cows might allow only those that produced the most milk to have children. Over many generations, this would produce cows with much higher yields of milk. It's thought that the domestication of many animals and plants by early humans was done in this manner – though it's not known if it was done intentionally.

Instead, Darwin's great revelation was to understand that selection happened naturally, too. Contests for survival meant that over many generations and millions of years, life develops to better match its environment. Apple trees, cheetahs and people don't choose which variations give them an advantage, it's just that those with an advantage – whatever that advantage might be in a given situation – are more likely to survive and have children. Darwin called this mechanism of evolution 'natural selection'.

He didn't realise it, but this mechanism was later able to explain why cloned potatoes are so vulnerable to blight. We saw that a single potato could produce 1,225 cloned potatoes in just two generations but that those potatoes would all be 'genetically identical' (a term we'll explain in a moment). Under favourable conditions, this gives our clone potatoes a huge advantage as they don't need to reproduce with another potato to produce offspring. But if there's a parasite, organism, predator or unfavourable change in the environment that is effective at killing potatoes, the whole population is equally susceptible. A blight organism which has evolved to be good at attacking the original plant will be just as good at attacking all the cloned plants, too. The entire crop would have no defence and so would rapidly be consumed by the blight. In fact, this can happen with crops that aren't cloned but have little variation.

But now imagine 1,225 potatoes that are all varied in some way. Some potatoes might have particular traits or genes – a term we'll discuss shortly – that are better at resisting blight, and that would make them more likely to survive and pass on that resistance to the next generation of potatoes. Variation makes them harder to kill off.

That's all very well for potatoes, but we now know that this survival-through-variation is what happens with fast-evolving human diseases, too. It's why you can catch influenza – the flu virus – every year, even if you were vaccinated the year before. Influenza evolves very rapidly and a flu jab that stops one kind of influenza won't necessarily stop the new kind that comes round the next year. Doctors are concerned that many other serious diseases – such as tuberculosis – are also evolving in such a way that the medicines we currently use to treat them will one day no longer work against them.

'I thought this far in the future they'd have cured everything.'

'The human race moves on but so do the viruses. It's an ongoing war.'

$$\partial^3 \sum x^2$$

Rose Tyler and the Tenth Doctor, *New Earth* (2006)

Evolution doesn't just show us how plants, animals and diseases are in competition with one another. It also reveals how we are related.

In *Listen* (2014), Clara and the Doctor meet Colonel Orson Pink, a man from about a hundred years in Clara's future. Clara is struck by how much Orson looks like a man she knows in her own time – Danny Pink. Then she discovers that Orson owns a plastic toy soldier, which he says is a 'family heirloom'. The toy is broken – the soldier isn't carrying a gun – which makes it distinctive. Clara recognises it as the same toy she once gave to Danny.

So, Danny and Orson share three things: the same looks, the same surname and the same toy soldier. The implication is that all three things have been inherited, meaning Orson is related to Danny.

Inheritance explains why people in families look similar. All living organisms (and many viruses) have a sort of instruction manual embedded into each of their cells, a coiling molecule called deoxyribonucleic acid, or DNA. These instructions aren't written in English. Instead, DNA is made up of a long sequence of four particular molecules – guanine, adenine, thymine and cytosine. We might think of the molecules as letters in an alphabet – G, A, T and C – which can spell out words.

Just as we can use the four letters E, I, L and V to spell out English words with different meanings – Evil, Live, Veil, Vile – the particular sequence of G, A, T and C dictates the different ways cells will develop and function. Although there are only four letters in this language of DNA, those letters can be used any number of times. Most cells in human beings contain DNA with sequences of 6 billion letters – about 10,000 times as many letters as appear in this book! That's a lot of information, just right for making something as complicated as you or me.

We inherit the DNA in our cells from our parents – half from each. We can see how brothers and sisters have been 'built' from similar sets of instructions because they often look very similar.

In clones and identical twins, those instructions are exactly the same. Stretches of DNA that provide information for particular functions – such as making eyes or ears – are called 'genes', so scientists call twins (and clones) with exactly the same DNA 'genetically identical'. However, twins can often behave very differently from one another.

Our genes don't fully determine the way our lives turn out – other factors are important.

The Tenth Doctor's companion Martha Jones looks very like her cousin, Adeola (seen in *Army of Ghosts* (2006)) – because both characters were played by actress Freema Agyeman. In fact, cousins can look similar to each other because they inherit half their DNA from the same source – that is, cousins don't share the same parents but they share one set of grandparents. Second cousins (that is, the cousins of your cousins) are less likely to look like you because you inherit much less of your DNA from the same source as they do – from a shared set of *great*-grandparents. The less DNA we share with someone, the further back our most recent common ancestor must have lived. It has been estimated that the most recent common ancestor of all human beings alive today may have lived as recently as between 2,000 and 4,000 years ago – not the first ever human, but the most recent individual who would appear on the family tree of everyone. But we don't just share DNA with human beings. As we said before, DNA is found in the cells of all living organisms and many viruses.

Darwin didn't know about DNA; the structure of it wasn't discovered until 1953, seventy years after his death. Yet he realised that his theory of evolution by natural selection explained the great diversity of life on the planet. When he published his theory in 1859, he called it *On the Origin of Species* – species being the basic units of biological classification, given in a two-part Latin name such as *'Homo sapiens'* for you and me.

Darwin argued – and DNA supports the theory – that all species on Earth are part of one huge family. It has been estimated that humans could share as much as ninety-eight per cent of our DNA with chimpanzees, and it's thought we shared a common ancestor with them some 6 million years ago. By using fossil evidence, we can estimate the rate at which genes have evolved over time – creating a 'molecular clock' with which we can deduce when different species diverged from one another. It's estimated that we shared a common ancestor with cheetahs – and other types of cat – some 85 million years ago, and with plants such as the apple tree and potato at some point in the Mesoproterozoic Era, some 1 billion to 1.6 billion years ago.

Darwin also argued that since we're so closely related to other apes we might learn much about ourselves from ape behaviour. In fact, studying apes has shed light on how evolution might develop behaviour as well as physical characteristics. We can see how working together as a group, agreeing systems of leadership and even friendship and kindness might have given our ancestors an advantage in the contest to survive. It's even been argued that heroism and self-sacrifice are evolutionary traits – by dying to save others, an individual can ensure the survival of their family or kinship group if not themselves. The more we've studied apes and their closeness to human beings, their ability to think rationally and with self-awareness, even to use sign language, the more there have been calls to grant legal protections to them. The Ninth Doctor clearly doesn't think we've evolved all that far from our cousins.

'Listen, if I did forget some kid called Mickey—'

'He's not a kid!'

'— it's because I'm busy trying to save the life of every stupid ape blundering about on top of this planet, all right?

The Ninth Doctor and Rose Tyler, Rose (2005)

Darwin's discovery had an extraordinary impact. In scientific terms, it led to whole new areas of scientific research, and further discoveries such as the structure of DNA and why cloned potatoes are vulnerable to blight. But it affected more than science. The *Doctor Who* story *Ghost Light* (1989) captures something of this. It is set in 1883, the year after Darwin's death, but his theory is cited in arguments about religion, class, politics and race.

The theory of evolution changed the world. After Darwin, economists argued that, just as competition in the natural world causes each new generation to be better adapted to its environment, competition was good for business, and those businesses that survived would evolve to better fit their markets. Today, some economists argue that if organisations such as schools and hospitals have to compete to achieve the best results, they can improve the services that they offer to the public.

People also worried how the human race might evolve in future, and how they might help to ensure that we evolved in the right direction – whatever that might be. Some even suggested that only those people with traits considered to be desirable should be allowed to have children – an idea called eugenics. Many apparently respectable people – including H.G. Wells and Winston Churchill – spoke in support of eugenics in the early twentieth century, and eugenics programmes of different kinds operated in many countries. However, the terrible reality of what these ideas could mean in practice was shown during the Second World War, when the Nazis systematically murdered millions of Jews and other people they considered to have undesirable traits.

After the Second World War, international laws were brought in to prevent such abuses happening again – but trying to influence human reproduction is something that still goes on today. Forced sterilisation – a medical process that prevents people from having children – on a widespread or systematic basis has been recognised as a Crime against Humanity with the jurisdiction of the International Criminal Court, but it still occurs. People have been sterilised because they have certain diseases, or represent 'undesirable' racial, sexual or social groups. In some countries, criminals have been sterilised, as if criminality were somehow an inherited trait.

But surely this is missing the point of Darwin's discovery. Apple trees and cheetahs didn't consciously select the traits that gave them an advantage. We don't know what threats or pressures we'll face in future contests, so the traits we might think are desirable now won't necessarily help our species survive – as we saw with the tasty cloned potatoes that were destroyed by blight.

Even so, natural selection can't help with big, fast changes such as pandemics of disease or catastrophes. In Chapter 5, we talked about the meteor collision that is thought to have wiped out the dinosaurs.

Except that *some* dinosaurs survived. Until the collision, it was an advantage to be a large, powerful dinosaur; afterwards, it's thought that dust and debris in Earth's atmosphere blocked the warmth of the Sun and created an 'impact winter'. In these changed conditions, large, powerful dinosaurs were at a disadvantage. Being small meant you could keep warm more easily and required less of the scarce food; being able to fly meant you cover more distance in looking for that food. So small, flying dinosaurs survived in these new conditions, and their descendants are still alive on Earth today – we call them birds.

Perhaps something like that happens in the *Doctor Who* story *New Earth* (2006). In the year 5,000,000,023, Cassandra insists that she is the last human in existence. However, she has a very narrow sense of what 'human' means. Rose points out that there are plenty of others living on the planet New Earth, but Cassandra dismisses them out of hand.

'There's millions of humans out there. Millions of them.'

'Mutant stock.'

'They evolved, Cassandra. They just evolved, like they should. You stayed still. You got yourself all pickled and preserved, and what good did it do you?'

Rose Tyler and Cassandra, *New Earth* (2006)

At the end of the story, Cassandra dies, but humanity lives on – *because* it has evolved. In fact, many of *Doctor Who*'s most effective monsters are monstrous because they've tried to control evolution...

THE PIPER

MARK MORRIS

There was no doubt about it. Barry Jenkins was lost.

As water dripped from the roof of the arched tunnel, and effluent flowed along the narrow central channel beside the concrete walkway on which he was standing, he consulted his map again. It was as he had thought. That wall in front of him simply shouldn't exist. Maybe the lads in the maintenance depot were playing a joke on him because he was new? Maybe this was an initiation test to see if he could find his way through the maze of Central London's sewer system with a dud map?

Sighing, he trudged forward. He guessed he would just have to take the detour to the right and see where it led. Reaching the opening, he peered into it suspiciously. It was dark and narrow. He could only hope that ahead of him was a left turn, which at least would mean he'd again be going in roughly the right direction. Light from the lamp on his hard hat played along the wet wall, which, by rights, shouldn't be here. He tapped the wall, scowling.

Something tapped back.

He recoiled, then grinned. It must have been an echo. The lads at the depot would be hooting with laughter if they could see how jumpy he was. Setting his face determinedly, he marched into the narrow passage. Sure enough, there was a blacker opening ahead on his left. *Now* he was getting somewhere.

Light slithered into the opening as he approached it. Aside from the drip of water all was silent. Barry peered into the blackness, craning forward so that the light could stretch as far as possible. And then he jumped as he heard scurrying sounds from the tunnel ahead.

Although he couldn't see anything, he knew what was causing the sounds. Rats. They didn't generally bother him – they tended to flee from humans – but on this occasion he felt uneasy. He wasn't sure why at first, and then he realised. It was because the sounds were not growing fainter, but *louder*.

The rats were moving *towards* him!

He waited, unsure what to do. Were the rats *really* heading in his direction or were the weird acoustics in the tunnel only making it seem that way? The light from his lamp probed the shadows ahead…

And then he saw them!

Red eyes. Glinting in the darkness. First one pair. Then another.

And then – he gasped – *dozens* of them!

Abruptly the scurrying sounds stopped. Barry stood motionless, hardly daring to breathe. The red, glittering eyes seemed to regard him with an almost inhuman intelligence. Cautiously he took a step backwards.

And with a hideous, screeching cry that echoed off the tunnel walls, the rats rushed towards him!

The tall, white-haired man in the purple smoking jacket strode through the hospital corridor like a visiting dignitary. In his wake hurried a short, pretty blonde girl with an exasperated expression on her face.

'Where's the fire, Doctor?' she gasped.

The white-haired man cast a puzzled glance over his shoulder. 'Fire?'

'What I mean is, can't you slow down? Why the big rush?'

The Doctor sighed. 'My dear Jo, you really must cultivate a sense of urgency. According to the Brigadier—'

'Pass please, sir.'

The order, cutting off the Doctor mid-flow, had been issued by an armed squaddie whose beret bore a circular badge identifying him as belonging to UNIT. His muscular form blocked the double doors that the Doctor had been approaching.

With a withering look the Doctor said, 'Don't be absurd, man. Surely you recognise me?'

Before the squaddie could reply, the blonde girl, Jo Grant, produced two UNIT passes.

'We're here to see the patient,' she said. 'Didn't the Brigadier tell you we were coming?'

'Captain Yates did, miss,' replied the squaddie. 'But the Brigadier gave orders not to allow anyone through without authorisation. No exceptions, he said.'

The Doctor harrumphed.

Once their passes had been verified, the Doctor and Jo passed through the double doors into an area that seemed a world away from the bustle of the rest of the hospital. The sense of hush was almost expectant. A bespectacled, harried-looking man in a white coat rose from a nearby desk and scurried forward, hand outstretched.

'Dr Raith,' he said. 'You must be the scientists from UNIT.'

The Doctor was already peering over Raith's shoulder. It was Jo who took his hand. 'I'm Josephine Grant. This is the Doctor.'

Instead of saying hello, the Doctor asked, 'Where's the patient?'

Responding to his authoritative tone, Raith turned smartly. 'This way.'

As they marched along the corridor, Jo fell into step beside him. 'What's wrong with the patient, exactly?'

Raith gave her an anxious look. 'It's probably best if you see for yourself.'

'He was a sewer worker, wasn't he? We heard he was attacked in the tunnels, that his injuries were... unusual.'

Raith laughed without humour. 'Unusual is putting it mildly. Here we are.'

The sign on the door read: ISOLATION – AUTHORISED PERSONNEL ONLY. The two UNIT soldiers standing sentinel checked their passes again, then Raith produced latex gloves and surgical masks in sealed plastic bags from the pockets of his white coat.

'If you could wear these? For your own protection.'

'I really don't think that's...' the Doctor began, then noticed Jo frowning at him. 'Oh, very well.'

When they were masked and gloved, Raith led them into the isolation chamber. A bed surrounded by white drapes dominated the featureless room. Aside from gentle bleeps and clicks from unseen machines beyond the drapes, all was quiet. Raith crossed the room and drew one of the drapes aside, ushering Jo and the Doctor forward. As soon as Jo set eyes on the patient she gasped.

'Good grief,' murmured the Doctor.

The young man was lying on a crisp white sheet, naked from the waist up. His stomach and chest were etched with a fine tracery of metallic circuitry, which appeared either to have embedded itself into his flesh or to be growing out of it. To Jo the circuitry resembled a tree, with branches fanning out like dark veins around the man's ribs, across and down his arms, and up his neck. Tiny white lights, set at points where the fibres split into smaller tributaries, winked and flashed, as though alive.

'What's happening to him?' Jo murmured.

The Doctor's face was grim. 'I'm very much afraid, Jo, that the poor chap is turning into a machine.'

Jo wrinkled her nose. 'Bit whiffy, isn't it?'

Their guide, a stocky Irishman called Joe McGowan, grinned. 'You get used to it after a while, miss. Give it five years and you'll not notice a thing.'

With McGowan and Jo were the Doctor, Brigadier Lethbridge-Stewart and three UNIT squaddies. The soldiers were armed with rifles, the Brigadier with his trusty service revolver, which he clutched in his leather-gloved hand. McGowan, the Doctor and Jo wore hard hats with lamps attached. The overlapping beams played across the curved, dripping walls of the sewer tunnels and gleamed on the water flowing along the central channel.

It was the Doctor who had insisted on retracing Barry Jenkins's steps and Jo who had insisted on accompanying him. The Brigadier had raised a token protest but knew that Jo had faced far greater perils in her travels with the Doctor. Most recently the two of them had returned from a planet full of man-eating plants, invisible aliens and Daleks! A London sewer tunnel was small potatoes by comparison.

McGowan, leading the way, suddenly halted. 'That's odd.'

The Doctor appeared at his shoulder. 'What is?'

'That wall.' McGowan pointed. 'It shouldn't be here.'

'Let me see.' The Doctor took the map, his eyes skimming across it. Half-turning to Jo and the Brigadier, he said, 'He's quite right, you know.'

'Renovations?' suggested the Brigadier. 'Channelling the flow, that sort of thing?'

McGowan gave him a pitying look. 'There speaks a man who knows nothing about what's under his own two feet.'

'I'll have you know—' began the Brigadier, but the Doctor waved him to silence.

'Shh.' He had moved across to the wall and was standing with his ear pressed against it.

'What is it?' hissed Jo.

The Doctor produced a stethoscope from a jacket pocket and used it to listen to different sections of the wall, umming and ahhing as he did so.

Finally, in a dry voice, the Brigadier said, 'In your own time, Doctor.'

The Doctor arched an eyebrow. Stuffing the stethoscope back into his pocket, he said, 'Do you know what this is?'

'Surprise us,' said Jo.

'It's a box.'

'A box?' repeated the Brigadier.

The Doctor nodded. 'A stone box. The question is – what's inside?'

The Brigadier stepped forward and rapped on the wall with the butt of his revolver. 'Could get a couple of my chaps to blow a hole in it for you.'

The Doctor winced. 'Or we could employ more subtle methods.' With a grin that simultaneously quadrupled his wrinkles and made him appear boyish, he produced a hammer and chisel so archaic they looked as though they could very well have once belonged to Mary Anning and began to tap the wall.

'Take a long time to—' the Brigadier began – and then the squealing started.

It came from the opening on their right, a shrill, terrifying cacophony, like a hundred panes of glass shattering at once. As the UNIT troops ran forward, the Doctor and the Brigadier whirled towards the sound, the Brigadier raising his revolver and pointing it into the tunnel.

McGowan clutched Jo's arms and looked at her wild-eyed. 'What in the Lord's name is that? It's like a million banshees all wailing at once.'

Jo was scared too, but McGowan's panic made her feel almost calm. 'It's animals,' she said. 'I think.'

'*Look!*' McGowan screamed.

Jo twisted her head. Through the crush of bodies in front of her, she glimpsed multiple red points of light swirling through the blackness towards them. She was baffled at first, and then, as the lights drew closer, she recognised what they were.

Red eyes. And now the light from the Doctor's lamp was picking out the first wave of the creatures surging towards them.

They *looked* like rats. Small, sleek, scampering on four legs, tails snaking behind them.

But these rats were not black or brown. They were not covered in fur.

They were silver. They gleamed.

They were robot rats! Made of metal!

The three UNIT troops began to blaze away, the din of their rifles deafening in the confined space. Bullets ricocheted off the rats, raising sparks. A few of the creatures were ripped apart by gunfire, but the majority kept coming – a squealing, scuttling wave of metal.

'Retreat!' roared the Brigadier, letting off more shots.

McGowan was already halfway up the tunnel, running as fast as he could. Jo, the Doctor and the Brigadier followed, the UNIT troops bringing up the rear.

Suddenly one of the soldiers screamed. Jo whirled, to see him go down, his body immediately engulfed by a twitching, writhing mass. The Brigadier sprang forward, but the Doctor shouted, 'No! Let me!'

Before the Brigadier could protest the Doctor pointed his sonic screwdriver. The sound that came from it was so piercing that Jo clapped her hands over her ears. Dimly she was aware of the Brigadier and the soldiers covering their ears too. The effect on the rats was spectacular.

They began to jerk and spin, to go haywire. A few sparked and became instantly motionless, but most, once they had recovered from their momentary disorientation, turned and fled back into the darkness from which they had come.

'Well done, Doctor!' yelled the Brigadier. 'Handy little device, that weapon of yours!'

The Doctor turned off his sonic screwdriver with a frown. Almost primly he said, 'The sonic screwdriver isn't a weapon, Brigadier. My intention was to confuse the creatures, not destroy them.'

'Even so,' the Brigadier said. 'Seems to have done the trick.'

As the two soldiers pulled their downed colleague back to his feet, the Doctor wandered across to pick up one of the inert rats. Giving it a cursory examination, he dropped it almost absentmindedly into the pocket of his purple jacket.

Gingerly rubbing one ear, the Brigadier asked, 'So what *were* those things, Doctor?'

'A deterrent,' the Doctor said, and peered thoughtfully back up the tunnel. 'Whatever's behind that wall doesn't seem terribly keen on house calls.'

Although the man in the isolation chamber did nothing but lie there, Dr Raith was terrified of him. He wished the fellow had not been brought to the hospital; that the responsibility for his care belonged to someone else. It was not that he was afraid the man might die. What *really* frightened him was not knowing what his patient would eventually become. That odd chap from UNIT had said Jenkins was turning into a machine – but how could that be? And yet the results of their various examinations seemed to corroborate the Doctor's diagnosis.

Raith was sitting at his desk, staring glumly at the man's X-ray results, when the peace of the Isolation Unit was shattered by several thumps and a crash. His head snapped up. He had no doubt the sounds were coming from the isolation chamber which housed their patient. He could only suppose the man had woken up and was now flailing about, distressed and confused. Wishing he were anywhere but here, he jumped up and ran towards the sounds. He arrived to find the two UNIT guards facing the door, training their rifles on it.

One of them turned to him nervously. 'He don't sound too happy in there, does he, Doc?'

Raith was about to reply when the door of the isolation chamber burst open.

For a moment nobody moved. Raith goggled at his patient in horror. In the thirty minutes since his last examination, the man's condition had worsened considerably. The complex network of circuitry now covered his entire upper body, including his face, which stared blankly out through eyes filmed over with a silvery sheen. Hesitantly Raith stepped forward.

'Mr Jenkins, why don't you...'

His voice tailed off. Jenkins' mouth had dropped open, as though on a hinge, and Raith could see something *moving* in there.

Suddenly a mass of silver worms, each about the size of a finger, poured from Jenkins's mouth. Moving with lightning speed, they flowed towards the two soldiers and began to slither up their bodies.

As the men screamed and dropped their rifles, Raith turned and fled. But he wasn't fast enough to outrun the worms.

Within seconds they were on him.

Although the Brigadier would never have admitted it aloud, he desperately needed the Doctor's advice. Something had gone badly awry at the hospital and the Brigadier had no idea how to deal with it. According to Sergeant Benton, the place was overrun with silver worms, which were infecting people, turning them into machines like that poor chap in the Isolation Unit. There was apparently no stopping the things. They were multiplying and spreading at an alarming rate. The Brigadier had ordered Benton to quarantine the hospital and seal every exit – but it was only a matter of time before the worms escaped into the wider world.

As he strode towards the UNIT laboratory, he heard the familiar trumpeting bellow of the Doctor's TARDIS.

'No!' he shouted, breaking into a run. 'Don't you dare, Doctor! I absolutely forbid it!'

But as he burst through the doors he saw the familiar blue box fading away. The Brigadier couldn't believe it. Where the blazes had the Doctor gone now?

Standing at the six-sided console the Doctor said, 'We've arrived, Jo.'

Jo looked dubious. 'But where? You know what the TARDIS is like. We might just as easily be in Timbuktu.'

The Doctor looked pained. 'The old girl homed in on energy signals emanating from the chamber. We're right on target.'

Jo raised her eyebrows. 'Well, there's only one way to find out, isn't there?'

They emerged from the TARDIS into a dank-smelling stone chamber strewn with debris. Jo switched on the torch she was holding and shone it around. The debris, which she had thought was rubble, was actually bits of machinery. There were cogs, circuit boards, engine parts and all manner of other paraphernalia.

'It's a scrapyard,' she said, torchlight playing over a nearby heap of metallic components, which gleamed silvery grey.

The Doctor was about to reply when, from behind the heap of components, they heard the scrape of movement.

They froze. Slowly the Doctor raised a warning hand, indicating that Jo should stay still. He edged towards the metal hummock and peered over the top. As he did so something rose up from behind it with a clicking and a whirring and a creak of metal.

It was a figure. Huge and dark and shadowy. The Doctor jumped back as Jo jerked the torch upwards.

Pinned by the bright beam of light the figure was revealed as a metal man, scorched and battle-scarred. It had an accordion-like control unit on its chest and strange jug-like handles projecting from the sides of its head. Its blank metal face comprised black circles for eyes and a slit for a mouth. Its left arm was a clockwork lash-up of cogs and levers. From the right side of its mangled chest spilled a mass of plastic tubing and exposed circuitry.

Jo blanched. 'Oh, heck.'

'A Cyberman,' breathed the Doctor

Jo's instinct was to turn and run back into the TARDIS, but she kept her torch beam trained on the huge creature. 'Where's it come from?'

'At a guess I'd say it's a casualty of their last invasion. It must have been injured and taken refuge in the sewers. It's been rebuilding itself ever since from whatever bits of machinery it can salvage and cannibalise.'

'Did it build the rats, too?'

The Doctor nodded. 'To bring it machine parts and spread the Cyber-infection. Even damaged, the Cybermen are single-minded, resourceful and highly dangerous.'

Since rising to its feet, the Cyberman had not moved. It seemed to be acclimatising itself. Suddenly it emitted a metallic rattle.

'What's it doing?' hissed Jo.

'Trying to speak. But its voice box must be damaged.' The Doctor raised his hands placatingly and flashed Jo a smile, though she could see he was worried. In a soothing voice he said, 'Don't worry, old chap, we won't hurt you.'

At once the Cyberman lunged forward, crashing through the heap of components. It raised its arms, metal hands grasping, and made a beeline for Jo. She stumbled back, torchlight jerking erratically over the creature's metallic surface. The Doctor rushed forward to try to stop it, but it swept him aside with ease.

Still tottering backwards, the heel of Jo's boot came down on a chunk of metal and she fell. Dropping the torch, she landed with enough impact to jolt the breath from her body. The Cyberman loomed over her, its fingers creaking open as it reached towards her face. Jo opened her mouth, trying to scream...

But then the Cyberman stopped moving.

For a moment it resembled a clockwork toy whose winder had run down. Jo blinked as a matrix of crackling blue electricity began to dance and spark around its head. Then came a muffled bang from inside its blank-faced helmet and black smoke began to pour from its slit of a mouth.

Like a downed statue, the huge figure toppled towards her. Jo thought she was about to be crushed, but then hands grabbed her and yanked her out from under the falling Cyberman. As it crashed to the floor, she sobbed with relief and clung to the Doctor.

'What... happened?' she gasped.

The Doctor indicated the metal rat he had taken from his pocket. It was crouched on the floor close by, its eyes blinking red.

'The Cyberman's brain was malfunctioning, which meant its defences were down. Before coming here, I modified this little fellow to transmit a signal to short out the Cyber implants in our friend's head.'

'You knew he'd be here?' said Jo, looking at the Cyberman.

'Educated guess,' the Doctor said. Producing his sonic screwdriver, he added almost sadly, 'Time to finish the job.'

He turned the screwdriver on and applied it to the edge of the Cyberman's faceplate. As the plate came loose and the Doctor prised it off, Jo caught a glimpse of what remained of the once-human face beneath. She turned away, feeling sick, and tried to concentrate on remaining as professional, and as scientifically detached, as the Doctor.

'What are you going to do?'

'That poor chap at the hospital was impregnated with living technology – Cyber technology. If I know the Cybermen, they'll be using him to create potential new recruits as we speak. But if I can transmit the right signal from our friend's brain I can not only lure all the Cyber rats back here, I can also draw out the Cyber technology from whoever it's infected and neutralise it.'

'Kind of like the Pied Piper and his pipe,' Jo said brightly.

The Doctor smiled. 'Kind of.'

Sergeant Benton knew the situation was hopeless, but there was no way he would ever give up – it simply wasn't in his nature. He would keep fighting until he could fight no longer – even if, in this instance, 'fighting' meant 'running away', or more specifically trying to keep one step ahead of the remorseless tide of silver worms, which were sweeping through the hospital, converting patients and medical staff alike into robotic zombies.

Together with a rag-tag group of survivors he had picked up en route – a Scottish porter called Don, a young woman called Mary who had been visiting her sister, a traumatised young boy who had seen both his parents engulfed by silver worms, and a dark-haired nurse called Holly who was still clutching the plastic bag of blood samples she had been transporting from one part of the hospital to another – Benton was fighting a desperate rearguard action. Evacuating and locking down the hospital, as per the Brigadier's orders, had proved an impossible task, such was the speed at which the worms had infiltrated the building's many floors and corridors. Even getting his own little group to safety had so far been beyond him. Each time they headed for an exit, they found their route blocked, either by yet another flowing wave of worms or by the lurching approach of converted humans, their skin glittering with circuitry.

In the past half-hour, Benton and the rest of his group had seen dozens of people converted. It was a horrific process, the worms flowing up and over the bodies of their victims like a slick of living metal, finding ingress through nostrils, mouths, ears, even the pores of the skin itself. The worms made no distinction between the young and the old, the healthy and the infirm. If it was living, breathing flesh it was all fair game to them.

It seemed that there was no way of stopping the worms' relentless progress, no way of stemming the flow. As far as conventional weaponry was concerned, it was the same old story. Bullets were useless against the worms, whereas opening fire on the converted humans was, of course, entirely out of the question. Puppets of an (he assumed) alien intelligence they may be, but they were still people, and therefore hopefully not yet irredeemable.

Benton's group were now on the hospital's fourth floor, having fled up a flight of stairs from the floor below with a horde of converted humans in hot pursuit. The sergeant was concerned not only by the fact that his party was being forced gradually upwards as each potential avenue of escape was denied them, but also by how much longer certain of them could keep going. Don the porter, who must have been nudging 60, was sweating and wheezing with exertion, and even Benton himself was hampered by having to carry the little boy, who was trembling like a frightened kitten, his face buried in the sergeant's chest.

'This way!' Benton shouted, leading the group at random along an unoccupied corridor. He rounded one corner, then another, alert for an exit that might, by some miracle, lead them down through an as-yet worm-free part of the hospital to safety.

His heart leaped with hope as the five of them rounded yet another corner and found themselves flanked by two double sets of lift doors. Just beyond the lifts was another door – this one glazed with reinforced glass, above which a sign read STAIRS.

Murmuring a silent prayer, Benton hurried across to the door and tugged it open. He listened for a moment. Silence.

'Is it safe?' asked the nurse, Holly, who was standing behind him, trying to peer over his shoulder.

Benton, the little boy still clinging to his chest, shrugged. 'I can't guarantee it, miss, but I think it's our best bet.'

They started down, Benton moving cautiously, the rest of the group trailing him like shadows. As they reached the door leading out on to Floor 3, he allowed himself to believe that maybe, just maybe, they might make it out in one piece, after all.

They were halfway down the next flight when Benton suddenly halted.

'What is it?' hissed Holly.

He put a finger to his lips. 'Listen.'

They all froze. From somewhere below them came a rustling sound, like the stealthy march of fire through dry grass.

'I think we should go back,' said Benton.

'What do you—' began the young woman, Mary. But then they all saw what was making the sound, and the words dried in her throat.

Worms. Thousands of them. They suddenly appeared at the bottom of the stairs that the group had been descending and began to flow towards them like rising floodwater.

'Back!' yelled Benton. 'Everybody back!'

But no sooner had the words left his mouth than the door to Floor 3 above them crashed open and more worms spilled through, accompanied by a lurching mob of converted humans.

Benton looked wildly up and down, but there was nowhere to go; they were trapped!

He clutched the little boy to him as Holly screamed and Mary whimpered and curled into a ball, her hands over her head. Benton closed his eyes, wondering what it would feel like to be converted, whether it would be painful.

He was doing his best to prepare himself for the experience when everything stopped.

For a moment he wondered whether this was part of the process, whether the conversion was already taking place, and that the first things to be subsumed were the subject's senses.

Certainly he could no longer hear anything. The metallic rustling of the worms had stopped, as had the lumbering advance of the converts.

Tentatively he opened an eye.

He was surprised to see that the carpet of worms that had been flowing up the stairs were now motionless, as were the mass of worms that had been descending towards them from above. And the converted humans now resembled deactivated robots. Their heads had drooped forward and their hands hung loose by their sides.

He waited, tense, expecting the worms to start moving again at any moment.

But when they did, it was in an unexpected direction. To Benton's astonishment, the worms suddenly turned in a rippling wave and began to *retreat*, to head back in the direction from which they had come. And what was even more astonishing was that those worms that were controlling the human converts began to follow the lead of the general mass, pouring from the mouths, noses, ears and even from underneath the fingernails of their victims, and joining the unexplained and seemingly miraculous exodus.

The convert that was closest to Benton, a bearded man in a blue hospital gown, dropped to his knees. Benton watched as the threads of alien circuitry retreated and eventually disappeared from his skin and the silvery sheen faded from his eyes.

The man blinked, coughed, took a deep breath, then fixed his bewildered gaze on Benton.

'What am I doing here?' he asked in a croaky voice. 'What's going on?'

Benton couldn't help but grin at him. 'Your guess is as good as mine, mate,' he said.

Twenty-four hours later, the mopping up operation was complete. UNIT troops had cleared the dead Cyberman and the inert Cyber rats from the sewers, and all those infected by Cyber worms in the hospital had made a full recovery.

When Jo walked into the UNIT laboratory, however, she found that another battle was raging. Good friends though they were, the Doctor and Brigadier were at loggerheads – and not for the first time.

'Research facility!' the Doctor roared. 'Are you insane, man?'

The Brigadier's response was equally acerbic. 'I assure you, Doctor, that all alien materials are handled with the utmost respect and delicacy. Furthermore, the security measures—'

'Security!' scoffed the Doctor. 'The Earth won't be secure until that technology has been utterly destroyed.'

'What's going on?' Jo interrupted.

The Doctor glared at her. 'This dunderheaded species of yours, Jo, appears intent on breaking open Pandora's Box.'

Jo raised her eyebrows at the Brigadier, who frowned.

'The Doctor is opposed to the government policy to transfer all recovered alien technology to a secure research facility, where it can be studied under laboratory conditions. Technology that could be of great benefit to mankind. For example, Dr Raith says we could use all these Cyber-doodads to help the sick and the dying...'

Jo had to admit it sounded reasonable. She turned to the Doctor. 'Perhaps he's right?'

'Of course he's not right!' snapped the Doctor. 'Mark my words, Brigadier, Cyber technology is a plague and one day it will infect you all.'

But it was clear the Brigadier refused to be swayed. The Doctor turned to Jo for moral support, but saw that she couldn't understand his anger either.

Grabbing his cloak he swept from the room. As he strode away his voice echoed back along the corridor.

'When it does, just don't expect me to be there to pick up the pieces.'

A door slammed. There was a moment's silence.

'He will be, though, won't he?' Jo said finally.

The Brigadier sighed. 'I hope so, Miss Grant. I truly do.'

TWELVE
MAN AND MACHINE

'It's an inhibitor. It's not activated. I need you to switch it on.'

'What does it inhibit?'

'Emotion. It deletes emotions.
Please. I don't want to feel like this.'

Danny Pink and Clara Oswald, *Death in Heaven* (2014)

We talked in Chapter 2 about the many problems space presents to the human body, such as weightlessness weakening our bones and tissues. That presents major challenges if we are to send people to live on the Moon or Mars, let alone further out into the universe. But in 1960 two scientists proposed a radical solution.

In an article published in *Astronautics* magazine, American neuro-scientist Manfred E. Clynes and psychiatrist Nathan S. Kline suggested that instead of going to all the trouble of building Earth-like environments in space for astronauts to live in, it was more logical to alter astronauts' bodies to suit the conditions of space. Just as, they said, 'in the past evolution brought about the altering of bodily functions to suit different environments,' (as we saw in Chapter 11), we might now make biomedical, physiological and electronic modifications to the human body. In effect, we could use science to evolve our bodies artificially.

This wasn't an entirely new concept. Science fiction writers had already explored the idea of mechanically adapting people to the conditions of space, such as American author Cordwainer Smith in his short story 'Scanners Live in Vain', first published in 1950. But these stories generally explored the disturbing psychological effects of such a transformation, whereas Clynes and Kline spoke about their proposed modifications as a kind of liberation. They argued that a person in space would no longer need to be 'a slave to the machine', having constantly to check and adjust systems to be sure of staying alive. Instead, an automatically 'self-regulating man-machine system' would mean the modified human was 'free to explore, to create, to think, and to feel' in space. Creating such a man-machine would, they enthused, 'not only mark a significant step forward in man's scientific progress, but may well provide a new and larger dimension for man's spirit as well'.

We can see the lasting influence of Clynes and Kline's article in the word they invented to describe their space-travelling man-machine. Since the 1940s, studies of control systems and effective action in animals and machines had been labelled 'cybernetics', from a Greek word for governor or pilot. Clynes and Kline called their man-machine a 'cybernetic organism' – or 'cyborg'.

It has been argued that cyborgs already existed in real life before we had a word for them. Some people say that a person driving a car (or another machine) can be a cyborg because the controls and responses become such second nature – an extension of the body – that in effect it becomes a single unit.

It's also been argued that the word cyborg wasn't widely used until it featured in a book by American journalist David Rorvik, *As Man Becomes Machine* (1971). Certainly, the term didn't appear in *Doctor Who* until *Terror of the Zygons* (1975). But by then, the makers of *Doctor Who* had already created one of the series' most successful monsters, a race of self-regulating man-machines called Cybermen – first seen in *The Tenth Planet* (1966).

In fact, there are two important differences between the Cybermen in *Doctor Who* and the man-machine cyborgs proposed by Clynes and Kline. Cyborgs were a solution to the problem of sending people into

The Doctor's scientific adviser

The creation of the Cybermen was the result of the production team on *Doctor Who* making a conscious effort to get their science right. In early 1966, the series had a new producer and a new script editor: Innes Lloyd and Gerry Davis. Both men wanted to make the series more directly relevant to its viewers.

They did this in a number of ways: they phased out stories set in the past (at least, those that didn't include monsters); they set several stories in the present day and near future; and they sought a professional scientist to act as an adviser on the programme – the only time that has ever happened on *Doctor Who*.

Davis met with four noted scientists from very different fields. Dr Alex Comfort was a physician and psychiatrist who had just published books on the biology of ageing (a subject we'll return to in Chapters 14 and 15). Eric Laithwaite was a professor of heavy electrical engineering. The astronomer and TV presenter Patrick Moore later appeared as himself briefly in the *Doctor Who* story *The Eleventh Hour* (2010). Lastly, Dr Christopher 'Kit' Pedler was a surgeon and pathologist whose chief interest was the retina in the eye. One thing united this diverse group of scientists: they were not merely expert in their particular areas but also good at communicating scientific ideas to the general public in an engaging way.

Of the four scientists, Pedler seemed the best fit for the needs of *Doctor Who*. When Davis asked him how the programme might work the Post Office Tower – which at the time was a newly completed landmark on the London skyline – into a story, Pedler suggested the idea that became *The War Machines* (1966), which we'll discuss more in Chapter 13. When Davis proposed a story about Earth turning out to have a twin planet (which we talked about in Chapter 1), Pedler – already interested in the field of cybernetics – conceived a story about the man-machines that would live there.

space, but space exploration was not the reason that people from the planet Mondas turned themselves into Cybermen. We're told in *The Tenth Planet* that they were getting weak, their life spans getting shorter. As a result, cybernetic scientists devised 'spare parts' to patch up the failing human bodies until they could be almost entirely replaced by machine components.

It's an important distinction because it's hard to imagine anyone volunteering to have machine parts inserted into their bodies so that they could go into space. We can understand it more if the machine parts are a short-term fix to save a sick person's life. In fact, that happens now: each year, some 40,000 patients in England are fitted with pacemakers. A pacemaker is an electrical device containing a battery and computer circuit that is implanted into the body to keep the heart beating regularly. It's one of a number of medical devices that can be fitted into the bodies of sick patients – for example, some kinds of hearing aid are fitted surgically. The devices don't always need to be electrical, either. Some people have excess fluid in their heads which puts pressure on the brain and can prove deadly. Cerebral shunts use simple valves to drain this fluid from the skull via plastic tubes. Artificial limbs might not be electrical, but they have become increasingly sophisticated in design.

These devices all help people who would otherwise suffer to live active, normal lives. But imagine a person who kept on being ill, and so needed to be fitted with ever more devices. On a world such as Mondas, where people were continually ill, there'd be good reasons for scientists to develop new and better devices to help them: artificial hearts instead of pacemakers; artificial hearing instead of hearing aids; artificial brains instead of cerebral shunts. But if you went to go so far as to replace the people's brains, would they be people any more?

In fact, the Cybermen don't go that far – they keep their human brains. In *The Tenth Planet*, they still have human hands, too. One Cyberman in that story denies that the conversion process has turned them into robots, but reveals that something fundamental has been lost:

'Our brains are just like yours except that certain weaknesses
have been removed ... You call them emotions.'
Cyberman Krail, *The Tenth Planet* (1966)

$\partial^3 \sum x^2$

Clynes and Kline argued in favour of modifying people not just to free them to explore space but so that they could feel it, too. However, they didn't really address the psychological impact of being converted into a man-machine. In *The Age of Steel* (2006), we discover that the Cybermen's emotions are blocked by an 'inhibitor chip' implanted into them. The Doctor switches off these chips by remote control, allowing the Cybermen to feel emotions again – and to understand what they have become. As a result their heads explode.

That seems key to the enduring success of the Cybermen as monsters: many stories include scenes of people being converted into Cybermen where it is a terrifying thing. It scared audiences in 1966 and continues to scare us today. In *Dark Water* and *Death in Heaven* (2014), Danny sees losing his emotions and becoming a Cyberman as a fate worse than death.

The Cybermen's lack of emotions is often used in *Doctor Who* to explain how they behave: cold and logical, they want to convert us to be like them because they think it's an improvement. But perhaps something else can explain the Cybermen's history of conquest and destruction. Note that the Cybermen in *The Tenth Planet* have individual names: we meet Gern, Jarl, Krail, Krang, Shav and Talon. In all other Cybermen stories, they are no longer individuals. Science can give us an insight into the consequences of removing a person's individuality.

'I did my duty for Queen and Country.
I did my duty for Queen and Country...'
The Cyberman formerly Yvonne Hartman, *Doomsday* (2006)

$\partial^3 \sum x^2$

In July 1963, American psychologist Stanley Milgram became interested in the argument made by Nazis who had been put on trial after the Second World War. Although they admitted committing terrible acts, these Nazis said that could not be held responsible because they'd been following orders. Was that a fair excuse? Milgram aimed to answer that question scientifically.

He devised an experiment involving three people: the person conducting the experiment and two volunteers, who were told they were helping a study of memory and learning. The experiment required one volunteer to be the 'teacher' and the other the 'learner' – and, to decide who would be which, the volunteers drew slips of paper. The volunteers were then put in separate rooms where they could hear but not see one another. The volunteer whose slip said 'teacher' was given a list of questions to ask the learner. If the learner got an answer wrong, they would receive an electric shock, administered by the teacher. With each wrong answer, the power of the electric shock would be increased.

Before asking the first question, the teacher was given an electric shock to understand what it felt like. Of course, because the roles of 'teacher' and 'learner' had been chosen randomly by choosing slips of paper, the teacher would know that they could very easily have been the learner and so suffered what happened next.

What the teacher didn't know was that *both* slips of paper had said 'teacher', and the person in the role of the learner was only pretending to be a volunteer. In fact, they were part of the experiment, too. When the learner – on purpose – answered a question wrongly, the teacher administered electric shocks, but that was also a trick. The learner just pretended to be in pain. After a series of 'shocks', the learner would start banging on the wall, begging the teacher to stop – but the person conducting the experiment would advise the teacher to go on. After more 'wrong' answers, the learner would become silent, as if the shocks had left them unconscious. But still the teacher would be told to administer more shocks.

The real purpose of the experiment was to see how much pain the teacher would be prepared to inflict on a total stranger just because they'd been told to do so by a figure of authority – the person running the experiment. The horrible result was that Milgram reported that in twenty-six of the forty times he ran the experiment (i.e. sixty-five per cent), teachers were prepared to inflict an electric shock after the learner had become silent. Many teachers questioned what they were doing or showed clear signs of distress – but they still obeyed.

Over the years, there have been a number of concerns about Milgram's experiment – questions about how he gathered data, doubts that his results can be applied to the behaviour of the Nazis in the Second World War, and the ethics of conducting such an experiment in the first place. But conducting the experiment again, and in different locations round the world, has produced broadly similar results. A range of other, subsequent experiments have built on Milgram's findings and given us a better understanding of a process called deindividuation.

When we are in groups, in the presence of authority figures or feel anonymous, our behaviour can become bolder, more impulsive and less likely to consider risks. It's been shown that making people wear a uniform – at school, in the police or the army – makes them feel less like distinct individuals, so they act more as a group. That can have positive results: it can make us work better together. But deindividuation can also be behind negative behaviour, too. It has been used to explain riots – when, because they're part of a crowd, people commit crimes and acts of violence they would never normally dream of. Sometimes those in riots dress alike, or share logos or symbols, even if they're not consciously wearing a uniform.

Technology can play a part in deindividuation, too. For example, people who are generally shy and polite can become more aggressive while driving a car – because being inside the car makes them feel safe, anonymous and strong. We can imagine how the same person might behave if they were turned into a Cyberman: they might be bolder and more aggressive not because of the loss of their emotions but because the metal suit makes them powerful and also look just like all the other Cybermen.

'Everyone shares the same information. A daily download published by Cybus Industries. You lot, you're obsessed. You'd do anything for the latest upgrade.'
The Tenth Doctor, *Rise of the Cybermen* (2006)

The twin planet concept of Mondas gave Kit Pedler and Gerry Davis a narrative excuse to explore a 'what if' scenario for human development. In *Rise of the Cybermen* (2006), the makers *of Doctor Who* tried to make the connection between the Cybermen and ourselves feel closer by presenting a different origin story for the Cybermen, this time on a parallel version of Earth. Here, it's not weakness and old age that make many people modify themselves; rather they are tricked into being upgraded by their love of mobile technology and new applications. John Lumic, the inventor of the Cybermen on this alternative Earth, says his previous 'inventions have advanced the whole planet', and calls the process of becoming a Cybermen 'the ultimate upgrade'. He almost makes it sound attractive.

We can also see deindividuation at work all around us today in the way people use mobile technology. With social media, we can share all kinds of information – news, entertainment, the details of our lives – but there's a tendency to share material we know our peer group will value or approve of. That reinforces the values of that group, and makes it even harder for members to share something different. As part of that group, and safely anonymous or at least physically remote from other people on the internet, we're more likely to be outraged if the group's values are challenged. That means we are more likely to respond with fury. Online, we might insult and threaten people in a way we would never do in person. There are even specific terms for this online behaviour, such as 'trolling' and 'flaming'.

We might illegally download music, films and TV programmes from the internet when we'd never break the law in the offline world. We can tell ourselves that 'everyone' is doing it, that our individual actions won't make any difference. But that's missing the point: we do it *because* we're acting as part of a group, and as a group activity – with many individuals all acting just as we are – this kind of online behaviour can sometimes wreck livelihoods and lives. When we feel safely anonymous in a large group of people who all seem to agree with us, it's easy to lose our fear of consequences.

> 'You have fear. We will eliminate fear from your brain.'
> The Cyber Controller, *The Tomb of the Cybermen* (1967)

In *The Tomb of the Cybermen* (1967), a man called Eric Klieg solves a series of logical puzzles to gain access to the honeycomb of 'tombs' where the last Cybermen are frozen. He tells the Doctor (who surreptitiously helps him with some of the puzzles when he gets them wrong) that 'everything yields to logic', and is certain that proving his intelligence to the Cybermen will convince them to ally themselves to him.

In Chapter 1, we cited the Doctor's claim that 'Logic ... merely enables one to be wrong with authority.' And Klieg has got it wrong here. The Cybermen set the logical puzzles so that only those with intelligence would be able to get through – just the right kind of specimens for being turned into Cybermen. It has all been a trap.

We'll talk more about the problems of logic in a moment, but it's interesting that this story takes place on the Cybermen's adopted home planet, Telos. 'Telos' is the Greek word for goal or purpose, and was used by the ancient Greek philosopher Aristotle in the fourth century BC to discuss his ideas about things having an ultimate purpose. For example, Aristotle claimed that the telos or intrinsic purpose of an acorn was to become an oak tree.

Teleological thinking has sometimes been applied to evolutionary biology, usually to argue against Darwin's theory of natural selection (which we discussed in Chapter 11). In a famous example, Darwin himself wrote in *On the Origin of Species* that it seems 'absurd in the highest possible degree' that the human eye, 'with all its inimitable contrivances for adjusting the focus to different distances, for admitting different amounts of light, and for the correction of spherical and chromatic aberration, could have been formed by natural selection'. Some have argued that the eye couldn't have evolved by chance, that there must have been some kind of plan or purpose from the start. That is a teleological argument.

Yet Darwin went on to refute that suggestion, explaining that the eye could have started in our distant ancestors as very imperfect and simple – such as a nerve rendered sensitive to light – that would have given that ancestor a slight advantage and so been passed on to its children. Over millions of years and many generations, slight improvements in the ability of this sensitive nerve would continue to offer advantage, so the eye could slowly develop into the form we know it today. In fact, fossil evidence shows us exactly this kind of development, and the presence of many different kinds of eyes across the animal kingdom makes it clear that vision can develop in lots of different ways.

So why would the writers of *The Tomb of the Cybermen* call the Cybermen's planet Telos? The word suggests that the Cybermen consider themselves to be humanity's ultimate form – what humans were always meant to be: evolution with purpose. From the Cybermen's point of view, if we could only get past our primitive, emotional objections and look at things logically, we would all agree with them.

That certainty is a chilling thought. Without fear, the Cybermen have no reason to doubt that they might be wrong. In fact, time after time in *Doctor Who* that's the Cybermen's downfall. Just as Klieg in *The Tomb of the Cybermen* makes assumptions about his own importance, the Cybermen's logic is clouded by their own sense of superiority. In *The Tenth Planet*, they assume they can save their planet by bringing it closer to Earth and draining energy – but, apparently because Mondas is weaker than Earth, it is the one that's destroyed. In *Silver Nemesis*

(1988), the Cybermen take charge of a special Time Lord weapon which they assume they'll be able to use to their advantage – but it has already been programmed to destroy their space fleet. In *The Time of the Doctor* (2013), the Doctor uses a logical line of argument to convince a wooden Cyberman to shoot itself. The Cybermen assume that they're the superior form of humanity, but humanity keeps on defeating them.

The Polish mathematician and biologist Jacob Bronowski argued in his influential BBC series on the history of science, *The Ascent of Man* (1973), that certainty is the opposite of scientific knowledge. Science, as we have seen, is a provisional series of statements based on evidence and testing, with tests that can be repeated. Those tests depend on doubt.

We can use machines to extend and enhance life. We can send machines into space and expand the reach of human consciousness and understanding. Technology allows us to share what we have learned much more quickly and easily. But our machines can also make us overly confident. It's not just that without fear we have no science. Worse, we become monsters.

But what of machines that are more than extensions of human consciousness – machines that can think for themselves?

THE GIRL WHO STOLE THE STARS

ANDREW CARTMEL

The sun came out from behind a dark bank of clouds and gleamed on the armoured black limousine as it cruised along the narrow streets of Canterbury towards the Westgate. The sleek modern steel-and-glass surfaces of the vehicle contrasted strangely with the ancient grey ragstone walls and drum towers of the squat medieval city gate. The limousine passed smoothly through it and on to the A290, the old Whitstable Road, climbing steadily northwards, uphill, towards the University of Kent.

The Doctor, Ace and Raine were following at a discreet distance in the pale blue VW Karmann Ghia they'd collected from the house in Allen Road that morning. The Doctor was a small man in a straw hat and neat, dark jacket with a paisley scarf at his throat. Ace and Raine were both young women, both dark haired and attractive, but within those parameters they could hardly have been more different – Ace tough and compact, Raine languid and elegant.

The Karmann Ghia followed the limousine through the stone gates, passing between the squat fortress towers and out into the sunlit road beyond. Ace was at the wheel; she offered a low, steady and highly critical commentary of the other drivers in the thickening traffic. They drove along the Whitstable Road and took a left turn onto University

Road, the gradient of the hill growing steeper as they approached the campus. The traffic had thinned now, but there were increasing crowds of people on foot, streaming past on either side, also heading towards the university. The limousine they'd been following was parked close to the square brown brick buildings of Darwin college. A large cordon of protesters were being forced steadily away from the car by a mixture of campus security officers and local police.

The protesters mostly appeared to be students, but there were people of every age in the group, including a number of small children and a baby in a papoose. Everyone, except the children, seemed to be holding placards. Three burly men in matching shiny grey suits, short cropped hair and sunglasses stepped out of the limousine, holding the door open for a much smaller, younger man with long fair hair tied back in a bun. He was dressed in jeans, a tweed jacket and sneakers. The three burly men were busily scanning the crowd, while apparently scratching their armpits.

'They've got guns in shoulder holsters,' said Ace.

'They're taking security very seriously,' said the Doctor.

'Who *is* that bloke?' Ace watched as the young man was quickly surrounded by the bodyguards and the small group began to press through the crowd, towards the college buildings.

'Raymond Luthier,' said the Doctor. 'An old student made good, come here to speak about his achievements.' He scanned the mass of protesters. 'Apparently not everyone is pleased about them.'

'He's made a fortune from his computer business,' said Raine. 'Like that Facebook chap.'

'Luthier has stirred vastly more controversy than any Facebook chap,' said the Doctor. He nodded at the crowd, holding placards which carried slogans such as *Canterbury Says NO to the Canterbury AI* and *AI = Against It!* and *If it's Artificial it's not Intelligence*. 'Of course, it's partly envy. Only a few short months ago he was in their midst. Just another undergraduate.'

'And now he's practically a billionaire,' said Raine.

'He does seem to be on his way to that dubious status.'

'Because he's invented artificial intelligence?' said Ace.

The Doctor frowned thoughtfully. 'Well, this so-called Canterbury AI which he's developed is something called a black box Artificial Intelligence.'

'That doesn't sound at all sinister,' said Raine, suddenly hugging her elbows close to her body as if she was cold, although it was a warm and sunny day. 'Not one little bit.'

'It simply means that no one knows how his software works. You put a question into it, and out comes an answer – invariably correct. But how it arrives at the answer is a mystery. It certainly displays all the qualities of intelligence, despite this obdurate opacity. In a sense it's a classic example of the Turing test.' The Doctor smiled and set off at a brisk pace, in the opposite direction to Raymond Luthier, his bodyguards, and the mass of protesters. Ace and Raine followed, glancing back the way they'd come in surprise.

'Aren't we listening to his talk, then?' said Ace.

'No. In fact, we are going to take advantage of the distraction caused by his visit to break into the university administration office and obtain certain useful information.'

'Couldn't we get this information from a computer?' said Ace.

'Unfortunately, not. It's extremely well protected. Using a firewall developed by a certain AI, presented to the university free of charge by a certain ex-student.'

'Nobody likes a creep,' said Ace.

'So instead we shall obtain the information by old-fashioned means.'

'Old ways are best,' said Raine.

The Doctor smiled. 'All we need is someone who can pick the locks on the doors and then open the no doubt equally well-locked filing cabinets.'

'It's nice to feel wanted,' said Raine.

The Doctor scrutinised the envelope on which he'd copied down the address which Raine had found – as predicted – in a locked filing cabinet. 'We should be there soon,' he said.

It had begun to rain and Ace switched the windshield wipers on, as they drove towards the little seaside village of Beltinge. By the time they arrived, the rain had stopped and the day was sunny once more. Everything had a freshly washed look – except for the rather dilapidated house that was their destination. It was a pretty enough little cottage, but neglect had given it grimy windows and an overgrown lawn. There were three bicycles lying on their sides in the long grass, rusting slowly, and a plastic crate full of empty beer bottles stood by the front steps, as though that was as far as someone had got with recycling them.

The Doctor knocked on the door and a young woman answered. 'Ms Gulpin?' said the Doctor. 'Ms Gina Gulpin?'

'Yes?' She peered at them warily from under a fringe of hair that had been dyed dead black. Her eyes were grey and she had an unhealthy indoor pallor, oddly offset by a sprinkling of freckles on her cheeks. She was wearing indigo leggings, a black miniskirt and a navy blue sweatshirt with the words *Rocketpunk Manifesto* in large white letters. Long silver shapes dangled from each of her earlobes.

The Doctor smiled his most ingratiating smile. 'We want to ask you about Raymond Luthier.'

The look of wariness vanished, to be replaced by one of frank disgust. 'That rat,' she said, and turned away from the door, leaving it wide open for them to follow.

'We used to be friends, can you believe that?' said Gina Gulpin.

The four of them were sitting in the chaotic lounge which ran the length of the back of the house. A series of windows in the rear wall overlooked a small orchard of pear trees. On the outside sill of the central window stood a decorated ceramic plant pot, devoid of plants and soil but brimming with rainwater. The room was crowded with furniture – two sofas and five armchairs, all mismatched, as well as a long wooden table with a line of computers on it. The walls were decorated with posters of lurid pulp science fiction magazine covers from the 1930s and 1940s – bulbous rocket ships, bug-eyed monsters, women in pointy metal bras. There were fast-food takeaway cartons perched on every surface, some of them only recently opened judging by the intense tang of curry hanging in the air. ('Jaffrani Hyderabadi Biryani,' said the Doctor, sniffing with what might have been approval.) Only the computers looked clean and well maintained.

'We were supposed to work on our first year project together,' said Gina. 'But then he started getting all Secret Squirrel about things. Wouldn't help me with my work. Wouldn't tell me what *he* was working on. Next thing I knew he was knee-deep in venture capitalists and launching this AI thing.'

'You didn't want to go to the university today and hear his talk?' asked Raine.

'I'm well out of there. I was compelled to stay away by a complete lack of desire to see his smug, smiling face.'

'That and the restraining order,' said the Doctor.

Gina Gulpin glanced at him. 'All right, yeah. You have no concept of how frustrating it was. He was clever, but not *that* clever. But suddenly he pulls this so-called AI out of his...' She looked at the Doctor. 'His hat,' she concluded.

He smiled at her. 'If the Canterbury AI is a genuine artificial intelligence – and to all appearances it *is* – then it could be very dangerous.'

Gina shook her head, her jet-black fringe of hair swaying and her silver earrings jiggling. Seen close up, they could be identified as miniature rocket ships. 'If it is real, he didn't make it himself. He must have got someone smarter to do it. In all modesty, I'm the smartest person he knows. And I didn't do it.'

'Well, we should be able to answer these questions soon enough,' said the Doctor.

Ace looked at him. 'How are we going to do that?'

'By breaking through one of the most secure firewalls in the world and hacking into Raymond Luthier's artificial intelligence.'

'Not wishing to repeat myself, but how—'

'We use the software that our friend has designed for just that purpose.' The Doctor smiled at Gina Gulpin.

'Excellent plan,' she said, smiling back at him.

'So, this is a virtual reality system?' said Ace, looking sceptically at the two battered armchairs Gina had dragged in front of a computer on the table. Each armchair had what looked like a modified cycling helmet lying on a cushion in it, attached by cables to the computer. The computer itself was very large, and very pink, with a *Hello Kitty* sticker on the top of it.

Gina nodded. 'I set myself the task of designing software that could get past just about any security measures anyone's invented yet. To make it easy and intuitive to use, I gave it a VR interface.' She grinned happily. 'And I decided not to do any of that *Burning Chrome* cyberpunk stuff. Instead the simulation looks like this.' She waved a hand at the pulp science fiction posters on the wall. 'Classic space battles. Planets. Starships. Alien suns.'

'And the information we're seeking,' said the Doctor. 'The data core in Raymond Luthier's AI. That will look like...'

'Three stars burning at the heart of an alien solar system.'

'Why three?'

'Because four's too many,' said Gina. 'And two isn't enough.'

The Doctor nodded. 'And the countermeasures? The software designed to stop intruders?'

Gina sighed as if it was all too obvious to explain. 'They will manifest as alien spaceships. Armed with missiles.'

'But I'll be armed with missiles, too,' said Ace. 'Right?'

'And really powerful engines, plus lots of reserve fuel, which will give you loads of delta-v.'

The Doctor looked at Ace. 'You remember our little discussion about delta-v when you were on the good ship *Vancouver*?'

She grinned. 'How could I forget?'

'And what is my part in all this?' said Raine.

'You steal the stars,' said the Doctor. 'And bring them back to us.'

'Right. I see. Steal the stars.'

'Using a giant toroidal magnetic field,' said the Doctor. 'You create a jet of plasma from the star to move it.'

Perhaps bored by this explanation, Gina left the room.

'Giant toroidal magnetic field?' Raine was frowning. 'I thought someone said something about "easy and intuitive".'

'Essentially,' said the Doctor, 'it will be like a balloon with a small puncture, using the escaping gas to drive itself.'

'I have an idea,' said Raine. 'Why don't you go with Ace instead of me? You're very comfortable with toroidal fields and all that.'

'I would,' said the Doctor, picking up one of the headsets which looked like a bicycle helmet, and turning it over in his hand. 'Only these things are designed to work on a *human* brain.'

'Oh yes,' said Raine. 'That.'

Gina came back in from the kitchen, carrying another carton of takeaway curry and sat down on the sofa, picking up a game console with a long lead which ran back to the big pink computer on the table. The Doctor put a hand on Raine's shoulder. 'Don't worry about the details. You will just operate a simple control panel on your "starship". Subjectively it will be as easy as cracking a safe.'

'Except for one thing,' said Gina from the sofa. 'If you get dead in there you'll be dead in real life. Don't forget that.'

'Charming,' said Raine, and sank down in the armchair on the right of the pink computer. Ace was already in the one on the left, and had put on her headset. Raine did the same.

'Now you have to hold hands,' said Gina. 'Your two spaceships will be linked together when you enter the home system and approach the Portal. Once you go through the Portal, you will be in the alien system

— Raymond's AI. Then if you let go, your two ships will detach and manoeuvre independently. Link up again when you're ready to come back through the Portal. I'll close it behind you to make sure none of Raymond's security software follows you back through.' She lifted up the game console. 'It could be nasty if it does.'

Ace reached across and took Raine's hand. It was warm and slick with sweat.

'This doesn't mean we're going out or anything,' said Raine.

'One last question,' said Ace, leaning back in her armchair, the headset covering her eyes and the top of her face. 'Why haven't you used this to hack in to the Canterbury AI yourself?'

'Do I *look* crazy?' said Gina.

Falling.

Through infinity.

The binary starship plunged on its fast, steep interplanetary orbit towards the Portal, floating in space like the giant blue-green iris of an immense eye. The eye seemed to widen in recognition as it saw them coming. In its centre a disc of blackness expanded – and suddenly stars were visible. Alien stars, in unknown constellations.

The binary ship which was the linked consciousness of Ace and Raine fell through the Portal. There was a shimmer, like the shimmer in your head between waking and sleeping. And suddenly they were there.

Three suns burned, a blue-white glare at the heart of a planetary system. And from those planets spaceships were already rising in an attack formation. The binary ship split in two. Raine's craft blazed its engines and shifted into an orbit around the triad of stars.

Ace's craft continued falling on its original trajectory, until the enemy started to fire on her. And then she began a game of evasion and counter-strike. The enemy's missiles had very high acceleration, but very low delta-v. With her powerful engines and large fuel reserves, Ace was able to dodge them easily, changing orbits whenever necessary.

That wasn't the difficult part.

The difficult part was firing her own missiles, to intercept enemy strikes against Raine. Raine was too consumed with her own manoeuvres to pay any attention to defence, so Ace had to guard Raine's back, while keeping herself alive. She shifted orbit, watching a missile glide through the phantom locus of her old position, a glittering white arrow heading out of the solar system, on an eternal trajectory, never to find a target.

And she fired her own in response.

She destroyed three of the enemy spacecraft and nineteen of their missiles – at first all of these were aimed at her, but then towards the end the enemy seemed to realise what Raine was doing and concentrated its efforts on her. Ace managed to intercept every missile they fired, and she wasn't too worried.

Until they stopped firing missiles.

And something rose from the red atmosphere of a giant planet below. A spaceship, but one unlike any of the others. Jagged, angular, black.

And big.

Far bigger than any of the others. Vastly larger than Ace's or Raine's.

And moving *much* more quickly.

Just then Ace got the signal that Raine was finished. Ace's engine flared and she moved into a Hohmann transfer manoeuvre to match orbits with Raine. She fired her engine again, their orbits synchronised, and the two ships docked, linked, and became a binary once again.

Between them and the red planet, the jagged black ship was rising fast, a fattening spider-shape. Then the red planet turned black and the jagged ship vanished utterly into shadow. Because the light was gone. The three stars were moving, abandoning their home system. Rushing back along the same orbit Raine and Ace had followed here.

Back towards the Portal.

The stars blazed. The binary ship followed. The jagged giant pursued. It was coming after them, closing fast. Ace fired her missiles at it. Every missile she had. No point saving them now. Once they were through the Portal she wouldn't need them any more.

Every missile hit its target.

None of them made any difference.

The jagged ship kept coming.

It didn't matter. The three captive stars were approaching the Portal. It was bigger than Ace remembered. The black disc at its centre expanding to infinity. Big enough to swallow the triad of stars. They passed through and disappeared. The binary ship followed close behind. The jagged giant was almost on them now, looming over them, dwarfing them…

But it didn't matter, because as soon as they were through the Portal they would be safe.

The Portal would close behind them.

Ace and Raine passed through the Portal. There was a shimmer, like the shimmer in your head between sleeping and waking. And suddenly they were back.

Safe.

Home.

Now the Portal would close behind them.

The Portal didn't close.

The huge jagged black ship began to nose through, into the home system.

The Portal didn't close.

Ace reached for the controls, to fire missiles, to try and stop it. But there were no missiles left…

The jagged ship was now a quarter of the way through the Portal.

The Portal didn't close.

Something was happening on the jagged ship's fuselage. A massive hatch was opening.

The Portal didn't close.

Something was emerging. A weapon of some kind.

Then the Portal closed.

Like a guillotine coming down, it scythed shut and neatly sliced off the head of the jagged ship. Whatever the weapon had been, it was cut in two. The rest of the ship's bulk was left behind forever, wherever it was, in another galaxy. The severed head of the ship spun lazily, dead and helpless, spilling glittering components into the vacuum. Lifeless and off on its own endless trajectory.

Ace pulled the headset from her sweating brow and yelled, 'You said you'd close the Portal!' She looked around the room. In the armchair beside her Raine looked pale and stricken, slowly removing her own headset with shaking hands. Behind them, on the sofa, Gina was clutching the thing that looked like a games controller. She had a chagrined expression on her face and she was dripping with water. Over her head, the Doctor was holding the plant pot from the windowsill, the one which had been full of rain.

'You were supposed to close the Portal,' hissed Ace.

'I fell asleep,' said Gina, wiping rainwater out of her eyes.

'Fell asleep!'

'You were in there for hours,' said Gina. Then she nodded at the takeaway carton, tipped on its side on the sofa. 'Plus I had a big lunch.'

'I woke her up,' said the Doctor, putting the plant pot down. It was empty now he'd poured its contents on Gina.

'Why weren't you in here to make sure she didn't fall asleep in the first place?'

'I'm afraid I was out there, admiring the orchard,' said the Doctor, nodding at the garden beyond the window. He handed Ace a pear. She passed it to Raine, who studied it for a moment, then began to eat it fastidiously and hungrily. Gina came and sat at the big pink computer.

'Let's see what you've got,' she said.

Then she began to laugh.

'It's not an AI at all,' said Gina. 'It's a massive scam.'

'A scam?' said Ace. She glanced at the Doctor 'But you said it works.'

'Oh, it works all right,' said Gina. 'It's a cunningly disguised gateway for the most massive crowd-sourcing project of all time. Raymond got rich not by inventing a super-intelligent inhuman mind, but by exploiting millions of very human minds, all over the developing world, and paying them a pittance.'

Raine came and perched on the arm of Gina's chair, staring at the computer screen. 'But surely these people must have realised what they were doing. Why didn't they blow the whistle?'

'That's where we come to the one bit which I have to grudgingly admit actually *is* rather clever,' said Gina. 'The so-called Canterbury AI minces up the task into a vast number of tiny chunks, all of which are worked on separately.'

The Doctor nodded, 'So each person only contributes a microscopic part of the whole – like one piece of Lego in a vast structure. None of them has any idea what the finished product will look like.'

'Exactly.'

'But his game is over now,' said the Doctor, smiling. 'Thanks to Raine and Ace.' He leaned close to Gina. 'Can you release the "AI" online as a resource open for everyone to use, with the crowd-source workers receiving a fair share of the revenues?'

Gina nodded and chuckled as she began to type at the keyboard. 'He's going to find that the price of his stock can go down as well as up.'

Ace looked up as Raine rose to her feet and walked towards the door.

'Where are you going?'

'Out in the garden, to pick a few pears,' said the girl who stole the stars.

THIRTEEN

ARTIFICIAL INTELLIGENCE

'Your trouble is, Drathro, that you've no
concept of what life is.'

'I have studied my work units for five centuries.
I understand all their responses. What you would call life.'

'Understanding is not the same as knowing.'

The Sixth Doctor and L3 robot Drathro, *The Trial of a Time Lord* (1986)

In *The War Machines* (1966), the First Doctor faces a terrible foe – a computer that can use a telephone line to communicate with other computers. In *The Green Death* (1973), people's movements through a building are watched by automated cameras linked to a computer. In *The Greatest Show in the Galaxy* (1988–1989), the TARDIS is invaded by a robot who takes over the controls to play a video advertising a circus.

At the time these stories were broadcast, these were all imaginative science fiction ideas. Today, the internet, CCTV and sophisticated electronic junk mail are all part of our daily lives – but there's an important difference. In *The War Machines*, *The Green Death* and *The Greatest Show in the Galaxy*, these artificial systems can speak, and even argue with the Doctor. They're intelligent, thinking machines.

At least, we don't consider the computers today that run CCTV or send junk mail as being intelligent – but then, that depends on what intelligence means. The word comes from the Latin for perceiving or understanding. Surely a CCTV camera perceives whatever it is recording and when we give a computer an instruction, such as typing the T on the keyboard, it 'understands' how to respond and puts a T on the screen.

Over the years, scientists have tried to devise ways to more accurately measure and assess intelligence. In 1912, German psychologist William Stern proposed the intelligence quotient or IQ test. Modern versions of the IQ test include studies of comprehension, reasoning, memory and processing speed. A 'norming sample' of participants taking the test is used to work out an average rate of intelligence – given as 100. Once this average has been found, anyone else taking the test can see if they are above or below the average and to what degree.

Studies have shown that those with higher IQ scores are likely to be more healthy, live longer and earn more in better jobs. Yet some are sceptical of using IQ to predict future behaviour, and argue that IQ is often an indicator not of the intelligence a person was born with but the way their upbringing and environment has shaped their responses – in Chapter 11, we talked about the debate about the differences between nature and nurture. In fact, IQ seems not to be innate; it's the sort of test you can train for. Others point out that IQ only gives a partial picture of the subject's mental ability: for example, the test does not measure creativity, emotional intelligence or experience.

There's something of this debate in the *Doctor Who* story *The Ribos Operation* (1978), in which the Doctor and his new companion Romana are sent on a quest to collect pieces of the Key to Time. Romana is highly intelligent. She claims to have graduated from the Time Lord Academy with a triple first, while the Doctor only scraped through with fifty-one per cent at the second attempt. But, as the story shows, she's naive, inexperienced and lacks the ability to think laterally and deduce from evidence – essential skills if she is to help recover pieces of the Key. She might be intelligent, but she has a lot to learn from the Doctor.

Three stories later, *The Androids of Tara* (1978) begins with the Doctor playing chess against his robot dog, K-9. Romana looks briefly at the board and concludes that K-9 will win in twelve moves. K-9 corrects her: he'll do it in eleven. The Doctor stares at the board doubtfully.

'Mate in eleven? Oh yes, oh yes. Well, that's the trouble with chess, isn't it? It's all so predictable.'

The Fourth Doctor, *The Androids of Tara* **(1978)**

It's a funny scene, but the Doctor has a point. He might not be good at exams or chess, but he has a knack for thinking in ways that aren't expected. Battling monsters requires a different *kind* of intelligence.

We talked in Chapter 8 about how a team of British mathematicians led by Alan Turing was able to crack Nazi secret codes in the Second World War, and how that work resulted in a new invention – the programmable computer Colossus, designed by Tommy Flowers. In fact, Colossus was only part of the solution to cracking the codes, and what actually happened can tell us a lot about the nature of intelligence – and how it applies to machines.

The Nazis used radio to send instructions and news to their forces spread all over the world. The British and other Allied forces could listen in to these messages but couldn't understand them because they were in code. Obviously, cracking that code would make a huge difference to the progress of the war, so sizeable resources and some of the brightest minds were devoted to the problem.

The Nazi codes were produced on Enigma machines, which looked like normal keyboards but contained rotating discs called rotors. If you input a letter into the machine, such as pressing the letter T on the keyboard, the rotors turned and produced a different letter as the output – for example, the next letter in the alphabet: U. If you had just one rotor in your Enigma machine, substituting each letter typed on the keyboard for the next letter along in the alphabet, you might produce a message from English words that said:

UIF TDJFOUJGJD TFDSFUT PG EPDUPS XIP

But with such a simple system, it wouldn't take your enemies long to crack this code – if you use a pen and paper, you can decipher it pretty quickly, can't you?

To make such a code harder to break, instead of substituting each letter in exactly the same way – moving up or down the alphabet by a given number of letters – you could randomise the substitutions: every T swapped for U, but every H swapped for A and every E swapped for Z, and so on. But there were ways around that, too. For example, E is the letter most frequently used in the German language – and in English, too – so you could check your coded messages for the most frequently used letter, and then assume that was E. The next most common letters in German are N, S, R and I; in English they are T, A, O and N. You could also look for the most common letter pairs (in English: TH, HE and AN) and the most common double letters (in English: LL, EE and SS).

It might take some trial and error – in the English words used to produce the coded message above, E appeared four times, but so did C, O and T. However, deducing just a handful of the substitutions would give you most of the letters in a word, allowing you to guess the rest – revealing yet more substitutions that might help with other words. Having decoded most of the words in a sentence, you could probably work out the rest. You might have worked out what the coded message above said before you'd decoded all of it.

To make codes harder to break, the first Enigma machines contained three separate rotors. Each time a letter was pressed, the rotors turned inside the machine by different amounts. That meant that the first time you pressed the T on the keyboard the machine might substitute a U – but the next time you pressed the T, the rotors would be in different positions so the machine would substitute something else, such as a J. That made the code much more secure: you couldn't just puzzle it out with pen and paper. You'd need an Enigma machine of your own (or understand how one worked) and you'd also need to know the positions of the three rotors when the coded message was sent.

If each rotor was divided into 26 – so that you could adjust it to substitute a T for any letter in the alphabet – then three rotors meant there were 26 x 26 x 26 or 17,576 possible starting combinations. A fourth rotor added to later machines meant 456,976 possible combinations. Special plugboards added to the machines made the codes even more secure: a plugboard with 10 leads in it meant more than 150 trillion possible combinations. That presented a serious challenge to anyone trying to crack the codes. But the Nazis also changed the settings they used on the Enigma machines every 24 hours. If breaking the codes was to be of any practical use, it had to be done very quickly every day.

In the 1930s, Polish mathematicians cracked some of the simpler versions of the Enigma code using machines which they called 'crypto-logical bombs' that could cycle through all the 17,576 possible starting combinations of a three-rotor system in about two hours. The Polish codebreakers also spotted clues in the coded messages that could help narrow down the search. Some words or phrases appeared regularly in messages, such as beginning with the word 'Anx' – the German for 'to' – followed by a space and then someone's name.

When the Enigma machines became more complex, these clues – called 'cribs' by the British – became very important. Alan Turing improved upon the design of the Polish codebreaking machine, and used the Polish name for it, 'bombe'. The first British bombe, produced in 1940, could use any known part of the message to help crack the whole of the code, in what is called a 'known plaintext attack'. Finding an effective crib greatly increased the speed at which the British could decode the Nazi messages. Later bombes, and the first programmable computer – Colossus, built in 1943 – were more sophisticated at cracking codes, but all still relied on cribs.

Turing's efforts inspired the *Doctor Who* story *The Curse of Fenric* (1989), in which brilliant mathematician Doctor Judson has built a computer that he assures his old friend Commander Millington can break the Nazi codes. Millington has his own methods, as the Doctor and his companion Ace discover as they explore the army base and discover the most unlikely room:

'This is a perfect replica of the German naval cipher room in Berlin. Even down to the files…'

'Commander Millington's a spy?'

'Oh no, no, no, no. He's just trying to think the way the Germans think, to keep one step ahead.'

The Seventh Doctor and Ace, *The Curse of Fenric* **(1989)**

It's a remarkable sight: a perfect recreation of a Nazi office in the middle of a British army base, but it's indicative of exactly the kind of creative, unconventional thinking that really was used to crack the codes.

This kind of thinking required a certain kind of intelligence – and a creative approach to recruitment. In January 1942, the *Daily Telegraph* ran a competition with £100 offered to anyone who could solve a particularly difficult crossword in under twelve minutes. The crossword was a mix of general knowledge, anagrams and riddles. As well as the cash prize, those who took part were contacted by the War Office and offered work in codebreaking.

There were overlaps between solving crosswords and cracking codes. Deducing the answer to the crossword clue 1 Across would provide you with letters in some of the Down clues – just as working out some of the substitutions in a code could make it easy to work out the rest, as we saw before. More than that, it often helps in solving a crossword to get inside the mind of the person who set it, knowing their particular habits and preferences, the kinds of clue they like to set. Codebreakers learnt to get inside the minds of the Nazi operators sending the coded messages, too. One codebreaker, Mavis Batey, even deduced that two operators both had girlfriends called Rosa – and used the name in their messages. Ironically, this creative, different kind of thinking required to crack the codes depended on the ability to think just like someone else – to imitate them.

After the war, Turing continued to work on developments in computers. His Automatic Computing Engine, or ACE, was one of the earliest computers to store electronic programs in its memory – before then, computers such as Colossus had to be rewired manually before starting any new task. As computers became more sophisticated and capable of more complex tasks, some people started to ask whether they would one day be able to think for themselves – and how we would be able to judge the moment when they did.

Turing also applied himself to this problem, and in 1950 published a short paper on the subject: 'Computing Machinery and Intelligence'. He begins by arguing that the question 'Can machines think?' is tricky, because it depends on our definitions of intelligence. As we've already seen, there are lots of different kinds of intelligence, so instead Turing proposed a game: without seeing them and only judging their answers to a series of questions, can we tell a computer and person apart? Turing's argument was that if a computer can imitate us well enough to fool us into thinking that it's a person, it must present the same apparent intelligence as a person. We don't test the intelligence of living people before we speak to them – we assume it's there. So why don't we assume intelligence in a computer, too?

At the time, Turing's imitation game – now better known as the 'Turing test' – was an interesting thought experiment. But today, we are used to computer systems that could well pass that test. Companies increasingly offer a customer support tool on their websites that makes us think we're chatting to a person but is actually an automated system. Computer viruses are often contained in messages that apparently come from our friends or other trusted sources. There's also an example related to *Doctor Who*.

For three months in 2006, British Telecom had a system that translated text messages into voice messages on a telephone landline – and used Fourth Doctor actor Tom Baker as the voice. It took Baker eleven days to record 11,593 sounds and phrases that the automated system could then assemble in different combinations to match the content of text messages. It even knew to translate abbreviations such as 'xx' to 'kiss kiss' and 'gr8' to 'great'. Some people had fun sending messages that made the automated voice say daft things – or even 'sing' famous songs. But a few people who knew Tom Baker in real life found it a bit confusing: for them, the automated system passed the Turing test.*

Today, we're used to automated systems predicting our responses. Online shops offer us deals and recommendations based on our previous purchases. Social media recommend people or news stories we might want to engage with based on our current network of friends. Some of these predictions might be wrong, but the more sophisticated systems can make surprisingly accurate matches – as if they know us better than we do ourselves.

Already, voice recognition systems are used in automated phone lines – you are asked to say 'yes' or give other simple answers when prompted. As these systems improve, we'll find ourselves talking to more and more computers, and those computers will have ever more sophisticated ways of predicting our responses, so that it will become ever more difficult to know if the person we're talking to is a person or not.

When it gets to that point, aren't they then people, too?

'The trouble with computers, of course, is that they're very sophisticated idiots. They do exactly what you tell them at amazing speed, even if you order them to kill you.'
The Fourth Doctor, *Robot* (1974–1975)

We can use *Doctor Who* to explore our problematic attitude to artificial intelligence. In the series, there is often a clear distinction: artificial

---

* It's a good job British Telecom used only the Fourth Doctor's voice and not a copy of his mind – that caused a lot of problems for the computer system Xoanon in *The Face of Evil* (1977).

intelligence is not on the same level as human (or alien) life. When battling the generally quite friendly, intelligent robot in *Robot*, the Doctor has few of the moral quandaries he does when facing even the Daleks. He destroys the robot but (as we saw in Chapter 9) lets the Daleks live.

In fact, his companion Sarah argues against both these decisions. She tells him the Daleks are 'the most evil creatures ever invented. You must destroy them.' While, upset by the destruction of the robot, she says something that implies that it had passed the Turing test – and the Doctor agrees.

'I had to do it, you know.'

'Yes, yes, I know. It was insane and it did terrible things, but at first, it was so human.'

'It was a wonderful creature, capable of great good, and great evil. Yes, I think you could say it was human.'

The Fourth Doctor and Sarah Jane Smith, *Robot*

The Doctor describes his robot dog K-9 as his 'best friend' on more than one occasion, but in *School Reunion* (2006) he seems happy to send K-9 to his death to stop the Krillitane invasion. Well, he's not happy, exactly – but we can't imagine him allowing a human companion to make the same kind of sacrifice. Does it make it OK that he can rebuild a robot companion after it is destroyed? And what about when, in *Planet of Fire* (1984), the Doctor terminates the 'life' of robot companion Kamelion and then *doesn't* rebuild him? Kamelion asks the Doctor to terminate him, but it's something that the Doctor would surely never do with a human companion.

We can see a general distrust of computers running through a lot of *Doctor Who*: as we've already seen, *The War Machines* and *The Green Death* are about evil computers. *The Face of Evil*, *The Girl in the Fireplace* (2006) and *Deep Breath* (2014) are about machine intelligences that have gone wrong – with deadly consequences. The point of *The Ice*

Warriors (1967) is to not rely on machines; in *Destiny of the Daleks* (1979) we see the limits of battle computers that cannot think creatively; in *The Two Doctors* (1985), the Doctor speaks proudly of a scientist who hated computers and worked out a famous theory using pen and ink. His attitude seems best summed up in *Inferno* (1970):

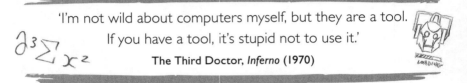

'I'm not wild about computers myself, but they are a tool. If you have a tool, it's stupid not to use it.'

The Third Doctor, *Inferno* (1970)

But there are exceptions. The Doctor is genuinely moved in *The Time of the Doctor* (2013) by the death of Handles, the reprogrammed, severed head of a Cyberman. That seems to be because he and Handles have spent more than 300 years together – the Doctor has become emotionally attached to Handles whether or not he thinks Handles is really alive.

Of course, the Doctor has had an even longer-standing relationship with another machine intelligence:

'I always leave the actual landing to the TARDIS herself. She's no fool, you know.'

'You speak as if she were alive.'

'Yes. Yes, I do, don't I?'

The Third Doctor and Mike Yates, *Planet of the Spiders* (1974)

For a long time, we might have excused the Doctor calling the TARDIS 'old girl' or speaking of it as being alive as an affectation. While exiled on Earth, he also gave a name to his car, Bessie, and talked to her affectionately, but we don't think of Bessie as alive.

However, in *The Doctor's Wife* (2011), the consciousness of the TARDIS – referred to in the story as its 'soul' – is deposited in a woman called Idris. For the first time in the hundreds of years they have been together, the Doctor and the TARDIS can talk to each other directly, and it turns out that the TARDIS – like the automated systems on websites we discussed earlier – understands the Doctor's needs better than he does:

'You didn't always take me where I wanted to go.'

'No, but I always took you where you needed to go.'

'You did. Look at us talking. Wouldn't it be amazing if we could always talk, even when you're stuck inside the box?'

'You know I'm not constructed that way. I exist across all space and time.'

$\partial^3 \sum \int \chi^2$ **The Eleventh Doctor and Idris, *The Doctor's Wife* (2011)**

The implication is not that the TARDIS is now, for the first time, alive, but that it has always been alive – just in a different way. Its intelligence or being hasn't changed by being transferred into Idris, just the way it is able to communicate. Yet at the end of the story we're told something else.

'I've been looking for a word. A big, complicated word, but so sad. I've found it now ... Alive. I'm alive.'

'Alive isn't sad.'

'It's sad when it's over. I'll always be here, but this is when we talked, and now even that has come to an end.'

$\partial^3 \sum \int \chi^2$ **Idris and the Eleventh Doctor, *The Doctor's Wife***

It's as if 'alive' doesn't mean intelligence or understanding: it's to do with looking and sounding like a human. The human Idris dies and the consciousness of the TARDIS returns to the time machine, apparently no longer alive.

But later, the Doctor talks to the TARDIS, requesting a destination. For a moment there's no response and he thinks that he's been silly: of course the ship can't hear him. Then levers on the console start moving on their own and the Doctor is delighted...

We're not told explicitly what that means – but the people making *Doctor Who* assume we have intelligence. So, what do you think?

THE MERCY SEATS

DAVID LLEWELLYN

'In Aprille and the Kingdom of Castile
We came upon a hostelrye genteel
And there bigan this tale of misterie,
About the Doctor, Skeletons and me.'

From 'Tales of My Young Manhood' by Geoffrey Chaucer
Written c.1373, manuscript discovered in the British Library, June 2193

'OK,' I announced, slapping my hand against the table. 'I've got one. So there are these two chickens, right?'

Everyone else groaned; even Matilda, who was heavily with child.

'Not this again…'

'You told us the chicken story in Pamplona,' said her husband, Johannes the cobbler. 'And it wasn't even funny the first time around.'

'Mind you,' said William of Bristol. 'Anything's better than the one about him being kidnapped in Rheims. Every single tavern, Peachfuzz here tells us his story about Rheims.'

William was the eldest of our group, a veteran of what we then called the Twenty-Seven Year War, and he called me Peachfuzz on account of my embarrassing excuse for a beard. I hated the name.

'*Fine!*' I snapped, and sat back down, my arms folded across my chest. 'I'd like to see you lot do any better.'

THE SCIENTIFIC SECRETS OF DOCTOR WHO

Met with a chorus of shrugs, I pointed to our newest member; the curiously dressed Scotsman with alarming eyebrows who had joined us only a few miles back.

'How about you?' I said. 'You've hardly spoken a word since supper.'

The stranger glanced up. 'Who, me?'

'Yes, you. What did you say your name is, again?'

'The Doctor.'

'Very well, then, *Doctor*. Tell us a story.'

'I don't *tell* stories,' said the Doctor. 'Usually, I *am* the story.'

'Then perhaps someone *else* could tell one,' sighed William of Bristol.

'Do we even *need* to tell stories?' asked Hugo the tailor. 'I know it's *traditional*, but quite frankly I think we all ran out of amusing anecdotes halfway across France.'

'I don't know,' said Isabel, his wife. 'I haven't told the one about my Uncle Ralf's pig yet.'

Hugo sighed, and through clenched teeth muttered, 'No one wants to hear about your uncle's pig.'

We six travellers – not including this Doctor – were almost a thousand miles from home, and 130 from our destination; the church at Santiago de Compostela. Readers will no doubt be aware that this pilgrimage across the Kingdom of Leon and Castile is one of the holiest in all of Christendom, yet we had spent almost every single mile of it bickering with one another. This latest argument might have lasted a lot longer had our evening not been very suddenly – and rudely – interrupted by a band of angry-looking villagers, who entered the tavern armed with pitchforks and daggers and swords.

'We've come for the pilgrims,' announced their ringleader.

Matilda gasped. Johannes opened his mouth to say something, but thought better of it. Hugo chewed his lower lip while his wife downed the rest of her sherry in a single gulp. William of Bristol began with a 'Now, look here,' but was shoved back into his seat. As for me… well, let's just say I learned some very important lessons about chivalry and derring-do in Rheims and know *exactly* when to keep my trap shut.

Out of the corner of my eye, however, I noticed that the Doctor was grinning with the mischievous anticipation of a schoolboy who has placed a thistle on his schoolmaster's chair.

The tavern's owner, a plump little man, came out from behind the bar, and said, 'Listen, Fernando. These people are *pilgrims*. We don't want any trouble here. What's the matter?'

'You know what,' the man replied angrily. 'For years, not a single plague death. Then, just when we think it's safe to bring our children back, it starts again. And just like the last time, it's these foreign pilgrims who bring death to our door. Why, only last night we lost another two souls.'

At the mere mention of the word 'plague' the tavern fell silent. There was still plague in these parts? But hadn't it died out some two decades ago? All eyes turned to us, and the tavern owner hung his head and sighed.

'I'm sorry,' he said. 'But you'll all have to leave. With *them*.'

The cart was little more than a wooden cage on wheels, built for carrying chickens and pigs, and it smelled *exactly* as you might expect. What's more, there was barely enough room for the seven of us to stand, let alone sit. Matilda, the pregnant woman, was short of breath, and it took three of us, Johannes and Hugo holding her by the arms and Isabel gently fanning her face, to stop her from fainting altogether.

'Where are you taking us?' asked the Doctor.

'To Bembibre,' said the rather gruff Fernando, his voice raised above the clattering of wooden wheels and horses' hooves. 'You'll be quarantined there till we know what to do with you.'

'Quarantined?' said the Doctor. 'Fantastic! Where?'

'We haven't decided yet,' replied Fernando.

'How about the church?'

'Actually... That's not a bad idea.'

I laughed. For one thing, our Scots friend seemed inappropriately cheerful. For another, I knew there was no church in Bembibre, and told him as much. 'Any pilgrim worth his salt knows *that*.'

'Peachfuzz is right,' said William of Bristol.

'Who says?' said the Doctor.

'Our map?' said I.

'Old map, is it?'

'Fairly. Why?'

'The Church of the Blessed Miracle appeared overnight,' said Fernando. 'Twenty years ago, it was.'

'One minute an empty patch of land,' said the Doctor. 'Next... *Ta-daa!* A church.'

'That truly is a miracle!' said I.

'Unlikely,' said the Doctor. 'Miracles are just the universe's way of papering over the cracks.' He turned to me. 'And what sort of a name is "Peachfuzz"?'

'My name's Geoffrey,' I replied, bitterly. 'Of London. Son of the late John Chaucer, the vintner. You may have heard of him.'

'*Chaucer?*' said the Doctor. '*Geoffrey* Chaucer? You're *the* Geoffrey Chaucer?'

Assuming this was sarcasm, I simply nodded.

'How old are you?' he asked.

'Twenty-three.'

'Oh, *great*,' said the Doctor. Then, turning to one side as if addressing some invisible friend: 'You travel through all of space and time, and when you finally meet one of the greatest poets in the *galaxy*, he's on his gap year.'

'Who are you talking to?' I asked.

The Doctor looked at me with a curious expression and then at the empty space to his left. He sighed.

'No one,' he said. 'Old habits. There's usually someone there.'

I was about to question him further when Matilda let out a gasp. From inside his coat the Doctor produced a curious metal stylus, which he pointed at her belly, and for a moment the instrument chirruped and glowed with bright green phosphorescence.

'What are you *doing*?' said Matilda.

'Excellent!' said the Doctor, ignoring her completely. 'The baby'll be with us in under an hour. Let's just hope Fernando here can get us to the church on time.'

I was bemused. 'I must say,' I told him. 'You seem in very high spirits, considering we're about to be locked up in some Castilian backwater.'

'Yes, well,' said the Doctor. 'Who says that wasn't my plan all along?'

The Church of the Blessed Miracle stood on a low hill, perhaps a hundred yards from the edge of Bembibre. I don't know what I was expecting. A spire of pure gold, perhaps, or choirs of cherubim and seraphim dancing in the clouds above. Instead, it was a grey and rather drab little building with a stubby spire, and looked much like every other village church we'd visited on our pilgrimage. Without ceremony, Fernando and his men herded us inside and then the doors were closed and locked behind us with an ominous, echoing clunk.

Only moments before, and just as the Doctor predicted, Matilda had gone into labour, and it seemed she might give birth at any second. To make her more comfortable – or as comfortable as she could be – we pooled together our cloaks and shawls and turned one of the wooden pews into a makeshift bed. Her husband Johannes sat beside her, holding her hand.

'Just remember to *breathe*,' he said.

'What in *blazes* do you think I'm doing?' Matilda barked. 'I *knew* this was a stupid idea. My sister was right. We *should* have stayed in Sidcup.'

'This is *perfect*!' said the Doctor.

On the verge of losing my temper with this strange, strange man, I took him to one side, and in a low, hushed voice said, 'You speak as if this is part of some plan. Now, I don't like to pick holes, but what plan could this possibly be a part of?'

'This place,' said the Doctor. 'The church appeared twenty years ago, yes?'

'If you say so.'

'And what else happened here, twenty years ago?'

I shrugged.

'The *plague*,' said the Doctor. 'Not just any old plague, but the Black Death. That's the plague turned up to eleven, with bells on. Thousands died. Millions.'

'Of course!' I said. 'It was the same in London.'

'But why would something just *appear* here in the middle of a plague?'

'Perhaps the Almighty wished to provide them with a place of solace...'

The Doctor gave me a wordless look and shook his head. 'What if,' he said, 'death is a substance? Something valuable, like gold, or edible, like... I don't know... cheese?'

'I haven't the slightest idea what you mean.'

'Of course you don't,' said the Doctor. 'You're human.'

If we hadn't been standing on sacred ground, I would have punched him in the nose. And what did he mean by 'You're human'? Was he not? Before I could ask him, the Doctor produced the very stylus we had seen earlier, and the room was suddenly illuminated with that same unearthly green light.

I looked around the church but saw nothing out of the ordinary. The walls were painted with Biblical scenes, though I can't say I recognised any one of them. At the far end of the nave was an altar flanked on both sides by four large wooden misericords, or 'mercy seats', and framing each of them a life-sized skeleton, carved from the same dark wood, and wielding a scythe.

'When you die,' said the Doctor, 'where does that energy go? The *chemical* energy, oh, that becomes worm food. Yum yum, lucky worms. But what if there's something *else*?'

He aimed his stylus at the church's walls, and those rather fascinating eyebrows of his furrowed together with considerable intensity.

'Beautiful,' he said.

'I've seen more accomplished frescoes,' I remarked.

'Not the paintings, the *walls*,' said the Doctor. 'You'd expect them to be made of mud or stone, but they're a proamonium-titanium alloy with a dense network of inner circuitry and a holographic shell.'

'Could you repeat that in Middle English?'

'This isn't a church. It's a spaceship.'

'That doesn't exactly help. A *space* ship?'

From behind us, we heard a sudden, piercing scream.

'Push!' said Johannes the cobbler. 'Push!'

'I *am* pushing!' snapped his wife.

'Doctor?' said Johannes. 'Some assistance?'

'From me?' said the Doctor. 'Yes. Right. Of course.' He rushed over to Matilda's side. 'Remind me again... How many heads do these things have?'

For several moments, the gentlemen in the room turned our backs to preserve Matilda's modesty. Then, with a squawk and a squeal, there was a brand new person in the world, and Matilda was cradling it, or rather *him*, a baby boy, in her arms.

'Perfect!' said the Doctor. 'Right on schedule.'

'*Perfect?*' said I. 'We can't stay here. Not now. We don't know what those villagers are planning. If they think we're carrying the plague...'

'They'll burn this place down,' said the Doctor.

'Exactly.'

'Which, if I'm wrong, might be the best thing for it.'

'Are you mad? We'd all *die*.'

'But so would *they*,' said the Doctor, pointing to the wooden skeletons.

'What *are* you talking about? Those are carvings.'

'And that's *exactly* what they want you to think.'

'They? Who are "they"?'

'In layman's terms I'd call them an energephagic transdimensional chameleoform, but seeing as this is the fourteenth century, let's just call them "nasty wooden beasties".'

I laughed, and it echoed around the church, for a moment drowning out the baby's first squeals. 'You *are* mad. We're the *only people in here.*'

Striding down the nave, the Doctor aimed his stylus first at the altar and then at the carved wooden skeletons.

'Doctor... They're made of *wood.*'

'Why do humans always assume aliens would disguise themselves as humans? You're not the only organic life on the planet, you know.'

Leaning in close, he tapped the stylus against one of the wooden skulls: *Knock-knock-knock.*

'Hello. Wakey wakey. Rise and shine.'

Again he tapped the skull, which sounded, to my ears, exactly like a block of wood and nothing more.

I was beginning to lose my patience.

'Doctor, if, indeed, you *are* a doctor... Matilda just gave birth. Now isn't the time for childish games.'

And that, with diabolical timing, was when the skeleton moved; its head tilting to one side and its jaw falling open with a wooden squeak. I very nearly befouled myself, and could only splutter: 'Did it...? Did that thing just...? Can it...?'

'Yes, yes and yes,' said the Doctor. 'We should probably step away from them now. No sudden moves.'

'But they're wooden sculptures. What could they possibly do to us?'

'Oh, I don't know... Kill us and feast on our dying breaths? You see, *that's* why they were here in the first place. The plague. They didn't start it; they fed on those it killed. A bumper harvest. Then nothing. But why didn't they just *leave*?'

As quietly as we could, the Doctor and I inched our way backwards down the nave; the skeleton never once taking its hollow eye sockets off us, not even for a second. Much to my horror, the thing detached itself slowly from its seat, standing to its full height, and the remaining skeletons followed suit. The creak and groan of wood separating from wood quickly alerted my fellow pilgrims.

'By the saints!' cried Isabel.

Looking up from her new-born son, Matilda screamed. Her husband Johannes was dumbstruck, and could only stare at the skeletons aghast as they made their way forward, two in the aisle and one in each nave, matching each other step for step.

'Listen, fellas,' said the Doctor. 'I don't suppose I could interest you in a game of chess? Or perhaps a quick round of Ker-Plunk?'

The skeletons took another creaking step forward, and in perfect synchronisation raised their scythes.

'OK,' said the Doctor. 'Everyone get behind Matilda.'

'Doctor?' I said, looking at him askance. 'Have you lost your mind?'

'Cower behind a woman?' said William of Bristol, and true to his nature he puffed up his chest and bellowed, 'Never! Have at you, vile demons!' Then, with fearsome bravery – or foolishness – he drew his dagger and gave charge.

'Don't!' yelled the Doctor, but it was too late. Our companion was within feet of the skeletons when one of them lowered its scythe, and with the curved wooden blade tapped the crown of his head. In an instant, the old warrior's eyes grew dim, and his lifeless body slumped to the ground. Then, looming over him, the skeleton opened its jaws and began to breathe in, and from William's corpse there rose a silver, ghost-like mist that hovered briefly in the air before vanishing into the skeleton's open mouth.

Johannes helped Matilda to stand, and our party retreated to the entrance of the church. Behind us, Hugo and Isabel had begun battering at the door, and from outside I thought I heard voices and the jangling of keys, but all seemed hopeless. Even if the villagers released us, there was surely little they could do to fend off our hellish adversaries. I turned to the Doctor, hoping that he might have the answer, and saw only that same mischievous grin of anticipation that I'd first witnessed in the tavern.

'Doctor?' I said. 'Do something!'

'Wait for it,' said the Doctor. 'Wait for it...'

The skeletons were now mere yards away. Cowering on the ground, Matilda held her baby to her chest and began to pray. Whether it was through hunger or fear, I know not, but the babe let out a cry that sang throughout the church, and all at once the skeletons paused and did something that none of us – save, perhaps, the Doctor – could possibly have expected: they *screamed*. Then, stretching out their gnarled and knotted fingers, they pointed not at Matilda, but at her baby, and as a chorus began to howl and wail in anguish. The Doctor's eyes grew wide, and a brief, ecstatic laugh escaped him.

'Yes!' he said, and then, turning to the others: 'I love it when I'm right. Which, granted, is most of the time. But still...'

Swiftly, the skeletons retreated to the church's altar and they began twisting and turning at details carved from wood, but to little effect. The altar itself glowed briefly, and from within it came a low and menacing hum, but both faded as soon as they began.

'That's it!' said the Doctor. 'They *couldn't* leave. Engine failure!'

He left us, and with cautious steps made his way towards the altar.

'What *is* he doing?' asked Johannes.

'I've no idea,' I replied.

As the Doctor came near, the skeletons raised their scythes again and hissed.

'No!' said the Doctor. 'I'm not here to harm you, or... you know... throw babies at you, or anything like that. I'm here to help.'

'Help *them*?' said Isabel. 'Why would he help those *monsters*?'

Once again, the Doctor held aloft his mysterious stylus, and placed it against the altar. It chirruped and it shone, and in the blinking of an eye the altar began to glow, and that low, throbbing sound grew louder and louder.

Suddenly, and with fortuitous timing, the church door was flung open and a grey beam of moonlight flooded the building, just in time for the villagers outside to see the events unfolding within.

Leaving the skeletons, the Doctor gestured to us that we should run (we needed little persuasion) and together we helped Matilda to her feet and bolted for the open door. Glancing back into the church, I saw what I'd thought was an altar now shining with a brilliant and blinding white light. From beneath us came a deep and sinister rumbling, and we were no sooner out of the church than the earth surrounding it began to crumble and crack.

Pilgrims and villagers alike fled down the hill, Matilda still clutching the baby to her chest. The noise was almost deafening, and slowly the whole structure twisted itself out of the earth and began rising up into the night sky. Then, with a colossal boom that stripped the leaves from nearby trees and rumbled across the neighbouring valleys like thunder, it was gone.

'It's a miracle!' I said.

'Why not?' said the Doctor, and together we sat, exhausted, on the ground.

We were on the outskirts of Bembibre. The sun had risen, and we were ready to move on to the next town, and the next. The Doctor, however, had given us his apologies. He would not be joining us for the rest of our journey.

'You *knew*,' I said. 'You knew those demons were in there. You knew the church was evil.'

'Not *evil*,' said the Doctor. 'Alien.'

'How can you say those things weren't evil? They killed William.'

'In order to eat. I don't remember reading anything about Geoffrey Chaucer being a vegetarian.'

'Another of your foreign words.'

'Precisely.'

'How?' I asked him. 'How could you possibly have known those creatures would be frightened away by a *baby*?'

'Call it an educated guess,' said the Doctor. 'But it wasn't the baby that scared them. Not really. It was life. *New* life. The opposite of death.'

'You mean it conquers death?' I said, in absent thought. 'That's a splendid idea for a story.'

'Not what I said,' said the Doctor. 'But go for it.'

Then, without saying another word, he walked away towards a small, blue, tomb-like edifice at the side of the path; an odd construction that none of us had noticed before. Through a narrow door in its side, the Doctor entered the blue box, and seconds later we witnessed one final miracle when, to our surprise, it vanished, leaving not a single trace that it was ever there.

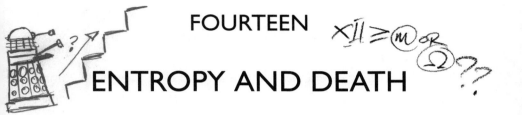

FOURTEEN
ENTROPY AND DEATH

'Four minutes [to live]? That's *ages*! What if I
get bored? I need a television, couple of books.
Anyone for chess? Bring me knitting.'
The Eighth Doctor, *The Night of the Doctor* (2013)

You are going to die. You might live for decades yet, but eventually
you'll die. As the Ninth Doctor tells Cassandra in *The End of the World*
(2005), 'Everything has its time and everything dies.' You, Cassandra
and the whole universe have a limited existence. Yet, surprisingly, it
was the development of steam engines during the Industrial Revolution
which helped us to understand why everything must eventually end.

In *The Mark of the Rani* (1985), the Sixth Doctor resists helping
English engineer George Stephenson with his design for a steam-
powered engine that Stephenson hopes will be capable of extraordinary
speed – fifteen or perhaps even twenty miles an hour. 'You'll find the
answer,' says the Doctor later, rather than interfere in the course of
history. 'And when you do, your invention will take off like a rocket.'

The story is probably set sometime in the 1820s because in (the real)
1829 a steam locomotive called Rocket took part in competition run by
the Liverpool & Manchester Railway. Rocket won the competition and
its designer, Robert Stephenson, went on to provide the steam engines
that worked the very first public transport system powered solely by
machines. Robert Stephenson was helped in designing Rocket by his

father, George – the man the Doctor met in the story – and for this and other work on the new method of transport, George Stephenson is often referred to as the 'father of railways'.

At the time, steam engines had a number of uses: they could pump water out of mines or drive machinery in factories, enabling people to extract raw materials and turn them into useful products more efficiently than ever before. In the early 1800s, the first engines using steam at high pressure were introduced – meaning much more power could be produced by a smaller engine. Developments continued, making engines smaller, faster and more powerful.

Yet there had been little published science on the workings of steam engines until French physicist Nicolas Léonard Sadi Carnot published *Reflections on the Motive Power of Fire* (1824). Carnot's attempts to understand the laws of physics that dictated how steam power worked led to a whole new field of science known as thermodynamics, from the Greek for heat power. But thermodynamics doesn't just explain how heat is moved around inside steam engines. It can also show how the universe will end.

A steam engine works by transforming energy from one form into another, eventually converting it into something useful like the motion of a piston to drive a pump or the spinning of a wheel to move a train. Coal is burned with oxygen to make carbon dioxide, in the process liberating heat energy. This heat energy is used to boil water into steam, which then expands. The expanding steam pushes on a piston which begins to move and can be made to do useful work. The chemical energy stored inside the coal has been converted into heat energy and then, via the water, the steam and the piston, into energy of motion. Sadi Carnot reasoned that the process which ultimately drove the engine was the tendency for heat energy to flow from a hot region to a cold one, until the temperature of the whole system was the same everywhere.

On a molecular scale, heat is really just the random motion of all of the atoms and molecules which make up an object. The more heat energy the object contains, the higher the average speed of its particles and the higher its temperature. The atoms and molecules are constantly colliding with each other and transferring energy from one to another, so the energy is constantly being redistributed around the object rather than being concentrated in just a few particles. If two objects with different temperatures are placed in contact, their atoms and molecules will begin to knock against each other, transferring energy between them. Overall, the atoms and molecules from the hotter object will transfer more energy to those in the colder object and there will be a net flow of heat until it is evenly spread between them and the objects are at the same temperature. This transfer of heat from a warm object to a colder one is known as the First Law of Thermodynamics.

The design of a steam engine allows some of this heat flow to be harnessed to do useful work. But scientists soon realised that no engine could ever be 100 per cent efficient because at every stage a fraction of the energy would be wasted: some of the energy from the burning coal will always warm the container rather than the water, some of the energy of the expanding steam will always warm the piston rather than push it, and some of the energy of the moving piston will be turned back into heat by friction with its surroundings. By improving the design of the engine, the amount of waste could be reduced and the efficiency improved, but no matter how hard you try the waste can never be entirely eliminated.

This is not just true of steam engines: any process which involves the transfer of energy from one form to another, or from one object to another, will involve some wastage as heat. When we fire a gun, chemical energy from the gunpowder is converted into the energy of the motion of the bullet, but inevitably some of it also heats the barrel of the gun itself or is turned into the sound of the gun firing (which eventually heats the air). When we switch on an old-fashioned lightbulb, the energy carried by the electrical current is converted into light, causing the metal filament in the bulb to glow, but a fraction of the energy is also converted into heat, causing the filament to get hot. Modern energy-saving lightbulbs use other, more efficient, methods to convert electrical energy into light energy, but a certain amount of heat is still produced.

What's true of steam engines, bullets and lightbulbs is also true of the universe as a whole: in every process occurring across the cosmos, from the orbit of planets to the shining of stars and the turning of galaxies, some energy is inevitably being converted into the random motion of particles – heat. In the long term, the tendency is for temperature differences across the universe to be evened out, as stars pour their heat and light into the frozen blackness of space and clouds of gas expand, collide and cool. This led the nineteenth-century physicist Lord Kelvin to imagine what we now call the 'heat death' of the universe: a time in the far future when all available energy has been converted to the random motions of heat and this heat is spread evenly across the whole universe. With no differences in temperature to cause energy to flow from one place to another, no useful work could be done and engines, bullets, lightbulbs and even life itself would be impossible.

One way of thinking about this process is that the universe is slowly but inexorably changing from an 'ordered' state, in which matter and energy are concentrated into complex structures like galaxies, stars, planets and people, to a 'disordered' state where they are spread out more randomly. Scientists have given a name to this universal quality of disorder – entropy. Its inevitable triumph is summarised by the Second Law of Thermodynamics, which states that entropy always increases.

We have an instinctive understanding of entropy because in some ways it defines our sense of the direction of time. If we put a dollop of strawberry jam in our porridge and stir it in, we expect the porridge to become pink as the molecules of the jam and the porridge are randomly mixed together. However long we stirred for, we would be extremely surprised to see the jam begin to separate out into a dollop again – and if we saw a film of this happening we would guess that the film was being played backwards.

Technically, it's not impossible for stirring to cause the jam and the porridge molecules to separate out again, just very, *very* unlikely. We can think of it as a game of probabilities: if we imagine all the ways we could arrange the trillions of porridge molecules and the trillions of jam molecules in a bowl, the vast majority of these would involve a random mix of porridge and jam – a disordered state. Only a small fraction of the possible arrangements would involve an ordered state, with all the porridge molecules neatly in one part of the bowl and all the jam molecules in another.

The same is true of any other system which involves a very specific arrangement of matter and energy. If we drop a cup of tea, it will go from an ordered state, in which silicate molecules are arranged in a cup shape and water, milk and tea molecules are confined to a cup-shaped volume, to a disordered state in which fragments of china and splashes of tea are spread randomly on the floor. There are simply far more ways to go from an ordered state to a disordered one than the other way round, so as time progresses teacups smash but shards of china and pools of liquid never spontaneously combine to form steaming cups of tea.

One intriguing exception to this rule of ever-increasing entropy is life. Living things are by definition highly ordered structures which depend on complex arrangements of molecules and carefully controlled flows of energy in order to function. Throughout their lifespans, living organisms seem to be able to keep entropy at bay, continuously maintaining their ordered state in apparent defiance of the Second Law of Thermodynamics. But this is only a partial victory: life maintains itself at the expense of its surroundings, pumping heat and excreting waste materials back into the environment – and the total entropy of the universe is still increased.

'Entropy increases! The more you keep putting things together the more they keep falling apart!'
The Fourth Doctor, *Logopolis* (1981)

Ideas of entropy on a personal and a universal scale are explored in the *Doctor Who* story *Logopolis* (1981). Here it is revealed that the universe should have reached the point of heat death long ago but entropy has been kept at bay by the mathematicians of the planet Logopolis, who have found a way to siphon it off into neighbouring universes (what the inhabitants of these other universes think of the plan is never mentioned). Through the actions of the Doctor's arch enemy, the Master, the vital gateways are closed and entropy begins to claim the galaxies, stars and planets of our universe – including the home world of the Doctor's companion, Nyssa.

In the story, the Fourth Doctor is able to halt the process and prevent the universe from collapsing into the ultimate disordered state, but only at the cost of his own life. However, this seems to be only a temporary – if long-lasting – reprieve: in *Utopia* (2007), the TARDIS travels forwards to the year 100 trillion, to an exhausted universe of fading stars and dying planets.

Just as the Fourth Doctor gave his live to save the universe, so all living things must eventually die. Life may be a process of holding entropy at bay but this can only be a temporary victory. Eventually all living systems begin to fail: ageing and death are, of course, examples of the inevitable trend towards increasing entropy.

'The Time Lords are an immensely civilised race. We can control our own environment, we can live for ever, barring accidents.'

The Second Doctor, *The War Games* (1969)

There are several ways that medical scientists can think about ageing. One is in terms of the general wear and tear that a body undergoes during a lifetime, which is determined to some extent by lifestyle and chance. For a time, your body can withstand and even repair much of the daily damage that it incurs but eventually the effects accumulate until something tips it over the edge – the straw that breaks the camel's back

But if we could entirely limit the damage done to a body, how long might a person live for? The longest human lifespan on record (with good evidence to confirm the claim) is that of a French woman, Jeanne Calment, who lived for 122 years and 164 days between 1875 and 1997. In her long life, she had watched the Eiffel Tower being built, and once even sold coloured pencils to the artist Vincent van Gogh – 100 years later, she remembered him as 'dirty, badly dressed and disagreeable'.

A scientist who tried to investigate the secret of Calment's longevity could find nothing exceptional about the way she lived, but it was discovered that several members of her family had also been long-lived: her brother died at 97, her father at 94 and her mother at 86, while ancestors in the seventeenth and eighteenth centuries had lived into their 70s – well above the average of the time. While Calment's environment – she lived all her long life in Arles in southern France – might have helped, it seemed her longevity was inherited.

Another way to think about ageing is that there are biological limitations – a bit like the biological clocks we discussed in Chapters 7 and 8. Senescence, from the Latin word to mean 'growing old', is the scientific name for ageing – either of cells or a whole organism. In cellular senescence, there seems to be a limit on how many times cells can divide and reproduce. Research suggests that this is the result of telomeres, which 'cap' the end of our DNA, a little like the plastic tips at the end of a shoelace. When we're young, a telomere contains thousands of repetitions of a six-letter DNA sequence. When a cell divides, some of the telomere is lost – and after several divisions, too much has been lost for the cell to divide again. It can still play a useful part in the body – senescent cells seem to play a role in battling a number of diseases – but recent experiments suggest that removing senescent cells from the body can increase resistance to age-related diseases, suggesting that cellular senescence is directly linked to ageing. However, the senescence of a whole organism is much more difficult to understand because it is so complicated, involving many separate processes all happening at once.

People often equate the process of ageing with age-related diseases, such as heart disease, cancer, arthritis or dementia. There are ways to combat these diseases. As we saw in Chapter 8, it's been shown that an active mind can reduce the risks of dementia. But what we understand about telomeres suggests that lifespan is hardwired into our DNA.

It has also been suggested that all living creatures have a limited average number of heartbeats or breaths – so that lifespan is defined by the speed of our biological clocks, called our 'metabolic rate'. If this is true, the slower our clocks run, the more time it takes us to reach our limit of heartbeats, so the longer we live. There is evidence to support this theory in general: we can compare the heart rates of different animals that have different lifespans. However, different species seem to have different limits. In fact, lifespan is probably a mixture of many different factors.

In *Doctor Who*, it seems that the Time Lords have worked out how to control all these different factors. Of course we know that Time Lords are able to regenerate, restoring their ageing or damaged bodies to a new, healthy state – perhaps by resetting their biological clocks (we'll discuss the process in Chapter 15). But even between regenerations Time Lords seem to age much more slowly than humans – a single incarnation of a Time Lord can live for hundreds of years. In *The Time of the Doctor* (2013), the Eleventh Doctor lives in a town called Christmas for a thousand years. He ages, but at a much slower rate than a human.

That said, this rate of ageing in Time Lords seems related to regeneration. In *The Sound of Drums* (2007), the Master can use what he calls the Doctor's 'biological code' to age him by a hundred years – a process that would kill most humans. In the next episode, *Last of the Time Lords* (2007), the Master ages the Doctor even more, turning him into a small, wizened creature. But the Master claims he's done this by suspending the Doctor's 'capacity to regenerate', which somehow lets us see all 900 years of the Doctor's life at once.

Whatever the mechanisms by which humans and Time Lords age, the different rates of ageing causes problems for the Doctor when he travels with human companions.

'I don't age. I regenerate. But humans decay.
You wither and you die. Imagine watching
that happen to someone who you—'

'What, Doctor?'

'You can spend the rest of your life with me, but I
can't spend the rest of mine with you. I have to live on.
Alone. That's the curse of the Time Lords.'

$\partial^3 \sum^7 x^2$ **The Tenth Doctor and Rose Tyler, *School Reunion* (2006)**

If we didn't outlive our loved ones – if they all had long lives, too
– there would still be problems. In fact, some scientists think death
might play an important role in evolution.

As we saw in Chapter 11, food and resources in any environment
are often limited. The theory is that once a living organism has raised
its offspring to adulthood, it will then compete with them for those
limited resources. It would seem to be an advantage to the species – if
not the individual – for the parent to die once the offspring is fully
grown, as that means the offspring doesn't have to compete for the
limited food, and so is more likely to produce offspring of its own.
Again, other factors may also play a part: in some species such as
humans, different generations tend to cooperate rather than compete.
But in a crisis, human adults will often put children's needs ahead of
their own. We're used to the idea of putting 'women and children first'
– and perhaps that's not just part of our culture, but also hardwired
into our cells. Dying so others can live isn't just about morality – it's
a good tactic for the long-term survival of the species or the genes we
share with our family or kin groups.

In *The Brain of Morbius* (1976), the Fourth Doctor meets the
Sisterhood of Karn, whose elixir can prolong life for centuries. As the
Doctor explains, the fact that the sisterhood can all live very long lives
means that nothing ever changes in the sisterhood, which leaves them

unprepared for a contest with the evil Morbius. As the Doctor tells the sisterhood's leader, Maren:

'Death is the price we pay for progress.'

The Fourth Doctor, *The Brain of Morbius*

Maren later concedes the point and dies to save the Doctor's life. Change is how we survive. Of course, on several different occasions – including when he visits Karn again in *The Night of the Doctor* – the Doctor survives death by changing his whole persona…

THE CONSTANT DOCTOR

ANDREW SMITH

'Looks like we're joining a party!'

Nyssa was first out of the TARDIS. They had landed in a side street of a sprawling alien city, and as she stepped into the main thoroughfare she was struck by the colour, bustle and noise of a metropolis in celebratory mood.

She was reminded of the Festival of the Harvest Moon back on Traken, but on a much larger scale. Everywhere there were flags, balloons, banners and ribbons. Many of the hundreds of people who thronged the street were dressed in gaudy, brightly coloured costumes with patterned face masks. Stalls and makeshift entertainments lined the middle of the street.

The Doctor, Adric and Tegan joined her and took in the scene.

'Is it some kind of carnival?' Tegan asked.

The Doctor said, 'A celebration of some kind, certainly.'

At the sound of approaching music, Nyssa looked round and saw a group of young men and women moving in their direction through the crowds. Four of them played strange musical instruments, spirals of metal whose surfaces responded melodically to the players' touch. The others were skipping and hopping to the music and handing out slips of printed, glossy paper.

A young man at the front of the small parade thrust one of the pieces of paper into Nyssa's hand. 'Happy Freedom Day, friend!' he cried.

'Freedom Day?' said Nyssa.

The young man looked curious. 'Don't you know?' Then he looked at her companions, nodded his understanding and spread his arms wide. 'Of course. You are visitors. Welcome to Lemaria!'

'Thank you,' said the Doctor.

Adric asked, 'What's Freedom Day?'

'Why, friend, it is the anniversary of Lemaria's liberation! Ten years since we were saved from the cruel alien race who invaded Lemaria and enslaved us!'

'What happened, exactly?' asked Tegan.

The young man saw that his friends had moved on some way into the crowds and he ran after them. He called back over his shoulder, 'Read the flyer! Come and see! You'll love it!'

Adric asked, 'What's a flyer?'

The Doctor pointed to the piece of paper in Nyssa's hand. 'That. It's an advertisement.'

Nyssa looked at the paper.

The
CAPITAL HISTORICAL SOCIETY
presents

THE LIBERATION OF LEMARIA!

A re-enactment

Performed every half hour
****
Venue: The Public Amphitheatre, Capital Square
Admission: FREE

The Doctor said, 'Can I see?' and took the paper from Nyssa. He scanned it and said to Tegan and Adric, 'They're putting on a theatrical performance. A depiction of the events of ten years ago.'

Adric and Tegan stepped close to the Doctor to read the flyer. As they did, Nyssa looked around. And up.

Oh.

She took a few steps into the street to get a better look at the side of the building next to them.

The Doctor said, 'It must be an extremely concise history, if they're performing it every half hour.'

'Shall we have a look?' asked Adric.

The Doctor said, 'Amateur dramatics aren't really my thing.'

Nyssa called, 'Doctor?' and pointed up.

The Doctor, Tegan and Adric joined her and looked up, following her finger.

Tegan said, 'Well now.'

Adric said, 'Is that… ?'

The Doctor said, 'Ah.'

On the wall was an enormous mural. From its depiction of hundreds of fallen, lizard-like bodies and exploding spacecraft, and the accompanying portrayal of cheering Lemarians, this was clearly an illustration of the planet's freedom from the 'cruel alien race' that had enslaved them.

Which was fine, thought Nyssa. Except, at the very centre of the painting, taking pride of place, was the unmistakable likeness of a familiar blue box .

Adric answered his own question. 'It is. It's the TARDIS!'

Nyssa said, 'If it's the TARDIS, who's that?'

She pointed to the figure of a man standing in the open TARDIS doors, looking out with a wave and acknowledging the Lemarians' cheers. He was old. *Really* old. With thick shoulder-length white hair. He wore a dark frock coat over a dress shirt with a black ribbon tie, and checked trousers. She supposed there was only person it could be.

'He's you,' said Nyssa. 'In the future, when you're old.'

The Doctor sighed, and said, 'Well, yes. But also no.'

They found the venue for the performance in a communal square at the far end of the main street. Tiered stone seating rose in a semicircle in front of a simple wooden stage.

The amphitheatre was filling up as the time travellers took their seats. The Doctor guided his companions to the back row.

On their way here they had seen more murals, and some banners, similarly depicting the TARDIS and various likenesses of this other Doctor. He was clearly revered by the Lemarians.

Tegan and Adric had been as surprised as Nyssa to learn that the elderly-looking man in the mural was yet another version of the very same man standing next to them.

While her friends had produced a flurry of questions for the Doctor (all of which had been deflected by his decision that they should indeed come to see this performance), Nyssa had become quiet, and had withdrawn into her thoughts.

She knew, as they all did, that the Doctor could alter his appearance and even his personality. They had seen it. He had changed in front of their eyes from a tall, curly-haired and sometimes abrasive man into the blond-haired, much more affable young Doctor with whom they now travelled. The Doctor called it 'regeneration', a means by which Time Lords extended their lives.

Her friends found the Doctor's regenerative ability fascinating and exciting. But for her it was a reminder of what had happened soon after she had first met the Doctor. Of when she had lost her father, his life and likeness stolen as part of another Time Lord's regeneration. The way the Doctor's people could cheat their way round death.

She brushed a tear from her eye and shook her head, steeling herself to subdue her emotions before they were noticed.

As they settled to await the performance, Adric said, 'So you were here before. You saved this planet.'

The Doctor shrugged. 'It seems so.'

Nyssa said, 'You don't remember?'

The Doctor said, 'There have been quite a few planets. And it would have been a long time ago.'

'You don't recognise those lizard things in the paintings?' asked Tegan.

The Doctor said, 'There have been quite a few lizard things.'

'Maybe this will jog your memory,' she suggested.

'Perhaps,' said the Doctor. 'Although it looks like it will be a minimalist show.'

Nyssa considered the stage dressings. A black drape dappled with white dots – presumably a starscape – had been hung as a backdrop. The stage was decorated with a few stones and plants, and a further drape had been hung to obscure the far left side of the performance area.

Adric said, 'How many of you have there been, Doctor?'

The Doctor hesitated before answering, 'Well … Including me, five.'

'Five?!' The volume of Tegan's reaction drew a disapproving look from a stern-faced woman in front of them.

Nyssa said, 'It's starting.'

There was a flourish of music. The group of musicians who had passed them in the street appeared to the right of the stage. They struck up a rousing overture.

Then the young man who had spoken to Nyssa strode out, centre stage, and bowed.

'Lemarians and most welcome visitors! Greetings! Prepare to be regaled with the story of how, ten years ago this very day, we the people of Lemaria were released from years of enslavement to the evil, brutal Megrati!'

At that, a figure leapt onto the stage from behind the obscuring drape, accompanied by a sting of music. He was dressed in the lurid costume of a lizard man, with clawed hands and feet and a bulbous head from which hung a forked tongue.

'That's not very convincing,' scoffed Tegan.

The lizard-man gave an exaggerated roar and reared up, showing his claws for the audience.

The Lemarians in the audience booed.

The young narrator continued, 'The Megrati had come to our world professing friendship...'

A male and female Lemarian walked onstage. Seeing the Megrati they overacted looks of horror. The Megrati spread its arms in a placatory, reassuring gesture. The man and woman immediately relaxed and smiled at the creature.

Nyssa doubted that events would have been anything like as straightforward as this. But she could make allowances for dramatic licence.

The narrator said grimly, 'But no sooner had we taken them into our trust than they showed their true colours!'

Nyssa gave a small gasp as the Megrati swiped at the Lemarians. Although his costume claw missed them by a good two feet, they screamed and fell. The Megrati again roared and clawed towards the audience, who again booed.

'Oh, please,' said Tegan.

The narrator cried, 'The Megrati killed tens of thousands of Lemarians before they accepted our surrender! And what a grim, hopeless existence then awaited us... slaves of the Megrati!'

The 'dead' Lemarians jumped nimbly to their feet and rushed behind the curtain. They reappeared moments later with metal collars round their necks and chains on their ankles. The male Lemarian was carrying a whip that he helpfully handed to the Megrati.

The Megrati cracked the whip and the two Lemarians wailed.

'For twenty long years we suffered, and many died, under the yoke of the Megrati,' said the narrator. 'But then came the traveller... The Doctor!'

The drape that had been obscuring the left of the stage was dropped. Revealing the TARDIS.

The audience burst into rapturous applause.

Nyssa smiled at the Doctor, who was looking more than a little embarrassed.

'At least they put some effort into that prop,' he muttered. 'Though it's not quite right.'

A moment later, the TARDIS door opened and a man stepped out. The audience cheered.

Nyssa considered this man, dressed as in the mural – frock coat, ribbon tie and checked trousers. An obvious wig of flowing white hair finished off the costume.

The 'Doctor' struck a pose, clutching his lapels and tilting his head back.

Beside her, the real Doctor shook his head. 'This is a pantomime.'

On stage, a young girl with thick dark hair joined the elderly-looking Doctor, who placed a protective arm around her and said, 'Well, child, shall we explore this strange new world, hmm?'

The girl said, 'Oh yes, let's, Grandfather!'

Nyssa felt herself react as if from an electric shock. She turned to the Doctor and saw that Adric and Tegan were also staring at him in amazement.

The Doctor looked extremely uncomfortable. He drew breath as if he was about to explain. Then he pointed, a sudden jerk of his finger towards the side of the stage – to a man carrying a tray of foodstuffs.

'Hunka burgers,' said the Doctor. 'All part of the experience of live drama. This will be my treat.'

And with that he rushed off down the steps.

Tegan shook her head. 'That's one way to get out of a difficult conversation.'

Nyssa turned to Adric, who had travelled with the Doctor the longest – as he liked to remind her and Tegan. 'Did you know he had family?'

Adric shifted uncomfortably in his seat. 'I suppose it never came up,' he said.

Nyssa returned her gaze to the stage, where the 'Doctor' was leaving his granddaughter to confront the Megrati, who was dominating the two Lemarians with his whip.

'You, sir, will desist from this monstrous behaviour!'

And with that he snatched the whip from the Megrati's hand and threw it aside.

The audience gave a collective gasp.

Adric said, 'He's a bit different.'

Tegan said, 'I didn't like him at first, but he's growing on me.'

The stage Doctor was now breaking off the chains of the Lemarian slaves and berating the Megrati.

Tegan laughed. 'I think I would have liked this old Doctor. You tell 'im, Doc!' Then her smile fell. She looked to be considering her words. She said, 'When he changed, from curly hair to our one... For the longest time, I thought it was kind of creepy.'

'I felt the same,' said Adric. 'I'd got to know him. That other him. I liked him. When he regenerated, it took me a long time to accept that he was... well, him. The Doctor.'

Nyssa said, 'I wonder if he knows what effect it has on others. He's a Time Lord. To him regeneration is natural. Maybe he forgets what it's like for those of us who only ever have one face, and one body.'

Tegan shook her head. 'If it's weird for us, it must be worse for him. Imagine what it must be like: losing almost everything that made you who you were, and suddenly being someone new.'

On stage, the Megrati was walking off with its head hung low while several Lemarians jeered at it. Models of space saucers on strings appeared from over the backdrop, swung from side to side, then flew off out of sight in an apparent depiction of the Megrati hordes leaving the planet.

'I think I do remember something about this,' said a voice behind them.

The Doctor climbed over the back of their seats a little awkwardly with four greasy blue *somethings* in buns in his hands. As he took his seat he went on, 'It was over very quickly. There was already a resistance faction among the people. I just gave them a helping hand. The Lemarians were brave, and in the end they succeeded. They drove out the Megrati.'

'In their spacecraft on strings,' Tegan laughed.

The Doctor smiled. 'You're meant to use your imagination.'

'Although,' said Adric, 'they've done a good job with that TARDIS prop. Except for that funny thing on the doors, the white circle.'

The Doctor explained, 'That's a St John ambulance symbol, the TARDIS had one of those at the time. But you're right.' He paused and leaned forward, staring at the blue box. 'In fact, it's a *very* good copy...'

Tegan said, 'Has anyone else noticed his voice? Is it just me, or does he sound Scottish?'

'What's Scottish?' asked Nyssa.

The Doctor turned his attention to the actor, who was now retreating to the TARDIS and saying, 'Perhaps I'll return in a hundred years and see how your world is flourishing. So you'd better get on with rebuilding it, hadn't you, hmm? You're safe now from the Megrati...'

The actor paused. He turned his head to the sky, as though looking for something, then turned back to his audience. 'You have my word.'

The audience applauded and cheered, and it seemed the play was over. The 'Doctor' took a bow, and the other cast members joined him on the stage. As they enjoyed the adulation, the 'Doctor' beamed at the audience, his eyes picking over the seats. But when his eyes found the seats where the time travellers were sitting, he did an odd thing.

He smiled.

Nyssa thought for a moment he was smiling directly at her. But then she caught a movement out of the corner of her eye and turned to look at the Doctor.

He was smiling, too. And now he lifted his Panama hat, doffing it towards the man on stage.

Then a terrible thunder shook the seats underneath them. Part of the stage fell forward, nearly crushing the actors. There were cries of terror from the audience and from the surrounding streets.

'An earthquake!' yelled Tegan.

'If we're lucky,' said the Doctor. 'No, don't run. We're safer here, I think.'

Adric pointed into the sky. 'Look!'

Nyssa had seen many types of spacecraft during her travels with the Doctor. She had even seen warships. But she had seen nothing like the enormous craft descending from the sky above; hundreds of metal darts, each more than three miles long and bristling with weapons. So huge, even though the ships were a hundred or more miles above them.

Nyssa recognised them as full-size versions of what the audience had just seen hanging on strings as part of the performance. The audience recognised them, too, and stared in dumb-founded horror.

The Megrati had returned.

The gun ports on the Megrati ships turned downwards, ready to fire.

Nyssa said nervously, 'Are you sure we shouldn't run?'

The Doctor said, 'I doubt there's time.'

Then, a reddish yellow ball of energy materialised on stage. When it faded, in its place was a Megrati. Not some man in a rubber suit, but the real thing. Green scales rippled over a muscly, eight-foot frame. Saliva dripped from its oversized, chipped fangs. In one hand it held a whip. In the other a large and threatening blaster.

The crowd reacted in terror.

'Who summons me?!' cried the Megrati.

And now the crowd looked bemused.

The Megrati snarled in frustration. 'Before you die, before we take our revenge on you, I will know, who summoned the Grand Megrati!'

The stage Doctor placed himself in front of the Megrati and said, 'That was me. I detected your invasion fleet when it was still twelve parsecs from here. I sent you that invitation – not a summons – because I thought you and I should have a chat when you arrived. Then I came here, thought I'd join the party while I waited.'

The Megrati looked this strange figure up and down. 'Who are you?'

'Oh, how soon you lot forget. Have a guess.'

The Megrati uttered a roaring laugh. Then the roar became a snarl, and it raised its whip hand.

The stage Doctor's hand shot out and gripped the Megrati's wrist. The alien brought its blaster up, but the Doctor kicked out and the weapon flew from its hand.

The Megrati snarled, 'Who are you?'

The stage Doctor said, 'I'm the man who's going to stop this before it starts. You are going to turn your fleet around, now, and leave.'

'You're a madman,' said the Megrati.

'If not, I will destroy your fleet.' The stage Doctor reached into his jacket and produced something that he pointed into the sky. 'Beginning with your Command Ship.'

The Megrati said, 'You are one man. Against an army. You cannot defeat us.'

'You wouldn't be the first to think so.' The stage Doctor looked up at the largest of the warships in the sky above. The Command Ship. Then he looked back at the Megrati.

'MCD engines, yes?' he asked.

The Megrati hesitated, then growled, 'Yes.'

The stage Doctor nodded. 'Megamonolithic Crystal Drive. The poor sentient being's answer to Hyperdrive. Terribly good at getting you from one side of a galaxy to another...'

The object in the stage Doctor's hand now emitted a shrill tone, and glowed a vivid emerald green.

Nyssa recognised the tone of a sonic screwdriver. Her heart leapt.

The stage Doctor went on, 'But MCD crystals are highly susceptible to targeted sonic beams.'

There was an explosion at the rear of the Command Ship. Its engine casings erupted, shattered by eruptions of white hot power. The vessel pitched upwards, its hull straining, groaning like some great wounded animal.

'Your crew will have time to abandon ship,' said the stage Doctor.

He lowered the sonic screwdriver, and released his grip on the Megrati. It backed away from him, continuing to look up.

The Command Ship rose slowly in the upper atmosphere. Smaller explosions erupted sporadically along the hull. Escape pods appeared in swarms from openings along the vessel's underbelly and sped away towards other ships in the fleet.

'My ship!' the Megrati protested. 'How did you do that?!'

Nyssa heard her Doctor, next to her, say quietly, 'Sympathetic destruction.'

On stage, the Doctor in the frock coat said, 'Sympathetic destruction! The crystals in your engines are networked to the crystals that power the rest of the ship. I set up a resonance and they vibrated to destruction. Once that starts, there's nothing you people can do about it but get to the lifeboats.'

The Megrati fumed.

'Now,' said the stage Doctor, determinedly, 'give the order. Call off your attack and leave. Or I'll do the same with every ship you've got.'

For a moment, the Megrati didn't speak. It looked again to the heavens, where the Command Ship was now a lifeless, scarred hulk, drifting away.

Then it lifted a scaly wrist and spoke into a communicator band. 'Fleet… Stand down. Agrylus, you are now the Command Ship. Teleport me aboard.'

The Megrati snarled at the stage Doctor as it waited to leave.

The stage Doctor said, still loud enough for everyone to hear, 'Never return. If you do, there won't be any warnings next time. And you'll have no fleet left.'

The Megrati made no reply. A moment later it was enveloped in the same reddish yellow energy field in which it had arrived, and it faded away.

Everyone looked up. Sure enough, the Megrati ships were turning to leave.

A voice in the crowd cried out, 'Do it! Don't let them get away! Do the same to all their ships!'

There was immediate support from pockets of the audience.

'You've got them at your mercy!'

'Kill them!'

'Deal with them once and for all!'

The stage Doctor turned to the crowd with such a look that they fell quiet. Then he sighed. 'Is that what you want? Is that what you really want? Shall I kill them?'

No one answered.

'After all,' the Doctor continued, 'like you say, that would deal with them once and for all... Hey, maybe you're right.' He held out his sonic screwdriver. 'So come up here. Take this from me. And you can do it yourself. Well?'

No one moved. Then a movement right beside her made Nyssa jump. But it was only her Doctor, leaning forward, elbows on knees, hands crossed, as raptly interested in what would happen next as anyone.

After a long moment, the stage Doctor smiled. 'Well, then. They're leaving... and so am I.'

Nyssa's Doctor sat back with a broad grin on his face.

The stage Doctor went to the TARDIS and opened the doors. He paused on the threshold and said to his audience, 'I'll see them safely out of this star system... In the meantime, why not carry on with your party? You've got something to celebrate.'

As the majority of the audience burst into applause, Nyssa smiled. Whatever face the Doctor wore, she thought, he is always the Doctor.

The stage Doctor gave a deep, theatrical bow.

His white wig dropped to the stage, revealing a tidy, shorter crop of dusty-grey hair underneath.

He straightened, a bit awkwardly, and backed towards the police box.

With just a quick smile towards the rear seats, he ducked inside and closed the door.

Adric said, 'He's left his granddaughter behind.'

Tegan sighed and gave him a shove. 'Adric, you dill.'

Then the air was filled with an all too familiar groaning, rasping sound. And the TARDIS faded from the stage.

FIFTEEN

REGENERATION

In *Deep Breath*, Clara struggles to come to terms with the Doctor's latest regeneration. Although she's seen the Doctor's previous incarnations, it's still a shock that the young-looking man she knew – and loved – is dead, and in his place stands an older-looking man with angry eyebrows and a Scottish accent.

In *Doctor Who*, regeneration involves a change of appearance and the healing of wounds and diseases. Apparently, it can sometimes involve a change of gender, but seems always to involve a change of personality – yet the regenerated person keeps the same memories. They are a different person and yet they are the same, which is why regeneration is such a strange and unsettling concept.

Yet it's not a wholly *alien* concept. Regeneration happens on Earth, too. Perhaps fittingly, one of the first scientists to really investigate regeneration on Earth was himself a Scottish doctor.

In 1763, the Scottish surgeon John Hunter arrived in London after three years working for the British army in France and Portugal. Struggling to find work in the capital as a surgeon, Hunter worked in a dentistry practice instead. At the time, sugar was very cheap – largely because of the huge number of unpaid slaves involved in its production – and lots of people in London had bad teeth that caused them pain. Hunter's dental practice didn't just remove people's bad teeth, it offered to replace them.

If you were poor but had apparently healthy teeth, Hunter's dental practice would offer good money to buy them. The healthy teeth would then be extracted and transplanted into the toothless mouth of a rich person, who would pay handsomely for the service.

As accurate medical records were not kept at the time, it's difficult to know how well the transplants worked, or how often they led to the spread of other diseases. But Hunter, as a surgeon, was interested in the principles of transplanting, and conducted a number of experiments. He successfully transplanted the claw from a cockerel onto its comb, and even tried implanting a human tooth into another cockerel to see if it was possible to do a transplant between different species of animal. Today, we might find those experiments crude, not to mention cruel, but Hunter learnt valuable lessons about the importance of transplanted tissue being fresh and of matching the size of transplanted organs.

This research paid off for him. In 1767, he was elected a fellow of the Royal Society – which remains to this day an academy of the most distinguished scientists – and the following year he was made a surgeon at St George's Hospital in London. He even became surgeon to King George III. But Hunter continued to study animals – and had access to the King's menagerie of interesting creatures. When one of these died in 1776, Hunter became the first person ever to dissect an elephant.

Since his days in France and Portugal, Hunter had collected specimens of animals. As a distinguished surgeon, he was sent more – including rare specimens of kangaroos collected from James Cook's voyage to Australia in 1768–1771. He also collected specimens of unusual humans – bits of bone that showed examples of particular diseases or medical complications, and even the whole skeletons of people who were very short or very tall.

Hunter used his collection to teach both the public and the next generation of surgeons. After his death, his collection was given to the Royal College of Surgeons where, as the Hunterian Museum, it continues to be used to teach surgeons. The public can visit, too, and the cockerels on which he experimented with transplants are still on display.

Importantly, while other doctors of the time taught human anatomy, Hunter was keen on comparing the structure and function of animal bodies, too, and the different ways that bodies can adapt to or compensate for damage done to them. This comparative work led to major scientific advances: one of Hunter's students, Edward Jenner, investigated a mild disease called cowpox, which dairymaids caught from their cows. Jenner's interest was that these dairymaids seemed not to catch a more common and deadly disease called smallpox. He gave people cowpox – and they were then immune to smallpox. His discovery – vaccination – takes its name from 'vacca', Latin for cow.

We now know that when we get the mild disease cowpox, our bodies easily develop antibodies to neutralise it. Cowpox is similar in structure if not in effect to smallpox, so antibodies developed to neutralise cowpox will neutralise smallpox, too. Jenner's vaccination – and the improved versions that followed it – led to the World Health Organization announcing in 1980 that smallpox was the first disease to be eradicated, via a vaccination programme carried out worldwide.

Comparative anatomy had other uses, too. In 1824, the doctor and geologist Gideon Mantell visited Hunter's collection, and found that the teeth of a specimen of iguana there looked like tiny versions of giant fossilised teeth Mantell had acquired some years earlier. This led Mantell to name the fossilised creature he'd discovered Iguanadon – 'Iguana-tooth'. Along with the fossilised remains of two other creatures, Iguanadon would later be used to define a new kind of animal: the dinosaur.

But Hunter had been interested in iguana because of a remarkable feature of its tail. Like many lizards, if an iguana is caught by its tail – for example, by a predator – it can let its tail break off and so escape.

Eventually, the tail will grow back – in a process called regeneration. That process always fascinated Hunter. In fact, one of his earliest animal specimens, collected while he was in Portugal in the early 1760s, is still on display as object 2222 in the Hunterian Museum.

The specimen is of a lizard called a Lacerta – and it has two tails. Hunter's own notes describe how if a lizard's original tail is only partly detached, or if a new tail is split while early in its growth, two tails will be formed. There, in a glass jar in the museum, is something rather like what happens to the newly regenerated Tenth Doctor in *The Christmas Invasion* (2005), when he regrows his severed hand.

> 'Quite by chance I'm still within the first fifteen hours of my regeneration cycle, which means I've got just enough residual cellular energy to do this…'
> **The Tenth Doctor, *The Christmas Invasion* (2005)**

We now know that all life on Earth is able to regenerate to some degree. Segmented worms – such as the earthworms you might find in a garden – can regenerate their bodies if they are cut in half crossways. In fact, both halves will regenerate into complete worms, creating two genetically identical worms where once there was just one. (Something like this happens in *Journey's End* (2008), when the Tenth Doctor siphons off excess regeneration energy into the hand severed in *The Christmas Invasion* – which, as a result, grows into a second, separate version of himself.)

The reason earthworms can regenerate like this is because their bodies contain clusters of stem cells. Stem cells are useful because, through a process called cellular differentiation, they can become more specialised for different roles in the body. It's a bit like the Doctor's sonic screwdriver – a single tool that can do lots of very different jobs. In human adults, stem cells can differentiate in ways that help repair different kinds of damage to the body. But in human embryos, stem cells have a much greater range of differentiation: they can become specialised in *any* of the ways the body needs.

Earthworms retain these kind of embryonic stem cells into adulthood, which is why they can wholly regenerate when they've been cut in half. Some larger animals retain stem cells like this, too. It's how iguanas and lizards can regrow their tails, while many amphibians can regrow lost limbs.

This kind of regeneration doesn't always happen immediately. For example, as crabs grow they get too big for their hard, protective shells. As a result, they must periodically shed their shells and – hiding away because they are vulnerable – grow new and roomier ones. This process – called 'moulting' – is somehow linked to regeneration, because while it is happening, the crabs can also regrow any limbs or claws they might have lost.

One Earth creature is even known to be able to regenerate the whole of its body. *Turritopsis dohrnii* are found in the Mediterranean Sea and also in the waters round Japan. They start their lives as tiny larvae called *planula*, which then settle on the seafloor as tube-shaped polyps, and from these polyps grow jellyfish. But when *Turritopsis dohrnii* jellyfish get old or sick or face danger, they can become polyps again – in effect, going back to their childhood state in a form of rejuvenation.

'Ben, do you remember what [the Doctor] said
in the tracking room? Something about,
"This old body of mine is wearing a bit thin."'

'So he gets himself a new one?'

Polly and Ben Jackson, *The Power of the Daleks* (1966)

The mechanism for this extraordinary process is transdifferentiation – the ability of stem cells to specialise into particular forms and then turn back again into stem cells. *Turritopsis dohrnii* seem able to grow old and regenerate many times, which is why they are more commonly known as immortal jellyfish.

If human beings could somehow tap into that mechanism of transdifferentiation, could we regenerate our whole bodies, too? In *Doctor*

Who, that's what happens in *The Lazarus Experiment* (2007), in which 76-year-old Professor Richard Lazarus is 'reborn' as a man of about 40.

'Hypersonic sound waves to destabilise the cell structure, then a metagenic program to manipulate the coding in the protein strands. Basically, he hacked into his own genes and instructed them to rejuvenate.'

The Tenth Doctor, *The Lazarus Experiment* (2007)

Of course, as the story makes clear, such technological innovation comes with risks. If we can make our cells change, how do we make sure they change only by the right amount or into the right things? As we saw in Chapter 14, our bodies comprise a whole series of complicated systems and processes – and if we get those out of sync, the result can be deadly.

In *Doctor Who*, the result can be even worse than that. When Lazarus manipulates his own cells, something in his DNA is activated that causes continual change, transforming him into a huge monster. In another story, *Mawdryn Undead* (1983), the Fifth Doctor meets aliens who have stolen a Time Lord machine designed to help when their regenerations go wrong. With it, the aliens hope to be able to regenerate themselves – but instead the result is to lock them into a continual cycle of degeneration and renewal. In eternal agony but unable to die, the aliens ask the Doctor to help them end their self-inflicted torment.

In real life, research is ongoing into the ways that stem cells might help us regenerate our bodies safely. But though we cannot yet regenerate our entire bodies, we partially regenerate all the time. Scars, bruises and sunburn are all signs of your skin regenerating, working to heal different kinds of damage. It's thought we replace all of our skin every two weeks or so.

Other parts of our bodies can regenerate, too. The endometrium in the uterus of human women entirely regenerates as part of a monthly cycle. (It also regenerates cyclically in the females of great apes, though at different rates to humans.) We seem able to regrow the tips of our fingers and toes if they are damaged, and human livers have been known to regrow themselves from just a quarter of the original tissue.

Individual cells in our bodies are continually dying and being replaced and it's sometimes claimed that we regenerate *all* our cells over a period of seven to ten years. If that were true then are we the same person now that we were eleven years ago?

> 'You take a broom, you replace the handle, and then later you replace the brush. And you do that over and over again. Is it still the same broom? Answer? No, of course it isn't.'
> **The Twelfth Doctor, *Deep Breath* (2014)**

Versions of this question have been debated for a long time. The Greek historian Plutarch included it in his book, *Lives of the Noble Greeks and Romans*, in the first century AD. In Plutarch's version, the hero Theseus owns a ship, and when its timbers decay they are replaced. After several hundred years of these repairs none of the original timbers remain. Plutarch tells us that the philosophers of his time were divided about whether that meant it was the same ship.

Whatever the case for Theseus's ship, it seems that we humans don't in fact regenerate all our cells. Cardiomyocyte cells in the heart are replaced very slowly, and the rate decreases as we age. Even those of us who live to be very old are unlikely to have replaced more than half our cardiomyocyte cells by the time we die. Scientists have also attempted to study whether neurons in the human brain regenerate or stay the same throughout our lives.

Surprisingly, the way they do this is to use nuclear weapons. The atomic bombs dropped on Japan at the end of the Second World War in 1945 and subsequent testing of ever more powerful nuclear weapons increased levels of carbon-14 – a radioactive isotope – in the atmosphere. The levels have decreased ever since, but scientists know by exactly how much.

Carbon-14 in the atmosphere finds its way into our food and, once eaten, into our cells as they are created. The amount of carbon-14 in a human cell is therefore determined by the amount in the atmosphere when the cell was formed. That means we can measure the amount of carbon-14 in a cell, compare it to the known rates in the atmosphere over the years since 1945, and deduce the year in which the cell was created.

This technique was used by Jonas Frisén, a professor of stem cell research at the Karolinska Institute in Sweden, to test cells in various parts of the human brain. In 2013, Frisén and his team published evidence that perhaps 700 neurons are created in the hippocampus of the adult brain every day. It seems that not all neurons are replaced, and that neurons created in later life do not survive as long as those we are born with. In short, we are still not quite sure how and to what extent our brains regenerate – but scientists are working to find out.

Even so, there's a big difference between the kind of regeneration that repairs our bodies and what happens to the Doctor in *Doctor Who* – when he becomes an entirely new person.

'If I'm killed before regeneration then I'm dead. Even then, even if I change, it feels like dying. Everything I am dies. Some new man goes sauntering away and I'm dead.'
The Tenth Doctor, *The End of Time* (2009–2010)

At the end of *The Time of the Doctor* (2013), the Eleventh Doctor looks old and wrinkled, his memory is failing and he has to use a walking stick. He has used the last of his allotted twelve regenerations, and he is going to die. However, the Time Lords then give him a whole new regenerative cycle – and something odd happens.

When Clara finds him in the TARDIS, the Eleventh Doctor looks young again. The regenerative process has healed him – but it can't stop there. He just has time to say goodbye before he becomes someone else.

That also happens in *The End of Time*: before the Tenth Doctor becomes the Eleventh Doctor, regenerative energy heals his cuts and bruises and he has time to journey in the TARDIS and look in on his old friends. In *Journey's End*, the Doctor used regenerative energy to heal himself from the effects of being shot by a Dalek and was then able to stop the process before he became someone else – as we've already discussed, by siphoning off the rest of the regeneration energy into his spare hand.

The suggestion is that regeneration involves a great deal of energy – which is difficult to control. That energy can also be used to destroy spaceships in *The Time of the Doctor*, and wrecks the control room of the TARDIS in *The End of Time*. It seems that the Doctor often has trouble controlling the outcome of his own regenerations, and despite claiming several times that he's always wanted ginger hair, he has yet to manage it. In fact he always seems rather surprised by his new appearance and when different incarnations of the Doctor have met each other – for example in *The Three Doctors* (1972–1973) or *The Day of the Doctor* (2013) – they rarely approve of each other's personality quirks or fashion sense.

Perhaps because they're triggered by violent or traumatic situations, the Doctor's regenerations often leave him in a weakened state and can lead to erratic and confused behaviour. In *The Christmas Invasion*, the Tenth Doctor is unconscious for hours while the alien Sycorax threaten London, while in *The Twin Dilemma* (1984), the newly regenerated Sixth Doctor even tries to strangle his companion Peri.

It seems that the Time Lords are aware that regeneration might not always go smoothly. In *Castrovalva* (1982), the Fifth Doctor seeks refuge in a part of the TARDIS called the Zero Room which seems designed to provide a calming environment in which Time Lords can recover from the stress of regeneration. As we discussed in Chapter 14, the Time Lords also have an arrangement with the Sisterhood of Karn, who provide them with a restorative elixir to help when regenerations go wrong – as we see in *The Brain of Morbius* (1976).

Others seem able to control the wild energy of regeneration. In *The Christmas Invasion*, alien 'pilot fish' are attracted to the newly regenerated Doctor because he is bursting with energy – he says they could use him as a power source. In *Let's Kill Hitler* (2011), River Song is able to heal the Doctor by using up her all remaining regenerations in one go. The Doctor returns the favour in *The Angels Take Manhattan* (2012), using a small amount of regenerative energy to heal River's broken arm.

For other Time Lords, regeneration seems not to be a random process at all. In *The War Games* (1969), they offer the Doctor a choice of faces for his next incarnation. In *Destiny of the Daleks* (1979), the Time Lady Romana seems to regenerate effortlessly, appearing in a selection of different bodies before deciding on one that she likes (which looks just like a woman she met in the previous story). Perhaps the Doctor would find regeneration easier if he didn't do it in the middle of a crisis.

Even so, the Doctor, seems to exert a certain amount of control over his new form as he sometimes adopts the faces of people he's met in the past. Actors Colin Baker and Peter Capaldi both played other characters in *Doctor Who* before being cast as the Doctor, which means that the Sixth Doctor looks like a Time Lord called Maxil from *Arc of Infinity* (1983) and the Twelfth Doctor looks like a human, Caecilius, from *The Fires of Pompeii* (2008).

'Have you seen this face before? … It's funny, because I'm sure that I have. You know, I never know where the faces come from. They just pop up. Zap. Faces like this one … Why did I choose this face? It's like I'm trying to tell myself something.'

The Twelfth Doctor, *Deep Breath*

Why would the Doctor's unconscious make him look like Caecilius? We've not yet been given a definite answer to that question, but one possibility is what Caecilius represents.

In *The Fires of Pompeii*, the Tenth Doctor and his companion Donna visit the Roman town in AD 79, and meet Caecilius and his family. However, when the nearby volcano erupts, the Doctor knows that the town and its people will be smothered by hot ash and pumice. He ensures that established history is not changed, then he and Donna leave in the TARDIS.

Donna, horrified at the fate of all those people they're leaving behind, begs him to go back. The Doctor insists that he can't – just as he can't change history to save his own people, his own family, from the Time War. Donna continues to plead with him.

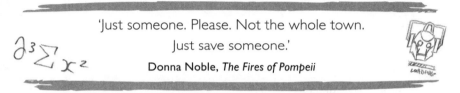

> 'Just someone. Please. Not the whole town.
> Just save someone.'
> **Donna Noble, *The Fires of Pompeii***

He relents. They save Caecilius and his family while the rest of Pompeii is lost. So is the Twelfth Doctor's appearance his unconscious way of ensuring that he remembers that act of mercy – and Donna's insistence that he save those he can?

Whatever the case, the suggestion is that when the Doctor regenerates, it involves something more than his cells starting over again in a random manner. Somehow, his experience is part of the process, too, shaping the new man he'll become. The things he has learnt and suffered, the people he's loved and lost, are able to physically change him.

The Twelfth Doctor in the latest episodes is thousands of years older than the First Doctor in *An Unearthly Child* (1963), and yet he seems younger, more energised, more daft, more exciting, more alive. That's not solely down to his ability to regenerate. What keeps the Doctor young is his attitude: his eagerness to engage and question, to be astounded by what he learns, to change.

We might even argue that the secret to the Doctor's longevity is that he's a scientist.

'I held back death...'

Doctor Who presents many remarkable ways to hold back the ageing process. Here are some examples.

Regenerate

The Time Lords of Gallifrey can regenerate twelve times – though in special circumstances they can also be granted a whole new regenerative cycle. The Master is offered a new regenerative cycle in *The Five Doctors* (1983); the Doctor is given one in *The Time of the Doctor* (2013).

Manipulate your cells

Perhaps related to regeneration (because the research seems to have been guided by the Master), Professor Richard Lazarus was able to manipulate his cells to lose some thirty years in *The Lazarus Experiment* (2007) – but there were nasty side effects.

Surgery

In *The End of the World* (2005) and *New Earth* (2006), the Lady Cassandra seems to have been sustained by continual, ever more drastic surgical interventions.

Stop time

In *The Pirate Planet* (1978), the evil Queen Xanxia is suspended in the last seconds of life using time dams – but the process requires so much energy that her people ransack entire planets to supply it.

Chemical supplements

In *The Caves of Androzani* (1984), the bats of the planet Androzani Minor leave deposits of a substance called Spectrox which, when properly refined, can 'hold back the ravages of time' and keep people young.

Steal other people's youth
In *The Talons of Weng-Chiang* (1977), war criminal Magnus Greel uses a futuristic process called 'organic distillation' to drain the 'life essence' from young women and transfer it to himself.

Steal other people's bodies
The Master, having used up his allotted twelve regenerations, takes over other people's bodies in *The Keeper of Traken* (1981) and the television movie *Doctor Who* (1996).

Upgrade to a computer
When River Song and her friends die in *Silence in the Library / Forest of the Dead* (2008), the Doctor uploads her into the computer 'data core', where she can 'live' in a virtual world for ever after.

Upgrade to a Cyberman
In *Dark Water / Death in Heaven* (2014), the minds of the dead are uploaded to a computer and then downloaded into Cybermen. Led by a Cyber-converted Danny Pink, these Cybermen die to save the Earth – but one, apparently a Cyber-converted Brigadier Alistair Lethbridge-Stewart – survives.

Become immortal
In *The Five Doctors* (1983), we're told that the Time Lord Rassilon can never die – and will share his immortality with those who want it. Unfortunately, that means they become part of the stone decorations on his tomb.

FURTHER READING

We've endeavoured with this book not to cover the same ground as Paul Parsons' *The Science of Doctor Who* (Icon Books: 2006), in which you can find out – among other exciting things – about *real* sonic screwdrivers and deflector shields.

Lawrence M. Krauss's *The Physics of Star Trek* (1995) was the first of these books to explore the science behind a fictional series. But our mix of new stories followed by chapters on the real science owes most to the series *The Science of Discworld* by Terry Pratchett, Ian Stewart and Jack Cohen – four volumes of which have been published since 1999.

What follows are some recommendations for further exploring topics discussed in this book. It's by no means a definitive list, and we've aimed to suggest books for general readers.

PART I – SPACE

1. Alien Life and Other Worlds

http://www.planethunters.org/ – where you can help search for planets

Jacob Bronowski, *The Ascent of Man* (1973) – a TV series detailing the history of science, available as a DVD and book

Bill Bryson, *A Short History of Nearly Everything* (2003)

Ben Goldacre, *Bad Science* (2009)

Lewis Wolpert, *The Unnatural Nature of Science* (2000)

2. Space Travel

https://www.zooniverse.org/#space – explore the Moon and Mars, and explore the stars and galaxies

Andrew Smith, *Moondust* (2009)

In the Shadow of the Moon (www.channel4.com/programmes/in-the-shadow-of-the-moon/on-demand) – it includes President Nixon's untransmitted TV broadcast in the event of Neil Armstrong and Buzz Aldrin being stranded on the Moon

BBC Archive collections: Moon Landings (www.bbc.co.uk/archive/moonlandings/) – an archive of BBC programmes relating to the Apollo missions

3. The Multiverse

Brian Greene, *The Elegant Universe: Superstrings, Hidden Dimensions and the Quest for the Ultimate Theory* (1999)

Michio Kaku, *Parallel Worlds: The Science of Alternative Universes and Our Future in the Cosmos* (2006)

http://space.mit.edu/home/tegmark/crazy.html – Max Tegmark's website, with links to articles on his idea of a multiverse of different levels

BBC Archive collections: Richard Feynman – Fun to Imagine (www.bbc.co.uk/archive/feynman/) – a series of six short films in which the Novel Prize-winning physicist discusses the mysterious forces that make ordinary things happen.

4. The Power of the TARDIS

The Life Scientific: Dame Jocelyn Bell Burnell (www.bbc.co.uk/programmes/b016812j)

Stephen Hawking, *A Brief History of Time: From the Big Bang to Black Holes* (1989)

Stephen Hawking with Leonard Mlodinow, *A Briefer History of Time* (2005)

5. The Future of Earth

Take part in climate science (www.zooniverse.org/#climate)

Rachel Carson, *Silent Spring* (1962)

Panorama: The Impact on Earth (20 July 1969), including Julian Pettifer's report on the benefits of the space programme to that date (www.bbc.co.uk/archive/moonlandings/7606.shtml)

Robert Poole, *Earthrise: How Man First Saw the Earth* (2008) – with a sample chapter at the author's website (www.earthrise.org.uk/sample%20chapter.htm)

Martin Rees, 'Is This Our Final Century?' (www.ted.com/talks/martin_rees_asks_is_this_our_final_century?language=en)

Learn more about 'killer' asteroids at www.killerasteroids.org/

PART 2 – TIME

6. The Laws of Time

Pedro Ferreira, 'Instant Expert: General Relativity' (www.newscientist.com/special/instant-expert-general-relativity)

James Gleick, *Chaos: Making a New Science* (1988)

J. Richard Gott, *Time Travel in Einstein's Universe: The Physical Possibilities of Travel through Time* (2002)

7. The Practicalities of Time Travel

Conn and Hal Iggulden, *The Dangerous Book for Boys* (2006) is full of practical tips that would help a would-be *Doctor Who* companion – whether you're a girl or a boy

Dava Sobel, *Longitude* (1995)

Tom Wolfe, *The Right Stuff* (1979) – Wolfe interviewed the test pilots and astronauts from the early days of the space programme, people with the 'right stuff' to take incredible risks to put the first Americans into space

8. Time and Memory

Susan Corkin, *Permanent Present Tense: The Unforgettable Life of the Amnesiac Patient, HM* (2013)

David Eagleman, 'Brain Time' (2009) (https://edge.org/conversation/brain-time)

David Eagleman, *Incognito: The Secret Lives of the Brain* (2011)

Steve Taylor, *Making Time: Why Time Seems to Pass at Different Speeds and How to Control It* (2007)

The Infinite Monkey Cage #9.2 'The Doors of Perception' (www.bbc.co.uk/programmes/b03j9lvb)

9. What is a Time War?

Jacob Brownoski, 'Knowledge or Certainty', in *The Ascent of Man* (1973)

Graham Farmelo, *Churchill's Bomb: A Hidden History of Britain's First Nuclear Weapons Programme* (2013)

Andew Hodges, *Alan Turing: The Enigma* (updated edition 2014) – the author's website also contains much information on Turing (www.turing.org.uk/)

William Lanouette, *Genius in the Shadows: A Biography of Leo Szilárd, the Man behind the Bomb* (1992)

Jim Ottaviani and Leland Myrick, *Feynman* (2011)

10. The History of Earth

William of Newburgh, *The History of English Affairs* (1861 translation by Joseph Stevenson, http://legacy.fordham.edu/halsall/basis/williamofnewburgh-one.asp)

Greg Jenner, *A Million Years in a Day: A Curious History of Everyday Life* (2015)

Ian Mortimer, *The Time Traveller's Guide to Medieval England: A Handbook for Visitors to the Fourteenth Century* (2008)

Ian Mortimer, *The Time Traveller's Guide to Elizabethan England: A Handbook for Visitors to the Sixteenth Century* (2012)

J.M. Roberts and Odd Arne Westad, *The Penguin History of the World* (sixth edition, 2013)

An Age of Kings (1960), released on DVD by Illuminations in 2013

Retronaut – the photographic time machine (www.retronaut.com)

PART 3 – HUMANITY

11. Evolution

Dorothy L. Cheney and Robert M. Seyfarth, *Baboon Metaphysics: The Evolution of a Social Mind* (2007) – a study of wild baboons that seems to shed light on human behaviour!

Richard Dawkins, *The Ancestor's Tale: A Pilgrimage to the Dawn of Life* (2004)

Steve Jones, *Almost Like a Whale: The Origin of Species Updated* (1999)

Take part in evolutionary science experiments at www.wormwatchlab. org/

12. Man and Machine

Manfred E. Clynes and Nathan S. Kline, 'Cyborgs and Space', *Astronautics* (September 1960) – http://web.mit.edu/digitalapollo/ Documents/Chapter1/cyborgs.pdf

Nick Harkaway, *The Blind Giant: Being Human in a Digital World* (2012)

Stanley Milgram, *Obedience to Authority: An Experimental View* (1974, republished 2010)

Jon Ronson, *So You've Been Publicly Shamed* (2015) – which explores how people are attacked for 'transgressions' on social media

David Rorvik, *As Man Becomes Machine* (1971)

A History of Ideas: Rewiring the Brain (www.bbc.co.uk/programmes/ p02hj624) – part of a series of short animations exploring big questions about how we live today

13. Artificial Intelligence

Nick Bostrom, *Superintelligence: Paths, Dangers, Strategies* (2014)

N.J. Mackintosh, *IQ and Human Intelligence* (1998)

Alan Turing, 'Computing Machinery and Intelligence', *Mind* (1950) – http://loebner.net/Prizef/TuringArticle.html

Bletchley Park Podcast Extra E28: Mavis Batey (https://audioboom. com/boos/1736751-bletchley-park-podcast-extra-e28-mavis-batey)

14. Death

Nicolas Léonard Sadi Carnot, *Reflections on the Motive Power of Fire* (1824) – English translation from 1897 at http://archive.org/stream/reflectionsonmot00carnrich#page/n7/mode/2up

Atul Gawande, *Being Mortal: Illness, Medicine and What Matters in the End* (2014)

Henry Marsh, *Do No Harm* (2014)

Sam Parnia, *Erasing Death: The Science that is Rewriting the Boundaries Between Life and Death* (2014)

Eric D. Schneider and Dorothy Sagain, *Into the Cool: Energy Flow, Thermodynamics, and Life* (2005)

15. Regeneration

Damien Broderick, *The Last Mortal Generation: How Science Will Alter Our Lives in the 21st Century* (1999)

Wendy Moore, *The Knife Man: Blood, Body-Snatching and the Birth of Modern Surgery* (2005) – which covers the life and work of John Hunter

Christopher Thomas Scott, *Stem Cell Now: A Brief Introduction to the Coming Medical Revolution* (2006)

ACKNOWLEDGEMENTS

As good scientists, Simon and Marek tested this book carefully. Our willing subjects (or lab rats) were: Simon Belcher, Dr Debbie Challis, Jenny Guerrier, Thomas Guerrier and Tim Guerrier.

We also sought advice from experts in particular areas. Chapter 1 was read by Dr Chris Naunton of the Egypt Exploration Society and Alice Stevenson of the Petrie Museum of Egyptian Archaeology, UCL. Simon discussed the ideas in Chapter 5 with actress Katy Manning who played companion Jo Grant, and some of the ideas in Chapter 7 with Chris Wild, curator of Retronaut.com. Chapter 8 was read by Dr Niall Boyce, editor of medical journal *Lancet Psychiatry*. Chapter 10 was read by Edward James, Emeritus Professor of Medieval History at University College, Dublin. Chapter 11 was read by Mark Carnall, curator of the Grant Museum of Zoology, UCL. Of course, any remaining errors remain the fault of Simon and Marek.

Ben Aaronovitch, Natalie Barnes and Dr Radmila Topalovic provided advice and guidance we've used in this book – even if they weren't aware they were doing so.

Grateful thanks to Justin, Albert, Charlotte and everyone at BBC Books for all they've done to make the book happen, and to Grant Berry, Mike Sarna and the staff of the Royal Museums Greenwich for graciously allowing Marek time off his other duties to travel in time and space.

INDEX

Note: page number in **bold** refer to illustrations

HIS NAME IS
STILL
MUDD

THE CASE AGAINST DOCTOR SAMUEL ALEXANDER MUDD

Edward Steers, Jr.

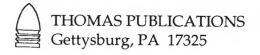

THOMAS PUBLICATIONS
Gettysburg, PA 17325

veritas praevalebit
(truth will prevail)

To Pat,

who has been cheerfully living with
Abraham Lincoln for these many years.

CONTENTS

FOREWORD

Historical myths fall into two general categories: those that spring up spontaneously and those that are manufactured. All three of the principal myths that grew out of the Lincoln assassination were manufactured:

1. That Secretary of War Edwin M. Stanton conspired with others to assassinate Lincoln,
2. That John Wilkes Booth escaped at the Garrett farm and died a suicide on January 13, 1903, under the alias David E. George, in a cheap hotel at Enid, Oklahoma Territory, and,
3. That Dr. Samuel A. Mudd was convicted in 1865 and sent to prison by a vengeful government only because he followed his Hippocratic oath and set the broken leg of John Wilkes Booth.

The fabrications that once supported the "Stanton was involved" myth have been utterly demolished in recent years by scholarly research; the "Booth escaped" myth, already in tatters, was reduced to nonsense by the testimony of expert witnesses in a 1995 civil suit in a Baltimore court. The third myth—that Dr. Samuel A. Mudd was "railroaded" into prison—continues to have life and attract support. It is this myth that Dr. Steers challenges in his carefully researched book.

The "Dr. Mudd was innocent" theme began to take shape in a book entitled *The Life of Dr. Samuel A. Mudd* by Nettie Mudd Monroe, published in 1906. Mrs. Monroe hardly knew her father. He died January 10, 1883, on Nettie's fifth birthday. However, she had many family papers available to her, as well as the recollections of her mother, Sarah Mudd, who lived on until 1911. The tone of later public relations efforts on Dr. Samuel A. Mudd's behalf was set in the last sentence of his son-in-law's introduction to Nettie's book. On April 14, 1906, D. Eldridge Monroe wrote:

> *Has not the time arrived to fully vindicate the name of Dr. Samuel A. Mudd, who was so cruelly and unjustly called upon to suffer—and to remove from that name the faintest shadow of doubt that may exist regarding his complicity in the great crime committed in Ford's Theatre, in Washington, forty-one years ago?*

In the late 1920s a young physician, Dr. Richard D. Mudd, began to interest himself in establishing the innocence of his grandfather, Dr. Samuel A. Mudd. His political and public relations efforts have been continuous, skillful, and effective. Over time, Dr. Richard D. Mudd developed a simple appeal, stated over and over and over and over again:

Dr. Samuel Mudd was a kindly country physician. He was arrested, tried, and convicted by a vengeful and hysterical government for the sole reason that he kept his Hippocratic oath and set the broken leg of John Wilkes Booth—a man he did not recognize. He was innocent of any complicity in the conspiracy.

This simplistic defense attracted conspiracy buffs and "true believers" looking for a cause. Dr. Samuel A. Mudd soon became fashionable, and promoting his innocence was worth votes to politicians without any bad side effects. It was not necessary to do any research or to read dreary testimony; just declare yourself in favor of exonerating the poor man, and then stand virtuously on the side of truth and justice.

For a good example of how this worked, the Michigan legislature adopted Concurrent Resolution No. 126 in July 1973. It followed almost precisely the routine used by Dr. Richard Mudd in his public relations campaign: a country doctor doing his bounden duty by setting the broken leg of a man who came to his door asking for professional help.

It was not until the Mudds pressured the Army Board for the Correction of Military Records to expunge the record of Dr. Mudd's conviction that things began to go sour. Researchers started reading the official transcript of the trial in the National Archives. Dr. Mudd, they learned, was not the saintly man depicted in Mudd propaganda. He had treated some of his slaves harshly, shooting one man—who survived—and flogging a young woman. More, he knew Booth and knew him well—actually Booth had been a guest in Mudd's home. He had been involved with Booth in a plan to capture Lincoln and carry him off to Richmond. Further, he had helped Booth to escape on April 15, knowing who he was and what he had done. Then he lied repeatedly to Federal investigators. In short, Dr. Mudd was guilty as set out in the specification in that he did "...advise, encourage, receive, entertain, harbor and conceal, aid and assist the said John Wilkes Booth...."

In 1992 the Army Board for the Correction of Military Records (ABCMR) recommended to the Secretary of the Army that he set aside the conviction on the ground that the military commission lacked jurisdiction to try Dr. Mudd. On July 22, 1992, this recommendation was denied by Acting Assistant Secretary of the Army William D. Clark who stated that it was not the role of the ABCMR to settle historical disputes or to act as an appellate court. The Mudds asked the new Secretary of the Army to review this decision. Assistant Secretary of the Army Sara E. Lister upheld Clark's decision on February 2, 1996, stating that: "Any further Army action would be an ill-advised attempt to alter legal history by non-judicial means. It would improperly disturb the importance of the finality of both judicial and executive decisions."

This would seem to have ended the matter. But no, the Mudd "innocence" machine is versatile if nothing else. Congressman Steny Hoyer of Maryland has introduced H. R. 1885, a bill which would order the Secretary of the Army to "set aside" the 1865 conviction of Dr. Samuel A. Mudd. Perhaps he is not serious but merely trolling for votes among the numerous Mudds, their kin, and followers in his congressional district. Still, it is incredible that Mr. Hoyer seems to believe that Congress can legislate innocence.

This book by Dr. Edward Steers, Jr. takes the reader through the complexities of the Dr. Samuel A. Mudd case with a sure hand and in an organized manner. For the very first time a respected Lincoln scholar has challenged the Mudd myth. It is about time.

James O. Hall
McLean, Virginia
July 22, 1997

Acknowledgements

Even as the body of Abraham Lincoln lay comatose in a rear bedroom of the Peterson house opposite Ford's Theatre, the government began to gather information about the terrible crime which John Wilkes Booth had just committed. Today, one hundred and thirty-two years later, the gathering and sifting of such information goes on, and occasionally new information is uncovered which adds light to the dark shadows surrounding Booth's act.

Among the many people who have spent untold hours researching the assassination of Abraham Lincoln, one person stands paramount. For over fifty years James O. Hall has searched the records and recorded the facts and myths which poured out of the Lincoln assassination, leaving not even the smallest pebble unturned in his search to understand every aspect of that momentous event. Today, every student and scholar in the field of the Lincoln assassination owes an enormous debt to James O. Hall. Much of what we know today about Lincoln's murder we learned from him. I am personally indebted to Mr. Hall for generously sharing his extensive files and scholarship with me, and for his thoughtful review of this work. If there is any failing or error in it, it is only because I failed to follow or inadvertently overlooked Mr. Hall's advice.

I would also like to acknowledge the invaluable assistance of Joan L. Chaconas, former president of the Surratt Society and Lincoln Group of the District of Columbia, for her review and editorial help with the manuscript. Joan Chaconas is a tremendous source of knowledge on the history of the District of Columbia and the events surrounding the assassination of Abraham Lincoln, and is always generous in her willingness to help find answers for those who have questions.

Finally I would like to acknowledge the staff and leadership of the Surratt Society, Surratt House Museum, and writers for the *Surratt Courier* (newsletter) for providing a wonderful resource from which students of the Lincoln assassination can continuously learn.

INTRODUCTION

In 1979, President Jimmy Carter wrote a letter to the grandson of Dr. Samuel A. Mudd[1] in which he stated:

> ...*I want to express my personal opinion that the declarations made by President Johnson[2] in pardoning Dr. Mudd substantially discredit the validity of the military commission's judgment.[3]*
>
> ...*A careful reading of the information provided to me about this case led to my personal agreement with the findings of President Johnson.[4] I am hopeful that these conclusions will be given widespread circulation which will restore dignity to your grandfather's name and clear the Mudd family name of any negative connotation or implied lack of honor.*

President Carter's hope that his letter would receive widespread circulation was realized. Simultaneous with Dr. Richard Mudd's receipt of it, Carter released his letter to the media through newsman Roger Mudd.[5] The media and the American public universally accepted Carter's letter as absolving Samuel Mudd of any wrongdoing or involvement in the horrendous murder of Abraham Lincoln by John Wilkes Booth.

Not to be outdone by his presidential counterpart, Ronald Reagan also wrote a letter eight years later to Richard Mudd expressing his personal belief that Samuel Mudd was, "...indeed innocent of any wrongdoing."[6]

In the intervening years since Samuel Mudd's pardon by Andrew Johnson and President Carter's letter, the perception of Dr. Mudd has become one of a simple country doctor who, in administering the Hippocratic oath, fell victim to a vengeful and hysterical government. That perception has been fueled by significant forces including Hollywood, television, the print media, and politicians. State legislatures[7] have passed resolutions exonerating Mudd and calling for the official reversal of the findings of the military tribunal that convicted and sentenced him. Efforts even exist for the issuance of a commemorative postal stamp honoring the doctor.

Much of the effort to rehabilitate Dr. Mudd has come from his grandson, Dr. Richard Dyer Mudd, who for over seventy years has waged a tireless battle to overturn the results of the military tribunal which convicted Dr. Mudd. Beginning with Franklin D. Roosevelt and ending with Jimmy Carter, Richard Mudd has petitioned every president on his grandfather's behalf.[8]

While successfully influencing public opinion, especially through the news media, Richard Mudd's efforts have fallen short of overturning his grandfather's conviction as an accomplice of John Wilkes Booth. President Carter, in his letter to Richard Mudd, astutely stated the reality of Mudd's situation when he wrote:

> Regrettably, I am advised that the findings of guilt and the sentence of the military commission that tried Dr. Mudd in 1865 are binding and conclusive judgments, and that there is no authority under law by which I, as President, could set aside his conviction. All legal authority vested in the President to act in this case was exercised when President Johnson granted Dr. Mudd a full and unconditional pardon on February 8, 1869.[9]

Samuel Mudd had been tried, convicted and sentenced by a military tribunal, and President Johnson's pardon established neither guilt nor innocence, but merely set Mudd free. Samuel Mudd in accepting President Johnson's pardon ended all recourse which he might have sought in pursuit of his claimed innocence.[10]

In his letter President Carter suggests that if any authority did exist in which he, as president, could set aside Samuel Mudd's conviction in 1865, he would do so. This is unfortunate, for both the legal authority of the military commission that tried Samuel Mudd, and its finding that Mudd was guilty as an accomplice of John Wilkes Booth, were correct.

Dr. Richard Dyer Mudd, grandson of Samuel A. Mudd, examining a jewel box made by Samuel A. Mudd while serving his prison sentence at Fort Jefferson.

Courtesy Dr. Richard D. Mudd.

While President Carter's letter (and subsequently President Reagan's) was a humanitarian expression intended to show sympathy for Dr. Samuel Mudd and his descendants' plight, it has no legal status nor was it intended to have legal status. And while Richard Mudd was greatly heartened by President Carter's expressions, they fell short of his lifelong effort to declare the military tribunal illegal, and declare his grandfather innocent of all wrongdoing.

While the majority of monographs and articles written about Samuel Mudd are universally in agreement of his innocence, there has not been enough discussion of the primary source materials which exist concerning the question of Mudd's complicity in the murder of Abraham Lincoln. While some of the evidence has had limited distribution, all of it is available to any individual who is willing to seek it.[11]

It is important to examine the wealth of evidence that exists within the writings and documents surrounding the events of Abraham Lincoln's murder so far as Dr. Samuel Alexander Mudd is concerned. The considerable bulk of information which has come to light over the past several years is primarily the result of one individual, James O. Hall. James Hall has proven to be an indefatigable researcher in pursuit of every detail associated with the murder of Abraham Lincoln. Equal to his tireless efforts in search of the truth is his boundless generosity in sharing his discoveries and extensive knowledge with any serious researcher. All any student of this tragedy need do is ask, and they shall receive. Few, if any, vocational historians have equaled the discoveries of James O. Hall in ferreting out the details related to Lincoln's murder.

Two of the principal myths of the Lincoln assassination must be challenged. First, that Dr. Samuel Alexander Mudd was an innocent victim stemming from his humanitarian efforts to render medical assistance to an injured man, and second, that the military tribunal which decided Mudd's fate was an illegal, rogue tribunal that unjustly punished him.

Presumably the individuals who reviewed Dr. Mudd's case and advised President Carter on his innocence in 1979 did not avail themselves of all of the historical materials nor of the several persons who are familiar with this evidence. This is not a criticism of those individuals, however, for much of the social consciousness of the nation has perceived Mudd's innocence for nearly a century. And while perception may be reality to most, it unfortunately belies the historical fact. His name is still Mudd.

1

A HORSE THIEF POINTS THE WAY.

John Fletcher's fears had been confirmed. He had warned the young man to return his rented horse by the supper hour, and now he was already several hours overdue. Fletcher had been troubled by the man's tardiness on previous occasions. When he had not returned by 10:30 p.m., Fletcher walked the short block from his stables to Pennsylvania Avenue to see if his overdue horse and rider were anywhere in sight. Incredibly, at that very moment, young Davy Herold was slowly making his way down Fifteenth Street toward the Avenue on Fletcher's horse.[1]

Four hours earlier, David Herold and three other men had met in a boarding house located just one block east of Ford's Theatre. There they reviewed their respective assignments one more time before setting out on their sinister plan. If each man carried out his murderous task according to plan, the president, vice-president and secretary of state would lie dead, leaving the nation in bloody disarray.

Herold had been assigned by the ring leader, John Wilkes Booth, to accompany Lewis Powell [alias Paine] to the home of Secretary of State William Seward. Herold would guard Powell's horse while he murdered the convalescing Seward.

Forcing his way into Seward's home, Powell made his way to Seward's bedroom where he proceeded to wreak his carnage. Frightened by the blood-chilling screams coming from the house, Herold abandoned Powell's horse, and galloped off in the direction of Fourteenth Street leaving the would-be assassin to fend for himself.

Fleeing the scene, Herold turned onto Pennsylvania Avenue where he came into Fletcher's view. Fletcher called out to Herold, demanding that he bring his horse back at once. The startled Herold pulled back on the reins, and spurring his mount, galloped down the Avenue and turned north onto Fourteenth Street with Fletcher running breathlessly in his wake. After racing a short block up Fourteenth Street, Herold turned east onto F

4

Street and headed at full gallop toward the Navy Yard Bridge according to a prearranged plan. It was approximately 10:30 p.m. on the night of April 14, 1865, the Good Friday preceding the Easter which would come to be known as *Black Easter*.

John Fletcher managed the stables owned by Thompson Naylor located on E Street just south of Pennsylvania Avenue. It was here that Davy Herold had rented the horse which he was now riding so vigorously into the night.

Only moments before, Fletcher had strolled up to the Union Hotel on Pennsylvania Avenue where he downed a glass of whiskey with another of his customers, a man named George A. Atzerodt. Fletcher thought Atzerodt a disheveled low-life who only recently frequented his stables together with his sidekick, Davy Herold. Atzerodt had stabled his own horse with Fletcher earlier in the day, calling for the horse around 10:00 p.m. Before riding off, Atzerodt asked Fletcher to join him in a drink, and the two men walked to the Union Hotel.

It seemed to Fletcher that Atzerodt was already "in his cups," and appeared wobbly from having spent most of the day in whiskey. After downing their drinks the two men parted. Fletcher gave little thought to the crazy German's remark that his spirited horse would be "...good upon the retreat" this particular night.[2]

Atzerodt had been assigned by Booth to assassinate Vice President Andrew Johnson who was resting in his room at the Kirkwood Hotel located at the corner of Twelfth Street and Pennsylvania Avenue. Earlier that same morning, Atzerodt had taken a room in the Kirkwood in anticipation of his bloody task. Still wobbly from alcohol, Atzerodt got as far as the hotel bar before his courage evaporated. Like Herold, Atzerodt fled his assigned task, and began wandering about the city at the very moment Herold was racing toward the Navy Yard Bridge.

Atzerodt was not Fletcher's problem however. The stable manager had to contend with getting his horse back from Davy Herold. Watching Herold turn east onto F Street, Fletcher turned and ran the few blocks back to his stables where he quickly saddled his own horse and set out after the fleeing thief. He remembered overhearing Atzerodt and Herold earlier, talking about a place called White Plains located across the Eastern Branch in Maryland and correctly assumed that Herold was headed in that direction. The city was fairly quiet except for the clatter of hoof beats which Fletcher noted as he raced past Tenth Street on his way toward the Navy Yard Bridge.

Riding hard, Fletcher arrived at the bridge located at the foot of Eleventh Street next to the Washington Navy Yard. He was stopped by the military pickets guarding the bridge who controlled all of the traffic into and out of the city. The bridge crossed the Eastern Branch of the Potomac River[3] connecting with a small settlement located on the eastern bank known as Uniontown. Sergeant Silas T. Cobb was in charge of the pickets on duty this night, and challenged Fletcher as he pulled up to the guard post out of breath.

The "Assassination" Conspirators.

John Wilkes Booth
Library of Congress

George Andrew Atzerodt
Library of Congress

Lewis Thornton Powell alias Lewis Paine (Payne).
Library of Congress

David E. Herold.
Library of Congress

7

Fletcher told Cobb his story of the stolen horse and asked if a young man had recently passed over the bridge. The sergeant told Fletcher that two men had recently passed over the bridge not minutes apart, the second man answering to Fletcher's description. Fletcher was sure the second man was Herold, and probably assumed the first man was his sidekick Atzerodt. Fletcher then asked Cobb for permission to cross over into Uniontown so that he might continue his pursuit of Herold and recover his stolen horse. As with the two before him, Cobb agreed to let Fletcher cross over, but told him he could not allow him to cross back before morning. Although the threat of a Confederate attack on Washington was no longer a reality, illegal trafficking into the city was. So, while there seemed no danger in letting someone leave, some control was still exercised over persons entering the city. A 9:00 p.m. curfew barring all unauthorized traffic into the city was still in effect. Those were Cobb's orders.[4]

Angered by the soldier's decision, and unable to stay away from his stables until morning, Fletcher wheeled his horse around, and rode back into the city returning to his stables on E Street.

Frustrated, Fletcher was not yet finished. After he stabled his horse he walked the short distance to police headquarters on Tenth Street where he reported the theft of his horse to the detective on duty. He was told that the police had picked up a stray horse near the Lincoln Hospital in southeast Washington, and had stabled it at the headquarters of the 22nd Army Corps commanded by Major General Christopher Columbus Augur.[5]

Accompanied by police detective Charles Stone, Fletcher walked over to the army headquarters a few blocks north. He was shown a saddle which he recognized as belonging to the disheveled little German whose name he momentarily forgot. He told Augur that he had the owner's name on a card back at his stables. Fletcher and Stone then returned to the stables to retrieve the card for General Augur. Written on the card was the name, *George A. Atzerodt.*

Fletcher was shown the horse which the police had brought in sometime around midnight. It was a large, brown horse distinguished by having lost one eye — the very same horse that Fletcher had saddled on many an occasion for the friendly Atzerodt. Fletcher must have been puzzled. The saddle was not on the horse Atzerodt had stabled only hours before, but Fletcher knew that the saddle belonged to the German. Still, he assumed that the two men that passed over the Navy Yard Bridge around eleven o'clock that evening were Davy Herold and his cohort, George Atzerodt.

Atzerodt, of course, had not passed over the bridge ahead of Davy Herold as Fletcher assumed.[6] That rider was John Wilkes Booth, fleeing his act of murder at Ford's Theatre only minutes before. Booth and Herold would shortly rendezvous at a prearranged location just over the District line where they planned to meet with Atzerodt and Lewis Powell. Unknown to Fletcher, it was Powell who had been riding the one-eyed horse whose owner was John Wilkes Booth.[7]

Important is the fact that Fletcher's information clearly linked Davy Herold to George Atzerodt, and within a matter of hours, Atzerodt, whose saddle was now in the custody of General Augur along with the stray, one-eyed horse, would be directly linked to John Wilkes Booth.[8]

Washington City's provost marshall, Major James O'Beirne, fearing a possible threat to Vice President Andrew Johnson's life, sent police detective John Lee to the Kirkwood Hotel, located at Twelfth and Pennsylvania Avenue, to guard him. Johnson, having relocated to Washington as a result of his election as vice president, had rented a room at the Kirkwood Hotel until he could find a suitable house.

When Lee arrived at the hotel on the evening of the 15th, he questioned the barkeeper and night clerk, a man named Michael Henry who, in the course of their discussions, told Lee that "a suspicious appearing character" had registered in Room 126 on the morning of April 14.[9] Lee proceeded to Room 126, and after forcing the door, searched the room. Among the items he found was a bankbook with the owner's name clearly written inside, *John Wilkes Booth*.[10] The "suspicious appearing character" that Lee referred to was George A. Atzerodt, Davy Herold's friend.

In less than twenty-four hours following the shooting of Lincoln, officials had a clear link between John Wilkes Booth and George Atzerodt, and thanks to John Fletcher, Augur linked George Atzerodt to David Herold. Augur had reason to believe that Herold and his friend had fled over the Navy Yard Bridge into southern Maryland. Who else might have fled over the bridge was uncertain for a time, but by mid-morning General Augur's staff came to believe the first bridge-crosser was Booth.

As a result of Fletcher's visit to army headquarters, Augur assembled a troop of the 13th New York Cavalry under the command of Lieutenant David D. Dana, and sent them over the Navy Yard Bridge and into southern Maryland. Shortly after noon on Saturday, April 15, Lieutenant Dana and his troopers arrived at the small village of Bryantown, some thirty miles southeast of Washington. Here they commandeered the local tavern and set up their headquarters.[11]

Fifteen hours after the assassination attempt at Ford's Theatre, Lieutenant Dana and the men of the 13th New York Cavalry were as close to the assassin Booth as any of the military would come over the next eleven days. Three miles to the north of Dana and his troopers, his broken leg now splinted, John Wilkes Booth was resting fitfully in the home of the good doctor, Samuel Alexander Mudd.

2

JEFFERSON DAVIS SAYS NO.

At what precise moment John Wilkes Booth decided to change his plans from one of capture to one of murder is not clear. The idea of capturing Lincoln was an old story—one that had a varied cast of characters including the nephew of a former president of the United States, and two officers of the Confederate States Army.[1]

Joseph Walker Taylor, a major in the Confederate Army, was the architect of one of the earliest plots to capture Lincoln. Walker Taylor, as he was known to his friends, was well connected in all respects. A Kentuckian like Lincoln, Taylor was the nephew of former president Zachary Taylor, and first cousin to Major General Richard Taylor, C.S.A., who was in command of the District of West Louisiana.[2] More importantly, he was first cousin to Sarah Knox Taylor, daughter of President Zachary Taylor, and the first wife of Confederate President Jefferson Davis.

Walker Taylor was on the staff of General Simon Bolivar Buckner who was stationed at Fort Donelson in western Tennessee in 1862. When Ulysses S. Grant successfully encircled Fort Donelson, Buckner was given command of the post so that he could surrender it to Grant.[3] While Buckner was forced to accept Grant's "unconditional surrender" terms, Walker Taylor had other plans. Wounded in the cheek and neck, Taylor decided to join forces with Nathan Bedford Forrest and successfully slip out of the fort the night before its surrender, then make his way to Louisville where he began a convalescence from his wounds.

As his health steadily improved, Taylor decided to make a clandestine visit to Washington, D. C. where he stayed with his uncle, Union Brigadier General Joseph Taylor, brother of Zachary Taylor. Young Taylor knew that he would not be betrayed by his elderly uncle. Like many families, the Taylors had members serving on both sides of the conflict. Walker Taylor was one of four brothers with divided allegiance; two were officers in the Union army while two served as officers in the Confederate army.

While convalescing in Washington, Taylor boldly attended a White House reception where he was introduced to the president. Lincoln, noticing Taylor's wounds, asked in what battle he had been wounded. When Taylor replied, "Fort Donelson," Lincoln commended Taylor for the great victory, and bravery of the Union forces in the fort's capture.[4] The smile that must have crossed Taylor's face can only be imagined.

After several days of observing Lincoln's daily routine, Taylor hatched his plot to capture the president, and take him south to Richmond where he would become a bargaining chip in negotiating prisoner exchange. While Taylor believed his plan was certain to succeed, he felt protocol required that he receive the approval of President Davis which he felt confident he would get.

According to Colonel William Preston Johnston, Davis's aide-de-camp,[5] Taylor traveled from Washington to Richmond in the summer of 1862 where he joined Davis and Johnston for breakfast at the Confederate White House. During the course of their meeting Taylor outlined his plan to capture Lincoln one evening while the president made his routine trip to his summer quarters at Soldiers' Home in the northern part of the city.[6]

Taylor's plan was simple:

> Lincoln does not leave the White House until evening, or near twilight, and then with only a driver, he takes a lonely ride two or three miles in the country to a place called Soldiers' Home, which is his summer residence. My point is to collect several of these Kentuckians whom I see about here doing nothing and who are brave enough for such a thing as that, and capture Lincoln, run him down the Potomac, and cross him over just where I crossed, and the next day will have him here.[7]

Davis listened intently before responding to Taylor's scheme. "No sir, I will not give my authority to abduct Lincoln," Davis said pointedly.[8] He did not believe such a plan could be successfully carried out without the high probability of Lincoln being killed. Davis' answer to Taylor was direct:

> I suppose Lincoln is a man of courage. ...He would undoubtedly resist being captured. ...I could not stand the imputation of having consented to let Mr. Lincoln be assassinated.[9]

Of course, Davis was right. In any attempt to capture the president of the United States, the probability that the president or, for that matter, someone else close to the president, would be killed was extremely high. Davis put an immediate end to Taylor's plan to capture Lincoln.

In 1889, only weeks before his death, Davis wrote to Taylor asking him to record the details of his proposal together with his (Davis') refusal to sanction such a plot.[10] Davis wanted to use Taylor's statement to blunt recurring inferences that Davis was somehow involved or sanctioned Booth's

Jefferson Davis.

Library of Congress

Abraham Lincoln.
Last known photograph
taken on March 6, 1865 by
Henry F. Warren on the
White House balcony.

Edward Steers, Jr. collection.

successful attempt in 1865. While Davis may have prevented the possible killing of Lincoln in 1862, there are some today who feel that circumstantial evidence clearly points to his full knowledge, and even acquiescence in Booth's eventual murder of Lincoln three years later.[11]

By the summer of 1864, the military situation had changed dramatically. Any illusions of a short war with Confederate success had completely faded away. Although some felt uneasy about Lincoln's chances for re-election in the fall, stunning Union victories at Atlanta, and later in the Shenandoah Valley would insure four more years with Lincoln as president.[12] Any hope of a negotiated peace with the "tyrant in the White House" was beyond reach.

During the early spring of 1864, Colonel Bradley T. Johnson (soon to be promoted to brigadier general), a native of Frederick, Maryland, and officer in the Confederate army, disclosed his own daring plan to capture Lincoln. Johnson's plan had all the earmarks of success. Johnson was serving under the command of Major General Wade Hampton[13] when he was ordered to join Major General Jubal A. Early's army in the upper Shenandoah Valley. Johnson proposed his idea of capturing Lincoln to Hampton who, according to Johnson, gave his approval.[14] As with Taylor in 1862, it is unreasonable to believe that Johnson and Hampton would plan to carry out the capture operation without first clearing it with Confederate authorities, including Jefferson Davis. Before Johnson could begin implementation of his plan, however, he was ordered to take his Maryland brigade and join Early, as a part of Early's Army of the Valley.

Like Walker Taylor before him, Johnson saw the vulnerability of the summer White House. Johnson had proposed picking two hundred of his best men and horses, and after crossing the Potomac River into Maryland at White's Ford,[15] heading for the Soldiers' Home located three miles north of the White House. Here, at Soldiers' Home, Lincoln had established his summer residence in Anderson Cottage.[16] The Lincoln and the Stanton families had taken advantage of the cooler setting at Soldiers' Home in order to flee the disease-ridden summer months in Washington.

Lincoln was often accompanied to and from the Home by a detachment of cavalry which provided a modest guard. Occasionally, however, Lincoln would make the short ride alone much to the consternation of those concerned about his safety. Cavalry guard or not, a contingent of two hundred battle-hardened Confederate cavalrymen could easily overwhelm any guard and capture Lincoln.

Johnson's plan was to raid the Soldiers' Home one evening, capture Lincoln, and with five selected troopers send him east, then south over the Eastern Branch of the Potomac River into southern Maryland following the well-known route of the Confederate Secret Service. This plan and route closely resembled that of another would-be kidnapper, John Wilkes Booth.

Brigadier General Bradley T. Johnson, C.S.A.

View of Soldiers' Home, Scott Hall on right of picture, Anderson Cottage on left of picture. From a stereo card ca. 1866.

As the select party of five headed toward southern Maryland with their incredible prize, Johnson would take his remaining troopers, and retrace his steps west toward the Potomac recrossing the river at White's Ford, Point of Rocks, Shepherdstown or Williamsport depending on the enemy's response. Johnson was convinced that his large raiding party would draw the Federals away from the real quarry which would then allow them to safely slip through the thin Union lines and over the Potomac River into Virginia. It was a well thought out plan which had a high probability for success.

Reporting to Early, recently victorious over Major General David Hunter in the Upper Valley, Johnson outlined his plan (and Hampton's previous approval) to the irascible general. Early, readying his army for a daring attack on Washington, put Johnson on hold by telling him to forget any plans to raid Soldiers' Home until after the upcoming campaign.

Although Early failed in his bold attempt to enter Washington and sack the city, the Confederate effort sufficiently scared Washington to force Grant to respond with considerable force. Grant organized a new army, designated the Army of the Shenandoah, under Major General Philip Sheridan, and ordered it to eliminate all organized Confederate resistance in the Shenandoah Valley, and to lay waste to the considerable supplies in the valley which continued to feed Lee's Army of Northern Virginia.

The ultimate outcome of this effort by Union forces was the destruction of Early's army and the removal of Early from Confederate command. This ended any scheme of Johnson's to capture Lincoln, but by the time Early and Johnson were knocked out of the war in December 1864, John Wilkes Booth was well on his way to upstaging all other plans to capture the Union president.

Shortly past midnight on the evening of March 15, 1865, John Wilkes Booth and six of his cohorts rendezvoused at a popular restaurant only a few blocks from Ford's Theatre.[17] The group had gathered at Booth's command ostensibly to review their plan to capture the president. Once captured, the details of the escape were well laid out. It was the act of capturing Lincoln that was problematic to some members of Booth's cadre of compatriots.

There was dissension among the band of conspirators. Booth's familiarity and easy access to Ford's Theatre led him to favor it as the site for abduction. Lincoln was known to frequent the theater. To some in the group, capturing Lincoln from the theater was fraught with difficulty, and too easily prone to failure, and failure meant disaster. It would be better to pick off the president on one of his many trips about the city, especially his trips to and from Soldiers' Home. The problem with Soldiers' Home, however, was that the Lincoln family did not set up residence there until late spring which was several weeks away. Time was working against the conspirators and an ominous feeling had overtaken some in the group that the longer the delay the more likely they would be discovered. If they were to strike it had better be soon.[18]

Fortunately the opportunity presented itself within hours of the midnight meeting. The following day, March 16, Booth learned from fellow actor E. L. Davenport, that Lincoln would visit the Campbell Hospital on the northern outskirts of the District on the 17th to witness a play for the benefit of convalescing soldiers. Booth's contacts allowed him easy access to such information and his presence at such an event would be commonplace, arousing no suspicion.

Word went out to the anxious conspirators, to assemble in readiness for execution of their assigned roles. When Lincoln left the hospital to return to the White House following the performance, his carriage would be overtaken, and he would be spirited away, over the well-established escape route through southern Maryland, and over the Potomac River into Virginia. Once over the river, the safety of Richmond would be close at hand.

To the conspirators' chagrin, however, their plot failed when Lincoln changed his plans at the last minute in order to meet with a contingent of soldiers, and accept a captured Confederate battle flag as a token of Union victory.[19] To add salt to Booth's already festering wounds, Lincoln greeted the regiment from the balcony of the National Hotel on Pennsylvania Avenue, where Booth had made his residence on that very day.[20]

The abortive attempt on March 17 was the last straw for two of the conspirators. For Arnold and O'Laughlen, Booth's scheme was increasingly hapless. Fraught with danger from the outset, it appeared to the two Baltimore school chums to be too risky to warrant the effort. To Arnold and O'Laughlen, capture was not only risky, it required the careful coordination of too many people whose enthusiasm was increasingly suspect.

Contrary to some historical accounts, Booth did not hatch his plan to murder Lincoln on the morning of April 14. It was at some point between the failed capture attempt on March 17 and April 12 that Booth decided on assassination. We know this because by Wednesday, April 12, George Atzerodt was selling Booth's carriage and Lewis Powell was scouting the Seward House[21] familiarizing himself with its layout and the location of the bedridden Seward.[22] It appears that Seward was already a target, and Powell was the designated assassin.

Booth had gone to the National Theatre on April 13 to see if Lincoln was planning on visiting the theater that evening. On the morning of the 14th, George Atzerodt registered at the Kirkwood Hotel located at the corner of Twelfth Street and Pennsylvania Avenue. There, Vice President Andrew Johnson was living in a room only a few steps from where Atzerodt set up his own housekeeping.[23]

At what precise moment Booth knew of Lincoln's planned visit to Ford's Theatre on Friday evening is not clear. It is also not clear at what moment

Mary Lincoln decided that she and her husband would attend the theater Friday evening, and whether news of their visit somehow passed from the White House eventually reaching Booth. While Booth and several of his cohorts were active on Wednesday, April 12, it may have been in anticipation of a future visit not yet planned, or it may have been that word had leaked that Mrs. Lincoln was contemplating a theater visit in hopes of gaining an earned respite for her war-weary husband. In any event, sinister movements were underway.

On April 13 Booth paid a visit to the National Theatre on Pennsylvania Avenue, another favorite spot of Lincoln's. Ostensibly, Booth was trying to find out if Lincoln would be attending the performance there. On the morning of the 14th, he visited Ford's Theatre to pick up his mail. He met with Harry Clay Ford,[24] who managed the theater's daily operation. Ford confirmed that both Lincoln and Grant would attend the evening performance. Of course, the presidential box would be reserved for the illustrious guests of the Ford brothers.[25]

That evening, the popular American actress, Laura Keene, was performing in the British comedy entitled, *Our American Cousin*. The performance was a benefit for the popular female star in which she would receive the proceeds of the evening receipts as her pay as one of the star performers at Ford's. The performance was sold out and Booth, ever the dramatic thespian, would himself play to a standing room only crowd for what he believed would be his greatest performance.

There is reason to believe that John Wilkes Booth became involved in Confederate underground activities as early as the spring of 1863. Booth was originally involved in smuggling drugs (quinine in particular) south. By late summer 1864, several war measures were instituted which dramatically changed both the demeanor and strategy of the conflict.

Among Ulysses S. Grant's first moves as general-in-chief in March 1864 was his suspension of prisoner exchange. By not exchanging captured soldiers Grant was in effect instituting a policy of strangling the Confederate war machine. While the North had substantial reserves of manpower to draw upon, the South did not. Suspension of prisoner exchange meant that the already undersized armies of the Confederacy could only get smaller. The Northern strategists knew that such depletion of manpower would eventually hurt the Confederacy. The down side, of course, was that Northern prisoners had to survive in Southern prison camps under conditions of extreme deprivation as the Confederacy slowly ran out of food, medical supplies, and facilities to support even a substandard existence. The result of having to provide for Northern prisoners of war only added further strain on a Confederate supply system that was already failing. On the other hand, the North had to care for increasing numbers of captured Confederates, putting an ever increasing strain on their resources.

As conditions deteriorated further, Northern prisoners suffered dispro-
portionately under dwindling Confederate resources causing increasing protests in the North. In August 1864, Secretary of War Edwin McMasters
Stanton issued a "retaliation order" in which rations for Southern prisoners
of war were reduced to levels believed commensurate with those issued to
Northern prisoners of war. The result was brutal on both sides. Booth, of
course, focused only on the condition of Southern prisoners of war and his
anger and hatred for Lincoln only grew more virulent.

Forty months into the war conditions had changed dramatically. Chivalry and noble causes were rapidly crashing into a nightmare of devastation and brutality. To John Wilkes Booth, this was entirely the fault of
Union tyranny under the iron fist of the country's despotic Caesar, Abraham
Lincoln.

Booth's solution to the growing disaster facing the Confederacy was
actually quite reasonable from a strategic point of view and, if successful,
could prove of considerable help to the dying Confederacy. Booth, as several before him, proposed to capture Lincoln and take him to Richmond
where the authorities (Jefferson Davis) could force an exchange of Southern
prisoners for the Northern commander-in-chief. How many soldiers is a
president worth? Certainly a division and perhaps all of the divisions in
Union hands. Perhaps even a negotiated peace settlement.[26]

Walker Taylor, Bradley T. Johnson and John Wilkes Booth all proposed
to capture Abraham Lincoln, Commander-in-Chief of the United States
military forces as a military strategy to affect the outcome of the war. This
point should not be lost when discussing the Lincoln assassination story.
While kidnapping was a misdemeanor in 1865, capturing the commander-
in-chief was a military (war) action and fell under the jurisdiction of the
military. Virtually all of the plots against Lincoln were for the purpose of
affecting the outcome of the war, i.e. the military operations of the North.
Neither Taylor nor Johnson nor Booth had any personal designs in dealing
with a captured Lincoln. All of their efforts had but one objective, to affect
the military operations of the North.[27] It is also revealing that Taylor and
Jefferson Davis used the word "capture" in referring to Taylor's plot against
Lincoln.[28]

Whether Booth was even aware of prior plots to capture Lincoln such
as Walker Taylor's or Bradley T. Johnson's is unclear, but certainly it is not
unreasonable to believe that he had gotten wind of them at one point or
another. Some writers have even suggested that Booth, along with Atzerodt,
Arnold and O'Laughlen, simply rolled over from Bradley T. Johnson's plot
in the summer of 1864.[29] One thing is strikingly similar among all of the
proposals to capture Lincoln: the route of escape.

Throughout the war the Confederacy operated a clandestine secret service or underground which was officially within the Confederate Signal

The "Capture" Conspirators.

Michael O'Laughlen

Samuel Bland Arnold

John H. Surratt, Jr.

Edman Spangler

Service or, more accurately, Signal Bureau. Movement from the Confederacy into Maryland and Washington, D.C. was carried out over two principal routes; both were well laid out and staffed with Confederate agents. The principal route into Washington crossed the Potomac River from Mathias Point in King George County, Virginia to Allen's Fresh, Newport, Bryantown (Bryan Town), Surratt's Tavern and Washington.

According to a Confederate Signal Bureau document located in the National Archives[30], the Surratt Tavern was a specific stop along the underground route into the District of Columbia. At the time the document was written, the widowed Mary Surratt was operating the tavern and had not yet relocated her family to her house at 541 H Street in Washington. Her son, John Harrison Surratt, Jr., was serving as a Confederate courier and frequently traveled the route between Richmond and Washington carrying messages for the Confederate government. Mary was certainly aware of her son's activity and could not help but know that her tavern (and later boarding house) were Confederate safe houses.

The routes used by the Confederacy were for the safe conduct of "...letters, papers and light packages to the Dept." as well as for the safe conduct of people. It was this "safe route" through southern Maryland into Virginia that John Wilkes Booth had reconnoitered on several occasions in preparation for taking Lincoln to Richmond after his capture. To carry out such a plan required help, both directly in committing the act, and indirectly in assisting the safe transport south. Booth found a ready and willing cadre of individuals in developing his bold plan.

Booth needed two types of accomplices: those who would assist in the actual capture and those who would assist in facilitating the escape to Richmond.[31] These two groups were quite different in character. The first was put together as a tight conspiracy by Booth specifically for the purpose of capturing Lincoln while the second was already in place serving the Confederacy in a different role. Booth needed to tap into the second to assure the success of the first. He was able to do both which resulted in a very broad conspiracy across different organizational lines.

Among the first group, or inner circle, were Samuel Arnold, George Atzerodt, Davy Herold, Michael O'Laughlen, Lewis Powell, John Surratt and, of course, John Wilkes Booth.

Among the second group were a few who had knowledge of the plan to capture Lincoln and were prepared to aid in the flight to Richmond. Before his death twelve days after Lincoln's demise, over two dozen individuals would knowingly aid and abet the assassin of Abraham Lincoln. Dr. Samuel Alexander Mudd was well connected with his feet in both of these two camps.

3

SIC SEMPER TYRANNIS[1]

Sometime between 6:30 and 7:30 on Friday evening, April 14, John Wilkes Booth met with George Atzerodt, Louis Powell and Davy Herold in Powell's room at the boarding house of Mrs. Murphy.[2] Also known as the Herndon House, Mrs. Murphy's boarding house was located at the corner of Ninth and F Streets just one block from Ford's Theatre. Booth had arranged for Powell to stay there out of sight, to avoid any problems which might jeopardize his plans. It was here that the four conspirators met to go over their plan for the last time. Booth reviewed the role of each of the four men and each of their targets.[3]

Powell, along with Davy Herold as guide, would go to the home of William Seward to kill the secretary of state. Atzerodt, already registered in Room 126 at the Kirkwood Hotel, would call on Andrew Johnson and kill the vice president. Booth would take care of Lincoln.[4]

All was coordinated to take place at approximately 10:30 p.m. The four would then head across the Navy Yard Bridge and rendezvous just over the District line in Maryland at a spot known as Soper's Hill.[5]

After going over their plans one more time the four men melted into the surrounding neighborhood and waited until the assigned hour. As 10:00 p.m. approached all four assassins were within striking distance of their targets. Atzerodt, after leaving John Fletcher at the Union Hotel rode the two short blocks to the Kirkwood Hotel where he entered the bar for yet another swill of whiskey. Within a few feet of Andrew Johnson's room, Atzerodt's courage failed and he quickly left the hotel, mounted his horse and rode away.

At the moment Atzerodt's courage evaporated, Lewis Powell had talked his way into Seward's house located on Lafayette Square directly opposite the White House. Powell insisted that he hand-deliver a doctor's prescription to the bedridden Seward. Forcing his way into the house, Powell erupted in a rage and began attacking anyone who got in his way. Herold, waiting outside with Powell's horse, panicked on hearing the horrible screams coming from the house and, dropping the horse's reins, galloped off leaving Powell to fend for himself in escaping from the city. Powell's horse, owned by John Wilkes Booth, was characterized by having lost an eye.[6]

Booth, perhaps uncertain as to the resolve of his three cohorts, had no reservations as to his own. Arriving at the rear of the theater, he dismounted from his horse and called for Edman Spangler to hold the reins for the few minutes that he would be in the theater.[7] Spangler, working as a stagehand that evening, had his own work moving scene flats between acts. Spangler passed the reins of Booth's horse on to a young theater hand named "Peanuts" Burroughs.[8]

Once inside the rear door, Booth lifted a trap door set in the floor of the theater and made his way down a small set of stairs to the dug out cellar beneath the stage. Crossing beneath the stage area, he made his way up a second set of stairs and through another trap door which brought him to the opposite side of the back stage area. Here a door led into a small alley separating the theater from the Star Saloon which was immediately adjacent to the theater. By this manuever, Booth was able to pass from the rear of the theater to the front sidewalk on Tenth Street, leaving his horse carefully tended outside the rear door of the theater. Entering the saloon, he downed a brandy marking the time, and after a brief exchange with the barkeep slipped out the front of the saloon and entered the theater lobby through its front door.

A star figure of national renown, Booth had liberal access to the theater and its environs. Passing across the lobby, Booth climbed the stairs located on the left, and arriving at the area known as the dress circle, slowly made his way across the rear of the circle to the boxes located at the far end. Here the president and his party were enjoying the play being carried out on the stage directly below the two boxes.[9]

As Booth approached the outer door to the president's box he encountered Lincoln's personal valet and attendant, Charles Forbes.[10] After a brief exchange in which Booth presented Forbes with a card,[11] he entered the outer vestibule of the two boxes. Seated immediately inside the inner door were the president, Mrs. Lincoln, Major Henry Rathbone and his fiancee, Clara Harris.

Booth secured the outer door from any unexpected interruption by wedging a piece of wood, which he had previously hidden behind the door, between the door and the notch in the wall which he had carefully fashioned earlier in the day. With the outer door firmly secured, Booth slowly opened the inner door leading into the box where Lincoln and his companions were sitting. Raising his small derringer, he fired point-blank into the back of Lincoln's head.

Upper left: John T. Ford. Upper right: Harry Clay Ford.
Lower left: Laura Keene. Lower right: Ford's Theatre.

Major Henry Rathbone and his fiancee Clara Harris had accompanied President and Mrs. Lincoln to the theater and were sitting near them in the presidential box. On hearing the shot and Booth's dramatic shout of *Sic semper tyrannis*,[12] Rathbone jumped to his feet and attempted to subdue the assassin. Severely wounding Rathbone with his knife, Booth swung his legs over the balustrade and dropped to the stage ten feet below. Legend has Booth catching his spur in a flag of the Treasury Guard which was mounted vertically between the boxes. Other accounts of the time mention Booth catching his spur in the "National Standard." Both balustrades of the two boxes were covered with American flags at the time, and it seems more probable that Booth caught his spur in one of them as he swung his legs over the balustrade and dropped awkwardly to the stage below.[13]

Whichever flag ensnared Booth, it caused him to land off balance and resulted in a clean break of the fibula above the ankle in his left leg. The break did not effect the tibia, or weight-bearing bone. Although Booth was hurting, he remained quite mobile.[14]

Making his way across the stage, Booth dashed out of the rear door to his waiting horse still being cared for by young "Peanuts" Burroughs. Within minutes he was racing toward the Navy Yard Bridge and his first major hurdle in escaping the city and the authorities who were in a state of complete disorganization during the first minutes following the assassination.

Arriving at the Navy Yard Bridge at approximately 10:45 p.m., Booth was challenged by the guard, Sergeant Silas T. Cobb. Cobb questioned Booth briefly, and surprisingly, Booth not only gave his correct name, but also his correct destination. He said he was headed for Beantown located in southern Maryland.[15] Booth was not wearing a disguise.

Satisfied that Booth posed no threat to the army or the city, the unsuspecting sentry waved the killer across the bridge, sending him into the comparative safety of pro-Confederate southern Maryland. Booth's admitted destination of Beantown suggests that he was headed for the home of Dr. Mudd.[16]

Within minutes after Booth passed the sentries, a second rider arrived at the bridge. He too was challenged by Cobb, but unlike the first rider gave a false name. Also unlike the first rider, he gave a false destination. He also gave a false reason why he had overstayed his visit in the city, arriving at the bridge long after the curfew of 9:00 p.m. Davy Herold told Sergeant Cobb that he had been with a woman and had lost track of the time. Cobb seemed understanding. Certainly Herold's excuse seemed plausible. Like the first rider, Herold posed no threat leaving the city, and was waved across the bridge.[17]

Minutes later a third rider approached. As with the previous two, the rider was stopped. He gave his name as John Fletcher, and he told the guard that his purpose in crossing over the bridge was to recover his stolen

The Assassin's Targets.

Lincoln National Life Foundation

Abraham Lincoln

Edward Steers, Jr. collection

Vice-President Andrew Johnson

Edward Steers, Jr. collection

Secretary of State William H. Seward

Library of Congress

Ulysses S. Grant

horse from the thief Davy Herold. Cobb acknowledged that a man meeting Herold's description had passed over the bridge only minutes before, but said that if he allowed Fletcher to pass over the bridge he could not return until morning. Those were Cobb's orders and Fletcher could take them or leave them. Fletcher reluctantly chose to return to the city and seek another remedy to recover his stolen horse. As he wheeled his horse around and headed back into the city, the two horsemen were galloping as fast as their mounts would carry them up the road that ran between two of the forts which guarded the city from hostile forces.[18]

Sometime around 11:00 p.m., John Wilkes Booth and Davy Herold had passed into the relative safety of southern Maryland. Back in the city pandemonium reigned. By the time Secretary of War Edwin Stanton assumed effective control of the situation, Booth and Herold were approaching the tavern at Surrattsville well beyond the immediate grasp of the authorities. John Wilkes Booth had struck a daring and devastating blow against the United States and had won, or so it seemed.

It was close to midnight when the two fugitives made their stop at the crossroads tavern named for John Surratt. John Harrison Surratt, Sr. had died two and a half years earlier and his widow Mary had leased the tavern in the fall of 1864 to a man named John M. Lloyd.[19] The tavern, through the connection of John H. Surratt, Jr., was a "safe house" along the Confederate underground route from Richmond to Washington.[20]

Mary's ownership of the tavern, her son's role as one of Booth's conspirators, and the devastating testimony of John M. Lloyd, the tavern manager, all combined to send the woman to the gallows. Mary Surratt thus achieved the dubious distinction of becoming the first woman to be hanged by the United States Government.[21]

Arriving at the tavern, Herold dismounted and called for the manager, John Lloyd. After what seemed several minutes, an inebriated Lloyd came to the tavern door. Herold, irritated at Lloyd's delay in answering the door and sensing his inebriation, told him, "For God's sake Lloyd, make haste and get those things!"[22] Lloyd knew exactly what things he was to get without being told. He returned in a few minutes with two Spencer carbines, ammunition, the field glasses Mary Surratt had brought that day, and whiskey.[23] Due to the broken bone in Booth's leg, he had trouble balancing himself on his horse, and was unable to carry the second carbine. He told Lloyd to keep it.[24] Herold took the other carbine and passed the whiskey to Booth. After fortifying themselves with alcohol, the two men wheeled their horses about and galloped off with Booth telling Lloyd, "We have assassinated the President and Secretary Seward."[25]

Surratt House Museum

Photograph by Edward Steers, Jr.

Mary E. Surratt

The Surratt Boarding House

Photograph by Edward Steers, Jr.

Surratt House and Tavern

4

DR. MUDD TELLS HIS SIDE OF THE STORY.

Situated approximately fifteen miles south of Mary Surratt's tavern was the home of Dr. Samuel Alexander Mudd. Mudd, a country physician who maintained a modest tobacco farm, was well known among the citizenry of Charles County, Maryland. He lived in a large, frame farmhouse with his wife Sarah Frances Dyer, affectionately known as "Frank," and their four young children.

According to statements given by Dr. Mudd,[1] it was around 4:00 a.m. when he and his wife were abruptly awakened from their sleep by a pounding on their front door. Mudd was alarmed at the loud banging at such an early hour and initially feared that it was someone or some persons up to no good.[2]

After briefly conferring with his wife as to who should go to the door, Dr. Mudd decided to go himself. He found two men outside his door, one man sitting astride a horse while the other man stood holding the reins of the two horses. Mudd claimed not to recognize the duo. On inquiring as to who they were and what they wanted, he was told they were "two strangers from St. Mary's Co. who were on their way to Washington. While enroute the horse of the mounted man had fallen, and broken the rider's leg."[3]

Mudd satisfied himself that one of the riders was indeed in distress and appeared to need medical assistance. He opened the door and invited the two men into his parlor, laying the injured man on a sofa. Mudd then obtained a light and, after examining the injured man's leg, helped him upstairs where he laid him in a bed and proceeded to treat him. Even in the better light of the bedroom Mudd still claimed not to recognize either of his two guests.

The uninjured man urged Mudd to attend to the injury of his friend quickly so that they could continue on their journey to Washington. In order to examine the injured man more thoroughly, Mudd had to cut the man's boot from his leg and foot "longitudinally in front of the instep." Removing the boot, Mudd set it aside. After examining the injured man's leg, he concluded that, "...there was one bone broken about two inches above the ankle joint—what we call a 'direct fracture.'" The injury was not compound, and Mudd proceeded to set the fracture and splint the leg using an old band box which he cut up and fashioned into a splint.

With the injured man treated and resting in the upstairs bedroom, Mudd walked around his farmyard giving instructions to the hired help before returning to the house for breakfast.[4]

The young man accompanying the injured man was "knocking about" and Dr. Mudd invited him to join him in breakfast. The "talkative" young man, according to Mudd, gave his name as Henson (Herold) and his friend's name as either Tyser or Tyson (Booth), Mudd could not be sure which. The two men, Mudd told his interrogators, **were complete strangers and he did not recognize either of them.** [Emphasis added].

As the two men finished their breakfast, Mr. Henson (Herold) asked Dr. Mudd if he could borrow a razor as his friend felt that he might feel better if he shaved off his moustache. In his written statements Dr. Mudd insisted that the injured man, Mr. Tyser, (Booth) had long chin whiskers and a moustache when he first examined him. Complying with Mr. Henson's (Herold) request, Mudd provided the injured man with one of his razors.

After finishing his dinner (the noonday meal) later that day, Mudd looked in on the injured man and noticed that he had indeed shaved off his moustache, but had retained his lengthy chin whiskers. A short while later, Mudd's wife would inform the doctor of a rather remarkable observation. She noticed that the chin whiskers had become detached when the man (Booth) came down the stairs later that afternoon.[5]

Following the noontime meal, Dr. Mudd and Mr. Henson (Herold) rode over to Oak Hill, the farm of Mudd's father. Henry Lowe Mudd, Sr. lived a short distance to the southeast of Samuel Mudd's farm. Mudd had taken Henson (Herold) to his father's farm to see if he might obtain a carriage or wagon to transport the injured Mr. Tyser (Booth). Arriving at the farm, Mudd found his father away, but met his brother there. No carriage or wagon was available or fit for serious service so Mr. Henson (Herold) told Mudd that he would ride into Bryantown and try and find a wagon.[6] Mudd agreed to accompany Mr. Henson (Herold) into town, for he had several errands of his own to run. Bryantown was a small village located approximately five miles south of Mudd's farm.

Henson (Herold), whose horse was considerably more sprightly than Mudd's, soon outran the doctor by some distance. As they approached Bryantown, Henson (Herold) abruptly reversed himself and rode back to Mudd exclaiming, "I believe I will get my friend to go to Rev. Wilmer's on horseback."[7]

According to Mudd's statement, the young man then galloped off in the direction of Mudd's house. Mudd continued on into Bryantown where he claimed to have purchased several needed items including nails, calico cloth, and pepper for which he paid cash. It was while attending to his shopping in Bryantown that Dr. Mudd admitted first hearing the news of Lincoln's murder. He did not, however, state if he had also learned who the murderer was.[8]

On his return from Bryantown, Mudd stopped by the home of one of his neighbors, Francis Farrell. Here he found another neighbor, John F. Hardy. The men met by the front gate where Mudd told them of Lincoln's assassination, as well as that of Seward and Seward's son, Frederick.[9] According to Farrell,[10] on learning of Lincoln's murder, he asked Mudd who had assassinated the President. Farrell stated that Mudd told him, "A man by the name of Booth." Hardy then asked if the assassin was the same Booth who had been in the area last fall. Mudd stated that he did not know—that there were three or four men named Booth—but if it was that same Booth (namely John Wilkes), he was acquainted with him.[11]

After his conversation with Farrell and Hardy, Mudd proceeded to return home. It was around 5:00 p.m. when he arrived back at the farm. On approaching his house, Mudd stated, the two strangers were already mounted on their horses getting ready to leave. "...I returned home leisurely, and found the two men were just in the act of leaving." Mr. Hensen (Herold) rode up to Dr. Mudd and inquired the shortest way to the house of a man named Parson Wilmer who lived near the Piney Church. Mr Tyser (Booth) was already some "...fifty to seventy yards" from where Mudd stood when Hensen (Herold) rode back to ask directions. According to Mudd's statement, he told Hensen (Herold) the most direct route to Wilmer's house after which Hensen (Herold) rode off, joining his partner in the direction of Mudd's short cut through the Zekiah Swamp. The route to Wilmer's is nearly due west of the Mudd house and directly opposite from Bryantown and the 13th New York Cavalry.

Sunday morning, April 16, Dr. Mudd attended church at St. Peter's where he met his "brother physician" and cousin, George Mudd.[12] Following church services, as George Mudd was on his way to the home of Henry Lowe Mudd, Sr. for Sunday dinner, he stopped to talk with his cousin Sam. According to George Mudd's testimony,[13] Samuel Mudd had told his cousin about the two suspicious persons who had been to his house the day before. George Mudd told the good doctor that the authorities should be notified. Samuel Mudd was reluctant to inform the soldiers in Bryantown of the strangers' visit, and asked George Mudd to do it for him.[14] George Mudd said that he would.

The next day, Monday, April 17, approximately forty hours after the two suspicious strangers left Samuel Mudd's farm, George Mudd rode

Dr. Mudd's Neighborhood

the short distance from his own farm to the Bryantown Tavern, and informed Lieutenant Dana of the 13th New York Volunteer Cavalry of his cousin's visitors.[15] George Mudd also informed Dana that one of the strangers had a broken leg and that his cousin had set it. Of course, no one had even suggested that the injured stranger was the assassin of the president, John Wilkes Booth, and so the government still had no knowledge or reason to believe that the fugitive was seriously crippled with a broken left leg. Such information would have been of vital importance to the government in their manhunt for Booth and Herold. But Samuel Mudd, now informed that the assassin of President Lincoln was the famous actor John Wilkes Booth, still contended that he did not know the two strangers other than by the names they gave him, Henson (Herold) and Tyser (Booth).

Home of Dr. Samuel A. Mudd

The road leading from the rear of the Mudd home. Booth and Herold presumably left along this route around five o'clock Saturday evening, April 15, 1865.

Booth's Route to Dr. Mudd's House and the Way Around Bryantown

Surratt's Tavern

Baltimore

Washington

St. Peter's Church

Waldorf

Beantown

Dr. Samuel A. Mudd

Henry L. Mudd, Sr.

Piney Church

Bryantown
13th NY Cavalry

Zekiah Swamp

St. Mary's Church

N
0   1   2
miles

Hughsville

Oswell Swann

To Bel Alton &
Col. Cox's Home

As a result of George Mudd's information concerning his cousin, a team of detectives led by Lieutenant Alexander Lovett paid Dr. Mudd a visit on Tuesday morning, April 18, with the express purpose of interrogating the doctor about the two strangers.[16]

Mudd was questioned on Tuesday, April 18, and again on Friday, April 21, and according to Lieutenant Lovett's later testimony, again on Saturday, April 22.[17] From these interrogations two written statements were obtained from Mudd (see Appendices 1 and 2). The first statement is in Mudd's own hand and is undated (referred to as the "voluntary statement,") but presumably written down by Mudd sometime on Friday, April 21. The second statement was prepared by Colonel H. H. Wells after the Friday, April 21 interview (referred to as the "Wells statement"). This second statement was signed by Mudd and Wells on Saturday morning, April 22, when Mudd returned to Bryantown.

On Tuesday, April 18, Mudd was interrogated at his farm by Lieutenant Alexander Lovett and detectives William Williams, Joshua Lloyd
and Simon Gavacan with George Mudd in tow. When the soldiers and
George Mudd first arrived, Samuel Mudd was away from the house
tending to work on the farm. Mrs. Mudd sent word to her husband to
come, and while they waited for his return Lieutenant Lovett questioned
Mrs. Mudd.

Mrs. Mudd told the soldiers what little she knew about the two strangers,
stating that, "...one of them was a young man about eighteen or nineteen years
of age. The other, who had a broken leg, was a man over thirty years."[18] She
had left the room while the injured man was treated and the next time she saw
him, "...she missed a moustache that he wore on his face when he entered the
house." It was at this time that she also revealed a startling piece of information, almost casually, when she told the detectives that,

> ...her husband had furnished the man a razor for him to shave it off
> (his moustache) and when the man was leaving the house in the afternoon
> (Saturday approximately 4:00 p.m.) she took notice when he came to the
> foot of the stairs, that **his chin whisker became detached and that, she
> thought it was a false whisker.**[19]

When Mudd finally arrived at the farmhouse, there were more questions from Lovett. Mudd stated the essential facts as he claimed he remembered them. Two strangers came to see him; one had a broken leg caused
by his horse falling on him which he treated. Mudd stated that **the two
men were complete strangers to him, he had never seen them previously
and did not know who they were.**

Mudd described the injured man as having a moustache and rather
long chin whiskers. His companion was described by Mudd as, "a young
man about seventeen or eighteen."[20] Mudd further stated that the injured man asked for a razor so that he might shave off his moustache
which now, on reflection, Mudd thought suspicious. At the time of their
leaving, Mudd claimed to have directed the two strangers to the road
which would lead them across the Zekiah Swamp in the direction of
Parson Wilmer's house at Piney Church. According to Lovett's later
testimony, Mudd told the soldiers that he had heard of Lincoln's assassination while he was at church on Sunday morning, April 16.[21] Signifi-
cantly, Mudd never mentioned the "false whisker" to the detectives, and
equally significant, the detectives never asked Mudd about it waiting
instead for him to volunteer it. He never did.

On Friday, April 21, the four detectives, along with several cavalrymen,
returned to the Mudd farm to further their questioning of the doctor. The
men had grown suspicious and, according to Lovett, came with the intention of arresting Mudd and taking him into custody. After interrogating
Mudd at his farm, the soldiers took Mudd into custody to Bryantown where

a formal statement was written down by Colonel Wells following Mudd's second questioning.

It was during this second interrogation at the Mudd house that Mudd made a startling revelation to the soldiers. Lieutenant Lovett had decided it was time to search the Mudd household, and on informing Mrs. Mudd of his intent, Dr. Mudd suddenly told his wife to go upstairs and bring down the boot which he had removed from the injured man's leg. Mrs. Mudd dutifully retrieved the boot and gave it to a surprised Lovett.

Carefully examining the boot, Lovett found the name *J. Wilkes* inscribed along the inner top edge. When Lovett called it to his attention, Mudd said, "he had not taken notice of that before."[22] Lovett now raised the issue of the false whiskers and Mudd finally "...said he was satisfied the stranger was Booth." Mudd did not, however, tell Lovett and the detectives at what precise moment he had deduced that the injured man at his house was John Wilkes Booth.

Following his questioning of Mudd that morning, Lovett took Mudd to Bryantown, and turned him over to Colonel H. H. Wells who was now in command of the troop of soldiers quartered there. After traveling a short distance along the main road to Bryantown, Mudd made another startling revelation. He told Lovett that he indeed knew John Wilkes Booth. He said that he had been introduced to Booth in November 1864 by a local man named John Thompson while attending Sunday services at St. Mary's Church in Bryantown. After this meeting, Mudd claimed that Booth had returned home with him and spent the night as his house guest. The following morning Mudd had taken Booth to his nearest neighbor, George Gardiner, where Booth bought a horse.[23] A horse characterized by having lost one eye.

Mudd was shown a photograph (carte de visite) of Booth, and was asked if the injured stranger resembled the man in the photo. Mudd thought that the photograph did not look like the injured stranger at first, but on reflection said it did resemble him "across the eyes." Although Mudd had maintained that the injured man kept a shawl wrapped around his face, and kept his face turned toward the wall so that his appearance was not obvious, he nevertheless gave a detailed description of the injured man which closely matched the features of Booth.

At some point, while he was in Bryantown being questioned further, Mudd wrote out a statement in his own hand summarizing what he had verbally told the officers.[24] In this voluntary statement, Mudd wrote, "I first heard of the assassination of President Lincoln on Saturday afternoon about two or three o'clock in the afternoon." At another point in his statement, Dr. Mudd said he heard of the assassination while in Bryantown. From his statement it is not clear who he heard it from, but it is clear from John Hardy's testimony that Mudd also heard, while in Bryantown, that John Wilkes Booth was the assassin.

St. Mary's Church near Bryantown, Maryland. John Wilkes Booth met with members of the Confederate underground at this church on at least two occasions in 1864. The first time was on Sunday, November 13, 1864; the second, on Sunday, December 18, 1864. It was during the first meeting that Booth was introduced to Dr. Mudd by Dr. William Queen's son-in-law, John Thompson, and it was after the second meeting in December that Booth stayed the night at Dr. Mudd's house, and purchased the one-eyed horse from George Gardiner the next day.

Also in his voluntary statement Mudd described his two visitors:

...one was a very small one. I should call him a well grown boy. He looked to be about 17 or 18—to be a boy who had never yet shaved. The other was a man of medium size, with black hair. He had whiskers, and also a moustache. ...The older...I should judge to be about 30 or 35 years of age.

Mudd also described the injured man as having a shawl wrapped around his head and shoulders partly concealing his face.[25] Upon their request, Mudd made a pair of crutches for the injured man, and was paid twenty-five dollars for his services. Mudd then related:

No suspicion was aroused in my mind of anything being wrong with regard to these men. After I heard of the assassination and began to have suspicion as to these two men being in some way connected with it, a little circumstance occurred to me as confirmatory of such suspicions & which I had not thought of before. It was this. After breakfast the older one asked for a razor and some soap; which he got; and on my giving him the articles which I had prepared, a short time afterward, I noticed that his moustache had disappeared.[26]

Mudd concluded: "The injured man had a belt with two revolvers in it concealed under his clothing, which I discovered when he got into bed after having his wound dressed."[27]

The following morning, Saturday, April 22, Mudd returned to Bryantown for further questioning at the direction of Colonel Wells. It was at this time that Wells presented Mudd with a statement which Wells had prepared, and which Mudd was asked to read and sign.[28] While the second statement covers much of the same material in Mudd's earlier handwritten statement, it does contain certain new information. Mudd adds to his description of the injured man:

He was a man, I should suppose about five feet ten inches high, and appeared to be pretty well made, but he had a heavy shawl on all the time. I suppose he would weigh 150 or 160 pounds. His hair was black and seemed to be somewhat inclined to curl; it was worn long. He had a pretty full forehead and his skin was fair. He was very pale when I saw him, and appeared as if accustomed to in-door rather than out-door life. ...I did not observe his hand to see whether it was small or large.[29] I have been shown the photograph of J. Wilkes Booth and I should not think that this was the man from any resemblance to the photograph, but from other causes I have every reason to believe that he is the man whose leg I dressed as above stated.[30]

Mudd, in this second statement, acknowledges for the first time that a prior meeting with Booth had occurred. "I have seen J. Wilkes Booth. I was introduced to him by Mr. J. C. Thompson, a son-in-law of Dr. William Queen, in November or December last."

The introduction was only a preamble, however. Mudd further states that Booth had actually stayed the night at his house.

The next evening he rode to my house and staid (sic) with me that night, and the next morning he purchased a rather old horse, but a very fine mover of Mr. George Gardiner, Sr., who resides but a short distance from my house.

Then Mudd makes a very important statement. **"I have never seen Booth since that time to my knowledge until last Saturday night."** The statement is signed by Mudd, "Sam'l. A. Mudd," and by Wells, "Subscribed and sworn before me this 22nd day of April 1865 H. H. Wells Col. & P.M. Genl Def. S. of P."[31]

By now Lovett and Wells are certain that Mudd has been less than forthright in his several interviews with them. Lovett felt that Mudd was evasive in most of his answers, volunteering little. Each successive interrogation seemed to produce new and more valuable information on the identity and whereabouts of Booth and Herold. Convinced of Mudd's duplicity, Wells ordered the doctor taken into custody on Monday, April 24, and transported to Washington, D.C. where he was imprisoned in the old Capitol Prison (Carroll Annex) before being transferred to the eventual trial site at the old Washington Arsenal grounds (now Fort Lesley J. McNair.)

As Mudd arrived in Washington still uncertain of his fate, John Wilkes Booth arrived at the farmhouse of Richard Garrett near Port Royal, Virginia where he settled in after his trying and painful trip through southern Maryland.

5

THE MEETINGS.
NOT QUITE THE TRUTH, THE WHOLE TRUTH, AND NOTHING BUT THE TRUTH.

When the government presented its case against Dr. Mudd, it had damaging evidence—evidence sufficient to convict Mudd. It did not, however, have all of the evidence against the good doctor.

What did the government know about Dr. Mudd when it went to trial? It knew that John Wilkes Booth and David Herold had come to Mudd's house early on Saturday morning, April 15, around 4:00 a.m., only five and a half hours after Booth shot Lincoln. It knew Mudd gave medical assistance to Booth by splinting his broken leg as well as feeding him and giving him a place to rest. It knew that Mudd was a former slaveholder and Southern sympathizer who opposed the Lincoln administration. And it knew, from Mudd's own admission, that he knew Booth from a meeting in November 1864.

The government also knew more. It knew of a second meeting between Booth and Mudd — a second meeting which involved John H. Surratt, Jr., and would prove damaging to Mudd's claim of innocence. What the government did not know, however, was that a third meeting had occurred involving Mudd and Booth, and a Confederate secret service agent.

While Dr. Mudd attempted to trivialize his admitted meeting with Booth in November 1864, the government knew better. The government had evidence that Mudd and Booth had actually met on two separate occasions in 1864, not one as originally claimed by Mudd. The second meeting took place in December 1864 in Washington, D.C. This second meeting was revealed by one of the government's star witnesses during his testimony at the trial.

At first, Mudd failed to inform the authorities of any of his meetings with Booth. It was only during his trip to Bryantown to meet with Colonel

Wells that Mudd acknowledged that he had met with Booth in November 1864. Mudd then said, "I have never seen Booth since that time to my knowledge until last Saturday night (April 15)."[1] The second meeting, which Mudd had withheld from Wells, took place in late December at Booth's hotel room in Washington, and would be introduced during the trial by the government's key witness, Louis J. Weichmann.[2] The third meeting would remain hidden until years later.

According to Mudd's statement to Wells, it was during the November visit that Booth stayed as an overnight guest in his house. Mudd also stated that it was during this November visit that he took Booth to his neighbor, George Gardiner, where Booth purchased the one-eyed horse subsequently used by Powell. Again Mudd lied. Booth did not stay the night during his November visit, nor did he purchase the one-eyed horse at that time. It was during a third meeting between Mudd and Booth that Booth stayed the night and purchased the one-eyed horse.

A memorandum prepared by the desk clerk of the National Hotel where Booth lodged when in Washington shows that Booth checked out of his hotel room on Friday, November 11.[3] He checked back into the hotel on Monday, November 14. Booth did go to Bryantown on the 11th where he spent the night at the home of Dr. William Queen, a member of the Confederate underground in Charles County.

On Sunday, November 13, Booth attended St. Mary's Church, a short distance southeast of Bryantown, where he was introduced to Samuel Mudd by Queen's son-in-law, John Thompson. Mudd acknowledges in his statement given to Wells that this meeting did occur. Contrary to Mudd's statement, however, Booth did not spend the night at Mudd's house, but returned to Washington as evidenced by the memorandum of the hotel desk clerk, and a letter written by Booth dated at Washington on November 14.[4] These two items clearly place Booth back in Washington on Monday, November 14.

If Booth did not stay at the Mudd house on the night of November 13, and did not purchase the one-eyed horse the next day as Mudd claimed, when did he? This suggests that Booth visited with Dr. Mudd in Charles County a second time—a third meeting not revealed by Mudd.

Booth did indeed visit Bryantown a second time. He was back at the Bryantown Tavern on the evening of December 17. As on his November trip, he was picked up by Dr. Queen, and stayed the first night at Queen's home. The following day, after church services at St. Mary's, Booth met with Dr. Mudd at the Bryantown Tavern where Mudd had arranged a meeting with Thomas Harbin, a Confederate Secret Service operative. Harbin was responsible for certain undercover operations in the lower Maryland counties that bordered the Potomac River.

Harbin was an extremely competent agent and could play a vital role assisting in the successful passage of Lincoln should Booth's plan of capture succeed. Harbin had been postmaster at Bryantown and was well

The meeting at the Bryantown Tavern on December 18, 1864.

The second meeting involving Mudd and Booth occurred in December immediately before the third meeting in Washington. It was at this meeting that Mudd introduced Booth to Thomas Harbin, a Confederate operative. As a result of this meeting, Harbin agreed to assist Booth in his capture conspiracy.

Edward Steers, Jr. collection   Courtesy of James O. Hall   Courtesy of James O. Hall

John Wilkes Booth   *Dr. Samuel A. Mudd*   *Thomas Harbin*

Courtesy of Surratt House and Museum

Bryantown Tavern ca. 1890.

acquainted with Dr. Mudd. Mudd introduced Booth to Harbin and after a "private conversation" between the three men, Harbin agreed to help Booth in his plan to carry the captured Lincoln to Richmond.[5]

Following their meeting at the tavern, Booth returned to Mudd's home where he spent the night on December 18. The following morning, Monday, December 19, Mudd and Booth visited George Gardiner where Booth purchased the one-eyed horse. Booth then returned to the Bryantown Tavern where George Gardiner's nephew, Thomas Gardiner, delivered the one-eyed horse to Booth the next day.[6]

The memorandum of National Hotel clerk Bunker places Booth at the National Hotel on Monday, November 14, and Tuesday, November 15. Clearly, Booth could not have been in two places at one time. This leads to the conclusion that it was during his second visit to Bryantown in mid-December that Booth visited with Mudd and purchased the one-eyed horse from Gardiner. This conclusion is supported by the testimony of Thomas Gardiner and John F. Hardy.

Booth received his newly-purchased horse from Thomas Gardiner on Tuesday, December 20, and subsequently rode him back to Washington. He arrived back in Washington at the National Hotel and checked in on Thursday, December 22.

Although missed by the government, and many researchers since,[7] other evidence exists which places Booth in Charles County in mid-December. During Thomas Gardiner's testimony relating to Booth's purchase of the horse, and Gardiner's delivery of it to Booth, Gardiner was asked whether he had ever heard of Booth being in the neighborhood before. Gardiner stated that he, "...did hear that he (Booth) was in the neighborhood of Bryantown some time before that." Clearly Thomas Gardiner places Booth in the area of Bryantown on two separate occasions, both times at St. Mary's, and one of those two times at the home of Samuel Mudd.

A second witness, John F. Hardy, a neighbor of Mudd, also testified to seeing Booth at St. Mary's Church near Bryantown on two separate occasions. The first time was in November, and the second was "...about a month after" but "...before Christmas." John F. Hardy gives the following testimony:

> *Q. The Booth that was spoken of was the one who had been there looking at lands. Is that what you asked?*
>
> *A. I saw a gentleman there that went by that name (Booth): I did not know who he was.*
>
> *Q. Where did you see him?*
>
> *A. I saw him some time before Christmas, at church, one Sunday.... Some time again I saw him at the same place, and asked if that was the same man; and the answer was, "Yes."*

Q. *When did you first see him?*

A. *Some time before Christmas: it may have been November. I will not be positive.*

Q. *Endeavor to refresh your recollection as to the dates of the two occasions that you saw Booth in the country.*

A. *I cannot call the dates: I do not remember any dates at all.*

Q. *How long were the two times apart?*

A. *I think about a month. It might not have been quite that length of time, and it may have been a little longer.*

Q. *The first time was about the 1st of November?*

A. *I think it was sometime in November.*

Q. *Early or late November?*

A. *That I cannot answer; but I think it must have been some time in November. I think both times that I saw him there were before Christmas; I am pretty sure it was, each time that I saw him there: and it strikes me it must have been in November when I first saw him there.*[8]

Hardy also testified to seeing Booth "...riding on the Horse Head Road, by himself" a day or two after seeing him at St. Mary's Church the second time:

Q. *Did you ever hear of his being in that part of the country, at any other except those two times, before the assassination?*

A. *No, sir: a day or two after the second time that I saw him at church, I met him a little above Bryantown, riding on the Horse Head Road, by himself; but I only call that about one time, as I think it was the next day after Sunday. On Monday evening, I rode to Bryantown to see if I could get my horse shod; and I met Mr. Booth, or the same man they called Booth,—I do not know who he was,—a little above Bryantown riding by himself. He was riding a horse in the road leading straight to Horse Head, or he could not come to this point, to Washington, on the same road.*[9]

Two eyewitnesses place Booth in the Bryantown area on two separate occasions: the first in November, and the second in December 1864. And it was on the second visit, according to Thomas Gardiner, that Gardiner delivered the horse to Booth at the Bryantown Tavern, not on the first visit.

But the most damaging evidence that places Booth in Charles County in December 1864 is from Mudd himself. This startling revelation appears in an affidavit by Mudd written in 1865 in response to a sworn statement by the officer in command of the military guard escorting Mudd to his imprisonment at Fort Jefferson.[10]

Following their convictions on July 7, 1865, Mudd, O'Laughlen, Arnold and Spangler were transported to Fort Jefferson in the Dry Tortugas where they were to begin serving their sentences. A military guard, commanded by Captain George W. Dutton (Company C, 10th Regiment, Veteran Reserve Corps) accompanied the prisoners to the fort. Following his return, Dutton filed an affidavit with Brigadier General Joseph Holt, the judge advocate general, on July 22, 1865 describing a conversation he had with Mudd. In his affidavit Dutton makes a damaging claim regarding Mudd. He states that while enroute to Fort Jefferson, Dr. Mudd "...confessed that **he knew Booth when he came to his house with Herold on the morning after the assassination of the President.**" And further, that Mudd "...also confessed that he was with Booth at the National Hotel on the evening referred to by Weichmann in his testimony; that he came to Washington on that occasion **to meet Booth by appointment;** who wished to be introduced to John Surratt;..." Neither of these two statements concerning Mudd were new to the government which suspected the first, and had proven the second.

Dutton's statement reached Mudd in prison which prompted Mudd to file an affidavit responding to Dutton's claims.[11] In his affidavit, dated August 28, 1865,[12] Mudd denies Dutton's claim that he confessed to knowing Booth, but did admit to the meeting at the National Hotel in which he introduced Booth to John Surratt. In his response, Mudd let slip a piece of information damaging to his case and supporting Booth's second visit to Bryantown in December. On describing his meeting with Booth, John Surratt and Louis Weichmann, which occurred in Booth's hotel room on December 23, 1864, Mudd writes:

> "We (Mudd and Booth) *started down one street, and then up another, and had not gone far when we met Surratt and Weichmann. Introductions took place, and we turned back in the direction of the hotel. ...After arriving in the room, I took the first opportunity presented to apologize to Surratt for having introduced him to Booth—a man I knew so little concerning. This conversation took place in the passage in front of the room (hallway) and was not over three minutes in duration. ...Surratt and myself returned and resumed our former seats (after taking drinks ordered) around a centre table, which stood midway the room and distant seven or eight feet from Booth and Weichmann. Booth remarked that he had been down to the country **a few days before,** and said that he had not yet recovered from the fatigue. Afterward he said he had been down in Charles County, and had made me an offer for the purchase of my land, **which I confirmed by an affirmative answer;** and he further remarked that on his way up (to Washington) he lost his way and rode several miles off the track.*

This is an extremely revealing statement by Mudd made only two months after he began serving his life sentence. While Mudd trivializes his meeting with Booth and his introduction of John Surratt to Booth, he reveals an even more damaging fact which emerges for the first time. Mudd quotes Booth as saying that he had been down in Charles County "...a few days before." This would be a few days before December 23. Booth was actually in Charles County from December 17 until December 22 when he returned to the National Hotel.[13] Mudd also reveals that he met with Booth at this time stating that Booth, "...had made me an offer for the purchase of my land, which I confirmed by an affirmative answer."[14]

Mudd is telling the truth for one of the few times in this whole episode. Booth had made another visit to Charles County just before December 23, and met with Mudd a second time at St. Mary's Church. It was during this second visit that the Confederate agent Thomas Harbin told of his meeting with Booth at the Bryantown Tavern which Harbin claimed was arranged by Mudd. At this important meeting, Harbin agreed to assist Booth in the safe passage of the captured Lincoln to Richmond.

Hardy's testimony places Booth on the Horse Head Road which would have placed Booth off of the main road back to Washington. Mudd writes in his statement, "... he (Booth) further remarked that on his way up he lost his way and rode several miles off the track." This would confirm John F. Hardy's testimony that he saw Booth riding along the Horse Head Road.

Booth finally returned to the National Hotel on Thursday, December 22 after this important meeting at the Bryantown Tavern where, with the helpful introduction by Mudd, he had enlisted the services of Thomas Harbin in his capture scheme. The following day, Friday, December 23, a third meeting between Booth and Mudd occurred, this time to enlist the services of John H. Surratt.

On the 23rd, Mudd and his cousin, Jeremiah T. Mudd, came to Washington from Charles County for the purpose of Christmas shopping, according to Jeremiah Mudd's testimony.[15]

While in Washington, Dr. Mudd and his cousin separated and Mudd went on to meet Booth on Pennsylvania Avenue near Booth's hotel. Booth had wanted Mudd to introduce him to John H. Surratt whose reputation as a Confederate courier had been made known to Booth.[16] Mudd had agreed to introduce Booth to Surratt and came to Washington to meet Booth for this purpose. This arrangement was presumably made while Booth stayed over at Mudd's house on Sunday, December 18.

Meeting in front of the National Hotel, Booth and Mudd started to walk up Seventh Street in the direction of the Surratt house located at 541 H Street a few blocks to the north. As Booth and Mudd walked up Seventh Street toward the boarding house they met John Surratt and Louis Weichmann coming down Seventh Street in the direction of Pennsylvania Avenue. The four men stopped and introductions were made, after which Booth invited the three men to join him in his hotel room a short distance from where they were standing.

The meeting at the National Hotel on December 23, 1864.

The third meeting involving Mudd and Booth took place in Booth's hotel room on December 23, 1864 during which Mudd introduced Booth to John H. Surratt, Jr. As a result of this meeting Surratt joined Booth's conspiracy to capture Lincoln.

Edward Steers, Jr. collection

John Wilkes Booth

Courtesy of James O. Hall

Dr. Samuel A. Mudd

Courtesy of Surratt House and Museum

John H. Surratt

Courtesy of James O. Hall

The National Hotel, Washington, D. C.

According to Louis J. Weichmann's testimony,[17] and Mudd's own affidavit, the four men returned to Booth's room where he ordered drinks and cigars for all. Weichmann's testimony details much of the actions of his three companions during this meeting which are also confirmed five years later by John Surratt in his famous Rockville Lecture.[18]

During the course of the meeting, Mudd and Booth stepped into the hall for private discussions and later were joined by Surratt. At some point, Mudd, Booth and Surratt sat around a table conversing, while Weichmann sat so that he could hear their conversation, but could not discern what was being discussed. Weichmann described how Booth took an envelope from his pocket and drew "lines" on it as if drawing a map. After approximately thirty minutes, the meeting adjourned, and Weichmann continued his visit with Mudd in the lobby of the Pennsylvania House hotel where Mudd was staying along with his cousin.[19]

Whatever actually transpired during the meeting in Booth's hotel room, one fact is sure: just as Thomas Harbin before him, John H. Surratt became a key member of Booth's conspiracy to capture the president as a result of his introduction to Booth by Dr. Mudd.

Mudd appears to be a principal recruiter for Booth, at least in regard to two very important members of his team: Thomas Harbin and John Surratt. Of all the conspirators enlisted into Booth's gang, Harbin and Surratt were the most competent and experienced, and the two who were already active agents of the Confederate underground.

When Dr. Mudd swore in his second statement dated April 22, 1865, that he had, "...never seen Booth since that time (November 1864 meeting) to my knowledge until last Saturday night," he deliberately lied. The three meetings which are described above were not casual or incidental meetings in which Mudd happened across Booth. In at least two of the meetings, Mudd was the arranger and the principal without whose participation the meetings could not be held. In these two meetings, Mudd introduced two key individuals into Booth's conspiracy group: Thomas Harbin and John H. Surratt.

Mudd steadfastly maintained that when Booth and Herold arrived at his house on Saturday, April 14, he acted only in the role of a good doctor who, when faced with a stranger in desperate need of medical assistance, did what his Hippocratic oath required him to do—render medical assistance. And, that upon finally becoming suspicious of his two late-night guests, he took the necessary steps to inform the military authorities of their visit. According to Mudd's story, when questioned by the military, he related all of the facts as he remembered them and withheld nothing from the authorities. For these innocent acts, the good doctor claimed, he was taken into custody and eventually charged as an accomplice in the murder of the president, and in aiding and abetting John Wilkes Booth's attempt to escape.

Mudd could not have been more disingenuous in his statements to the authorities nor in his later claims of innocence. At each turn he was attempting to cover his trail by volunteering information only when he was reasonably sure it would be found out anyway.

It would appear that Mudd did not want the authorities to find out about Booth's second visit to Charles County when Mudd arranged the critical meeting with Thomas Harbin. So he condensed the meetings in November and December into a single visit by Booth, at which time Booth stayed the night at Mudd's house and purchased the one-eyed horse. Mudd knew the authorities had found out about Booth's visit to Charles County in November and he hoped to conceal the second, more damning visit and it worked. The authorities, and for that matter many researchers, never realized that there was a second visit in December 1864.[20]

It is now clear that the scenario Mudd presented was a lie, and that he deliberately withheld the facts from the authorities. He revealed bits of information only when they became obvious to his interrogators, at the same time twisting the truth to cover his activities. Knowing the details of the three meetings involving Mudd and Booth, it is beyond reasonable belief to accept Mudd's claim that he had met Booth only by accident, and that he did not recognize him on the morning of April 15 when he sought medical assistance. Dr. Mudd's deliberate deceptions were the only way he could hope to avoid the gallows with his other accomplices.

6

WHAT DID MUDD KNOW
AND WHEN DID HE KNOW IT?

Lieutenant Lovett testified at the conspiracy trial that Mudd claimed to have first heard of Lincoln's assassination on Sunday, April 16, while at church.[1] Mudd attended St. Peter's Church on that Sunday and while there sought the counsel of his cousin, George Mudd, soliciting his help in reporting to the military authorities in Bryantown the visit of the two men to his house.

Lovett's testimony is at variance, however, with Mudd's own statement in which Mudd wrote, "I first heard of the assassination of President Lincoln on Saturday afternoon (April 15) about two or three o'clock in the afternoon."[2] Several paragraphs later in that same statement Mudd writes, "I first heard of the assassination of President Lincoln at Bryantown."

Mudd wrote that his purpose in going to Bryantown on Saturday, April 15, was to, "...purchase some articles which were needed by the family; and I thought I would at the same time see about some nails that were intended for immediate use. I purchased at Mr. Bean's some calico & some pepper, for which I paid him."[3] While Mudd acknowledges hearing of Lincoln's murder while in Bryantown, he does not tell us if he also heard who the assassin was. Did he not ask? Did the informant who told Mudd overlook telling him who the assassin was or did he simply not know? By Saturday afternoon the authorities had released the name of John Wilkes Booth as the assassin of Lincoln.

While claiming to be forthright and willing to tell all to his interrogators, Mudd is silent about this important point in each of his statements. His neighbors are not. That Mudd learned in Bryantown that the assassin was John Wilkes Booth comes from the testimony of two of his own friends.

Francis R. Farrell, a neighbor of Dr. Mudd's, lived midway between the Mudd house and Bryantown. Mudd acknowledges in his voluntary statement, and again in Colonel Wells' draft, visiting with John F. Hardy and Francis R. Farrell on his return trip from Bryantown Saturday afternoon. Farrell was called as a prosecution witness and under examination by Judge Advocate John A. Bingham, he stated that Mudd told him of Lincoln's assassination. Farrell states, "I asked the question who assassinated the President; and the doctor replied, and said, '**A man by the name of Booth.**'" Mr. Hardy then asked him if it was, "...the Booth that was down here last fall.[4] The doctor said that he did not know whether it was or not; ...if it was that one, he knew him."[5]

According to both Farrell and Hardy, Mudd knew that Booth was the assassin of Lincoln on Saturday afternoon while Booth was still at Mudd's home. Mudd's only defense at this point would be his claim to not have recognized Booth while Booth was at his house.

Mudd also withheld information about his identity as a mail courier along the Confederate mail line between Washington and Richmond. He further failed to reveal that he had gone to Bryantown on Saturday, not to purchase supplies, but to make a mail drop for the Confederate underground only to be confronted by Union soldiers.[6]

Several miles to the south of Bryantown was the home of a man named Thomas A. Jones. Jones, age 41, was a farmer who worked a stretch of land that fronted along the Potomac River. This land was situated along a high bluff which presented a clear view across the river of Confederate Virginia.[7] Jones served as one of the Confederate mail operatives and underground agents along the line from Richmond to Washington, and reported to Samuel Cox, his superior in the underground in Charles County.

Thomas Jones played a crucial role in the attempted escape of Booth and Herold during the first days of their flight. After leaving Mudd's home around 5:00 p.m. on Saturday evening, Booth and Herold made their way several miles south to the home of Colonel Samuel Cox near Bel Alton, Maryland.[8] Cox's home, known as Rich Hill, was situated a short distance from Thomas Jones' home.

The route Booth and Herold took to Cox's home was directly opposite the route that Mudd told the soldiers he had sent the two strangers on. Mudd testified that he sent the two strangers west, toward Parson Wilmer's at Piney Church. The route Booth and Herold actually took made a wide sweep to the east around Bryantown, as if Booth had known that a troop of Federal cavalry was making its headquarters there. The wide sweep to the east of Bryantown brought them into contact with a man named Oswell Swann, a black tobacco farmer whose cabin was located southeast of Mudd's farm. Swann agreed to escort the two fugitives across the Zekiah Swamp to the home of Colonel Cox.[9]

Arriving around 1:00 a.m. on Sunday morning, April 16, Booth and Herold spent the next several hours with Cox and his adopted 18 year old son, Samuel Cox, Jr. Shortly after breakfast on Easter Sunday morning,

Photograph by Edward Steers, Jr.

Thomas Jones' home known as "Huckleberry." Jones hid Booth and Herold in a pine thicket not far from his home, and safely sent the two fugitives over the Potomac River and into Virginia. Many years later Jones wrote a book which described his role in aiding Booth and Herold in their effort to escape.

Thomas A. Jones

Courtesy of James O. Hall

Jones was visited by Samuel Cox, Jr. who relayed the message that Colonel Cox wanted to see him right away. The two men rode over to the senior Cox's home, Rich Hill, where Cox informed Jones that the two fugitives were hiding in a thicket not two miles south. He told Jones to care for the men and to get them safely across the Potomac River to Virginia.

Jones, whose role as a Confederate agent also included ferrying persons back and forth across the river, was well suited for such a task. According to Jones himself, he never questioned the Colonel's directive, but set about his task like a good soldier. In 1893, twenty-eight years after the events associated with his efforts, Jones wrote a book in which he detailed much of what he knew.[10]

Since the military was extremely active throughout the area in the first hours following the assassination, Jones felt that an attempt to cross the river immediately was too risky. He found the two fugitives hiding in a small pine thicket not far from the Cox plantation, and told them to stay low until the right moment arrived when he could put them into the river.[11]

Jones' help was vital to the survival of Booth and Herold. It was Jones who literally sustained the two men for five days by providing both provisions and newspapers from Sunday, April 16, through Thursday, April 20. Without Jones' capable help and careful monitoring of the military activities in the area, Booth and Herold would surely have been captured or killed in the effort.[12]

Rich Hill, the home of Samuel Cox.

Late Thursday evening, April 20, Jones came for the two men. After leading them to the edge of the river, he placed them in a boat and pushed them into the river and toward the Virginia shore. Booth and Herold did not make it to Virginia that night, but wound up back on the Maryland shore at the farm of John J. Hughes along Nanjemoy Creek, some distance to the north of where they were first launched by Jones. After hiding all day Friday and Saturday, April 21 and 22, Booth and Herold made a second attempt to cross the river which proved successful. They landed on the Virginia side early Sunday morning.

Later on the morning of April 23, Booth and Herold were placed in the capable hands of Thomas Harbin, the Confederate agent introduced to Booth by Mudd at the Bryantown Tavern only four months before.[13] The meeting between Booth and Harbin which Mudd had arranged in December now proved a godsend to Booth. Harbin made the necessary arrangements to see the two men safely to their next stop along the escape route.

Jones' efforts were heroic to the successful escape of Booth and Herold across the river into Confederate Virginia. Although arrested and thrown into old Capital Prison in the general roundup through St. Mary's County,

Courtesy James O. Hall

Courtesy James O. Hall

Colonel Samuel Cox

Samuel Cox, Jr.

Booth visited Cox after he left Mudd's house on Saturday evening. Years later, Samuel Cox, Jr. would write of Mudd's revelations concerning Booth and his visit on Saturday, April 15, 1865.

the authorities never knew of Jones' role in harboring and successfully aiding Booth and Herold in their escape.

Years later, Jones wrote the details of the events surrounding his summons by Colonel Cox to Rich Hill, and of hiding Booth and Herold in a pine thicket until successfully placing them on the Potomac. Subsequent to its publication in 1893, a copy of Jones' book was owned by Samuel Cox, Jr., and passed through his descendants where it was eventually examined by the Lincoln assassination researcher, James O. Hall.[14] Of particular interest in this privately held volume is a series of annotations made in various key parts of the book by Samuel Cox, Jr.

In 1877, according to Samuel Cox, Jr., after Dr. Mudd's release from prison, he and Dr. Mudd were candidates for the Maryland state legislature. The two men canvassed Charles County together during this period and, according to Cox, privately discussed the events of 1865 concerning John Wilkes Booth and Davy Herold.

Cox writes in his annotations that Mudd confided to him that shortly after setting Booth's leg Mudd had taken,

> ...letters he had but a short time had gotten through the contraband mail for distribution, and that in going to Bryantown to mail them[15] he was surprised to find the village surrounded by soldiers and upon being stopped by a sentry, ...he was horrified when told the president had been shot the night before, and, upon asking who had shot him **the fellow had answered Booth**.

These revelations are significant in themselves, but Cox relates even more damaging statements about Mudd:

> He (Mudd) then told me his first impulse was to surrender Booth, that he had imposed upon him, had twice forced himself upon him and now a third time, had come with a lie upon his tongue and received medical assistance which would be certain to have him serious trouble but he determined to go back and upbraid him for his treachery which he did. And that Booth had appealed to him in the name of his Mother whom he professed to love so devotedly and that he acted and spoke so tragically that he told them they must leave his house which they did and after getting in with Oswald Swann they were piloted to Rich Hill. Aug 7 1893 S Cox Jr.

Cox supports the claim that Mudd was not only thoroughly acquainted with Booth, but knew that it was Booth at the time he gave him medical assistance.[16] According to Cox's annotations, Mudd acknowledged that Booth had visited with him on two occasions in Charles County when he stated that Booth, "...had twice forced himself upon him...." Cox also reveals Mudd's confession to be a mail agent for the Confederacy going to Bryantown to mail Confederate letters he had recently received for distribution.

There is still further corroboration of Mudd's knowledge that his patient was the assassin Booth. Following Mudd's conviction and sentencing, he, along with Arnold, O'Laughlen and Spangler, was transported under military guard to Fort Jefferson in the Dry Tortugas off the coast of Florida. Commanding the guard that escorted Mudd and his fellow prisoners was a young officer, Captain George W. Dutton, Co. C, 10th Veteran Reserve Corps. Following his escort duty, Dutton, in a sworn affidavit, stated that Dr. Mudd,

> ...confessed that he knew Booth when he (Booth) came to his house with Herold on the morning after the assassination of the President; that he had known Booth for some time, but was afraid to tell of Booth's having been at his house on April 15, fearing that his own and the lives of his family would be endangered thereby.[17]

Dutton's affidavit corroborates the statements made by Samuel Cox, Jr. Neither Cox nor Dutton were associated in any way and there is no known evidence suggesting that they ever met or even communicated with one another at any time. Most importantly, Cox's annotations were not made until 1893, twenty-eight years after Dutton filed his affidavit with the judge advocate. Just as Cox's claims, Dutton's statement rings true. There would be no purpose to fabricating such a statement at the time since Mudd had already been charged, tried and sentenced, and was enroute to the prison where he was about to begin serving his sentence. Nothing was gained by Dutton, the judge advocate or the government by fabricating such a story post facto.

The statements made by Samuel Cox, Jr. and George Dutton make Mudd's claim that Booth wore a disguise, and that Mudd failed to recognize Booth, nonsense. To believe Cox and Dutton is further evidence that Mudd lied about what he knew and when he knew it. Upon learning of Dutton's affidavit, Mudd filed his own in response to it.[18]

In addition to the statements already discussed, there exists one other revealing document which is damaging to Dr. Mudd's case. When George Atzerodt walked into the bar of the Kirkwood Hotel around 10:00 p.m. on the night of the assassination, he was only moments away from carrying out the task Booth had assigned to him of assassinating Vice President Andrew Johnson.

Fortunately, Atzerodt's courage evaporated and he fled the hotel, mounted his horse and rode away in the direction of Ford's Theatre. Seeing the great commotion along Tenth Street in front of the theater, the frightened Atzerodt returned his horse to a stable on Eighth Street, and began wandering about the city, half drunk and half in terror. He boarded a horse-drawn trolley at Seventh Street and Pennsylvania Avenue, and made a round trip to the Navy Yard before returning to his old haunt, the Kimmel House (also referred to as the Pennsylvania House), where he flopped for the night.[19]

Early Saturday morning Atzerodt arose and walked to Georgetown where he boarded a stage for Rockville, Maryland, located to the northwest of the city. Atzerodt eventually made his way to Germantown, Maryland, some twenty-five miles northwest of Washington. He went to the house of his cousin, Hartman Richter, and safely settled down with his relatives, or so he thought.[20]

On Thursday, April 20, Atzerodt was taken into custody by a troop of Union soldiers and transported to Washington where he was eventually imprisoned at the Washington Arsenal along with other conspirators who had been arrested earlier. On May 1, 1865, between the hours of 8:00 p.m. and 10:00 p.m, Atzerodt was visited by his brother-in-law, John L. Smith, and the provost marshall of Baltimore, James L. McPhail.[21]

Smith, an assistant to McPhail, had gotten word of Atzerodt's arrest. He convinced McPhail to accompany him to Washington to seek permission to visit his brother-in-law and find out what sort of trouble he had gotten himself into.

McPhail and Smith were granted permission to visit the prisoner and interview him. During a two hour interview McPhail transcribed a lengthy statement from Atzerodt which failed to reach the authorities. Instead, McPhail apparently turned the statement over to Captain William E. Doster, former provost marshall of the District of Columbia, who had been appointed by the War Department as defense counsel for Atzerodt. Doster put the statement safely away among his personal papers where it remained until its rediscovery in 1978.[22]

In Atzerodt's statement describing his own role as a member of Booth's plot to capture Lincoln, Atzerodt confirms Thomas Harbin's role: "Thos. Holborn (Harbin) was to meet us on the road and help in the kidnapping." While Atzerodt reveals certain details of the conspiracy, he also mentions several individuals who were involved to varying degrees. In a surprising revelation, Atzerodt tells McPhail, "I am certain **Dr. Mudd knew all about it, as Booth sent liquors & provisions for the trip with the president to Richmond, about two weeks before the murder to Dr. Mudd's.**"

According to Atzerodt's statement, Booth entrusted Mudd with storing these supplies. Booth and his cohorts could then provision themselves after capturing Lincoln. That provisions were sent to Mudd's two weeks before the actual assassination suggests that Booth's decision to murder Lincoln occurred sometime between then and April 12.

Dr. Mudd's name surfaces yet again in connection with Booth's escape to Virginia. After Booth and Herold safely reached the Virginia shore Sunday morning, April 23, Herold made his way to the home of Mrs. Elizabeth Quesenberry, a Confederate agent who was well connected to Thomas Harbin. Harbin maintained a signal camp not far from the Quesenberry home. Leaving the injured Booth with their small boat,[23] Herold made his way to the Quesenberry home where he negotiated with the Confederate lady. Hearing Herold out, Mrs. Quesenberry knew who to send for. Within the hour, Thomas Harbin arrived and took charge of the two fugitives. Harbin passed Booth and Herold over to one of his operatives, a man named William Bryant, with instructions for Bryant[24] to get the men to the home of a wealthy planter by the name of Dr. Richard Stuart.[25]

Stuart had been engaged in drug smuggling for the Confederacy, and had even spent time in jail under suspicion of being a Confederate operative, but never for very long. While his precise role with the Confederate underground is clouded, he was a well-trusted Confederate operative in his own right in King George County, Virginia.

Mudd's introduction of Harbin to Booth in December at the Bryantown Tavern would now serve Lincoln's assassin well, emphasizing again the crucial role that Mudd played in Booth's operation to capture Lincoln. Without Harbin, Booth and Herold would have been stranded on the Virginia side of the river. Bryant, following Harbin's instructions, provided horses for the two men, and took them to the home of Dr. Stuart. It was around dinner time on Sunday evening when Bryant arrived with his two weary fugitives.

Booth and Herold were not well received by Stuart, who by now knew of Lincoln's murder and knew who Booth and Herold were. It was a "no win" situation for Stuart who, now that the war was over in Virginia, did not need to become involved in any way with Lincoln's assassination.

Although Stuart refused lodging and medical help to Booth, he did provide the two fugitives with food and allowed them to refresh themselves. After feeding the two, Stuart insisted that Bryant get them off of his property. He told Bryant to take them to the cabin of a free black named William Lucas, which adjoined Stuart's property.[26]

Two weeks after Booth's capture at the Garrett farm, Stuart was taken into custody[27] at which time he gave his interrogators a statement concerning the fugitives' visit on Sunday night.[28] In his statement Stuart said that one of the men had said to him that he had been recommended to the men by Dr. Mudd: "... they said Dr. Mudd had recommended them to me."[29] Stuart denied knowing Dr. Mudd personally, but acknowledged he knew of "...Mudds in Maryland." If Stuart is to be believed, Dr. Mudd knew where Booth and Herold were heading when they rode away from his property on Saturday evening, and that Stuart, a Confederate sympathizer and a fellow physician, was a required stop once the two reached Virginia. Importantly, Dr. Stuart's home was not on the way to Washington where Mudd had claimed the two men were headed when they left his house.

Richard Stuart's statement is further corroborated by the statement of William Bryant. Bryant had guided the fugitives from Quesenberry's house to Stuart's. In a deposition given by Bryant following his arrest on May 6,

Photograph by Edward Steers, Jr.

Cleydale, the summer home of Dr. Richard Stuart located in King George County, Virginia. Booth and Herold arrived at Cleydale Sunday evening, April 23, 1865. According to a later statement by Dr. Stuart, Herold had told Stuart that they were referred to him by Dr. Mudd.

Photograph by Edward Steers, Jr.

Cedar Grove, the home of Dr. Richard Stuart located on the Potomac River.

Bryant quoted David Herold as telling him, "I was recommended to Dr. Stuart to have something done to my brother's leg." Bryant elaborated further, "In going along I asked him what made him want to go to Dr. Stuart's; I mentioned other doctors who were more convenient. He said the reason was because he was recommended to Dr. Stuart."[30]

Of the handful of people who could have made such a recommendation, only Dr. Mudd is mentioned by name, and then by Richard Stuart himself. The government had both depositions in hand when it brought its charges against Mudd, and had no doubt that the doctor lied when he said he sent the two strangers off in the direction of Parson Wilmer's near Piney Church.

7

The case against Dr. Mudd

The case against Dr. Mudd[1] may be found in the government's specification which reads in part:

> ...*the said Samuel A. Mudd did, ...advise, encourage, receive, entertain, harbor and conceal, aid and assist, the said John Wilkes Booth, ...with knowledge of the murderous and traitorous conspiracy aforesaid, and with intent to aid, abet, and assist ...in the execution thereof, and in escaping justice after the murder of the said Abraham Lincoln...*[2]

The accusations against Mudd can be summarized as: 1) participating in the plot to assassinate Lincoln, and 2) knowingly aiding and abetting the escape of Lincoln's murderer. Certainly Dr. Mudd did not know of, or participate in, any plot to murder the president. The government, however, did not distinguish between the original conspiracy to capture Lincoln, and the ultimate conspiracy which resulted in his murder, and neither did the law. The murder of the president was an extension of the conspiracy to capture. Jefferson Davis had clearly understood that. In 1862, he had been correct when he concluded that any attempt to capture the president of the United States would surely result in killing, thus converting the plan of capture to one resulting in murder. The case against Mudd as a knowing accomplice in aiding Booth and Herold in their escape effort is substantial and compelling.

The appropriate venue for trying the accused, whether before a military tribunal or before a civil court, is a separate question from Dr. Mudd's guilt as an accomplice. It has no bearing on our consideration of the historical evidence in determining the guilt or innocence of Dr. Mudd. Too often, students of Dr. Mudd's case equate their belief that the military tribunal was the wrong court with Mudd's alleged innocence. The conclusion is frequently drawn that if it can be established that the tribunal was without legal jurisdiction, Mudd must be innocent. Mudd's guilt or innocence, and the jurisdiction of the tribunal are two separate questions and should not be confused.

On the one hand, the military tribunal may have lacked legal jurisdiction, but the accused could have been guilty. On the other hand, the military tribunal may have had legal jurisdiction, and the accused could have been innocent. The primary concern then, must be with the guilt or innocence of Dr. Mudd based on the evidence at hand, and not the jurisdiction of the military tribunal or whether he should have been tried in a civilian court.

In considering the case against Dr. Mudd, key questions center around whether Dr. Mudd had knowledge of a conspiracy to act against the president, knowledge which he withheld from the appropriate authorities, and which ultimately resulted in Lincoln's murder.

Was Dr. Mudd, in fact, a participant in the conspiracy to act against the president, from which he could withdraw prior to its commission only by reporting it to the authorities; and, did he knowingly aid and abet the assassins of the president after the act? These questions are linked, and fall heavily on the side of Mudd's guilt.

In judging Mudd's role in the conspiracy to capture the president, a conspiracy which led to his murder, consider the following facts of evidence:

Mudd's knowledge of, and acquaintance with, John Wilkes Booth.
1. The meeting in November 1864, in which Booth is first introduced to Mudd at St. Mary's Church in Bryantown.
2. The meeting at the Bryantown Tavern in mid-December 1864, (December 17-21) where Dr. Mudd introduced Booth to Thomas Harbin, and when Booth spent the night at Mudd's house and later purchased the one-eyed horse from his neighbor, George Gardiner.
3. The December 23, 1864 trip to Washington where Mudd meets Booth at the National Hotel and introduces him to Confederate agent John H. Surratt, Jr.

Whether Mudd knew that Booth murdered Lincoln, and when he knew it.
1. Samuel Mudd's statement that he had heard of the assassination while in Bryantown on Saturday afternoon (April 15).
2. Francis R. Farrell's testimony in which he states that Mudd told both himself, and John F. Hardy on Saturday afternoon that a man named Booth had murdered Lincoln.
3. Samuel Cox, Jr.'s statement that Mudd told him, in 1877, that while in Bryantown on Saturday afternoon, April 15, Mudd had heard of the assassination of President Lincoln, and that John Wilkes Booth was the assassin.

4. Samuel Cox, Jr.'s statement that Mudd told him that when he learned Booth was the assassin he returned home and ordered Booth out of his house.
5. Captain George W. Dutton's affidavit that Mudd told him on July 22, 1865, that he knew it was Booth whose leg he had set at his home on Saturday, April 15.

Evidence linking Mudd to Booth's conspiracy to capture President Lincoln.
1. Mudd's introduction of Thomas Harbin to Booth.
2. Mudd's introduction of John H. Surratt, Jr. to Booth.
3. Samuel Cox, Jr.'s statement which quotes Mudd as saying that he went into Bryantown on Saturday, April 15, to mail contraband letters which he had received earlier.
4. George Atzerodt's "lost confession" in which Atzerodt states that Booth had sent provisions to Dr. Mudd's house to be used for their flight to Virginia.
5. Dr. Richard Stuart's deposition which states that Herold had told him that Dr. Mudd had referred Booth and Herold to Dr. Stuart, implying that Booth would receive medical assistance.
6. William Bryant's statement that the two fugitives were referred to Dr. Stuart for medical assistance.

In the language of the law—would a reasonable person believe that Mudd was well acquainted with John Wilkes Booth? Would a reasonable person believe that Mudd had knowledge of Booth's conspiracy to capture Abraham Lincoln, and knowingly aided that conspiracy? Would a reasonable person believe that Mudd recognized John Wilkes Booth as the patient he gave medical treatment to early on the morning of April 15, 1865?

The three meetings involving Booth and Mudd which resulted in introducing John Surratt and Thomas Harbin into Booth's conspiracy, together with the statement by George Atzerodt that Booth had sent provisions to Mudd's to be used during the escape, clearly identifies Mudd as a willing conspirator in Booth's original plot.

Mudd's knowledge of the assassination, and that the assassin was John Wilkes Booth is evident from Mudd's own statements and the statements of Francis Farrell and John Hardy.

Mudd's knowledge that the injured man resting at his house on Saturday, April 15, was John Wilkes Booth is attested to by George Dutton and Samuel Cox, Jr., and from the evidence that Mudd and Booth had met on at least three prior occasions, and conducted business which furthered Booth's plot.

The evidence clearly shows that Mudd had knowledge of and participated in Booth's conspiracy to capture Lincoln. And following Lincoln's murder, he knowingly aided and abetted Booth in his escape.

There can be little doubt that Mudd recognized Booth when Booth came to his home early Saturday morning following the murder of Lincoln. Whether Booth had told Mudd that he had just murdered Lincoln is arguable. But what is not arguable is the fact that Mudd soon learned that Lincoln had been murdered, and that Booth was the murderer.

Knowing that his patient was the man accused of murdering the president, Mudd waited until Sunday morning church services to inform his cousin of the two visitors, and then asked his cousin to notify the authorities rather than inform them himself. George Mudd did not inform the authorities in Bryantown until Monday, April 17, more than forty hours after the two fugitives left Mudd's house. This delay proved crucial to Booth and Herold, allowing them ample time to reach Samuel Cox's plantation where they received much-needed help.

It was Dr. Mudd's contention then, and it is the contention of his defenders now, that Mudd did not know that the injured man he treated was John Wilkes Booth. This is based primarily on the claim made by Mudd that Booth wore a false beard while at Mudd's house, and effectively hid his features behind a shawl which he kept closely wrapped about his head and face.

A careful reading of the two statements given by Mudd shows that he gave an accurate description of Booth. Mudd's claim that Booth wore false whiskers to hide his identity is beyond belief when the evidence is carefully reviewed. Booth made no effort to hide his identity prior to arriving at Mudd's house, or after leaving the Mudd house. There is no evidence to show that Booth tried to hide his identity from any of the other people he came into contact with during his escape. Why would he choose to single out Mudd and attempt to disguise himself only in Mudd's presence?

Booth was well acquainted with Mudd as evidenced from their prior meetings. What purpose would be served by Booth hiding his identity from Mudd by wearing a disguise? The story of a false beard can only be found in Mudd's one statement of April 21, and nowhere else in the numerous encounters Booth had during his subsequent escape.

If Mudd truly did not know that his visitor was John Wilkes Booth, then when he subsequently found out in Bryantown that Lincoln had been murdered by Booth, it would have little consequence for the doctor other than being "horrifying news." But if Dr. Mudd knew that the injured man resting in his home was John Wilkes Booth, his obligation under the law was clear and unequivocal. Dr. Mudd was required to inform the authorities that the alleged murderer of the president was at his home. Mudd's only concern would be for the personal safety of his wife and children who were at that moment with Booth and Herold at the doctor's farm. The government believed that Mudd knew his injured patient to be Booth, and rightly concluded that Mudd knowingly aided and abetted his escape.

But the evidence suggests more than aiding and abetting. It strongly suggests that Dr. Mudd was a knowing and active participant in Booth's conspiracy to capture Lincoln, a conspiracy that resulted in murder. The evidence shows that Dr. Mudd met with Booth on at least three occasions. On two of these occasions he introduced Booth to two key individuals who became active participants in his conspiracy. These individuals were well known Confederate operatives, and they played key roles in Booth's plans. Further evidence suggests that Booth sent provisions to Mudd's house to be used by the escape party.

At the time of Mudd's first meeting with Booth at St. Mary's Church in November 1864, Booth was a well known leading actor with a national reputation. His family was considered the first family of the American stage. Booth's father, who died in 1852, had been the leading Shakespearean actor in England and later in America. Booth's older brother Edwin succeeded his father in that role. John Wilkes Booth's acting career was only a step behind his more famous brother. But whereas Edwin supported the Union, John's politics swung in the opposite direction. His views were well known and thought by most who described them as being in the extreme. A reasonable person would have no problem believing that Dr. Mudd knew of Booth well before they ever met, and had quickly become familiar with him after they met.

The fact that both Dr. Mudd and John Wilkes Booth shared a common passion for the Confederacy and desired its success was not incidental. Mudd, a former slaveholder, was more than just pro-Confederate; he felt that to lose the Confederacy would be to lose his special way of life.

Mudd was strongly opposed to black suffrage, and believed that blacks were beneath his dignity. In several letters which Mudd wrote while in prison to family members back home, he revealed his negative attitudes concerning blacks.

Within a few months of Mudd's imprisonment, on September 25, 1865, he attempted to escape from Fort Jefferson aboard the supply ship, *Thomas A. Scott*. The attempt failed when Mudd was discovered hiding beneath a plank in the ship's hold and he was returned to the prison. Mudd's defenders explain the escape attempt by saying that Mudd only wanted to reach Key West where he could obtain a writ of habeas corpus and hopefully secure his freedom.[3] Mudd himself refuted this claim by his apologists, and gave a different explanation for his attempted escape. On October 18, 1865 in a letter to his wife he wrote:

> *...it is bad enough to be a prisoner in the hands of white men, your equals under the Constitution, but to be lorded over by a set of ignorant, prejudiced and irresponsible beings of the unbleached humanity, was more than I could submit to....*[4]

Three days later, in a letter dated October 21, 1865, to his brother-in-law, Mudd reveals the real reason for attempting to escape:

> *No man can say naught against the Conduct of either of us up to the present, other than my individual effort to get away, and I plead my apprehensions...the humiliation of being guarded by an ignorant, irresponsible & prejudiced negro Soldiery, before an Enlightened People as a justification. We are now guarded entirely by negro soldiers & a few white Officers a skins difference. ...Could we have had the White Regiment, the 161st N.Y.V. to guard the place no thought of leaving should have been harbored for a moment.*[5]

Being placed under a negro guard was more than Mudd could bear, and forced his escape attempt. Mudd also writes to his wife, telling her his feelings about returning to a community in which blacks have become the majority:

> *I am sorry to hear of the death of George Garrico and Mr. Bean. Our white population is wonderfully diminishing by death and other causes. The negroes will soon be in the majority, if not already. Should I be released anytime shortly, and circumstances permit, I will use all my endeavors to find a more congenial locality.*[6]

Dr. Mudd's own writings show that he was anti-black, a view ardently shared by John Wilkes Booth. It is also clear that Mudd was sympathetic to Booth, and shared his political views completely.

It is not unreasonable to think that Mudd desired the Confederacy's success in separating from the Union. He was not alone in this view. That Dr. Mudd would have participated in some way to help bring about a successful separation between the Northern and Southern states is both reasonable and understandable.

Despite his statement in which he claimed to be a "Union man," Mudd's sympathies were clearly anti-Union.[7] Mudd lied to his interrogators when he claimed support for the Union. If Mudd was a Union man, as he claimed in his statement to Wells, it was only under a perverse Union that still believed in slavery and the inferiority "...of ignorant, prejudiced and irresponsible beings of the unbleached humanity...." With Mudd, as with so many others, it was Union our way or no way at all.

As with his position regarding blacks, Mudd has left a written record explaining his views on Northern society and Abraham Lincoln. In 1862, Mudd wrote a letter to Orestes A. Brownson, a Catholic scholar and publisher of a leading Catholic journal of the period entitled *Brownson's Quarterly Review*. In his letter, Mudd explains what he means by Union:[8]

> The South even those termed Seceders and Leaders of Secession—
> desire Union! Yes Union!
>
> The people of the South are differently constituted from those of the
> North—attributable to education and climate. ... they are more sensi-
> tive—their sense of honor is much more keen and they would sooner run
> the risk of death, than live with an injured reputation.

And further:

> The people of the North are Puritanical, long faced or Methodistic and
> hypocritical—they deal in Sympathetic language to hide their deception—
> their actions are Pharisaical, covert, stealthy, and cowardly. They are law
> abiding so long as it bears them out in their selfish interest, and praisers
> and scatterers and followers of the Bible so long as it does not conflict with
> their passions. They make good cow drivers, pickpockets and gamblers.
>
> ...Your people have so degenerated, that were it not for the foreign
> element—which you possess—there would be only war on parchment, as
> it is, there is just enough of true Yankee to make the rest good for nothing,
> but an expense to the Nation.

And finally, Mudd reveals his feelings about Lincoln and his Republican cohorts:

> ...I regret sincerely to see such a lack of Patriotism in the Present
> Administration and in the representatives of the North. They are dreamy
> and mystified—they rush headlong regardless of law and its consequences
> and skulk like sheep-stealing dogs, when another nation stands up in open
> contravention. **I confidently assert that if there was any other man
> at the head of the Government of true conservative and constitu-
> tional principals, the Revolution would immediately cease so far
> as the South is concerned.**

Was Mudd suggesting the removal of Lincoln? Mudd's vitriolic attack
on Brownson, and on Northerners in general, as well as his statements
regarding his black guards belies the humanitarian mantle he professed to
wear. Consider Mudd's pointed condemnation of Northerners as, "...law
abiding so long as it bears them out in their selfish interest...." One wonders how Mudd would have characterized his own behavior when dealing
with his lawful interrogators three years later. Mudd's letter to Brownson
would have surely helped to place a noose around Mudd's neck had it been
known at the time of his trial and subsequent sentencing.

Dr. Mudd's contribution to the capture conspiracy was not restricted to
arranging the introduction of Thomas Harbin and John Surratt to the plan.
Atzerodt's statement of May 1 that provisions were sent to Dr. Mudd's
farm by Booth to aid in the escape along the Confederate line is further
damage to Mudd's defense. Since Booth's original escape route did not

pass by Mudd's farm, it can be surmised that the provisions which Booth had sent were to be shipped to some other point along this original escape route.

The most damaging evidence against Dr. Mudd's case is that which supports the charge that he knew John Wilkes Booth at the time of his visit seeking medical care; that he subsequently learned that Booth had murdered Lincoln, and that he failed to turn Booth over to the authorities. Knowing that troops were in Bryantown, Mudd further aided Booth by sending him off in the direction of Samuel Cox and even recommending Dr. Richard Stuart to him.

Why would Mudd do such a thing? Evidence does support the view that when Booth arrived at Mudd's house in the early morning hours of April 15, Mudd knew nothing of Lincoln's assassination. The evidence also supports the view that Mudd would have no role in any plan to murder the President, albeit more from faintheartedness than a humanitarian concern. Why then would Mudd have jeopardized himself? The explanation is obvious. Mudd had become an active participant when he aided Booth's plan to capture Lincoln. Perhaps his participation was only around the edges at first, but eventually Mudd was sitting close to the center. Aiding and abetting Booth in the capture plan was one thing; murder was another. But once Mudd became embroiled in Booth's plan, there was no way out. Booth could and would implicate Mudd to the authorities with disastrous results. Mudd knew this.

When Mudd arrived in Bryantown the afternoon of April 15 and found out what Booth had done, he probably experienced panic, and then outrage. As he stood facing the military authorities in Bryantown, Mudd could have easily given Booth up, and ended it cleanly—except for one thing. Mudd knew that he was already deeply involved with Booth and his plans and that there was a trail which tied him close enough to Booth to hang him. Mudd had to do his best to cover that trail or point it in a different direction—away from himself.

Mudd was between a rock and a hard place. To give up Booth, Booth would have surely given up Mudd.[9] Mudd was in no position to tell the soldiers where Booth was unless he was sure that Booth would die in the attempt to capture him, and that was too uncertain. Mudd also had to consider his wife and children. They were with Booth at the very moment Mudd was in Bryantown. Mudd had to think it was possible that Booth would use them to his advantage in his effort to flee. Booth would not have given himself up without a fight, as evidenced by his final hours.

Mudd's only chance was for Booth to get out of his house, off of his farm, and as far away as possible, perhaps Mexico, Cuba or Europe. Mudd did the only thing he could do. He returned home, and as Samuel Cox, Jr. later wrote, upbraided Booth for his treachery and told him to get out fast.[10]

In doing this, Mudd surely told Booth that Bryantown was a hornet's nest, filled with angry soldiers who were looking everywhere for him, and that he had better skirt around Bryantown to the east and make his way to William Burtles' place or to Samuel Cox's home before attempting to cross the Potomac.[11]

Mudd's story that Booth and Herold wanted to go to Parson Wilmer's (also a good Union man) was a ruse. To have done so would have endangered them substantially more than swinging east where they eventually met Oswell (Oswald) Swann who successfully piloted them to Samuel Cox's house.

Unfortunately, the only way in which Mudd could have disassociated himself from Booth's criminal conspiracy would be by informing the authorities in time to successfully avert the crime. This Mudd could not do. His only chance was the hope that Booth would successfully escape the country, or be killed in the attempt.

Jefferson Davis knew the possible consequences of such a scheme as Booth's. In 1862 when Walker Taylor proposed his plot to Jefferson Davis to capture Lincoln and bring him to Richmond, Davis immediately understood the implications and likely consequences. Lincoln was a courageous man in Davis' own words, and would surely resist capture, making it likely that he might be killed. When one sets out to capture the president of the United States, it is almost certain that someone will die. Mudd's failure to realize this when he willingly embraced Booth's conspiracy to capture showed a serious misjudgment on his part and helped to cast his fate.

What of Lieutenant Lovett's contention that Mudd was evasive in his answers and concealed additional information which he knew was needed? Originally Mudd claimed he did not know Booth, had never met him, and that Booth disguised his appearance by wearing a false beard and hid his face behind a shawl. Mudd further stated that Davy Herold had told him that the two men were headed toward Washington when Booth's horse slipped and fell causing Booth to break his leg. Mudd told Lovett that when the two men left, he directed them to a short cut through the Zekiah Swamp in the direction of Parson Wilmer's (west). This was the opposite direction to the route Booth and Herold actually took. Mudd told Colonel Wells during his interrogation in Bryantown on Friday, April 21, "I have always called myself a Union man." All of the above are at variance with the facts. In each instance, Mudd lied.

That Mudd knew Booth and knew him well is clear from the evidence already discussed. That Booth was disguised so that Mudd did not recognize him is beyond belief. Booth readily identified himself at several stops along his twelve day escape route. He identified himself to Sergeant Cobb at the Navy Yard Bridge. He also identified himself to Samuel Cox, to Thomas A. Jones, Dr. Richard Stuart, and to the three Confederate soldiers that accompanied him across the Rappahannock River on Monday morning, April 24.[12] The only people Booth apparently withheld his identity from were the Garretts when he arrived at their farm on Monday afternoon. If Booth knew Mudd and knew that Mudd knew him, why would Booth seek to disguise himself from the doctor, and more importantly, in seeking medical care, how could he think that he could successfully fool an intelligent clinician like Mudd, who knew him from their three previous meetings?

And lastly, what is Mudd's real connection with St. Mary's Church near Bryantown? Mudd was a member and communicant at St. Peter's Roman Catholic Church a short distance to the east of his farm. He and his wife Sarah were married at St. Peter's and each of his children had been baptized at St. Peter's. St. Peter's is the church of record for Dr. Mudd, and is where he and his family attended services regularly. Yet the two times that Booth visited Dr. Mudd in Charles County, he met him at St. Mary's Church near Bryantown.

Booth's presence at St. Mary's Church in November, and again in December, is testified to by John F. Hardy who places him there on both occasions.[13] St. Mary's was the church of Dr. William Queen, the senior Confederate sympathizer in Charles County, and the man who brought Booth to that church on the two occasions that Dr. Mudd was known to have been there. That Mudd attended St. Mary's Church when Booth was there, furthering his plans, suggests that it was a rendezvous for important members of the Confederate underground. Mudd's presence on the occasion of Booth's two known visits to the church adds further credence to his involvement with Booth, and his plan to capture Lincoln.

When Mudd had successfully cleared his home of Booth and Herold at five o'clock on Saturday evening following his return from Bryantown, he could only hope that they would successfully escape. The best thing that could happen would be for Booth to die before implicating Mudd in his conspiracy. Mudd was caught in a terrible dilemma and all he could do was wait and hope that he would never hear another loud knock on his door in the middle of the night.

WE CANNOT ESCAPE HISTORY.[1]

In a recent biography of Samuel Mudd the author concluded his study with the following observation:

> *This gentle man lived his life well, marred only by some enthusiasms of early adulthood and finally by a sudden unexpected entanglement with an egotistical zealot who had committed a horrendous crime.*[2]

This gentle treatment of Dr. Mudd in which his role in Booth's conspiracy is reduced to an "unexpected entanglement" is consistent with the perception of Mudd for the past one hundred and thirty-plus years. Knowing what the members of the military tribunal knew at the time of the sentencing, life imprisonment for Dr. Mudd was appropriate. Knowing what historians know today, the tribunal would certainly have voted the death sentence for Mudd.[3]

While Mudd's crucial help to Booth did not prevent Booth's ultimate apprehension and death, it did prolong it. More importantly, Mudd's role in the conspiracy to capture not only lent credibility to Booth among key individuals in southern Maryland, but brought two very important members into the plot which eventually involved others. The participation of John Surratt placed a rope around his mother's neck. Even this tragedy has a fine thread which is connected to Mudd.[4]

When all of the evidence is carefully reviewed it is impossible to conclude that this "gentle man's" fate resulted solely from his administration of the Hippocratic oath as his defenders would have us believe. Booth's murder of Lincoln was the crime of the century, and when viewed from the perspective of historical hindsight, it may well have been the crime of the twentieth century as well. Certainly the political events which followed in the wake of Lincoln's death did not bode well for the nation as a whole. It is anyone's guess what course the nation would have followed had Lincoln

The conspirators, from an engraving by A. H. Ritchie in 1865. Conspicuously absent from the ring of conspirators charged by the United States government is the image of Dr. Samuel Alexander Mudd. This omission is found on nearly every composite drawing or photograph illustrating the accused conspirators. While doubts exist among many as to Mary Surratt's guilt, Dr. Mudd has been consistently portrayed as a victim of a hysterical government that rushed to judgment.

survived his theater visit and served out the remaining four years of his presidency.

None of the evidence suggests that Dr. Mudd was knowingly involved in Booth's deliberate act of murder. Mudd probably viewed Lincoln's murder as most intelligent Southerners did, a tragedy for the South. Imagine how Mudd must have felt now that the nation was in the hands of "...cow drivers, pickpockets and gamblers." A people "...so degenerated" that only the "...foreign element" in them allowed them to succeed.

Had the prosecution been aware of Mudd's letter to O. A. Brownson it surely would have used it to discredit him even further, and support the prosecution's contention that Mudd was vehemently anti-Union and sought Lincoln's removal as president. Of course, Mudd's views as expressed in his letter are nothing more than the expressions of a Confederate sympathizer who desired to turn back the clock to the peaceful antebellum days of slavery, but unable to do so because of the policies of Abraham Lincoln.

Mudd was a Southerner who lived by the social and moral standards of the South. He fully supported the Confederate cause, and was surrounded by Confederate sympathizers who actively supported that cause.

As a member of the Confederate mail line which followed one of the routes through southern Maryland (the one ultimately used by Booth in his escape), Mudd came into intimate contact with the key members of the Confederate Signal Service in southern Maryland. These members included Dr. William Queen, John Thompson, Samuel Cox, Thomas Harbin, Thomas Jones and John H. Surratt, Jr.

Perhaps it was only benign circumstances that brought Mudd into contact with Wilkes Booth, but it mattered little what brought the two together initially. The acquaintance, once made, was enough to eventually lead to Mudd's undoing. Mudd and Booth were believers in a cause that demanded the removal of Lincoln—one way or another.

That John Wilkes Booth was introduced to Dr. Mudd at St. Mary's Church in November by Dr. William Queen's son-in-law, John Thompson, was not the result of good manners following church services. Booth's visit later in December to the Mudd house, and his overnight stay were crucial to Booth's ultimate plans. The question is, why did Dr. Queen pass Booth along to Dr. Mudd of all people in southern Maryland? The answer must lie in Mudd's role, and his reliability as a key contact in Queen's eyes.

Mudd's subsequent role in arranging a meeting in which he introduced Booth to Thomas Harbin and still later, when he introduced John Surratt to Booth, played a crucial part in Booth's scheme to capture—then murder—President Lincoln. Mudd may well have been reluctant, even adamant, about involving himself with a man like Booth in his dangerous scheme to capture the president. But involve himself he did and while his involvement may be viewed as trivial by some, it proved crucial to Booth.

Mudd knew that it was John Wilkes Booth who came to his door on that fateful Saturday morning of April 15, 1865, and when confronted with the shocking news in Bryantown on Saturday afternoon that Lincoln had been killed by Booth at Ford's Theatre, he was caught in a terrible trap. Once aware of the situation, he did the only thing he could do to save his own neck. He returned home and told Booth to leave, and to avoid Federal troops by skirting around Bryantown. Having sent Booth off with a fore-warning, Mudd could only wait and hope for the best. In his own mind he knew he would never have involved himself in Booth's murder scheme. To the very end Mudd maintained his innocence, claiming to be a victim of a hysterical and vengeful government. While the government may have been hysterical and vengeful, it is hard to picture Mudd as a victim.

Since Dr. Mudd's death in 1883, a rising force has made its way into the cultural history of the country in an effort to reverse the role attributed to Mudd in the assassination of Abraham Lincoln. The first major effort of any wide standing was the biography of Samuel Mudd written by his youngest child, Nettie Mudd Monroe.[5] Only five years old at the time of her father's death, Nettie gleaned much of her information from her mother who lived until 1911. Nettie published her book in 1906 when she was twenty-eight years old and her mother was seventy-one. At the time of its publication the book was well received, but had limited distribution. Today, the original edition is found mostly in private libraries as a scarce collectible.

In 1936, a movie was made about Dr. Mudd by Twentieth Century Fox studio under the direction of John Ford entitled *The Prisoner of Shark Island*. The film, starring the talented Warner Baxter, was well received, and al-most overnight Samuel Mudd became a folk hero. The film was classic Hollywood, and stressed the theme of a mild-mannered country doctor who sought only to extend his healing powers to a sick and injured stranger. As a result of his good Samaritan efforts, Dr. Mudd was swept up in the military's dragnet and ruthlessly rushed to judgment by a vengeful and retribution-seeking government.

Pronounced guilty by a kangaroo court, Dr. Mudd was clandestinely shipped to Fort Jefferson on the Dry Tortugas, called Shark Island in the movie. Here Mudd spent the next three and a half years alternating be-tween physical abuse and mental torture. Not the least of Mudd's troubles, according to the Hollywood version, were large man-eating sharks that constantly circled within the prison moat ensuring a horrible death to all those who tried to escape.

While *The Prisoner of Shark Island* was more Hollywood fiction than fact, it was a well-made movie drama that focused people's attention on the Lincoln assassination and the Mudd story.

In 1995, Light Vision Films produced a documentary video tape en-titled, *Rewriting History: The Case of Dr. Samuel A. Mudd*. This eighty-minute documentary claims to examine, "...the hysteria and shock of 1865," and asks, "Was Dr. Mudd wrongfully tried and imprisoned?" In support of the video's thesis, several notables render their opinions on the innocence of Dr. Mudd, and the illegal jurisdiction of the military commission that tried him. Unfortunately, the documentary does not discuss the great body of evidence against Dr. Mudd nor does it offer any explanation of most of the events and statements raised in the current work and well-known to several of the experts who provided commentary in the video. Like *The Prisoner of Shark Island*, the documentary is a successful presentation of the views expressed by members of the Mudd family and other defenders of Dr. Mudd.[6]

One of the more egregious falsehoods that continues to permeate the accounts of Mudd's treatment by the government is that Mudd, along with the other male conspirators, was forced to wear a canvas hood by order of Secretary of War Edwin M. Stanton. Mudd was said to have endured this "...especially vicious torture" while in his prison cell.[7] His eyes and ears were covered with cotton, and the hood, which extended to mid-waist, was tied tightly about his neck and waist. He could not see or hear. He was held completely incommunicado as a result of this diabolical treatment.

According to one author, "...No explanation was given for this treatment...."[8] Perhaps no explanation was given because Mudd was never treated in such a manner. It is one more distortion in the story of Mudd.

The prisoners, including Dr. Mudd, were held at the Washington Penitentiary on the arsenal grounds in the District of Columbia in specially prepared cells under the command of Major General John F. Hartranft. Hartranft reported directly to his commanding officer, Major General Winfield Scott Hancock. Hancock had heard that Hartranft was granting Mudd special privileges as a result of Mudd being seated in the courtroom separately from the other prisoners who were confined in an area behind a low railing. In response to Hancock's request for an explanation of Mudd's seating arrangement, Hartranft wrote the following communiqué to Hancock:

> Hd. Qrs. Mil. Prison
> Wash. Arsenal. May 10th 1865
> 9:40 P.M.

Major Genl. Hancock
Comdg. Mid. Mil. Div.
General,
    In reply to your communication relative to my giving especial privileges to Dr. Mudd, I respectively state that the separation of Dr. Mudd from the rest of the prisoners was accidental and occurred as follows:
    On Tuesday, when the prisoners were taken into Court, Dr. Mudd and Mrs. Surratt happened to be the last of the prisoners brought in; the

other six were taken into the prisoners' dock and by seating the person in charge of each prisoner by his side, the room was all taken up. When the Dr. was brought in, he was placed on a chair, just in front of the other prisoners and outside of the railing. Mrs. Surratt was also seated near him.

To day the prisoners were brought in and seated in the same manner, I thinking that it would be more convenient for the Court to have them seated the same each day.

*Dr. Mudd has been treated since he has been in this prison, precisely the same as each of the other male prisoners, except that **he has not been hooded, which was in accordance with your instructions**.*

I disclaim all intention of granting Dr. Mudd any privileges.

I have the honor to be

> *Very Respectfully*
> *Your Obt. Servt.*
> *Bvt. Maj. Genl.*
> *Gov. and Comdr. Mil. Prison.*[9]

Hartranft's statement belies the persistent claim in numerous works that Dr. Mudd was hooded. The claim that Mudd was hooded, however, casts further suspicion on the behavior of the military tribunal.

Over the next several decades following *Shark Island*, historical writings picked up the theme of Mudd's innocence and brutal handling by the government with a seeming ignorance of much of the evidence surrounding

One of the hoods worn by the accused during their initial incarceration.

Engraving of prisoners being led from their cells showing use of hoods. Engraving from **Frank Leslie's Magazine, 1865.** *While many have written that Mudd was hooded during his early confinement, Major General John F. Hartranft, in charge of the prison and prisoners, wrote to his commanding officer, Major General Winfield Scott Hancock that Mudd, "...has not been hooded, which was in accordance with your instructions."*

Mudd's role in Booth's original conspiracy and subsequent escape. Despite the sympathetic treatment which Mudd generally received in historical treatises of the period, no serious effort existed to reverse the judgment of the court. This came later as a result of Mudd's grandson, Dr. Richard Dyer Mudd,[10] who mounted a campaign to "free" his grandfather as early as the administration of Franklin D. Roosevelt. Richard Mudd's attempts to seek presidential intervention on his grandfather's behalf met with repeated frustration. A measure of success did not come until the administration of Jimmy Carter.[11]

On July 24, 1979, President Jimmy Carter wrote a letter to Dr. Richard Mudd in support of his efforts on behalf of his grandfather, and of Carter's belief that his grandfather was innocent. Carter wrote that while he, as president, was unable to set aside Dr. Samuel Mudd's conviction, he agreed fully with President Andrew Johnson's statements in his pardon of Mudd. In particular, Carter quoted the following from Johnson's pardon:

...it is represented to me by intelligent and respectable members of the medical profession that the circumstances of the surgical aid to the escaping of the assassin and the imputed concealment of his flight are deserving of a lenient construction, as within the obligations of professional duty and, thus, inadequate evidence of a guilty sympathy with the crime or the criminal;

And ...in other respects the evidence, imputing such guilty sympathy or purpose of aid in defeat of justice, leaves room for uncertainty as to the true measure and nature of the complicity of the said Samuel A. Mudd in the attempted escape of said assassins ...

Carter concluded his letter with the following statement:

A careful reading of the information provided to me about this case led to my personal agreement with the findings of President Johnson. I am hopeful that these conclusions will be given widespread circulation which will restore dignity to your grandfather's name and clear the Mudd family name of any negative connotation or implied lack of honor.

When Dr. Mudd was offered and accepted a full and unconditional pardon on February 8, 1869, by President Johnson, the case of presidential exoneration or reversal of guilt was closed. As President Carter states, perhaps for the first time in the long history of efforts to exonerate Samuel Mudd,

All legal authority vested in the President to act in this case was exercised when President Andrew Johnson granted Dr. Mudd a full and unconditional pardon on February 8, 1869.

After nearly seventy years of continuous effort to "free" his grandfather, Richard Mudd was greatly heartened and pleased with President Carter's gracious letter.[12] The news media quickly followed up on the release of the letter, and declared that Dr. Samuel Mudd had finally been exonerated and declared innocent of any wrong doing by the president of the United States. Of course, Carter did no such thing. As he clearly states in his letter, all presidential authority was exercised by Andrew Johnson in 1869. President Carter merely added the considerable weight of his position at the time to express his personal opinion that,

...a careful reading of the information provided to me about this case led to my personal agreement with the findings of President Johnson.

Clearly Presidents Andrew Johnson and Jimmy Carter did not have all of the information provided to them when they concluded that,

...Dr. Mudd's guilt was limited to aiding the escape of President Lincoln's assassins and did not involve any other participation or complicity in the assassination plot itself....[13]

Not to be outdone by President Carter, President Ronald Reagan, on December 8, 1987, wrote to Dr. Richard Mudd extending his support on behalf of Dr. Mudd's grandfather.[14]   Like Carter before him, Reagan lamented his inability to do anything further on behalf of Samuel Mudd and concluded his letter by stating the obvious:

> But we'll have to accept that 'full unconditional pardon' is what we must settle for.

While Dr. Richard Mudd's initial reaction to President Carter's letter (and President Reagan's eight years later) was that the curtain was finally closing on his years of struggle to gain a presidential reversal of the military tribunal's action, the curtain was suddenly raised yet one more time.

On January 22, 1992, a hearing was obtained before the Army Board for the Correction of Military Records (ABCMR). This board consists of civilian members that hear claims concerning military records that are believed to be in error, and makes recommendations to the secretary of the army based on its findings. The board lacks any authority to change any record, but acting on evidence presented and reviewed, comes to its recommendations which it submits to the secretary of the army.[15]

Because of its nature, the board hears evidence only from the aggrieved parties as to the claim of error in the record. Lawyers representing the Mudd family together with family members were allowed to appear before the board and present their evidence. Opponents to the petition to correct or expunge the record were not allowed to appear before the board and present counter evidence. An examiner acting for the board presents the facts and relevant law in question to the board. The board may, and frequently does, put questions to the examiner as to the relevant law in the case.

The arguments presented to the board by the proponents stated that no basis existed in 1865 for the military jurisdiction over the accused Dr. Samuel A. Mudd.[16] On questioning, the examiner recommended that Samuel Mudd (and his family) be granted relief. It is important to note that the board did not consider the question of Dr. Mudd's innocence or guilt—only whether he was lawfully tried by a military commission.

The board heard the arguments and agreed with the court appointed examiner that relief be granted to the Mudd family in the case of Dr. Samuel A. Mudd. In its conclusion the board stated:

> ...the board finds no good reason why Dr. Mudd should not have been tried by a civilian court. It, therefore, unanimously concludes that the military commission did not have jurisdiction to try him, and that in so doing denied him his due process rights, particularly his right to trial by a jury of his peers. This denial constituted such a gross infringement of his Constitutionally protected rights, that his conviction should be set aside.[17]

When the board found "...no good reason why Dr. Mudd should not have been tried by a civilian court" it ignored the rulings by the Attorney General of the United States, James Speed, in 1865, and Federal District Court Judge Thomas Jefferson Boynton who presided over the District Court for the United States of the Southern District of Florida in 1867. Both Speed and Boynton ruled that the military commission had legal jurisdiction to try the accused conspirators. (These rulings are covered in detail in Chapter 10.)

The board's recommendation was forwarded to the secretary of the army's designee, William D. Clark, acting Assistant Secretary of the Army. Secretary Clark, in reviewing the record, denied the recommendation of the board. In his ruling, Clark wrote:

> *The ABCMR concluded that the military commission which tried Dr. Mudd did not have jurisdiction over civilians and recommended that Dr. Mudd's conviction be set aside on that basis.*
>
> *Accordingly, my denial of that recommendation **should not be taken as a determination of either the guilt or the innocence of Dr. Mudd.** It is not the role of the ABCMR to attempt to settle historical disputes. Neither is the ABCMR an appellate court. The precise issue which the ABCMR proposes to decide, **the jurisdiction of the military commission over Dr. Mudd, was specifically addressed at the time in two separate habeas corpus proceedings, one before the Chief Justice of the Supreme Court, the other before a U.S. District Court. There also was an opinion by the Attorney General of the United States.***
>
> *The effect of the action recommended by the ABCMR would be to overrule all those determinations. Even if the issue might be decided differently today, it is inappropriate for a non-judicial body, such as the ABCMR, to declare that the law 127 years ago was contrary to what was determined contemporarily by prominent legal authorities.*
>
> *Accordingly, I have rejected the ABCMR's recommendations and have denied the application for relief.*[18]

It is a wonder how the Army Board for Correction of Military Records was ever allowed to hear the petition in the first place based upon Clark's ruling. To plead the lack of legal jurisdiction of the military commission whereby the ruling declares that the ABCMR has no authority as a board to overrule judicial rulings seems to preclude its authority from the very beginning.

Nonetheless, this hearing is instructive to students of the conspiracy trial. It brings legally trained experts into the arena previously held almost exclusively by non-legally trained historians.

While Assistant Secretary of the Army Clark was still deliberating over the board's assessment of the hearing, and before his ruling, the University of Richmond School of Law, with the approval of Dr. Richard Mudd, staged a moot court in which a full adversarial hearing was held on the question of Mudd's trial. The school proposed an appellate hearing with experienced jurists trained in the law. This moot court brought the question of Mudd's trial even closer to professional legal scholarship.

Representing the defendant, Dr. Mudd, was the great-great-granddaughter of Brigadier General Thomas Ewing, Jr., who originally defended Dr. Mudd in 1865.[19]

The panel of judges listened to and asked numerous questions of the advocates for each side after which they deliberated and rendered a unanimous opinion. The three judges agreed in their verdict that the military commission lacked legal jurisdiction to try and convict Dr. Mudd. Interestingly, while the panel sat in judgment deliberating only on the question of the legal jurisdiction of the military commission, all three judges could not resist discussing the innocence of the defendant in their findings, leading us to believe that the historical intrigue surrounding Mudd is impossible to ignore even among leading jurists.

Unfortunately, it would seem that once again, the question of whether the military tribunal that tried Dr. Mudd had legal jurisdiction cannot be separated from the question of his guilt or innocence. Would the panel of judges have ruled otherwise if they were firmly convinced of Mudd's guilt? Presumably, they would still have ruled against the jurisdiction of the military commission, but one wonders.

These two quasi-legal events are carefully presented in a recent publication together with five commentaries by eminent scholars in support of one position or the other.[20] The student of the legal aspects of the Lincoln assassination and the military tribunal that followed it will find substantial grist from among these excellent writings.[21]

As the curtain was finally descending following these latest efforts to "free Dr. Mudd," it suddenly was raised one more time. On June 12, 1997, Congressman Steny Hoyer (D., Maryland 5th) with co-sponsor Thomas Ewing (R., Illinois 15th) introduced a bill into the House of Representatives seeking relief for Dr. Mudd.[22] The bill directs "...the Secretary of the Army to set aside the conviction of Dr. Samuel A. Mudd by a military commission in 1865 for aiding, abetting, and assisting the conspirators who assassinated President Abraham Lincoln."[23] The bill's findings state that:

> The conviction of Dr. Mudd was based on evidence of guilt that fell so far short of meeting the prosecution's burden of proof that such conviction amounted to a denial of due process of law which was so extreme as to constitute fundamental unfairness.
>
> Because the conviction of Dr. Mudd was not based on sufficient evidence and resulted in a denial of due process of law, the Secretary of the Army should set aside the conviction.[24]

In his remarks from the floor of the House, Mr. Hoyer stated:

> *Mr. Speaker, while it is clear that Dr. Mudd did set John Wilkes Booth's broken leg, there is absolutely no evidence to suggest that he was either a co-conspirator in the assassination of President Lincoln or even aware of the events which had occurred earlier that evening on Friday, April 14, 1865.*
>
> *I urge my colleagues to join me in ensuring that history is recorded accurately and that our Nation's most basic individual rights, embodied in the Constitution, are not violated at any time. Dr. Samuel Mudd's name and honor and that of his family, many of whom live in my district, hang in the balance. We ought to allow the findings and decision of the Army Board for Correction of Military Records, the most reputable and qualified entity to date which has reviewed this case, to stand, thus ending the 132-year-long disservice accorded to Dr. Samuel Mudd.*

Congressman Hoyer's remarks reflect the ongoing effort to revise the history of this sad epoch in our nation's past. Clearly Mr. Hoyer and the Army Board for Correction of Military Records (ABCMR) have not availed themselves of the primary source documents, including the statements of Dr. Samuel A. Mudd himself, which are readily available in this case. The failure of these two important entities to carefully review the entire judicial record before attempting to revise history is indefensible. The effort by the Legislative Branch to overturn the rulings of the Judicial Branch is without precedent, and amounts to an attempt to alter legal history by non-judicial means.

The best argument against such legislative tampering can be found in a letter by assassination historian James O. Hall to the editor of the *Maryland Independent*:

> *Perhaps it would be best for Congressman Hoyer to withdraw H. R. 1885 and leave the matter of Dr. Mudd's guilt or innocence to competent researchers and historians. They will have the last word anyway.*[25]

As the debate over the lawful jurisdiction of the military tribunal and the guilt or innocence of Dr. Mudd thickens, a clearer, more objective understanding of those momentous events surrounding the terrible death of Abraham Lincoln should eventually emerge.

The tendency of many writers and politicians to gloss over the role of Dr. Mudd[26] is no longer acceptable to students of the assassination. A more demanding review of the participants and events of that time is now being made. To accept Samuel Mudd as simply the good doctor who was victimized by an insane zealot is too simplistic and historically remiss. At some point, when all of the emotion is past, the whole truth will finally emerge. As Abraham Lincoln so astutely observed in the fall of 1862, *We cannot escape history.*

9

THE GOOD DOCTOR

Samuel Alexander Mudd (1833-1883) was born on December 20, 1833 at Oak Hill, the farm of his father, Henry Lowe Mudd, Sr. The senior Mudd's farm was located a short distance from the site of what would become Mudd's own farm in 1859.[1] Henry Mudd was a farmer of substantial means in Charles County, Maryland, where he owned several hundred acres of farm land along with several slaves needed to provide the considerable labor required for culturing tobacco. By the outbreak of the Civil War, tobacco was second only to cotton among the South's most profitable agricultural crops.

Henry Mudd was a strong advocate of education, and through a combination of public, private and home schooling, provided substantially for young Sam Mudd's schooling. At the age of seven, Sam attended public school for two years after which his father hired a tutor to teach his children at home. At fourteen years of age Sam attended the St. John's College in Frederick, Maryland where he received his first formal classical education. It was while at St. John's that young Sam met his future wife, Sarah Frances Dyer (1835-1911), who became known as "Frank" to Sam and his family.[2]

Sarah Dyer was attending a girl's academy in Frederick at the same time Sam was attending St. John's College. Following his course of instruction at St. John's, Sam returned home to Charles County only to leave shortly afterwards, and enroll in Georgetown College in the District of Columbia. Sam studied at Georgetown for three years, from 1850 to 1853. Shortly after returning home, Sam decided that his real interest lay more in medicine than farming. Under the able mentoring of his second cousin, Dr. George Mudd, he entered the Baltimore Medical College (later to become the University of Maryland Medical School) where he completed two years of medical training and received his certification to practice medicine as an M.D. in 1856.

Mudd's acquaintance with Sarah Dyer during the period they both attended school in Frederick blossomed into a courtship, which led to Mudd asking Sarah to marry him. Both Sam and Sarah were still in their teens when Sam proposed marriage, and Sarah told Sam that she would marry him, but not before he finished his education, and earned his medical degree. Sam agreed.

Having successfully graduated from Baltimore Medical College in 1856, Sam and Sarah were married on November 26, 1857 and set up housekeeping in the home of Sarah's brother, Jeremiah Dyer, who was a bachelor at the time.[3] Within the year, Sam and Frank purchased 218 acres from the original patent granted to Thomas Mudd, the progenitor of the Maryland Mudds. Sam then set about to have their own house built on the newly acquired tract, known as St. Catharine's. St. Catharine's traced its lineage back to Thomas Mudd in the year 1696, and at the time Sam acquired St. Catharine's, it had descended through the Mudd family for nearly one hundred and sixty-two years.[4]

While Sam and Frank waited for their new house to be built, their first child, Andrew Jerome, was born in November 1858. In 1859, the three Mudds moved into their newly-constructed home and Sam took up the dual role of farmer-doctor. Over the next six years, three more children were born to the couple: Lillian Augusta (June 2, 1860), Thomas Dyer (June 6, 1861),[5] and Samuel Alexander II (January 30, 1864). For the next thirteen and a half months, Sam and Frank and their four children would lead happy normal lives in the midst of family and friends in the rural southern community of Charles County, Maryland.

A Southerner by heritage and tradition, Samuel Mudd continued the life of a Southern planter and part-time physician that was a natural way of life among his peers. At one point, Mudd owned as many as eleven slaves who provided the labor for his tobacco farm, not always under happy circumstances.

During the trial of Dr. Mudd, the prosecution introduced six of his former slaves as witnesses against him.[6] The prosecution introduced these witnesses in an effort to show the court that Mudd had frequently harbored and cared for Confederate soldiers at his home, and secreted soldiers at various times in the woods near his house, supplying them with blankets and food.[7] The conclusion which the prosecution attempted to make to the court was that Mudd was more than a Confederate sympathizer; he was an active player in the rebellion.

During the testimony of Elzee Eglen, one of Mudd's former slaves, Eglen told of being shot by Mudd because he had not responded quickly enough to Mudd's orders.[8] Eglen was described during the trial as being "obstreperous." Clearly Mudd did not want to kill Eglen, but only wound him as a lesson for Eglen's tardiness in responding to his instructions. Other slaves testified to being whipped by him.[9] These incidents, along with the vituperations in his letter to Orestes Brownson and Mudd's derogatory references to blacks in his letters home while imprisoned, seldom appear in the numerous treatises about the doctor. By any standard, owning slaves and whipping and shooting them seems at variance with the ideals of the Hippocratic oath.

That Mudd was an educated man, a pious man and a respected caregiver among the citizens of Charles County is certain. But Mudd was also a man whose principles fully encompassed the Southern ideal that states' rights included the right of select individuals to declare certain other people as non-citizens whose status was only as property. Mudd strongly defended that principle and, like most of his neighbors with the exception of his mentor Dr. George Mudd, he supported the use of arms against his countrymen to preserve that principle.

Mudd's principles as a physician and a practitioner of the Hippocratic oath were at variance with his actions in support of the Southern cause. If he objected to anything involving the plot to capture Lincoln and change the course of the war, it was not the plot itself so much as the plotters. Booth and his band of cohorts were not of Mudd's ilk. But John Wilkes Booth had apparently used the right names in drawing Mudd into his scheme.

The government sentence of life imprisonment was a devastating blow to Mudd. His only hope of keeping his sanity in light of such a sentence lay in his belief that friends and family would be able to reverse the tribunal's ruling or at least gain a presidential pardon.

The military tribunal sentenced four of the accused conspirators to death by hanging: Mary Surratt, Lewis Powell, Davy Herold and George Atzerodt. Three were sentenced to life imprisonment: Samuel Mudd, Samuel Arnold and Michael O' Laughlen. Edman Spangler received a six-year sentence.[10] The death sentences were carried out on the arsenal grounds next to the very building where the prisoners had been incarcerated and tried. The remaining four were originally scheduled for imprisonment at the federal penitentiary at Albany, New York, but this was quickly changed to Fort Jefferson in the Dry Tortugas.

Fort Jefferson was the most remote of all federal forts within the jurisdiction of the United States, located approximately seventy miles off of Key West, Florida in the Gulf of Mexico. Some have speculated that the change was made by Stanton to keep the convicted men under military control and as remote from family and friends as possible. This speculation is consistent with Stanton's behavior and his authority at the time. If Stanton had wanted to isolate the prisoners within the military system, no better place existed than Fort Jefferson.

Mudd arrived at the fort near the end of July 1865, after a two week journey aboard a federal steamship. Life for Dr. Mudd at Dry Tortugas was varied over the next three and a half years of his imprisonment. Initially, Mudd was treated without deference to his professional position and training and served as a prison laborer.

Two months after he began serving his sentence, Mudd attempted to escape the island fortress by stowing away in the hold of one of the supply ships that infrequently stopped at the fort. Discovered, Mudd was treated harshly at first, confined in chains, and kept in a communal cell with several other prisoners—treatment not unusual for an attempted escapee.[11] The harsh treatment was short-lived, however, as Mudd himself described in one of his many letters home. In a letter dated October 5, 1865, ten days after his abortive escape attempt, Mudd wrote to his brother-in-law, Jeremiah Dyer:

> *I am taking my present hardship as a joke. I am not put back in the least. I will soon assume my former position, or one equally respectable. The only thing connected with my present attitude is the name, and not the reality. I have no labor to perform, yet I am compelled to answer roll-call, and to sleep in the guard house at night. This will not last longer than this week.*[12]

Meanwhile, life back on the farm was increasingly difficult for Mrs. Mudd and her four children. Much is made of Frank's plight who, left husbandless with her four children, was faced with the task of maintaining the farm in Sam's absence. She did have help, however. Jere Dyer, Frank's brother, assumed responsibility for overseeing the farm operation and Sarah certainly had Sam's father and his labor force to help make sure the farm continued to function and that Frank and her children were provided for.[13]

As time distanced the failed escape attempt, Mudd was assigned to the carpenter's shop at the prison. While it is not clear precisely what his official duties were within the prison shop, it is clear that Mudd had time to practice the art of cabinetry. Among the items which the family descendants proudly cite in their inventory of Mudd prison artifacts are a "ladies work box," an "inlaid center table," a presentation "cane," "wreaths and flowers made of collected shells," and several "cribbage boards."[14] At least Mudd's incarceration offered some intellectual stimulation and was not so harsh as to leave him debilitated and unable to fashion cabinetry.[15]

Dr. Mudd's first major break came in June 1867 with the outbreak of yellow fever at the fort. Although a life-threatening scourge, the fever proved a life saver to Mudd. A parasitic disease carried by the mosquito, yellow fever can often prove fatal. Within weeks scores of inhabitants at the fort came down with the disease. The only physician at the fort was Dr. Joseph Sim Smith, a Union surgeon who had been a classmate of Mudd's at Georgetown College.

Military tribunal and government prosecutors.

The last vestige of the old Washington Arsenal where the accused were tried. The trial was held on the third floor of the present building which has survived as an apartment building for officers at Fort Lesley McNair.

The final judgment. Of the ten individuals found guilty by the government, four were sentenced to hang: Mary Surratt, Powell, Herold and Atzerodt.

Fort Jefferson. Of the remaining six conspirators, four were sentenced to prison in Fort Jefferson: Mudd, O'Laughlen, Arnold and Spangler; Booth being dead and John Surratt still at large.

Smith arrived at the island shortly after the outbreak and was soon overwhelmed by the spread of the disease. He wisely enlisted the aid of his old school mate, Dr. Mudd. Within six weeks Dr. Smith and his young son were dead, leaving a widow and young daughter stranded on the island and surrounded by the yellow death.[16]

On Smith's death, Dr. Mudd assumed medical responsibility for the remaining inhabitants at the fort until aid came in the person of Dr. D. W. Whitehurst, a Key West surgeon. The two physicians labored day and night to care for the victims of the disease, but there was little that medicine could do other than attempt to relieve some of the symptoms. Medical science had not yet learned that the disease was transmitted by the mosquito and even if the islanders had known that fact there is little they could have done to eradicate the infestation that swept over the island.

Among those who fell victim to the fever were Sam Arnold and Michael O'Laughlen, Mudd's fellow conspirators. Arnold eventually recovered, but O'Laughlen died. Mudd himself eventually contracted the fever; but with care recovered in time to see the last of the epidemic blow out to sea.

As a result of Mudd's humanitarian efforts, he was given free run of the fort. A petition was signed by all of the inhabitants of the fort in support of Mudd for his heroic efforts, but the petition failed to reach the president. A new commandant arrived who returned the fort to its previous conditions, leaving Mudd in deep despair to ponder his ultimate fate.

Then, in February 1869, President Andrew Johnson issued a presidential pardon freeing Mudd "unconditionally."[17] Within two weeks, both Arnold and Spangler received similar pardons.[18]

Mudd returned home to his wife and four children and began to pick up the pieces. Over the next several years Sarah and Sam had five more children;[19] Sam resumed his farming and medical practice; and eventually he ran for the state legislature. In 1877, Mudd ran as a delegate for the state legislature along with his neighbor, Samuel Cox, Jr. The good people of Charles County saw fit to elect Cox, Jr. as their delegate while sending Dr. Mudd back home.

During the fourteen years following his release from imprisonment Mudd maintained a low profile, save for his one attempt at elective office. He maintained his innocence whenever pressed to comment on the momentous events surrounding Lincoln's death. In the end, his devotion to his medical practice is said to have resulted in his death. While administering to his patients in January 1883, Dr. Mudd contracted pneumonia and on January 10, 1883, at the age of 49, died. He was laid to rest in the church cemetery next to the building where he first met with John Wilkes Booth on that fateful Sunday in November 1864—St. Mary's Catholic Church.

10

INTER ARMA SILENT LEGES[1]

According to Colonel Wells' testimony, Mudd had undergone several interviews beginning on Tuesday, April 18 and ending on Sunday, April 23. After interviewing Mudd on Friday, April 21, Wells, now convinced of Mudd's duplicity, had his house staked out by troopers. On Sunday morning, Wells personally visited the Mudd farm and had Mudd show him the route the two fugitives took when they left on Saturday evening. Mudd pointed out tracks leading away from the rear of his house in the direction of the Zekiah Swamp.

Wells was satisfied that Mudd was lying about his relationship with Booth and his own role in Lincoln's murder. He was convinced that Mudd not only knew where Booth and Herold were hiding out, but that Mudd was rendering Booth medical assistance. On Monday morning, April 24, Wells sent a troop of cavalry to Mudd's house to arrest him and take him to Washington for further questioning. By now, the authorities had seven of the ten alleged conspirators in custody. Only Booth, Herold and John Surratt were still at large. Within forty eight hours Booth and Herold would be in custody leaving only John Surratt still free.[2]

Satisfied of Mudd's complicity in Booth's plot, the government charged Mudd as a conspirator in the murder of Abraham Lincoln. Also charged were seven other individuals (Booth being dead and Surratt still at large).

On May 1, 1865, President Andrew Johnson issued an Executive Order[3] directing that those accused in the former president's murder stand trial before a military commission composed of nine Union officers.[4] After seven weeks of hearings the commission handed down its rulings finding all eight individuals guilty. Four were sentenced to death by hanging (Mary Surratt, Lewis Powell, David Herold and George Atzerodt), three were sentenced to life imprisonment (Samuel Mudd, Samuel Arnold and Michael O'Laughlen), and one was sentenced to six years' imprisonment (Edman Spangler).

On July 7, 1865, the four conspirators sentenced to death were hanged on a special gallows constructed within the walls of the arsenal in the District of Columbia. Mudd, along with Arnold, O'Laughlen and Spangler were ordered transferred to the military prison at Fort Jefferson. With the conclusion of that final act, the punishments meted out by the military commission which had been charged with "removing the stain of innocent blood from the land"[5] became a matter of controversy that still swirls about the heads of historians and students alike.

Defenders of Mudd, as well as most writers on the subject, maintain that the military tribunal of 1865 was illegal and that Mudd was improperly tried and convicted. Unfortunately, the controversy surrounding the legality of the trial is often confused with the question of Mudd's guilt or innocence. The principal question arising from this unique episode is whether the military commission was a properly constituted body which had legal authority to try, convict and sentence the accused conspirators in the murder of Abraham Lincoln. Those who answer against the commission's authority cite as their principal justification for claiming its illegal basis the Supreme Court decision of 1866 known as *ex parte Milligan*.[6]

The serious student of the Lincoln assassination can readily cite this landmark decision in which the Supreme Court ruled that the military commission was without jurisdiction in those districts removed from military zones in which the civil courts were open and functioning and where no threat of military action existed. This ruling has been used by scholars and students alike as a blanket condemnation of the military commission that tried the Lincoln conspirators, and thus brand the commission that tried them as illegal. But is it so?

While the Supreme Court never issued a decision on the tribunal's jurisdiction in the cases of Mudd and his co-defendants, it did hear a petition on their behalf. In February 1869, the Supreme Court agreed to listen to arguments on behalf of Arnold and Spangler (Mudd had been pardoned only days before). The court heard oral arguments but issued no decision since Johnson preempted the court by pardoning both petitioners before the court could rule, leaving the question moot.[7]

Since that time, however, a series of rulings have been issued which bear on this question and warrant our review. In attempting to arrive at a conclusion concerning the status of the commission, however, we need to reach back to those opening days of the rebellion. This was a time when constitutional questions and civil liberties were being subjected to a series of executive actions which ultimately led to the commission's existence and sanction.

If the days between Lincoln's election and his inauguration were full of strife and discord, the ones immediately following were even more so. Lincoln's dilemma was to do everything within his power to avoid war without ensuring the permanency of secession. It was a precarious balancing act which was predestined to failure.

Acts of open hostility against the federal government increased with alarming frequency until open warfare finally erupted with the Confederate bombardment of Fort Sumter. Ten days later, Federal troops were involved in open rioting on the streets of Baltimore within forty miles of the national capital.

Experiencing increasing difficulty and frustration in dealing with individuals and groups opposed to the government's efforts to suppress the rebellion, Lincoln decided to move quickly to render harmless those people whom he deemed detrimental to the Union cause. On April 25, 1861, he issued an order to the commanding general of the army, Winfield Scott, authorizing Scott to suspend the privilege of the writ of habeas corpus along certain military lines, but only under the "extremist necessity."[8] Within two days, on April 27, Lincoln issued a second, similar order to Scott authorizing him to suspend the writ, "if necessary" along the military line from Philadelphia to Washington.[9]

Lincoln desperately needed troops and, having the experience of Baltimore on April 19 fresh in his mind, he meant to obtain them as quickly as possible without further hindrance. He had seized upon the opportunity of suspending the writ of habeas corpus as a military necessity. In the eyes of Lincoln and many of his supporters, civil processes were becoming increasingly ineffective. The increasing number of arrests for treason and the growing failures to stem the tide of opposition caused federal authorities to lose confidence in the courts, and to turn to the military, especially in areas where Southern sympathies ran high.

In suspending the writ of habeas corpus, Lincoln contended that he was authorized by the constitutional provision which states in part, "The privilege of the Writ of Habeas Corpus shall not be suspended unless when in Cases of Rebellion or Invasion the Public Safety may require it."[10] Lincoln interpreted this to mean that the president was empowered to suspend the writ if and when he deemed the safety to be in jeopardy.

Censure of Lincoln's action was immediate. Controversy swirled about the embattled president and his orders limiting civil liberties. His first hard test arose in a confrontation with the venerable eighty-four year old Supreme Court Chief Justice, Roger Brooke Taney.

On May 25, 1861, a troop of Pennsylvania militia had arrested a prominent Marylander named John B. Merryman in the early morning hours at his Cockeysville home. Merryman, whose sympathies and militant actions were clearly against the national government, was taken to Baltimore where he was confined in the military prison at Fort McHenry.

Merryman, an astute lawyer, immediately petitioned for his release on a writ of habeas corpus before Judge Taney who was then sitting as a circuit court judge for the District of Baltimore.[11] Taney promptly issued the writ ordering the military commander of the district, Major General George B. Cadwallader, to deliver Merryman to the court immediately. General Cadwallader asked Taney for more time so that he might consult with his commander-in-chief as to whether he should comply with the judge's order. Taney answered by sending the marshal for the District of Baltimore to Fort McHenry with orders to arrest Cadwallader on contempt charges. The marshal was met at the gates of the fort by an armed guard which refused his admittance, forcing him to return to Taney empty-handed. The military had stood down the prestigious chief justice, and old Taney knew exactly where to level his wrath.

On the 28th of May the aging Taney strode into an overflowing courtroom to tumultuous cheers and delivered a stinging oration. In his castigation of the newly elected president, Taney traced the history of the writ down through English common law to the U.S. Constitution, sharply pointing out that the president of the United States had no authority whatsoever to suspend this sacred and valuable right. He further admonished Lincoln by reminding him of his oath to uphold the Constitution and the law of the land, and directed him to start doing so now.

But outwitting Lincoln, as Taney and the rest of the country would soon learn, was no easy task. Sensing the difficulty of his position and realizing that he could gain little and lose much in a jousting match with the wily chief justice, Lincoln pocketed the judge's ruling and held his silence. Taney had had his day in court but lost to Lincoln and the weight of arms.

During the next year and a half Lincoln suspended the writ on five separate occasions, each time specifying special and narrow circumstances.[12] Then on September 24, 1862, he issued a sweeping order in which, "...all Rebels, and insurgents, their aiders and abettors" were subjected to martial law and trial by military commission, and further, suspended the writ of habeas corpus for all persons, "...confined by military authority."[13]

Up to this point the suspension of the writ had been supported by presidential authority only in narrowly defined cases. This new proclamation, however, had broad and sweeping implications. The suspension pertained only to those instances which involved military arrest of civilians presumably based on military necessity. While this suspension of the writ had a very precise applicability, it became an order for wholesale arrests.

The use of military commissions throughout the war was not in any way infrequent. During the four-year period approximately two thousand commissions sat in judgment over nearly thirteen thousand defendants and were not at all adverse to "harsh judgments."[14]

This relatively new form of justice actually had its origins during the war with Mexico in 1846. When General Winfield Scott took his American forces into Mexico he was faced with a dilemma which the American military had never before encountered. He was forced to improvise ways to deal with serious crimes committed by civilians within his military area which would have been triable in the civil courts in the United States. Not having such courts available to try American citizens for their alleged offenses while in Mexico, Scott established two courts on his own: the military commission, which handled civil offenses, and the council of war, which covered offenses against the "laws of war." Scott took these actions reluctantly and only after unsuccessfully petitioning the Congress of the United States for direction in this troublesome matter.

Scott's council of war did not survive the Mexican conflict, and was merged into the military commission which also assumed the responsibility for trying those cases involving offenses against the "laws of war."

It is interesting to note that the authority for military commissions throughout this period was without statutory basis. Their legal basis and utilization were never directly challenged before the Supreme Court during the four years of the Civil War save in one peculiar instance. In this one case where the Supreme Court had an opportunity to hear and rule on the legal jurisdiction of the military tribunal, it effectively avoided the issue by declaring that it lacked jurisdiction.

The case involved Ohio congressman Clement L. Vallandigham, a notorious Copperhead.[15] Vallandigham had been arrested by the military for his "anti-war" efforts in Ohio and elsewhere. He was brought to trial before a military tribunal in Cincinnati in 1863. Found guilty, he was ordered banished from Union soil to a point within the military lines of the Confederacy. Vallandigham filed a petition with the Supreme Court for a writ of habeas corpus and challenged the legal jurisdiction of the military tribunal that tried him.[16] Just two years after Chief Justice Taney had challenged Lincoln, the Court effectively sidestepped the tricky issue by ruling that it was without jurisdiction in the case, the military commission falling outside the Judicial Act of 1789. In so doing, the Court, in effect, gave its back-of-the-hand approval to the military commission as a war court. Interestingly, in the several cases which have come before the Supreme Court over the eighty-three year period involving military commissions, the court has never ruled against the authority of the military commission, only to its jurisdiction in specified instances.

The use of the military commission was put to its severest test following the assassination of Lincoln. With all but two of the charged conspirators in shackles, the new president, Andrew Johnson, issued an Executive Order on May 1, 1865, subjecting those charged with the former president's murder to stand trial before a military commission composed of nine Union officers.[17]

While the reasons for turning to a military trial may be varied, as has been speculated, we have only the written justifications of the principal jurist to guide us. Attorney General James Speed issued an official opinion on the legal jurisdiction of the tribunal as ordered by President Johnson.[18]

Speed's lengthy opinion, often rambling far afield, seems at times to attempt to legitimize the commission by sheer weight of words. Its essence, however, reduces down to two important and substantive points: that the offenses which the accused were charged with were offenses against the laws of war, and that the defendants were, in fact, "belligerents" who served as, "...secret, but active participants (spies) in the recent hostilities."[19] Thus Speed cast a net about the hapless accused which placed them in an exclusionary category, and denied them trial in the civil courts which lacked jurisdiction over such offenses and persons. The Supreme Court had already supported this notion in the Vallandigham case.[20]

In his opinion Speed asserts that, "If the question be one concerning the laws of war, he (the accused) should be tried by those engaged in the war—they and only they are his peers. The military must decide whether the accused is or is not a participant in the hostilities. If he is an active participant in the hostilities, it is the duty of the military to take him prisoner without warrant or other judicial process, and dispose of him as the laws of war direct."[21] This point which Speed effectively develops in his opinion to Johnson is not dismissed lightly. Some historians express the view that a certain hysteria of the times equated participation in the rebellion with participation in the assassination. While this position may have some basis in fact, it should not cloud or confuse Speed's conclusion that the accused conspirators were Confederate agents (belligerents) and therefore legally triable before a military tribunal. The distinction is important.

Despite the feeling by some that the attorney general was not guided by constitutional law in developing his opinion regarding the jurisdiction of the military tribunal, Speed was quite cognizant of the constitutional provisions which later came to haunt the commission and its advocates. In his opinion, Speed acknowledges the existence of the civil courts in the District of Columbia and their jurisdiction under normal circumstances, but dismisses their right to try the accused conspirators, writing,

> *The fact that the civil courts are open does not affect the right of the military tribunal to hold (the accused) as a prisoner and to try. The civil courts have no more right to prevent the military, **in time of war**, from trying **offenders against the laws of war** than they have a right to interfere with and prevent a battle.*[22]

It was the government's contention that the commander-in-chief of the armed forces had been murdered by enemy agents within a military zone which had been subjected to an invasion attempt by hostile forces at a time when martial law existed.[23] It further asserted that martial law supersedes civil law in every instance. The defense countered by challenging the legality of the military commission as a court in what should have been a strictly civil matter. The accused were civilians (not enemy belligerents) charged with what should be a civil offense, conspiracy to murder, and therefore should be tried in the civil courts of the District of Columbia which were open and functioning without difficulty. The defense further maintained that the need or justification for martial law ended with the surrender of Lee on April 9, 1865.

Not unexpectedly, the military commission ruled that the challenge to its legal justification was without merit and the trial proceeded over the continued protests of the defense. The question of the military commission's jurisdiction arose again, not just once, but several times over the next eighty years. The first hard test arose scarcely a year after the 1865 conspiracy trial in a case soon to become famous known as *ex parte Milligan*.[24]

Lambdin P. Milligan, a long-time resident of Indiana and a citizen of the United States, had been actively engaged in a series of overt acts in opposition to the federal government's prosecution of the war, playing a major role in organizing a chapter of the Order of the Sons of Liberty in 1863 within the state of Indiana. This group had as one of its objectives the forced take-over of certain government arsenals in the Midwest, together with the attempted liberation of thousands of Confederate prisoners of war from various Northern camps. This elaborate scheme by Milligan and his collaborators was no amateurish operation, and disastrous consequences of this internal threat to Union efforts were quickly recognized. Federal agents had successfully infiltrated Milligan's organization and closely monitored its activity. In May 1864, Major General Alvin P. Hovey, who commanded the military district encompassing Indiana, ordered the arrest of Milligan and several of his supporters.[25] Milligan was tried before a military commission in Indianapolis, found guilty on all counts and was sentenced to death by hanging.

Milligan, an accomplished lawyer who had been admitted to the bar with another accomplished lawyer, Edwin M. Stanton, immediately petitioned the United States Circuit Court for Indiana on a writ of habeas corpus following his conviction. Milligan's plea was based on his belief that he had been tried and sentenced by a military commission which lacked legal jurisdiction.

The court that received Milligan's petition consisted of Judge David McDonald and Supreme Court Justice David Davis who was sitting as a circuit court judge during the Supreme Court recess. Davis was strongly opposed to the death penalty and to the use of military commissions to try civilians during wartime, and these feelings were well known by those familiar with his career.

Davis felt that the military holding Milligan would ignore the circuit court ruling and would proceed to execute him under "Presidential authority." Davis shrewdly persuaded Judge McDonald to "oppose" him in their ruling to take advantage of a procedure whereby if two judges of a circuit court are divided on a question of law, they could take the question to the Supreme Court for an answer. Davis then convinced President Johnson to commute Milligan's death sentence to life imprisonment, thereby allowing a resolution of the issue before the Supreme Court which would not have been possible if Milligan had been executed.[26]

On March 6, 1866, the petition came before the Supreme Court in its spring session. Three questions were posed to the court on which Davis and McDonald claimed they were opposed:

1. *On the facts stated in said petition and exhibits, ought the writ of habeas corpus to be issued?*
2. *On the facts stated in said petition and exhibits, ought the said Lambdin P. Milligan to be discharged from custody as in said petition prayed?*
3. *Whether upon the facts stated in said petition and exhibits, the military commission mentioned therein had jurisdiction legally to try and sentence said Milligan in manner and form in said petition and exhibits stated?*

The justices listened to the two groups of advocates as they pressed their cases. The government position was argued by Henry Stanberry (soon to become Andrew Johnson's attorney general), Benjamin F. Butler and Attorney General James F. Speed. The thrust of their argument lay in the authority of the president of the United States to order certain persons charged with offenses against the laws of war tried before a military commission in those areas where martial law was in effect.

Representing Milligan were a group of distinguished Americans whose credentials were impressive. Opening the defense was James A. Garfield, future president and only admitted to practice before the court that very morning. Garfield was accompanied by J. E. McDonald who had defeated Milligan for the Democratic nomination for governor of Indiana the previous year only to lose to Oliver P. Morton, the man who persuaded President Johnson to commute Milligan's sentence. Rounding the quartet of defense attorneys was the prominent jurist, Jeremiah S. Black, former attorney general under Buchanan and currently a judge of the Pennsylvania Supreme Court, and David Dudley Field, the brother of sitting Supreme Court Justice Stephen S. Field.

The defense argued simply, if somewhat excessively, that Milligan was not, nor ever had been in the military service of the United States, that the civil courts in Indiana were open and functioning freely, and that constitutional guarantees of a civil trial by a jury of his peers had been denied him.

The importance of the Milligan case centered around three key points dealing with: the privilege of the writ of habeas corpus which had been denied to Milligan, the existence of martial law, and the constitutional guarantees concerning the preeminence of civil courts in time of peace and war.

The court ruling has since been hailed as a landmark decision in American jurisprudence and one of a dozen cases considered to be the foundation of American civil liberties. The court ruled unanimously that the only authority under which a military commission could exist was that derived from the "laws and usages of war," but that the laws of war can never apply to citizens in jurisdictions where the civil courts were open and functioning, and that the president has no authority, constitutional or otherwise, to order anyone to stand trial before a military commission under the circumstances described in Milligan's case.[27]

The prosecution's contention that the military commission was justified under the rule of martial law resulting from Lincoln's Proclamation of 1862 was held invalid. The court said that martial law can only apply in the case of actual invasion or civil war where the courts are closed and it is impossible to administer justice except by the power of the military. Martial law, therefore, was limited to the zone of actual combat, and not to an area where only the threat of invasion existed.

On the question of habeas corpus, the court neither affirmed nor denied the president's authority to suspend the writ saying, "Unquestionably there is an urgency which demands that the government should not be required to produce the persons arrested in answer to a writ of habeas corpus." But who is the government? The president or the Congress, or both?[28]

If the court still left that issue somewhat clouded, it did affirm that Congress in its Act of March 21, 1863, specified the conditions and circumstances associated with the suspension of the writ. Prisoners were not to be kept confined indefinitely, but their cases were to be presented to a grand jury at the next regular session. In the absence of an indictment by the grand jury, they were to be released immediately. If indicted, they would be tried in a civil court by a jury of their peers as guaranteed by the Sixth Amendment of the Constitution. Thus, while a person may be denied the privilege of having his jailers present him before a civil court to determine whether and on what grounds he should continue to be held, he must be taken before a grand jury and indicted or set free. This procedure was a far cry from what in fact was taking place throughout the North during the war; and it was this very practice that formed the basis for Milligan's plea.

Many historians have applied a broad brush to the Supreme Court's ruling in Milligan concluding that the court declared military commissions illegal in those areas where the civil courts were open and functioning. This is incorrect. Such a conclusion is an oversimplification and does not reflect the court's complete ruling. The decision was not so sweeping in its meaning and Justice David Davis, the man directly responsible for the Milligan case coming before the court, said as much in a letter which he later wrote discussing the decision. Davis maintained that the decision applied only to the trial of civilians in certain parts of the North during the war.[29]

It is important to understand that the Supreme Court did not rule that military commissions were illegal, only that their jurisdiction was carefully limited to certain conditions which must be met. The court felt that none of the requisite conditions existed in Indiana or applied to Milligan which would make him subject to military authority.

Certainly the Milligan case casts an ominous shadow over the Lincoln conspiracy trial, leading many students of this episode to declare it illegal. Among them were the lawyers of Dr. Mudd. Quickly following on the heels of the Milligan decision was a petition filed with the Supreme Court on behalf of Dr. Mudd and his cohorts. Mudd, Edman Spangler and Samuel B. Arnold were languishing off the Florida Keys in the federal prison at Dry Tortugas when the Milligan decision was released. The defendants claimed that *ex parte Milligan* applied equally to their case and that the military tribunal which had tried them (and hanged Mary Surratt, Lewis Powell, Davy Herold and George Atzerodt) was illegal.

On December 29, 1866, Chief Justice Salmon P. Chase reviewed the petition and returned it stating that, "...the petition should be addressed to a Court or Judge of the United States in the District within which the prisoner is held."[30] In August 1868, Mudd's lawyers followed Chief Justice Chase's direction and made application for a writ of habeas corpus to the United States District Court for the Southern District of Florida.

Hearing their petition was Judge Thomas Jefferson Boynton who presided over the District Court of the United States for the Southern District of Florida. Mudd's petition to Boynton went beyond citing *ex parte Milligan* by stating that, "...if the military commission was legal in their case," then President Johnson's proclamation of July 4, 1867, granting general amnesty to all persons associated with the rebellion applied equally to them.

Boynton, however, ruled against the petition denying its validity on both points.[31] The judge wrote that the Milligan decision did not apply to the Lincoln conspirators, and that Johnson's amnesty proclamation specifically excluded all persons being held in military prisons, and "...all persons who were engaged directly or indirectly in the assassination of the late President...or in any plot or conspiracy in any manner therein connected."

Boynton maintained that a sharp difference existed between the cases of Milligan and Mudd. Indiana was not in a military situation; that is, it had not been invaded and did not have a hostile army camped within or adjacent to its borders. In sum, it was not an active zone of combat, and the crime which Milligan was accused of was not against the laws of war. In contrast, Boynton considered Washington an active zone of combat and its commander-in-chief murdered, not from private malice, but as a military necessity to effect military and political objectives. Boynton wrote:

> *The president was assassinated not from private animosity nor any other reason than a desire to impair the effectiveness of military operations, and enable the rebellion to establish itself into a Government; the act was committed in a fortified city, which had been invaded during the war, and to the northward as well as the southward of which battles had many times been fought, which was the headquarters of all the armies of the United States, from which daily and hourly went military orders. The President is the Commander-in-Chief of the army, and the President who was killed had many times made distinct military orders under his own hand, without the formality of employing the name of the Secretary of War or Commanding-General. It was not Mr. Lincoln who was assassinated, but the Commander-in-Chief, for military reasons. I find no difficulty, therefore, in classing the offense as a military one, and with this opinion, arrive at the necessary conclusion that the proper tribunal for the trial of those engaged was a military one.*[32]

Strongly reminiscent of Speed's opinion two years earlier, Boynton finessed around the principal argument arising from the Milligan decision by placing the accused in an exclusionary category. Mudd and his compatriots were cast in a net they could not wriggle out of.

Mudd was not finished just yet, however. His lawyers were now prepared to take Boynton's denial to the Supreme Court. As the petition was being prepared, President Johnson issued his pardon of Dr. Mudd on February 8, 1869. Deleting Mudd from the petition, the application was filed with the court on behalf of Samuel Arnold and Edman Spangler on February 19, 1869. Being petitions for habeas corpus, they were expedited and arguments were heard on February 26, 1869. Before the court issued an opinion, however, President Johnson followed his pardon of Dr. Mudd by issuing pardons for Arnold and Spangler rendering a decision by the court moot. The petitions were dismissed on March 19, leaving all of the arguments in place with no decision. Regardless of the arguments for or against the military tribunal and Mudd's personal situation within the American justice system, he clearly had his day in court and was not denied post-trial due process.

If the Supreme Court had put to rest the question of jurisdiction of military tribunals with its decision in *ex parte Milligan* as many historians have concluded, its ruling was as gossamer as was the decision in Dred Scott. Immediately following the cessation of hostilities and the death of Lincoln, the radicals of Lincoln's party began sweeping through the

Southland with a vengeful force. The period of Reconstruction saw an expansive use of the military tribunal enforcing a policy of retribution against the defeated rebels. As the Northern victors established control throughout the Southern states, they solidified their power through military justice. Despite *ex parte Milligan* (which raised the Radicals wrath toward the Supreme Court to an unprecedented level), the military commission lived on in apparent disregard for the court's ruling. It should be remembered that the court in its Milligan ruling not only reaffirmed the jurisdiction of the civil courts where they were open and functioning, but narrowly defined the circumstances under which martial law could legally exist as it did throughout the reconstructed South.

Close on the heels of the Milligan decision, Johnson ordered a cessation to all military trials involving civilians. The Radicals, more determined than ever to carry out their purification program, maneuvered around Johnson and his "obstructionist" Supreme Court with the passage of the Reconstruction Act of March 2, 1867. The Act created five military districts in eleven southern states (Tennessee was excluded) and placed each under the command of a Union general.[33] Each district was subject to martial law, and the military tribunal continued to operate in defiance of *ex parte Milligan* under the protective umbrella of the Reconstruction Act.

Both President Johnson and certain members of the Supreme Court indicated their feelings that the act was unconstitutional. The radicals continued to live with a growing fear that their policies would eventually be blocked by these two adversaries. Soon after the Milligan ruling the court found itself embroiled in still another controversy which generated great heat. Two cases had come before the court involving test-oaths which required certain individuals to attest to their loyalty to the United States and to their never having served or aided the recently defeated Confederacy in any manner. The court, in a close five to four vote, held that the loyalty oaths were unconstitutional in that they imposed a punishment ex post facto.[34] Once again the radical members of Congress leveled their fury at the court and its "undoing" of all they were accomplishing. As the storm swirled about the heads of the justices, a third "reconstruction" case came before the already bruised bench which had the Radicals snarling even more viciously than before.

William C. McCardle, an ex-Confederate colonel and the editor of a Vicksburg newspaper, had been arrested and held for trial before a military tribunal. McCardle had been charged with the dual crimes of insulting Major General E. O. C. Ord and of strongly opposing the Reconstruction Acts in his newspaper's editorials. Upon his arrest, McCardle applied to the federal court for release on a writ of habeas corpus. The court denied McCardle's petition, and he promptly petitioned the Supreme Court for relief.[35]

The Radical members of Congress, now more sure than ever that the court would again rule on the wrong side of Reconstruction, quickly moved to block any further meddling by the justices. After the case had been presented and before the justices had convened to issue their opinion, both houses of Congress, in a single day, passed an act which selectively removed the court's appellate jurisdiction under the Act of February, 1867. When the court finally did convene, it had no other recourse but to dismiss the petition on the grounds that the Supreme Court lacked jurisdiction in the case, thus sending McCardle back to his military captors.[36] And so the rule of martial law throughout the South continued to be administered by the military through their tribunals in spite of Milligan.

For the next seven and a half decades the question of military tribunals lay in obscurity, all but disappearing from the American scene. It would probably have remained so if it had not been for its resurrection during the Second World War. The interval between the Civil War and World War II saw no circumstances in which military tribunals held court. Then, during the summer of 1942, eight German agents secretly landed along the coast of the United States; four on Long Island, New York, and four along the coast of Florida. Within two weeks all eight would-be saboteurs had been arrested by the FBI, and were brought to Washington, D. C.[37]

President Franklin Delano Roosevelt quickly issued a Presidential Proclamation calling for the establishment of a military tribunal, and at the same time denying the accused access to the civil courts.[38] Roosevelt's proclamation was strikingly reminiscent of Andrew Johnson's proclamation issued nearly eighty years earlier.

The defense attorneys for the eight prisoners petitioned the Supreme Court on a writ of habeas corpus and challenged the jurisdiction of a military tribunal citing *ex parte Milligan* as their defense. As in 1865, the climate was clearly against the defendants and any claim of civil liberties which they might present. The nation was engaged in a war which could clearly end in defeat, for the summer of 1942 was not a time of optimism for America and her military.

The Supreme Court, already in summer recess, startled the entire world by agreeing to reconvene in an emergency session to hear the defendants' petition. Here indeed was a headline event. Perhaps the court wanted to show the world, and especially totalitarian nations, America's great concern for civil liberties—even for those who would destroy the very Constitution they now sought to wrap around themselves.

The circumstances surrounding *ex parte Quirin* were similar in many ways to those associated with Milligan and with the Lincoln conspirators a century before. The United States was part of a military zone which had been penetrated by enemy belligerents. The accused were charged with offenses against the laws of war, and the president, by executive order, had made them subject to martial law thus denying a trial by jury in the civil courts. All this had been claimed by the government in 1865 and again in 1942.

The defense in citing *ex parte Milligan* pointed out to the court that the civil courts were open and functioning, that no invasion or threat of invasion was imminent, and that the civil authority was not compelled to operate with the support of bayonets.

In its ruling[39] the court took a turn which should seem curious to students of *ex parte Milligan*. The court held that the president had authority to create a military commission, and that indictment by a grand jury and a trial by jury were not applicable—the defendants were charged with "offenses against the laws of war." The ruling in 1942, more than any other, is strongly reminiscent of Attorney General James Speed's opinion of July 1865 in regard to the Lincoln conspirators.

So Quirin and his collaborators went on trial before a military commission and were found guilty and sentenced—all with the sanction of the Supreme Court.[40]

The Supreme Court's affair with the military commission did not end here, however. By the summer of 1945 the Allied Armies had reversed the dark days of 1942 and had rolled to total victory over the Axis Powers. With the final surrender of the Japanese forces in the Philippines, the military was once again challenged before the Supreme Court in its efforts to use the military tribunal as a final court of justice.

With the fall of the Philippines early in 1945, Japanese General Tomoyuki Yamashita, the "Tiger of Malaya," surrendered his Imperial Japanese 14th Army Group and became a prisoner of war. United States military authorities decided to charge Yamashita with responsibility for all of the atrocities committed by the soldiers under his command in the closing weeks of the war. While U. S. authorities acknowledged that Yamashita never ordered or condoned (or was even aware of) the atrocities being committed, he was nevertheless held responsible for all of their actions.

Once again the Supreme Court was asked to decide on the jurisdiction of a military tribunal in trying defendants when the civil courts were open and functioning, and once again, Milligan became the defense.[41]

While Yamashita was a military officer and an enemy belligerent, his crimes were crimes against civilians triable in the civil courts in the jurisdiction where the alleged offenses occurred. While there may seem to be little in common between Yamashita and the conspiracy trial of 1865, the questions answered by the Supreme Court in Yamashita have direct bearing on our consideration of the legal jurisdiction of the Lincoln conspiracy trial in 1865.

Eighty years after its ruling in *ex parte Milligan*, the Supreme Court went against its ruling of 1866 and said that the Congress of the United States had the authority to establish military commissions and that its authority was derived directly from the Constitution under Article I, paragraph 8, which states in part that Congress could "...define and punish...offenses against the Law of nations...," a principal clause cited by Speed in 1865 in support of his opinion to President Johnson. This latter decision, eighty years after Milligan, seems in sharp contrast to the court's original decision. The court went on to state that the authority of the military tribunal rested in the charge that the defendant was accused of "violations against the laws of war," and therefore should be tried before a military tribunal.

> *Neither congressional action nor military orders constituting the commission authorized it to place the petitioner on trial unless the charge preferred against him is a violation of the laws of war. We conclude that the allegations of the charge, tested by any reasonable standard, adequately allege a violation of the law of war and that the military commission has authority to try and decide the issue which it raised.*

As in the case of the Lincoln conspirators, Yamashita's trial took place after all hostilities had ceased. The Supreme Court pointed out in their ruling, however, that the **cessation of hostilities does not end the jurisdiction of the military commission.** This point is important to the issue of the Lincoln trial. Critics of the Lincoln conspiracy trial have claimed that the surrender of Lee's army ended all threat of military invasion and thereby eliminated the jurisdiction of the military court. Like Quirin, et. Al., Yamashita faced the military tribunal, was found guilty and was executed with the full sanction of the Supreme Court.

In these two modern wartime rulings the Supreme Court clearly defined the defendants as enemy belligerents who were rightfully charged with committing offenses against the laws of war and therefore fell under the jurisdiction of the military tribunal.

Reviewing the judicial record with respect to military tribunals over a period of eighty years, what conclusions may be drawn with reference to the case of the Lincoln conspirators? In its most famous case, *ex parte Milligan*, the Supreme Court clearly defined the circumstances in which martial law may legally exist.[42]

The court did not rule, as some claim, that military commissions were without jurisdiction where the civil courts were open and functioning. The military commission clearly had jurisdiction in those cases in which offenses against the laws of war were charged, and the Supreme Court sanctioned such authority on several occasions. The court made this clear in Milligan, and in Quirin and in Yamashita. The court went further in stating in Milligan that he was not an enemy belligerent and that he was not charged with offenses against the laws of war.

If we interpret the court's ruling in Milligan as only acknowledging the jurisdiction of military commissions in those circumstances in which the civil courts are closed and unable to administer justice, then it went against itself in Vallandigham, Quirin and Yamashita—all cases involving military tribunals in areas in which the civil courts were open and were carrying on their business unimpeded.

When, then, are military tribunals legal? They are legal in those cases where martial law exists and the civil courts are forced to close, or when the accused are enemy belligerents charged with violations of the laws of war. Quirin and Yamashita were defined as enemy belligerents charged with offenses against the laws of war. In Yamashita, the court ruled that persons charged with violations against the laws of war were rightfully tried by a military commission. In Quirin, the court ruled that the president of the United States has the authority to establish military commissions and that persons who are accused as belligerents or secret agents (spies) are subject to trial before such commissions.

How are these cases applicable to our understanding of the Lincoln conspiracy trial? The government's justification for a military trial was premised on the fact that the accused conspirators were, in fact, belligerents who were agents and sympathizers of the rebellion who operated in stealth and in concert.

In his opinion of July 1865, Attorney General James Speed developed the position that the defendants were enemy belligerents who conspired to murder the commander-in-chief behind military lines within an active war zone and thus committed offenses against the laws of war. They were not civilians or entitled to be considered as civilians. The original conspiracy was designed to capture the commander-in-chief of United States forces, a military offense. The accused having met the test as enemy belligerents, the president had the authority to establish the military commission before which they were tried.

The key factor, it seems, is not in the kind of court that administers justice, but in the alleged offense and the nature of the offender. Having decided these two questions, the proper jurisdiction (court) follows.

Certainly sufficient evidence exists which shows that Booth, Surratt, Atzerodt, and Mudd all performed services for the Confederacy as agents in moving supplies or people across military lines. Powell, O'Laughlen, and Arnold served in the Confederate army.[43] Only Mary Surratt, Herold, and Spangler are without any known ties to the Confederate Secret Service or military although many believe that since the two Surratt houses served as safe houses for Confederate agents it was not without Mary Surratt's knowledge and participation.

From the cases reviewed, it appears that the mood of the court is influenced by the state of the nation at the time of ruling. During wartime, the court favors a military position; during peacetime, the court favors a civil position.

Had the court issued an opinion on the petition of Arnold and Spangler in 1869, it appears likely that their decision would have been in favor of the legal jurisdiction of the military commission consistent with the court's later rulings in the twentieth century.

Judge Boynton made a clear distinction between Indiana and the District of Columbia in ruling on Mudd's petition before the District Court in Florida. That distinction comes through in the court's subsequent rulings during and shortly after World War Two.

While the question of Dr. Mudd's guilt or innocence is entirely separate from the legal jurisdiction of his trial, the historical evidence supports the legality of the military commission to try Mudd and his co-defendants.

Admittedly, the history of the military commission is sordid, but it nevertheless occupies an important place in American jurisprudence. The question of whether Dr. Mudd was legally tried and convicted, like so many other controversial incidents of the Civil War, must forever remain an arguable subject. One fact is clear, however, whatever history thinks of the military tribunal and its jurisdiction: Dr. Mudd was allowed every avenue of access to the American justice system, both before the U. S. District Court (Southern District of Florida) and before the Supreme Court of the United States.

While Mudd's proponents may be unhappy with the decisions rendered by the judicial system, they cannot claim that Mudd was denied due process following his conviction. The good doctor had his day in court, both military and civil, and despite the concerted efforts and good intentions of his defenders—his name is still Mudd.

APPENDIX

1

STATEMENT OF SAMUEL A. MUDD.
VOLUNTARY STATEMENT,
UNDATED, IN MUDD'S OWN HANDWRITING.

I reside in Charles County, Maryland, near Bryantown, about 25 miles from Washington. My house is, I suppose, between 18 & 20 miles from the nearest point on the Potomac river, and about 60 or 70 miles from the west shore of the Chesapeake. I am a physician by profession, and have been practicing some 9 years, having graduated in 1856 in Baltimore.

I first heard of the assassination of President Lincoln on Saturday afternoon (April 15) about two or three o'clock in the afternoon.

There are two or three physicians besides myself living in that immediate neighborhood. The village in which I live is a very small one, having only some 8 or 10 houses in it.

About 4 o'clock on Saturday morning, the 15th, two persons came to my house and commenced rapping very loudly at the door. I was very much alarmed at this, fearing it might be somebody who had come there not for any good purpose, and hesitated at first about going down. On their knocking very heavily the second time, I aroused my wife, and we conferred with one another a moment as to who should go to the door. She thought she had better go as it might be some one who came there with an evil intent. Knowing her nervous nature, however, I determined it would be better for me to go. I, therefore, concluded to do so. Before opening the door, however, I inquired who was there. They told me two strangers from St. Marys Co. who were on their way to Washington; but that the horse of one of them had fallen, and broken the rider's leg. Satisfying myself of the correctness of the statement of one of them having received an injury, by going to a window & seeing one of them in distress, I went and opened the door.

I took them into the parlor, and laid the injured man on the sofa, until I could get a light, when I took him upstairs. His friend urged me to attend to his leg as soon as possible, as they were very anxious to get to Washington ; and then it is my impression he enquired (sic) if they could not reach some point on the Potomac where they could get a boat to Washington.

I examined the injured leg, but did not give it a very thorough examination owing to the parties wanting it attended to in such haste. My examination was sufficiently thorough, however, to enable me to discover that there was one bone broken about two inches above the ankle joint—what we call a "direct fracture." In setting the limb, having no splinters, or anything of that sort at hand, I was compelled to cut up an old band-box and use it. I do not remember of their having assigned any reason for their great haste—other than that they had made an early start and were anxious to get to Washington as soon as possible.

As regard the personal appearance of these two men, one was a very small one. I should call him a well grown boy. He looked to be about 17 or 18—to be a boy who had never yet shaved. The other was a man of medium size, with black hair. He had whiskers, and also a moustache.

A photograph of Booth was afterwards shown me by a detective, but I did not observe any resemblance between the two men, though I must say that I have very often been shown likenesses of intimate friends, and failed to recognize them by their pictures. The last man I have described had a black streak down the side of his face.

These men remained at my house until 4 & 5 o'clock in the afternoon. I never saw either of the parties before, nor can I conceive who sent them to my house. They themselves gave me no intimation on the subject.

The man whose leg was broken had on a dark suit but I cannot tell whether he had on pants, coat & vest of the same material and color, or not. The injured man had very little to say. He had a heavy shawl which he kept around him; and he seemed to be laboring under considerable nervousness, or pain.

I was at home pretty much all day, and was in the room where they were at short intervals. The reason I took them upstairs was because I had no room downstairs. Including the entry recently built between the house and the kitchen, and the kitchen itself, there are five rooms on the lower floor, which is occupied by myself and wife.

I had very little conversation with these men during the day, though one (the smaller) seemed to be quite communicative, and well acquainted through out the whole neighborhood. Nothing was said by them leading me to infer that they had been engaged in any such deed as this assassination.

The small one also had on a dark suit, with black hair.

After the injured man had got off of his horse, the other one asked me if I could not have the two horses stabled, as one of them would not suffer herself to be hitched. I went after the boy, and he held them until the boy came.

I did not see the parties when they left in the afternoon. The small one said he would not need any one to assist him in putting the injured man on the horse as he had before put him on at the time he broke his leg; so I did not go out.

My family at this time consisted of my wife, four children, a widow lady, and a sister-in-law. There are three working hands on the place—two white and one colored. I think my wife saw them for a short time after dinner, when she went up to know whether they would have anything more, or desired any particular diet. I do not think any others of the family saw them.

They requested me to have a pair of crutches made after I set the leg when I got two arm pieces and whittled them out as best I could. I afterwards gave them to the old man who works on the farm to put a stick in.

They paid me $25 for my services, which they rather pressed me to accept. I told them a small fee would answer.

Before they left they inquired the way to the Rev. Wilmer's, an acquaintance of mine, who resides not far from Beantown. His house is about five miles from mine, round the road, and about 4 directly across. I think they took the road across as they inquired for the nearest road. He is regarded by neighbors as a Union man. I have always called myself a Union man, though I have never voted with the administration party. I have never heard any expression from my neighbors as to what they thought of me in that respect.

I do not think any of my neighbors saw these men at my house. I think I first communicated the fact of these men stopping at my house under these circumstances to Mr. John F. Hardy, and Frances Farrell. It was on Saturday evening when I did so if my memory serves me right.

This injured man had boots on, but whether he had spurs on or not I dismember. I had to cut the boot from the injured limb. This boot he left, and it is now in possession of the military authorities.

The names given by these parties—the young man Henson, and the other Tyson or Tyser. There are some Hansons down in our neighborhood who are regularly called Hensons.

I only saw one of these horses. That one was a small bay mare, with a natural tail as far as I could observe. I did not notice any white scars, or spots about him. This horse was a very lively one.

The older of these men I should judge to be about 30 or 35 years of age.

I first heard of the assassination of President Lincoln at Bryantown.

The injured man after having his leg set seemed to suffer a good deal of pain, and said he did not think he would be able to travel on horseback, and desired to get a carriage, buggy, or something of the sort that he might be enabled to continue his journey. I told him I had nothing of the sort, but that perhaps, he might get an old carriage from my father, and that as I was going to ride out that afternoon, the young man might go over there with me, and see if he could do so. After dinner, the young man ordered the bay mare, and then we rode over to my father's together. We found my father out, but saw my brother who was getting his horse ready to go to the Post Office, or to church. I asked him if he could lend a carriage. He said the carriage he had was old & very much out of repair, and unfit to travel in, any distance. While I was holding this conversation with my brother this young man stood just behind a house in front of the shed where I was engaged in talking.

My brother not being willing to take the responsibility of lending this carriage, the young man said he would go to Bryantown, and endeavor to get a conveyance there. He started off at a pretty fair gallop and I after him. He soon got a good distance ahead of me as his horse was quite a sprightly one, while mine was a very dull one. When he got a mile and a half beyond my father's house, he abruptly turned round and came back, meeting me as he did so. He seemed to be engaged in deep thought. As he passed me he observed, "I believe I will get my friend to go to Rev. Dr. Wilmer's on horseback." He, therefore, did not go to Bryantown—at least with me. My object in going there was to purchase some articles which were needed by the family; and I thought I would at the same time see about some nails that were intended for immediate use. I purchased at Mr. Beans some calico & some pepper, for which I paid him. I got back to the house between 4 & 5 o'clock. The two men were just getting ready to start when I got back. It was about 12 o'clock when we had dinner. One of the men, the young one, ate dinner with me. The other one had his dinner sent to him.

I was not where I could see these men mount their horses at the time of their departure. I was down at the front of my place below the swamp. In describing the way to Rev. Wilmer's I told them that in going across this swamp there would be but one fence to pull down between that place and the barn, which would lead them to the place where they desired to go.

No suspicion was aroused in my mind of anything being wrong with regard to these men. After I had heard of the assassination, and began to have suspicion as to these two men being in some way connected with it, a little circumstance occurred to me as confirmatory of such suspicions & which I had not thought of before. It was this. After breakfast the older one asked for a razor and some soap; which he got; and on my giving him the articles which I had prepared, a short time afterward, I noticed that his moustache had disappeared.

The pantaloons of this man were covered with mud in many places; and the appearance of his clothes would in other respects indicate that he had been riding very rapidly.

I mentioned my suspicion of these men, and the circumstance of the moustache being removed, the next morning to a "brother" physician, a relative of mine, Dr. Geo. Mudd and I think also to Mr. Wm. Mudd and Mr. T. L. Gardiner.

The injured man had a belt with two revolvers in it concealed under his clothing, which I discovered when he got into bed after having his wound dressed. I did not discover whether the other one was armed or not.

Appendix

STATEMENT DRAFTED BY COLONEL *H. H. WELLS* AFTER THE FRIDAY, *APRIL 21, 1865*, INTERROGATION OF DR. *MUDD* AND PRESENTED TO HIM ON SATURDAY, *APRIL 22, 1865* FOR APPROVAL AND SIGNATURE. KNOWN AS THE *WELLS* OR SECOND STATEMENT.

Statement of Dr. S. A. Mudd
In the matter of the murder of the President
April 21, 1865
Bryantown, Md. April 21, 1865

Dr. S. A. Mudd, residing 4 miles north of Bryantown, Maryland, being duly sworn deposes and says:

Last Saturday morning, April 15th, about four o'clock, two men called at my house and knocked very loudly. I was aroused by the noise, and as it was such an unusual thing for persons to knock so loudly, I took the precaution of asking who were there before opening the door. After they had knocked twice more, I opened the door, but before doing so they told me they were two strangers on their way to Washington, that one of their horses had fallen by which one of the men had broken his leg. On opening the door, I found two men, one on a horse led by the other man who had tied his horse to a tree near by. I aided the man in getting off of his horse and into the house, and laid him on a sofa in my parlor. After getting a light, I assisted him in getting upstairs where there were two beds, one of which he took. He seemed to be very much injured in the back, and complained very much of it. I did not see his face at all. He seemed to be tremulous and not inclined to talk, and had his cloak thrown around his head and seemed inclined to sleep, as I thought in order to ease himself, and every now and then he would groan pretty heavily. I had no proper paste-board for making splints, and went and got an old band-box and made one of it; and as he wanted it done hastily, I hurried more than I otherwise would. He wanted me to fix it up anyway, as he said he wanted to get back, or get home and have it done by a regular physician. I then took a piece of the band-box and split it in half, doubled it at right angles, and took some past (sic) and pasted it into a splint. On examination, I found there was a straight fracture of the tibia about two inches above the ankle. My examination was quite short, and I did not find the adjoining bone fractured in any way. I do not regard it a peculiarly painful or dangerous wound; there was nothing resembling a compound fracture. I do not suppose I was more than three-quarters of an hour in making the examination of the wound and applying the splint. He continued still to suffer, and complained of severe pain in the back, especially when being moved. In my opinion, pain in the back may originate from riding; I judge that in this case it originated from his fall and also from riding, as he seemed to be prostrated. He sometimes breathed very shortly and as if exhausted. He was a man, I should suppose about five feet ten inches high, and appeared to be pretty well made, but he had a heavy shawl on all the time. I suppose he would weigh 150 or 160 pounds. His hair was black and seemed to be somewhat inclined to curl; it was long. He had a pretty full forehead and his skin was fair. He was very pale when I saw him, and appeared as if accustomed to in-door rather than out-door life. I do not know how to describe his skin exactly but I should think he might be classed as dark, and his paleness might be attributed to receiving the injury. I did not observe his hand to see if it was small or large. I have been shown the photograph of J. Wilkes Booth and I should not think that this was the man from any resemblance to the photograph, but from other causes I have every reason to believe that he is the man whose leg I dressed as above stated.

In order to examine and operate upon his leg, I had occasion to cut his boot longitudinally in front of the instep. It seems that when he left my house, this boot was left behind. Yesterday morning my attention was called to this boot which is a long and top-boot. On making an examination of it, I find written on the inside in apparently a German hand, what I take to be "Henry Luz, maker 445 Broadway, J. Wilkes." I did not notice the writing in this boot until my attention was called to it by Lieutenant Lovett. (Boot produced and identified by deponent as the one taken from the leg of the wounded man.)

I have seen J. Wilkes Booth. I was introduced to him by Mr. J. C. Thompson, a son-in-law of Dr. William Queen, in November or December last. Mr. Thompson resides with his father-in-law, and his place is about five miles southwesterly from Bryantown, near the lower edge of what is known as Zechiah Swamp. Mr. Thompson told me at the time that Booth was looking out for lands in this neighborhood or in this county, he said he was not very particular where, if he could get such a lot as he wanted, whether it was in Charles, Prince George, or Saint Marys county; and Booth inquired if I knew any parties in this neighborhood who had any fine horses for sale. I told him there was a neighbor of mine who had some very fine traveling horses, and he said he thought if he could purchase one reasonable he would do so, and would ride up to Washington on him instead of riding in the stage. The next evening he rode to my house and staid with me that night, and the next morning he purchased a rather old horse, but a very fine mover of Mr. George Gardiner, Sr., who resides but a short distance from my house. I would know the horse if I should see him again. He is a darkish bay horse, not bright bay, with a tolerably large head and had a defect in one eye. Booth gave eighty dollars for the horse. I have never seen Booth since that time to my knowledge until last Saturday night.

When I assisted the wounded man into my house on Saturday morning last, the other party with him who appeared to be very youthful, took charge of the horse and said he would keep it and the other one until they could be put in the stable. As soon as I could I woke my colored man Frank Washington, and sent him out to put the horses in the stable, and the young man came into the house. After setting the wounded man's leg the best I could for the time, I think I walked around to my farm-yard and gave some directions, when I returned breakfast was ready; and this young man was up and knocking about. I asked him to come to breakfast. He did so, but the other man remained up stairs in bed. I did not know who this young man was, but he remarked that he had seen me. He appeared to be a very fast young man and was very talkative. He was about five feet two or three inches high I would not be positive as to his height. He had a smooth face and appeared as if he had never shaved, his hair was black; and I should consider his complexion dark. I did not notice his eyes very particularly. He wore a dark-colored business coat. I have seen the photograph of Harold, but I do not recognize it as that of the young man. He seemed to be well acquainted throughout the whole country, and I asked his name; he gave it as Henson, and that of the wounded man as Tyser or Tyson. I did not hear either of them address the other by the first name.

The only thing that excited my suspicions on reflecting upon these circumstances was that after breakfast, when I was about to leave for my farm-work, this young man asked me if I had a razor about the house that his friend desired to take a shave, as perhaps he would feel better. I had noticed that the wounded man had whiskers and a moustache when he came into the house. After dinner, I went to see the patient and although he kept his face partly turned away from me I noticed that he had lost his moustache, but still retained his whiskers. I did not pay sufficient attention to his beard to determine whether it was false or natural.

This young man asked me if I could fix up clumsily some crutches for his friend to hobble along with, and I went down to the old Englishman I had had there who had a saw and augur and he and I made a rude pair of crutches out of a piece of plank and sent them to him. This young man mentioned the names of several parties in this neighborhood whom he knew; among others, several here in Bryantown. He mentioned being in the store of William Moore; he did not say when. I think he said he knew Bean, who kept store here; and he knew very well Len Roby, Rufus Roby, & Major James Thomas, Sr. He inquired the way from my house to Bryantown, although he represented in the morning that they had come from Bryantown. He said he knew Parson Wilmer, who lives at a place called Piney Church, he said also that they had met two persons, a lady and gentleman, walking somewhere near Bryantown that morning, and inquired of them the way to my house, and that they also met a negro, but did not state where & that they also inquired of him the way to my place.

I saw only one of the horses which these men rode to my house. She was a bay mare, moderately long tail, dark mane and tail. I won't be certain whether she had a star in the forehead or not, she appeared to be a meddlesome, high-spirited animal. I saw her after dinner, between twelve and one o'clock, when this young man and I rode over to my father's place in order to see if we could get a carriage for the wounded man; but I found that the carriages were all out of repair except one and we could not get that one. He then concluded to go to Bryantown for a conveyance to get his friend over as far as his friend's Mr. Wilmer's. I then went down to Mr. Hardy's, and was in conversation with him fully an hour when I returned home leisurely, and found the two men were just in the act of leaving. The young man inquired of me the nearest way to Mr. Wilmer's. I told them there were two ways; one was by the public road leading by Beantown; the other led across the swamp directly across from me by which they could save a mile both are easterly. This road from my house is directly across in a strait (sic) line; it is not a public way, but by taking down a fence you can get through. They concluded to take this latter route, and I gave them the necessary directions. I did not see them leave my house. The man on crutches had the house when I got back, and he was some fifty to seventy yards from me when this young man came to me and began to inquire of me the direction. I do not know how or where Booth got a conveyance away from my house; he did not go in a carriage, but he undoubtedly went on horseback.

When they came there in the morning this young man said that one of the horses would not stand without tying and asked that both of them should be put in the Stable. He held one of the horses until I returned into the house with the wounded man, when I called a colored boy named Frank Washington and sent him round to take the horses to the Stable. I have also a white man named Thomas Davis, who has charge of my horses, and I judge that he saw the horses which were in the Stable during Saturday.

I judge that between four and five o'clock on Saturday afternoon they left my house. I do not know where they went, I have not been spoken to by any one for professional advice in their behalf since that time, and have not seen either of them since.

It is about four miles across from my house to Parson Wilmer's, and by the public road it is about five miles. I suppose they could go in about an hour or an hour and a half by walking their horses.

I suppose in a day or two swelling would take place in the wounded man's leg; there was very little tumifaction in the wound, and I could discover crepitation very distinctly. It would be necessary to dress it again in two or three days if it were left in a recumbent posture, but if moved at a moderate rate, I do not know as it would aggravate it very much unless it was struck by something. I do not know much about wounds of that sort; a military surgeon would know more about those things.

Sam'l. A. Mudd

Subscribed and sworn before me this
22nd day of April 1865   H. H. Wells
Col. & P. M. Genl Def. S. of P

APPENDIX

3

ANDREW JOHNSON'S PARDON OF DR. MUDD

Andrew Johnson, President of the United States of America.

To all to Whom these Presents shall come, Greeting:

Whereas, on the twenty-ninth day of June in the year 1865, Dr. Samuel A. Mudd was by the judgment of a Military Commission, convened and holden at the City of Washington, in part convicted, and in part acquitted, of the specification wherein he was inculpated in the charge for the trial of which said Military Commission was so convened and held, and which specification in its principal allegation against him, was and is in the words and figures following, to wit: "And in further prosecution of said conspiracy, the said Samuel A. Mudd did, at Washington City and within the Military Department and military lines aforesaid, on or before the sixth day of March, A. D. 1865 and on divers other days and times between that day and the twentieth day of April A. D. 1865, advise, encourage, receive, entertain, harbor and conceal, aid and assist, the said John Wilkes Booth, David E. Herold, Lewis Payne, John H. Surratt, Michael O'Laughlen, George A. Atzerodt, Mary E. Surratt and Samuel Arnold and their confederates, with knowledge of the murderous and traitorous conspiracy aforesaid, and with intent to aid, abet, and assist them in the execution thereof, and in escaping from justice after the murder of the said Abraham Lincoln, in pursuance of said conspiracy in manner aforesaid:

And whereas, upon a consideration and examination of the record of said trial and conviction and of the evidence given at said trial, I am satisfied that the guilt found by the said judgment against the Samuel A. Mudd was of receiving, entertaining, harboring, and concealing John Wilkes Booth and David E. Herold, with the intent to aid, abet and assist them in escaping from justice after the assassination of the late President of the United States, and not of any other or greater participation or complicity in said abominable crime;

And whereas, it is represented to me by respectable and intelligent members of the medical profession, that the circumstances of the surgical aid to the escaping assassin and the imputed concealment of his flight are deserving of a lenient construction as within the obligations of professional duty, and thus inadequate evidence of a guilty sympathy with the crime or the criminal;

And whereas, in other respects the evidence, imputing such guilty sympathy or purpose of aid in defeat of justice, leaves room for uncertainty as to the true measure and nature of the complicity of the said Samuel A. Mudd, in the attempted escape of said assassins;

And whereas, the sentence imposed by said Military Commission upon the said Samuel A. Mudd was that he be imprisoned at hard labor for life, and the confinement under such sentence was directed to be had in the military prison at Dry Tortugas, Florida, and the said prisoner has been hitherto, and now is, suffering the infliction of such sentence;

And whereas, upon occasion of the prevalence of the Yellow Fever at that military station, and the death by that pestilence of the medical officer of the Post, the said Samuel A. Mudd devoted himself to the care and cure of the sick, and interposed his courage and his skill to protect the garrison, otherwise without adequate medical aid, from peril and alarm, and thus, as the officers and men unite in testifying, saved many valuable lives and earned the admiration and the gratitude of all who observed or experienced his generous and faithful service to humanity;

And whereas, the surviving families and friends of the Surgeon and other officers who were the victims of the pestilence earnestly present their dying testimony to the conspicuous merit of Dr. Mudd's conduct, and their own sense of obligation to him and Lieut. Zabriskie and two hundred and ninety nine noncommissioned officers and privates stationed at the Dry Tortugas have united in presenting to my attention the praiseworthy action of the prisoner and in petitioning for his pardon;

And whereas the Medical Society of Hartford County, Maryland, of which he was an associate, have petitioned for his pardon, and thirty nine members of the Senate and House of Representatives of the Congress of the United States have also requested his pardon; Now, therefore be it known that I, Andrew Johnson, President of the United States of America, in consideration of the premises, divers other good and sufficient reasons me there unto moving, do hereby grant to the said Dr. Samuel A. Mudd a full and unconditional pardon.

In testimony thereof, I have hereunto signed my name and caused the Seal of the United States to be affixed.

Done at the City of Washington, this Eight day of February, A. D. (Seal) 1869, and the Independence of the United States the ninety third.

ANDREW JOHNSON
By the President
WILLIAM H. SEWARD
Secretary of State

APPENDIX

4

PRESIDENT JIMMY CARTER'S LETTER TO
DR. RICHARD D. MUDD, JANUARY 24, 1979.

THE WHITE HOUSE
WASHINGTON

July 24, 1979

To Dr. Richard Mudd

I am aware of your efforts to clear the name of your grandfather, Dr. Samuel Alexander Mudd, who set the broken leg of President Lincoln's assassin, John Wilkes Booth, and who was himself convicted as a conspirator in the assassination. Your persistence in these efforts, extending over more than a half century, is a tribute to your sense of familial love and dedication and is a credit to the great principles upon which our nation was founded.

Your petition and the petitions submitted to me on behalf of your grandfather by numerous members of Congress, several state legislatures, historians and private citizens have been exhaustively considered by my staff over the past two years. Regrettably, I am advised that the findings of guilt and the sentence of the military commission that tried Dr. Mudd in 1865 are binding and conclusive judgments, and that there is no authority under law by which I, as President, could set aside his conviction. All legal authority vested in the President to act in this case was exercised when President Andrew Johnson granted Dr. Mudd a full and unconditional pardon on February 8, 1869.

Nevertheless, I want to express my personal opinion that the declarations made by President Johnson in pardoning Dr. Mudd substantially discredit the validity of the military commission's judgment.

While a pardon is considered a statement of forgiveness and not innocence, the Johnson pardon goes beyond a mere absolution of the crimes for which Dr. Mudd was convicted. The pardon states that Dr. Mudd's guilt was limited to aiding the escape of President Lincoln's assassins and did not involve any other participation or complicity in the assassination plot itself—the crime for which Dr. Mudd was actually convicted. But President Johnson went on to express his doubt concerning even Dr. Mudd's criminal guilt of aiding Lincoln's assassins in their escape by stating:

"...it is represented to me by intelligent and respectable members of the medical profession that the circumstances of the surgical aid to the escaping of the assassin and the imputed concealment of his flight are deserving of a lenient construction, as within the obligations of professional duty and, thus, inadequate evidence of a guilty sympathy with the crime or the criminal;

"And...in other respects the evidence, imputing such guilty sympathy or purpose of aid in defeat of justice, leaves room for uncertainty as to the true measure and nature of the complicity of the said Samuel A. Mudd in the attempted escape of said assassins..."

A careful reading of the information provided to me about this case led to my personal agreement with the findings of President Johnson. I am hopeful that these conclusions will be given widespread circulation which will restore dignity to your grandfather's name and clear the Mudd family name of any negative connotation or implied lack of honor.

Sincerely,
signed Jimmy Carter

Appendix

President Ronald Reagan's letter to Dr. Richard D. Mudd (December 8, 1987).

THE WHITE HOUSE
WASHINGTON

December 8, 1987

Dear Dr. Mudd:

I have investigated the situation with regard to your grandfather, Dr. Samuel Alexander Mudd. I know how much you have done and the effort you've put forth to get his name cleared of the charge against him. I regret to say I've learned that, as President, there is nothing I can do. Presidential power to pardon is all that is within a President's prerogatives and that, of course, was done by President Andrew Johnson.

Believe me, I'm truly sorry I can do nothing to help you in your long crusade. In my efforts to help, I came to believe as you do that Dr. Samuel Mudd was indeed innocent of any wrongdoing. But we'll have to accept that "full unconditional pardon" is what we must settle for.

Sincerely,
signed Ronald Reagan

APPENDIX

6

"LOST" STATEMENT OF GEORGE A. ATZERODT[1],
STATEMENT OF GEO. A. ATZERODT TO PROV. MAR. MCPHAIL
IN PRESENCE OF JOHN L. SMITH ON THE NIGHT OF
MAY 1, 1865 BET. 8 & 10 PM.

James Wood[2] sometimes called Mosby boarded with Mrs. Murray an Irish woman on the corner of 9 & F St. in a three story house, front on the upper end of the P.O. and South End of Patent Office—with basement entrance on the left side going up 9th St. from Avenue. He was a little over six feet, black hair, smooth round face, gray coat black pants, & spring coat mixed with white & gray. Saw him last time on Friday evening about 5 o'ck with Booth. He sent for letters to the post office with James Hall. He was brought from New York. Surratt told me so. He said he had been a prisoner in Balte. near the depot. He was arrested for whipping a negro woman. Mosby was Wood's nick name—did not know him by any other name than mentioned. Gust. Powell now arrested in Old Capitol was one of the party. He went also by name of Gustavus Spencer, Surratt and Spencer came from Richmond, together just after it had fallen.

James Donaldson, a low chunky man about 23 or 24 years of age, small-potted, dark complexion (not very) deep plain black suit; only saw him one time & this was Wednesday previous to the murder, he was having an interview with Booth and told him to meet him on Friday eve & he replied he would and left and went up Penn. Avenue towards the Treasury building. I was under the impression he came on with Booth.

Arnold, O'Laughlin, Surratt, Harold, Booth and myself met once at a saloon or restaurant on the Aven. bet 13 & 14 St.

The Saml. Thomas registered on the morning of the 15th April at Penn Hotel, I met on my way to hotel, he was an entire Stranger to me. I left the Hotel alone on the morning of 15th of April. A Lieut. in room No. 51 will prove this. Surratt bought a boat from Dick Smoot & James Brawner living about Port Tobacco, for which they paid $300.00 and was to give one hundred Dolls. extra for taking care of it till wanted. Booth told me that Mrs. Surratt went to Surrattsville to get out the guns (Two Carbines) which had been taken to that place by Herold, This was Friday. The carriage was hired at Howards.

I saw a man named Weightman[3] who boarded at Surratt's at Post Office. he told me he had to go down the Country with Mrs. Surratt. This was on Friday, Also.

I am certain Dr. Mudd knew all about it, as Booth sent (as he told me) liquors & provisions for the trip with the President to Richmond, about two weeks before the murder to Dr. Mudd's.

Booth never said until the last night (Friday) that he intended to kill the President.

Herold came to the Kirkwood House, same evening for me to go to see Booth. I went with Herold & saw Booth. He then said he was going to kill the President and Wood, the Secy. of State. I did not believe him. This occurred in the evening about 7 1/2 o'clock. It was dark. I took a room at Kirkwood's. Both Herold & I went to the room left Herold's coat, knife, & pistol in room and never again returned to it. Booth said during the day that the thing had failed and proposed to go to Richmond & open the theatre. I am not certain but I think I stayed one night at Kirkwood's (Thursday) we were to try and get papers to Richmond from Mr. Johnson.

Booth spoke of getting the papers. He would get them out of the Theatre. Wood & Booth were apparently confidential with each other. Plenty of parties in Charles County knew of the kidnapping affair.

One of the men named Charles Yates, knew all about it, he went to Richmond during the winter he was to row the Presdt & party over.

Thos. Holborn[4] was to meet us on the road and help in the kidnapping. Bailey & Barnes knew nothing of the affair unless Booth told Bailey & he told Barnes. Booth had met Bailey on "C" St. with me. I did not meet Booth or any other of the party in Baltimore on or about the 31 of March.

Boyle[5] also killed Capt. Watkins near Annapolis last month, was one of the party, in the conspiracy.

I repeat I never knew anything about the murder.

I was intended to give assistance to the kidnapping. They come to Port Tobacco (Surratt & Booth) several times and brought me to Washington.- The pistol given me I sold or received a loan on it Saturday morng after the murder from John Caldwick[6] at Matthews & Wells, Store, High St. Georgetown. The knife I threw away just above Mrs. Canby's boarding house the night of the murder about 11 o'clock when I took my horse to stable. I had the horse out to help to take the President. I did not believe he was going to be killed, although Booth had said so. After I heard of the murder I run about the city like a crazy man.

I have not seen Arnold for some time, but saw O'Laughlin on Thursday evening, on the Avenue at Saloon near near U. S. Hotel. He told me he was going to see Booth.

Wood did not go on the street in day time for fear of arrest. When he first came to Washington he boarded at Surratt's. This was in Feby. He (Wood) went with Booth last of February to N. York.

Booth we understood paid the way. I know nothing about Canada. Wood told me he had horses in Virginia. Saml. Arnold & Mike O'Laughlin ought to know where the horses and pistols were bought.

Sam & Mike have a buggy and horse kept at stable in rear of Theatre. Booth had several horses at same place. I think the horses property was in Surratt's name. I sold one of the horses & paid part of the money to Booth and part to Herold, who said he would see Booth about it. The saddle and bridle belonging to Booth is at Penn House, where I left it. I overheard Booth when in conversation with Wood say, That he visited a chamber-maid at Seward's House & that she was pretty. He said he had a great mind to give her his diamond pin. Herold talked about powders & medicines on Friday night at Mrs. Condby's. Wood, Herold, Booth & myself were present. This was a meeting place because Wood could not go out for fear of arrest.

Kate Thompson or Kate Brown, as she was known by both names, put up at National & was well known at Penn House. She knew all about the affair. Surratt went to Richd with her last March & Gust. Howell made a trip with her to same place. This woman is about twenty yrs of age, good looking and well dressed. Black hair and eyes, round face from South Carolina & a widow.

I did not see Surratt for seven or eight days before the murder nor have I seen him since.

Miss Thompson or Brown had two large light trunks, one much larger than the other. Young Weightman at Surratts' ought to know about this woman. This remark made by me in Baltimore on the 31 of March alluded to blockade running & privateering altogether & Booth said he had money to buy a steamer & wanted me to go in it.

I was to be one of them. In this way I was going to make a pile of money.

Booth said he had met a party in N. York who would get the Prest. certain. They were going to mine the end of Kirk House, next to War Dept. They knew an entrance to accomplish it through. Spoke about getting friends of the Presdt. to get up an entertainment & they would mix in it, have a serenade &c & thus get at the Presdt. & party.

These were understood to be projects.

Booth said if he did not get him quick the N. York crowd would. Booth knew the New York party apparently by a sign. He saw Booth give some kind of sign to two parties on the Avenue who he said were from New

York. My Uncle Mr. Richter and family in Monty. Co. Md. knew nothing about the affair either before or after the occurrence & never suspected me of any thing wrong as I was in the habit of visiting and working in the neighborhood & staying with him. My father formerly owned part of the property now owned by Richter. Finis.

APPENDIX

7

AFFIDAVIT OF GEORGE W. DUTTON CONCERNING
CERTAIN STATEMENTS MADE BY
DR. SAMUEL A. MUDD, SINCE HIS TRIAL.

Camp Fry, Washington, D.C.
August 22, 1865.

Sir - I am in receipt of your communication of this date, in which you request information as regards the truthfulness of certain statements and confessions reported to have been made by Dr. Mudd while under my charge, en route to the Dry Tortugas.

In reply, I have the honor to state that my duties required me to be constantly with the prisoners, and during a conversation with Dr. Mudd, on the 22nd of July, he confessed that he knew Booth when he came to his house with Herold, on the morning after the assassination of the President; that he had known Booth for some time but was afraid to tell of his having been at his house on the 15th of April fearing that his own and the lives of his family would be endangered thereby. He also confessed that he was with Booth at the National Hotel on the evening referred to by Weichmann in his testimony; and that he came to Washington on that occasion to meet Booth by appointment, who wished to be introduced to John Surratt; that when he and Booth were going to Mrs. Surratt's house to see John Surratt, they met, on Seventh street, John Surratt, who was introduced to Booth, and they had a conversation of a private nature. I will here add that Dr. Mudd had with him a printed copy of the testimony pertaining to his trial, and I had, upon a number of occasions, referred to the same. I will also state that this confession was voluntary, and made without solicitation, threat or promise, and was made after the destination of the prisoners was communicated to them, which communication affected Dr. Mudd more than

the rest; and he frequently exclaimed, "Oh, there is now no hope for me."
"Oh, I can not live in such a place."

Please acknowledge receipt of this letter.

I am, General,very respectfully,
Your obedient servant,
George W. Dutton
Capt. Co. C, 10th Reg't. V. R. C., com'dg. Guard.

Sworn and acknowledged at Washington, D. C., this 23rd August, 1865, before me.

G. C. Thomas,
Notary Public.

APPENDIX

PARTIAL STATEMENT OF DR. MUDD IN RESPONSE TO G. W. DUTTON, FORT JEFFERSON, AUGUST 28, 1865.

1. That I confessed to having known Booth while in my house; was afraid to give information of the fact, fearing to endanger my life, or made use of any language in that connection—I positively and emphatically declare to be notoriously false.

2. That I was satisfied and willingly acquiesced in the wisdom and decision of the Military Commission who tried me, is again notoriously erroneous and false. On the contrary I charged it (the Commission) with irregularity, injustice, usurpation, and illegality. I confess to being animated at the time, but have no recollection of having apologized.

3. I did confess to a casual or accidental meeting with Booth in front of one of the hotels on Pennsylvania Avenue, Washington, D. C., on December 23rd, 1864, and not on January 15th, 1865, as testified to by Weichmann. Booth, on that occasion, desired me to give him an introduction to Surratt, from whom he said he wished to obtain a knowledge of the country around Washington, in order to be able to select a good locality for a country residence. He had the number, street, and name of John Surratt written on a card, saying to comply with his request would not detain me over five minutes. (At this time I was not aware that Surratt was a resident to Washington). I declined at first, stating that I was with a relative and friend from the country and was expecting some friends over from Baltimore, who intended going down with me to spend Christmas, and was by appointment expected to be at the Pennsylvania House by a certain hour—eight o'clock. We started down one street, and then up another, and had not gone far when we met Surratt and Weichmann.

Introductions took place, and we turned back in the direction of the hotel. Arriving there, Booth insisted on our going to his room and taking something to drink with him, which I declined for reasons mentioned; but finding that Weichmann and Surratt were disposed to accept, I yielded, remarking that I could not remain many minutes. After arriving in the room, I took the first opportunity presented to apologize to Surratt for having introduced to him Booth—a man I knew so little concerning. This conversation took place in the passage in front of the room and was not over three minutes in duration. Whilst Surratt and myself were in the hall, Booth and Weichmann were sitting on the sofa in a corner of the room looking over some Congressional documents. Surratt and myself returned and resumed our former seats (after taking drinks ordered) around a centre table, which stood midway the room and distant seven or eight feet from Booth and Weichmann. Booth remarked that he had been down in the country a few days before, and said he had not yet recovered from the fatigue. Afterward he said he had been down in Charles County, and had made me an offer for the purchase of my land, which I confirmed by an affirmative answer; and he further remarked that on his way up he lost his way and rode several miles off the track. When he said this he left his seat and came over and took a seat immediately by Surratt; taking from his pocket an old letter, he began to draw lines, in order to ascertain from Surratt the location and description of the roads. I was a mere looker on.

APPENDIX

9

REPORT OF LIEUTENANT ALEXANDER LOVETT.

Washington DC, April 29, 1865.
Major James R. O'Beirne
Provost marshal DC

Major .
I have the honor to submit the following report of service in pursuit and detection of the assassin of the President, and persons implicated in the assassination.

In accordance with your order I started on the night of Monday the 17th inst. with officers Simon Gavacan and William Williams and 9 mounted men of Provisional Cavalry and proceeded to Surattsville (sic) Prince Georges Co. Md. for the purpose of arresting any parties implicated in the late assassination. At this place we were joined by Officers Lloyd and Cottingham, left the latter at Surattsville (sic) and proceeded toward Newport Tuesday morning the 18th. Having ascertained that John M. Lloyd a resident in the vicinity, was suspected of being in complicity with the assassination, I arranged his arrest which was accomplished on Tuesday P.M. on the road between Newport and T. B. about 2 miles beyond the latter place. After his arrest, he made a partial confession to me in private of his implication in the crime, stating that he knew the whole party and to save himself would "come out" on all of them, and that though he supposed he might be hung, he would not hesitate to tell all he knew of the affair. He said he was acquainted with Booth and Harrold (sic), who had frequently visited his home before the murder, and had had their arms concealed in his (house) for a week or ten days before it was committed.

On Friday morning the 14th inst. Mrs. Sarrat (sic) called at his house and told him that the party engaged in the plot would be along that night requesting him to furnish them with the arms (secreted) with him. Booth and Harrold (sic) came along and stopped at his house between 12 and 1 o'clock that night and took the arms secreted there with him, with the exception of one piece a seven shooter carbine which Booth could not carry on account of sickness resulting from a fractured leg. His confession was much confused as he was very agitated and frightened and cried most of the time. He was left in confinement at Roby's P. O. under charge of Officer Cottingham.

We then proceeded on Wednesday the 19th to Bryantown where we obtained information which led us to suppose that Booth had his leg dressed by Dr. Samuel Mudd who resided about 4 1/2 miles distant. We started for his residence where we arrested the said Dr. Mudd. He stated that two men came to his house about daybreak on Saturday morning, April 15th, one mounted on a bay horse, and the other on a roan. One of them was assisted into his house, and requested to have his leg set, which he said had been broken by his horse falling upon him. Booth seemed very much excited and declined any further explanation of the accident. After the operation of setting the leg, the patient asked for a razor and soap and water with which he shaved off his moustache. He then asked if he could obtain a buggy anywhere in the neighborhood. Dr. Mudd tried to get a buggy from his father, but did not suceed (sic). They remained until about 3 or 4 o'clock P. M. during which time he had a pair of crutches made for the injured man. When he was helped upon his horse and in company with his accomplice was piloted through the swamp by Dr. Mudd himself. The doctor said he left them after passing through the swamp and that was the last he saw of them. Before being asked if he knew Booth, he at first denied that he did, but afterwards acknowledged that he did, having been around the neighborhood with him last fall, and in introducing to different parties, that he was with him when he purchased a horse from Squire Gardiner and that he was satisfied the injured man was Booth when he set his leg. I obtained a boot which was cut from Booth's foot in order to set his leg. Inside was the name "J. Wilkes." I took the prisoner to Bryantown and turned him over to Col. Wells commanding at that place.

I am Major Very
Respectfully
your obt. Sevt.
Alexander Lovett (signed)
1st Lt. 14th Co. 2 Bat. VRC

Official Copy
Jas. R. O'Beirne
Maj. 22d Rgt VRC
and Pro Mar. DC

10

OBITUARY OF SAMUEL A. MUDD.

Of interest in this brief biography of Mudd following his death is the statement that many residents of Charles County believed Mudd to have been a Confederate agent involved in the "forwarding of supplies and information."

Baltimore American, January 13, 1883

DR. MUDD DEAD
Wilkes Booth's Physician

The Man Who Set the Broken Leg of Lincoln's Assassin—His Trial and Sentence to the Dry Tortugas—How He Won a Pardon by His Heroism.

Dr. Samuel A. Mudd, who was sentenced to the Dry Tortugas for life for harboring J. Wilkes Booth, the assassin of President Lincoln, and who was subsequently pardoned by President Johnson, died on Wednesday last at his residence near Bryantown, Charles County, Md., after a brief illness. The career of Dr. Mudd was one of unusual interest and his name will go down in history as one of those connected with the terrible tragedy of April 14, 1865. The story of Dr. Mudd's connection with the case is as follows: On the night of April 14th, after Booth shot President Lincoln, he fled in company with Harold. As is well known, the assassin in jumping from the private box in Ford's Theatre occupied by the President, to the stage, broke his ankle. Harold stood by his side and the two fled into Charles County, Maryland. When the pursuers of the assassin, following on his trail, reached the residence of Dr. Mudd near Bryantown, two days after the shooting, the Doctor admitted to them that about daybreak on the 15th two men rode rapidly up to his house, and one alighted. The stranger asked the Doctor to set the broken ankle of his companion, and the latter was then assisted from the horse into the Doctor's house where his injury was attended to. They remained at the house during the day and departed at night fall, and Dr. Mudd always contended that this was the beginning and ending of his acquaintance with them; that he did not know who they were, and did not hear of the shooting of the President until the next Sunday. One of the witnesses at the trial of the conspirators, however, testified that when he went to Dr. Mudd's house to arrest him, on April 21st, the physician, finding that they were going to search the house, told his wife to bring down stairs an old boot leg, which had been cut open in order to get it off the injured leg of Booth. Inside of the leg was written in ink, "J. Wilkes." Later in the day Dr. Mudd admitted that the injured man was Booth, and principally on this admission he was convicted. President Johnson sentenced him, together with Spangler, Arnold, and McLaughlin, to imprisonment in the Albany penitentiary for life at hard labor, and subsequently sent them to the Dry Tortugas. While at the Dry Tortugas Dr. Mudd made several attempts to escape, and on one occasion succeeded in concealing himself in the coal hold of a British steamship outward bound. Just before the steamship sailed, however, he was discovered and sent on shore. When he had passed two years of his life therewith yellow fever became epidemic, and the island was deserted of many of the residents and physicians. Dr. Mudd then came forward, and making known his profession, volunteered to attend the sick. For several months he worked hard, and at one time was the only physician on the island who dared attend the victims of the yellow scourge. When the disease died out the residents forwarded a petition for Dr. Mudd's pardon to President Johnson. This President Johnson granted, and Dr. Mudd returned home much broken in health, and resumed the practice of his profession in Charles county, where he resided until the day of his death. During the war he had always been an unqualified sympathizer with the Confederacy, and was believed by many to have been an agent of the Confederate government in this state, for the forwarding of supplies and information. His reputation as an unqualified secessionist, and the fact that on one occasion prior to the shooting of Lincoln he attended church at Port Tobacco in company with Booth, were the principal grounds upon which public opinion was influenced against him before and after his trial. "Dr. Mudd," it was stated by a Charles County gentleman in this city last night, "certainly never contemplated the assassination of Lincoln by Booth or any of his confederates, but he did expect the abduction of Lincoln, and was heart and soul in favor of it. When Booth's vanity led him to commit the deed he of course had no intention of stopping at Mudd's house. He was bound for the south, hoping to get through to South America and thence to Spain. When the assassin's leg was broken, however, he went to Dr. Mudd, knowing he would receive help and sympathy. This was, I think, the real state of Dr. Mudd's connection with the affair." From the time the doctor was sent to the Tortugas, his wife, who with her children, continued to reside in Bryantown, with untiring perseverance never relaxed her efforts to secure the pardon of her husband. She succeeded in interesting prominent public men throughout the country in the case, and would probably have secured Dr. Mudd's release eventually if the petition from Dry Tortugas had not hastened matters. Several years ago, when the yellow fever threatened to become epidemic in the South, Dr. Mudd went to Washington, and tendered his services to the National Board of Health as a consulting physician to treat the cases, believing that his experience with the disease in the Dry Tortugas would be of much value. The Board of Health, however, declined his offer. A claim for compensation for attending the federal soldiers ill with the fever on the Dry Tortugas was filed before Congress a few years ago by Dr. Mudd, but was disallowed. Dr. Mudd was born near Bryantown, and was about 48 years of age. He leaves a wife, the sister of the late Jere Dyer, of this city, and several children. Dr. Mudd's sister was married to Mr. Dyer, his wife's brother, and now resides in this city. He leaves two brothers, now living in Charles County—Messers. J. A. Mudd and H. L. Mudd, Jr., both prominent farmers. His father, Mr. H. L. Mudd, who died about ten years ago, was formerly quite wealthy, but the enormous expenses attending the defense of his son, when he was tried, it is said swept away nearly all the property. The father of the doctor was untiring in his efforts to save his son, and engaged the best counsel to be had, among the number being the present Judge Stone, who had charge of the defense. Dr. Mudd was a cousin of Dr. George Mudd, late Republican senator and quite a prominent public man. The deceased ran for the House of Delegates with Mr. Samuel Cox on the Democratic ticket in 1877.

Photographs by Edward Steers, Jr.

The tombstone of Dr. Samuel Alexander Mudd and his wife, Sarah Frances (Dyer) Mudd in the burial ground adjacent to St. Mary's Church. In this cemetery are the graves of Dr. Mudd's father and mother, Dr. Mudd's neighbor, George Gardiner, and Dr. William Queen, a member of the Confederate underground.

APPENDIX

11

THE SAMUEL A. MUDD RELIEF ACT OF 1997
AND
H. R. 1885

105th CONGRESS
1st Session
H. R. 1885

To direct the Secretary of the Army to set aside the conviction of Dr. Samuel A. Mudd by a military commission in 1865 for aiding, abetting, and assisting the conspirators who assassinated President Abraham Lincoln.

IN THE HOUSE OF REPRESENTATIVES, June 12, 1997, Mr. Hoyer (for himself and Mr. Ewing) introduced the following bill; which was referred to the Committee on National Security - Subcommittee on Military Personnel

SECTION 1. FINDINGS.

The Congress finds the following:

(1) On June 29, 1865, Dr. Samuel A. Mudd of the State of Maryland was convicted by a military commission in Washington, D.C., of aiding, abetting, and assisting the conspirators who assassinated President Abraham Lincoln.

(2) The conviction of Dr. Mudd was based on evidence of guilt that fell so far short of meeting the prosecution's burden of proof that such conviction amounted to a denial of due process of law which was so extreme as to constitute fundamental unfairness.

(3) Because the conviction of Dr. Mudd was not based on sufficient evidence and resulted in a denial of due process of law, the Secretary of the Army should set aside the conviction.

SEC. 2. DIRECTION TO SET ASIDE CONVICTION.

The Secretary of the Army shall set aside the conviction of Dr. Samuel A. Mudd of the State of Maryland that was entered on June 29, 1865, for aiding, abetting, and assisting the conspirators who assassinated President Abraham Lincoln.

INTRODUCTION OF THE SAMUEL MUDD RELIEF ACT OF 1997

HON. STENY H. HOYER

in the House of Representatives THURSDAY, JUNE 12, 1997

Mr. HOYER: Mr. Speaker, I rise today to introduce legislation which seeks to clear the name of Dr. Samuel A. Mudd and set aside his conviction for harboring John Wilkes Booth, the assassin of President Abraham Lincoln. Due to the tremendous amount of controversy over Dr. Mudd's conviction, his case was reviewed by five high-ranking civilian employees of the Department of the Army in January, 1992. After all the testimony and evidence waspresented, the civilian panel unanimously declared Dr. Mudd innocent of the charges. However, without commenting on the facts in this case, the Acting Assistant Secretary of the Army declined to accept this decision based on jurisdictional grounds. I believe that Dr. Mudd deserves an official exoneration, and that the Department of the Army should follow the recommendations of its own civilian panel, and that of two former Presidents.

On April 14, 1865 President Lincoln was assassinated at Ford's Theater by the actor, John Wilkes Booth. Following the extensive manhunt for Booth that ensued, on April 21, 1865, Dr. Samuel Mudd, a gentleman farmer and physician, living in Southern Maryland, was arrested for 'aiding and comforting' Booth. Specifically, he was accused of setting Booth's leg which was broken when he jumped off the balcony onto the stage at Ford's Theater.

Dr. Mudd was represented by General Thomas Ewing, Jr., who served in the U.S. House of Representatives in the 1870's, representing Lancaster, OH. Because President Lincoln was also Commander in Chief, Dr. Mudd was tried before a military commission, known as the Hunter Commission. Although he was found guilty, Dr. Mudd was imprisoned, not hung as were four of Booth's alleged co-conspirators. After being imprisoned in the Dry Tortugas for 4 years, President Andrew Jackson pardoned him because of his devoted medical care of prisoners and guards in a yellow fever epidemic.

For more than 75 years now, Dr. Richard Mudd, the grandson of Dr. Samuel Mudd, has been working to have his grandfather's conviction set aside. He is now 96 years old and has devoted his entire adult life to this very important and worthy cause. His efforts to have the Department of the Army set aside the conviction have been, and continue to be, grounded in fact and have substantial support among historians throughout the Nation. Moreover, former Presidents Carter and Reagan have both written letters proclaiming their belief that Dr. Mudd was innocent.

In July, 1990, at the urging of Senator Biden, the Judge Advocate General of the U.S. Army determined that the U.S. Army Board of Correction of Military Records [ABCMR] had the jurisdiction to review such a case and to determine the feasibility of setting aside the conviction. For 2 years, the Mudd family collected historical information and prepared their case, which was presented to the Army in January, 1992. Their argument that Dr. Mudd's conviction should be set aside was based on the premise that the Army did not have jurisdiction over a civilian, who had a constitutional right to be tried by a jury of his peers in civil court. Moreover, his due process rights, they argued, had been violated because insufficient evidence of his guilt had been presented to the military commission.

Mr. Speaker, the five member board unanimously found that Dr. Mudd's conviction should be set aside and recommended such action to the Secretary of the Army. They had determined that the Hunter Commission of 1865 did not have the jurisdictional authority to try Dr. Samuel Mudd and that he had suffered a 'gross infringement of his constitutional rights.' These jurisdictional arguments were bolstered by a Supreme Court decision in 1886 (sic) that a citizen of the United States, who was not a member of the armed forces, could not be tried by the military when the civil courts are open and functioning. However, in a surprise decision in July, 1992, Acting Assistant Secretary William D. Clark declined to adopt the Board's recommendation. While this decision was appealed in August, 1992, no further action was taken until March, 1996.

In March, 1996, as over 130 years had passed since the assassination of President Lincoln, Assistant Secretary Sara Lister declined to adopt the board's recommendation to set aside Dr. Mudd's conviction, adding that her decision did not 'involve the substantive aspects of whether Dr. Mudd was actually guilty or innocent.' Rather, Assistant Secretary Lister found that it was improper to attempt to retry this case or determine the feasibility and appropriateness of a decision made over 100 years earlier. She thus found that she did not have the appropriate jurisdiction to set aside Dr. Mudd's conviction. She determined that 'It would be inappropriate for the Army to administratively correct the record of conviction or attempt to alter legal history by non-judicial means.'

However, Mr. Speaker, for those of us who believe that there is significant evidence and information proving Dr. Mudd's innocence, therefore agreeing with the ABCMR's 1992 decision, we cannot stand idly by and allow this conviction to stand. If the facts are clear and conclusive, as the ABCMR found in 1992 and as former Presidents Carter and Reagan have determined, then the Congress must act to set aside the conviction of an innocent man.

Despite the Army's claim that the appropriate time to appeal this decision was 130 years ago, we must understand the hysteria and upheaval that ensued immediately following President Lincoln's tragic assassination. It is clear that the pressure to round up and arrest all of those involved in the assassination led to a conviction that fell far short of meeting the prosecution's burden of proof requirement. Moreover, the process by which Dr. Mudd was found guilty clearly violated his constitutional right to a 'trial by jury.'

Governor Engler and state legislators from Michigan, including Senator William Van Regenmorter, and the Charles County Board of Commissioners in Maryland support efforts to have this conviction overturned. Moreover, there are hundreds of people throughout the Nation who are dedicated to seeing justice served and history recorded accurately in this case. I am introducing this legislation today with my colleague from Illinois, Representative Thomas Ewing, who himself is collaterally related to Samuel Mudd's lawyer. It directs the Secretary of the Army to set aside the conviction and specifically cites the denial of due process of law and insufficient evidence. Because Dr. Mudd was found guilty by a military court, his record can only be cleared by the U.S. Army.

Mr. Speaker, while it is clear that Dr. Mudd did set John Wilkes Booth's broken leg, there is absolutely no evidence to suggest that he was either a co-conspirator in the assassination of President Lincoln or even aware of the events which had occurred earlier that evening on Friday, April 14, 1865.

I urge my colleagues to join me in ensuring that history is recorded accurately and that our Nation's most basic individual rights, embodied in the Constitution, are not violated at any time. Dr. Samuel Mudd's name and honor and that of his family, many of whom live in my district, hangs in the balance. We ought to allow the findings and decision of the Army Board of Correction of Military Records, the most reputable and qualified entity to date which has reviewed this case, to stand, thus ending the 132-year-long disservice accorded to Dr. Samuel Mudd.

SELECTED BIBLIOGRAPHY

Since the endnotes which appear throughout this book cite all of the bibliographical sources used in this study, a source bibliography is unnecessary. Instead, a selective bibliographical listing of those books which will give the reader a full exposure to the events and persons associated with the murder of President Abraham Lincoln is presented. Also recommended is the *Surratt Courier*, a newsletter published by the Surratt Society (P.O. Box 427) in Clinton, Maryland (20735). This longstanding publication has proven to be an indispensible source of materials relating to the assassination of Abraham Lincoln not available elsewhere.

Arnold, Samuel B. *Defense and Prison Experiences of a Lincoln Conspirator.* Hattiesburg, MS: Book Farm Press, 1943.

Basler, Roy P., ed. *The Collected Works of Abraham Lincoln.* 9 vols. New Brunswick, NJ: Rutgers University Press, 1953.

Bryan, George S. *The Great American Myth.* Reprint. Chicago: Americana House, Inc., 1990.

Hanchett, William. *The Lincoln Murder Conspiracies.* Urbana, IL: University of Illinois Press, 1983.

Higdon, Hal. *The Union vs. Dr. Mudd.* Chicago: Follett, 1964.

Jones, John Paul, ed., *Dr. Mudd and the Lincoln Assassination. The Case Reopened.* Conshohocken, PA: Combined Books, 1995.

Kauffman, Michael W., ed., *Samuel Bland Arnold: Memoirs of a Lincoln Conspirater.* Bowie, MD: Heritage Press, 1997.

Jones, Thomas A. *J. Wilkes Booth.* Chicago: Laird and Lee, 1893.

Kunhardt, Dorothy Meserve, and Philip B. Kunhardt, Jr. *Twenty Days.* New York: Harper and Row, 1965.

Lattimer, John K. *Kennedy and Lincoln: Medical and Ballistic Comparisons of Their Assassinations.* New York: Harcourt Brace Jovanovich, 1980.

McHale, John E. Jr. *Dr. Samuel A. Mudd and the Lincoln Assassination.* Parsippany, NJ: Dillon Press, 1995.

Mudd, Nettie. *The Life of Dr. Samuel A. Mudd.* New York: Neale Publishing Company, 1906.

Oldroyd, Osborn H. *The Assassination of Abraham Lincoln.* Washington: 1901.

Pitman, Benn. *The Assassination of President Lincoln and the Trial of the Conspirators.* Philip Van Doren Stern: 1865. Reprint. New York: Funk and Wagnalls, 1954.

Poore, Ben Perley, ed. *The Conspiracy Trial for the Murder of the President, and the Attempt to Overthrow the Government by the Assassination of its Principal Officers.* 3 vols. New York: Arno Press, 1972.

Roscoe, Theodore. *The Web of Conspiracy.* Englewood Cliffs, NJ: Prentice-Hall, 1959.

Steers, Edward Jr. *The Escape and Capture of John Wilkes Booth.* Gettysburg, PA: Thomas Publications, 1983.

Tidwell, William A., James O. Hall and David Winfred Gaddy. *Come Retribution.* Jackson, MS: University Press of Mississippi, 1988.

Verge, Laurie, ed. *From War Department Files. Statements Made by the Alleged Lincoln Conspirators Under Examination 1865.* Clinton, MD: Surratt Society, 1980.

Weckesser, Elden C. *His Name Was Mudd.* Jefferson: McFarland and Company, 1991.

Weichmann, Louis J. *A True History of the Assassination of Abraham Lincoln and of the Conspiracy of 1865.* ed. Floyd E. Risvold, New York: Alfred A. Knopf, 1975.

The primary sources used in this study are:

The Trial Transcript, microfilm 599, sixteen reels, National Archives; The AGO Reward File, microfilm 619, four reels, National Archives; and the extensive files of James O. Hall.

NOTES

INTRODUCTION

1 Dr. Richard Dyer Mudd of Saginaw, Michigan, has devoted over seventy years to reversing the action of the military commission that tried his grandfather and found him guilty as an accomplice to John Wilkes Booth's assassination of Abraham Lincoln.

2 President Andrew Johnson issued Samuel A. Mudd a full pardon on February 8, 1869.

3 See Appendix 4.

4 See Appendix 3.

5 Clark Hughes, *Saginaw News*, December 15, 1987. Roger Mudd, while not a direct descendant of Samuel Mudd, is a collateral descendant.

6 See Appendix 5.

7 House Concurrent Resolution No. 126, Michigan legislature, *A Concurrent Resolution Expressing the Sentiment of the Michigan Legislature That Dr. Samuel A. Mudd Was Innocent of Any Complicity in the Assassination of President Abraham Lincoln*, July 17, 1973.

8 President Reagan was petitioned by other Mudd family members and not by Dr. Richard Mudd.

9 Letter from President Jimmy Carter to Dr. Richard D. Mudd, July 24, 1979, in the possession of Dr. Richard D. Mudd.

10 A presidential pardon goes beyond freeing a convicted individual or granting immunity from prosecution to one charged with a crime. It also relieves the individual of the consequences of his or her conviction. Thus, unlike a convicted felon, an individual so pardoned may vote, run for office, serve in the armed forces of the United States and enjoy all of the rights and privileges of an individual never charged or convicted of a crime. It does not, however, reverse the findings or conclusions of the individual's conviction as a result of his or her trial. In *ex parte Garland* (4 Wallace, December, 1866, 333) the Supreme Court stated that,"...in the eye of the law the offender is as innocent **as if** (emphasis added) he had never committed the offense." The court does not state that a presidential pardon views the offender as not having committed the offense. For a discussion of the meaning of a presidential pardon see Hall, James O., *Surratt Courier*, XX: No. 9, September, 1995.

11 Certain important primary documents reside in private collections, but photocopies have made their way into the public domain and public historical societies. The principal depository is the Surratt House Museum Library located in Clinton, Maryland.

CHAPTER 1

1 Fletcher's horse was named Charley. For Fletcher's account of the events on the night of April 14 see: Statement of John Fletcher, National Archives and Records Administration (hereafter abbreviated NARA), M599, reel 5, frames 414-421, and NARA, M619, reel 456, frames 299-307; also, Testimony of John Fletcher in Poore, Ben Perley, *The Conspiracy Trial for the Murder of the President*, I:326-341, New York: Arno Press, 1972, hereafter referred to as *Trial*.

2 Ibid., 328.

3 Now called the Anacostia River.

4   Testimony of Silas T. Cobb in *Trial*, I:252, and NARA, M-599, reel 4, frames 0172-0178.

5   The 22nd Army Corps occupied a series of sixty-nine forts and batteries which ringed the District of Columbia. It was responsible for protecting the city from Confederate attack. When Grant began his siege of Lee's army in front of Petersburg and Richmond, he stripped as many troops as he could from the Washington defenses where he felt they served little useful purpose. Most of the forts were now manned by skeleton crews of soldiers and invalid veterans known as the Veteran Reserve Corps.

6   Atzerodt, in fact, had not fled the city, but after wandering about, which including a trolley ride to the Navy Yard, he checked into his favorite hotel, the Pennsylvania House (also known as the Kimmel House). Rising early on Saturday morning, Atzerodt slowly made his way into Montgomery County, Maryland where he arrived at the home of his cousin Hartman Richter. Atzerodt was eventually taken into custody on Thursday, April 20. Statement of George A. Atzerodt, NARA, M-599, reel 2, frames 0045-0047.

7   The spot where Booth and Herold rendezvoused is believed to be at a point just over the District line known as Soper's Hill. It was located along the road to Surrattsville, now Clinton, Maryland. Statement of David E. Herold, NARA, M-599, reel 4, frames 0442-0485.

8   The one-eyed horse would be indirectly linked to Dr. Samuel A. Mudd who introduced Booth to its former owner, George Gardiner, Mudd's nearest neighbor. Booth purchased the horse from Gardiner in December 1864 during the second of his two known visits with Dr. Mudd in Charles County, Maryland. Statement of Samuel A. Mudd, NARA, M-599, reel 5, frames 0212-0225.

9   Letter from Michael Henry to James O'Beirne, provost marshall of the District of Columbia, July 20, 1865, in the collection of Scott A. Balthaser. Photocopy in author's files.

10   NARA, M-599, reel 15, frame 0067.

11   Testimony of David D. Dana, *Trial*, II:68. The Bryantown Tavern was known locally as the Montgomery Tavern after its proprietor.

CHAPTER 2

1   Lincoln had been a target of kidnappers and assassins from the first day of his election in the fall of 1860. As Lincoln traveled from Springfield to his inaugural in Washington in February 1861, the famous detective Alan Pinkerton had successfully aborted a plot to murder Lincoln as he passed through the city of Baltimore. Lincoln received dozens of letters threatening his life while in the White House. He kept several of these letters carefully tied with a ribbon in one of the small cubby holes in his desk, presumably for later reading.

2   Richard Taylor (1826 - 1879) distinguished himself by repulsing Major General Nathaniel P. Banks' Red River Expedition in 1864 by defeating Banks' Army of the Gulf at Mansfield and Pleasant Hill which effectively ended Banks' career in Louisiana. Taylor surrendered the last Confederate force east of the Mississippi River in May 1865.

3   The senior officer in command at Fort Donelson was the former secretary of war under President James Buchanan, John B. Floyd. Floyd's second-in-command was Confederate Brigadier General Gideon J. Pillow. Floyd decided to escape Donelson along with Pillow and turned command of the fort over to Brigadier General Simon Bolivar Buckner for purposes of the surrender. Floyd and Pillow slipped out of the fort at night and escaped under the protection of the famed Confederate cavalryman, Nathan Bedford Forrest.

4   Louthan, Henry T., "A Proposed Abduction of Lincoln," *Confederate Veteran*, June 1908, 157-158.

5   Ibid.,158.

6   The Soldiers' Home was located approximately three miles due north of the Capitol building situated in the rolling countryside outside the city proper. Lincoln, as James Buchanan before him, moved his family to a cottage at Soldiers' Home each year to avoid the hot, humid and disease-laden city during the summer months. The Lincolns spent nearly a fourth of their tenure in Washington living at the Home.

7   Taylor apparently crossed the Potomac River from the Virginia side using one of the two main routes the Confederates secured to move between Richmond and Washington. It was the very same route which Booth had planned to use in his abduction escape and did use in his own escape effort.

8   Louthan, 157.

9   Ibid., 158.

10   Ibid., 158.

11   Tidwell, William A., James O. Hall and David Winfred Gaddy, *Come Retribution: The Confederate Secret Service and the Assassination of Lincoln,* Jackson and London: University Press of Mississippi, 1988.

12   Lincoln himself doubted his reelection chances and documented his reservations by writing a note to the effect that it was not likely that his administration would be reelected. Lincoln asked each of his cabinet members to sign the note *in camera* and carefully put it away to be read at a later date should his feelings come true. Of course, he was wrong as were the naysayers who sought his replacement as the Republican candidate in 1864.

13   Hampton succeeded Major General J.E.B. Stuart to command of the Cavalry Corps of the Army of Northern Virginia following Stuart's death at Yellow Tavern on May 12, 1864. Hampton was only one of three civilians without formal military training (Richard Taylor being the second) to attain the rank of lieutenant general in the Confederate army.

14   Brennan, John C., "General Bradley T. Johnson's Plan to Abduct President Lincoln," *Chronicles of St. Mary's,* 22:413-424, 1974. Also Johnson, Bradley T., "My Ride Around Baltimore in Eighteen Hundred and Sixty-Four," *Cavalry Journal,* September 1889, 250-260.

15   White's Ford was located substantially west of the District near Poolesville in Montgomery County, Maryland, and served as a major crossing point for Confederates from Virginia into Maryland. Mosby and certain of his command had crossed into Montgomery County here on several occasions.

16   Soldiers' Home consisted of a large main hall which housed the old inmates and three residences or cottages which normally housed the Home's administrators. The Lincolns stayed in the largest cottage named for Major Robert Anderson of Sumter fame who had been the Home's first administrator. The Stanton family occasionally stayed in a smaller cottage previously used by James Buchanan as his summer retreat.

17   Gautier's Restaurant was located on Pennsylvania Avenue near Twelfth Street, a half block from the Kirkwood Hotel and three blocks from Ford's Theatre.

18   Arnold, Samuel B., *Defense of a Lincoln Conspirator,* Hattiesburg, Mississippi: Book Farm, 1943.

19   Lincoln canceled his trip to Campbell Hospital at the urging of Indiana Governor Oliver P. Morton so that Lincoln could accompany Morton to the National Hotel where Morton and Lincoln received the captured flag from the 142nd Indiana Volunteer Infantry Regiment.

20 Washington *Evening Star*, March 18, 1865.
21 Atzerodt, *Lost Confession*. On May 1, 1865, while in custody at the Washington Arsenal, George Atzerodt gave a seven page statement to Baltimore Provost Marshal James McPhail. This statement, known today as the "Lost Confession," subsequently disappeared only to resurface in 1977. Joan L. Chaconas, past president of the Surratt Society, discovered the statement among the private papers of Captain William E. Doster, the court-appointed defense attorney for Atzerodt. A photocopy of the statement was secured. Subsequently the statement was sold at auction and resides in a private collection. Hereafter referred to as Atzerodt, *Lost Confession*. See Tidwell, William A., James O. Hall and David Winfred Gaddy, *Come Retribution*, Jackson: University Press of Mississippi, 1988, 416-418, for a full description of circumstances surrounding Atzerodt's lost confession. See Appendix 6 for full text.
22 Seward was recovering from a serious accident in which he had been thrown from his carriage and injured his neck nine days prior to the attempt on his life.
23 Testimony of Robert R. Jones, *Trial*, I: 110.
24 John T. Ford, owner of the theater, was away on business and not present when Booth visited the theater.
25 While visiting the theater that morning, Booth prepared for his murder attempt by hiding a piece of wood from a music stand and cutting a small hole in the plaster wall inside the outer box door. He would wedge the length of wood between the door and the wall securing it in the notch so that the door could not be forced open from the outside. Booth in effect, was locking himself inside the box with Lincoln and his guests.
26 This assumes that the power structure in Washington would be willing to deal for Lincoln. There are some who believe that getting Lincoln out of the way would result in an even harsher posture with the Confederate government and would result in federal authorities dragging their collective feet.
27 This became the justification for trying the accused conspirators before a military tribunal. See Speed, James, *Opinion of the Constitutional Power of the Military to Try and Execute the Assassins of the President*. Government Printing Office, Washington, 1865.
28 Louthan, Henry T., *Confederate Veteran*, 157 - 158.
29 Samuel Arnold, Michael O'Laughlen and Henry Atzerodt (brother to George Atzerodt, see NARA, M-599, reel 7, frame 0006, folder 2, containing a letter from Henry Atzerodt to George Atzerodt which is addressed to Dear Brother) were all members of Johnson's First Maryland Infantry and would have undoubtedly been among the chosen one hundred. See Brennan.
30 Gaddy, David W. "The Surratt Tavern — A Confederate "Safe House?"." *In Pursuit of...Continuing Research in the Field of the Lincoln Assassination*, Surratt Society, 1990, 129. This important document was discovered by Erick F. Davis among various Confederate papers in the National Archives.
31 Mudd's importance was to this second group, facilitating the escape to Virginia and hopefully, Richmond.

CHAPTER 3

1 "Thus Always to Tyrants," the motto of the state of Virginia. Booth is reported to have shouted this from the box immediately after firing the fatal shot. Others testified that he shouted from the stage after leaping from the box.
2 Statement of George A. Atzerodt, NARA, M-599, reel 3, frames 0596-0602.
3 Atzerodt, *Lost Confession*.

4   General Grant had originally accepted the president's invitation but then backed out after discussing it with Mrs. Grant. Julia Grant had suffered the insults of Mary Lincoln a month earlier during a visit to City Point at a military review and did not wish to experience such wrath again. The Grants left in the afternoon for New Jersey where their children were in school, and sent their regrets to the Lincolns. Booth knew this, having seen the Grants leave earlier in the day according to the statement of John Matthews. Grant, along with Major General Ambrose Burnside, had accompanied Lincoln to a performance at Ford's Theatre a month earlier where they saw Booth's brother-in-law, John Sleeper Clarke, star in a farce entitled, "Love In Livery." See *Evening Star*, "The President and General Grant at Ford's," February 11, 1865, 2, col. 6.

5   Statement of David Herold, NARA, M-599, reel 4, frames 0442-85. This statement is reproduced in *From War Department Files*, Laurie Verge, ed., Surratt Society, Clinton, Maryland, 1980, 1-21.

6   Powell would run from the house after thinking he had murdered most of the residents including Seward, and mounting his horse, ride toward the Navy Yard Bridge. He apparently became lost and abandoned his horse in the eastern part of the city and is believed to have hidden out in Glenwood Cemetery or Congressional Cemetery not far from the bridge. When arrested on Monday, April 17, at Mary Surratt's boarding house, Powell was carrying a pickax suggesting he had been hiding out in one of the two nearby cemeteries where such implements may have been available.

7   Edman Spangler was accused of being an accomplice in Booth's crime and received a sentence of six years' imprisonment. Witnesses testified that Spangler quickly shut the rear door of Ford's after Booth dashed through it, thus aiding Booth's escape. Spangler served three and a half years of his sentence together with Dr. Mudd, Samuel Arnold and Michael O'Laughlen at Fort Jefferson before being pardoned in 1869 by Andrew Johnson. Spangler returned to the farm of Dr. Mudd where he lived for the next six years before dying in 1875. He lies buried in the old cemetery of St. Peters Church, the church attended by Dr. Mudd.

8   Joseph "Peanuts" Burroughs was a young boy who served as a "gopher" running various errands for the staff and selling peanuts on the sidewalk in front of the theater, hence the name, "Peanuts" Burroughs. For his actions on the night of April 14, 1865, see *Trial*, I, 225-233.

9   Earlier in the day, Ford had the temporary partition separating the two boxes removed creating a single large box instead of two smaller boxes.

10   Lincoln was accompanied to the theater that night by John F. Parker, a member of the D.C. police force who served as one of his personal bodyguards. Parker was absent at the time Booth approached the box, but Lincoln's personal valet, Charles Forbes was sitting in the seat closest to the door. Parker was later charged by a police board of inquiry for failure to protect the president, but was acquitted of all charges and reinstated on the police force. Ironically, Forbes was a signatory to the charges leveled against Parker for "neglect of duty." Photocopy in author's files, original in a private collection.

11   Testimony of Theodore McGowan, *Trial*, I:194. For further details, see statement of Captain T. McGowen, NARA, M-599, reel 5, frame 0317 - 0322; and statement of Lieutenant A. M. Crawford, NARA, M-599, reel 7, frame 0481 - 0483. Both were seated near the door to the presidential box and saw Booth enter.

12   Translates to "Thus always to tyrants," the motto of the state of Virginia. Historical legend has Booth shouting this famous motto from the stage after his

jump from the box, but testimony given within a few hours of the event have him shouting the motto from the box after firing the fatal shot. Others claim he shouted something to the effect that, " The South is avenged!" from the stage after he gathered himself up following his dramatic jump. For a detailed discusson of eyewitness accounts of Booth's words see, Good, Timothy S., ed., *We Saw Lincoln Shot. One Hundred Eyewitness Accounts*, Jackson: University Press of Mississippi, 1995.

13   A national standard was originally on display as the flag which "avenged the martyred President" by ensnaring Booth thus causing him to land off balance and break his leg. That flag has disappeared, but a photograph of it while on display still exists in the National Park Service collection (Oldroyd Collection) which adds further to the mystery of which flag caught Booth and led him to seek medical assistance from Dr. Mudd.

14   For an alternate account of how Booth broke his leg see, Kauffman, Michael W., "Booth's Escape Route: Lincoln's Assassin On The Run," *Blue & Gray Magazine*, June, 1990, 17.

15   See testimony of Silas T. Cobb in *Trial*, Vol. I, 1865, 251.

16   Beantown is within the same neighborhood where Dr. Mudd's farm was located. Mudd stated that he lived "...near Bryantown," which was situated approximately five miles due south of Mudd's house. Beantown was situated approximately four miles due west of Mudd's.

17   Herold gave his name as "Smith" and according to Cobb, "...made use of a rather indelicate expression, and said he had been in bad company." Ibid., 252.

18   Forts Wagner and Baker were situated at the top of Good Hope Road in Uniontown. Booth and Herold probably passed between them shortly after eleven o'clock well in advance of any effort to alert the military forces to secure all avenues out of the city. The two fugitives were well ahead of the authorities who were still somewhat disorganized by the catastrophic events still unfolding back in the District. Fort Baker was in telegraphic communication with the military telegraph office, and around midnight began receiving messages from the military office in Washington. By that time Booth and Herold were out into Prince George's County, Maryland, and on the way to Surrattsville. See NARA, RG 393, Pt.2, 186.

19   For financial reasons, Mary Surratt decided to lease the tavern and move herself and young daughter Anna to the house she owned in Washington, D.C. Located at 541 H Street, within walking distance of Ford's Theatre, the house was used as a safe house for Confederate agents as well as a money-earning boarding house. Powell and Atzerodt stayed here at various times during the days leading up to that fateful Friday.

20   Gaddy, 129.

21   Mary Surratt made two visits to the tavern in early April 1865: the first on April 11 and the second on April 14, the day of the assassination. On April 14, she carried a package to Lloyd from Booth which later proved to be field glasses picked up by Booth later that night. During both of Mary Surratt's visits, John M. Lloyd testified that she had given him instructions to have ready items which would be picked up by persons later on. It was Lloyd's testimony along with Booth's numerous visits to the boarding house that convinced the members of the tribunal that Mary Surratt was an accomplice of Booth.

22   *Trial*, I:118.

23   Mary Surratt had met with Booth around noon on Friday and Booth asked her to take a small package to John Lloyd which proved to be a pair of field glasses. According to Lloyd, Mary Surratt also: "...told me to have those shooting-irons

ready that night, - there would be some parties call for them." Testimony of
John M. Lloyd, *Trial*, I:118. It is this testimony in particular that sent Mary to
the gallows.

24 Lloyd hid the second carbine in the tavern by carefully lowering it by an attached rope in the wall separating the kitchen from the dining room where it
was found by soldiers searching the tavern.

25 *Trial*, I:119.

CHAPTER 4

1 Two statements were given by Mudd. The first statement, undated and referred to as Mudd's "voluntary" statement, was written in Mudd's own hand
and given to Colonel H.H. Wells. The second statement was prepared by
Wells on April 21 following his interview with Mudd, and was certified by
Mudd with his signature, dated April 22, 1865. NARA, M-599, reel 5, frames
0212-0239. See Appendix 2.

2 In particular, Mudd claimed to have been anxious about a Confederate guerrilla who had frequented the area and whose demeanor was more that of a
lawless renegade than that of a Southern freedom fighter. John H. Boyle, Jr.
alias the Guerrilla Boyle, had appointed himself a Confederate enforcer in southern Maryland. He had murdered Union Captain Thomas W. Watkins on March
25, 1865 in his own home only three weeks prior to the loud knock on Mudd's
door. See Hall, James O., "The Guerrilla Boyle," *The Maryland Independent*,
May 7 and May 14, 1975, 1.

3 Voluntary Statement of Dr. S. A. Mudd. NARA, M-599, reel 5, frames 0226
through 0239. Reproduced by the Surratt Society. From *War Department Files.
Statements Made By The Alleged Lincoln Conspirators Under Examination, 1865.*
Surratt Society, 1980.

4 According to Mudd's statement he had three men as "working hands" on his
farm, "two white and one colored." Mudd originally owned six slaves prior to
Maryland's emancipation act in 1864.

5 On Tuesday, April 18, Lieutenant Alexander Lovett and his men visited the
Mudd farm to question Dr. Mudd. Mudd was working in the field and while
Lovett waited for him to return he questioned Francis Mudd, the doctor's wife.
Mrs. Mudd stated that as the injured man and his friend were coming down
the staircase to leave the house on Saturday afternoon (Dr. Mudd still being
absent in Bryantown) she noticed the whiskers of the injured man seemed to
come loose and fall away from one side of his face leading her to conclude that
they were false whiskers. Testimony of Alexander Lovett, *Trial*, I:263. Also:
NARA, War Department Records, file "L", R.B.P. 59, JAO.

6 Mr. Henson , according to Mudd's voluntary statement, was "... well acquainted
through out the whole neighborhood," and again, "This young man mentioned
the names of several parties in this neighborhood whom he knew, among others, several here in Bryantown. He mentioned being in the store of William
Moore; he did not say when." Indeed, Davy Herold was very familiar with
much of southern Maryland where he spent many days hunting and lounging
about. He also was well acquainted with many of the residents of Charles
County. Herold was familiar with Bryantown and knew how to get there from
Mudd's, a fact which did not seem to spark Mudd's curiosity about the two
strangers.

7 Parson Wilmer lived approximately five miles nearly due west of Mudd's farm.
To reach Wilmer's house the two men would have to cross over the Zekiah
Swamp.

8   "I first heard of the assassination of President Lincoln at Bryantown." Voluntary Statement of Dr. S. A. Mudd, NARA, M-599, reel 5, frames 0226-0239.

9   Lewis Powell in his attack on William Seward injured several other members of the household including Frederick Seward, Secretary Seward's second oldest son who served as assistant secretary of state. Frederick received several skull injuries from Powell's beating and was not expected to live. He eventually recovered, however, as did Seward and all the other injured members of his household.

10 *Trial*, III:418.

11 *Trial*, III:432. During the trial, Hardy testified that he had seen Booth on two separate occasions in the area: once at St. Mary's Church and a second time on the road near Bryantown. See *Trial*, III:433.

12 Dr. George Mudd (1826 - 1899) was a second cousin of Sam Mudd and lived less than a mile from Bryantown. Dr. Samuel Mudd passed by Dr. George Mudd's farm on both his trip to and from Bryantown the day before when he learned of Lincoln's assassination. Dr. George Mudd was known throughout the area as a Union sympathizer unlike his cousin. Like his cousin, he was a solid member in good standing in the surrounding community.

13 *Trial*, II:386.

14 Samuel Mudd's reluctance presumably stemmed from his fear of possible retribution by Confederate guerillas that might still be roaming the area.

15 *Trial*, II:391. This is the same group of soldiers that had been sent to Bryantown by General Augur as a result of John Fletcher's revelations earlier at army headquarters.

16 Lovett was accompanied by Detectives William Williams, Joshua Lloyd , Simon Gavacan, and several soldiers.

17 *Trial*, II:258.

18 Actually Booth was twenty-six years old and Davy Herold was two months shy of his twenty-third birthday (June 16, 1842).

19 Report of Lieutenant Alexander Lovett, NARA, M-619, reel 456, frames 0488 - 0490, AGO files.

20 David Herold gave the appearance of being much younger. Almost everyone described Herold as a boy or, at best, a young man who appeared to be a boy. Herold is frequently characterized by most writers as being "slow-witted" or acting simple at times. He actually was neither. Herold was clever enough to evade making serious mistakes during his interrogation on the monitor, *Montauk*, on April 27 and handled himself rather well. See NARA, M-599, reel 4, frame 0442 - 0485.

21 *Trial*, II:259. This may have been an attempt on Mudd's part to cover the delay in notifying the authorities until Monday, April 17.

22 *Trial*, II:261.

23 Booth purchased from his neighbor George Gardiner the one-eye horse which Powell rode the night of the assassination and which soldiers found roaming stray east of the capital. This was the horse wearing Atzerodt's saddle that was shown to John Fletcher at army headquarters between midnight and two a.m.

24 See Appendix 1.

25 Booth did not have a shawl at the theater or at the Surratt House. No mention of a shawl was made by John Lloyd in his testimony nor by Davy Herold in his testimony. If Booth had "a heavy shawl" when at Mudd's, where did he get it? Either he picked up the shawl at Dr. Mudd's house or Mudd fabricated the story of a shawl to support his claim that he did not recognize the injured man as Booth.

26 See Appendix 1.
27 When Booth entered the box at Ford's Theatre he carried a small derringer and a large bowie knife. The derringer (manufactured by Henry Deringer of Philadelphia and so marked) was recovered in the box early on the morning of April 15 by William F. Kent who turned it over to Lawrence Gobright, a member of the Associated Press. Gobright turned the derringer over to police chief A. C. Richards. See *Trial of John H. Surratt*, vol. I, Government Printing Office, 1866, p. 123. If Booth had two large revolvers as Mudd stated, he must have acquired them from Davy Herold after rendevousing with him at Soper's Hill or at Dr. Mudd's house. Both revolvers were recovered at the Garrett farm and are now in the Ford Theatre Museum.
28 See Appendix 1 for full statement.
29 Importantly, Booth had indelibly tattooed the initials "JWB" on the back of his left hand between the thumb and forefinger as a young boy. This distinctive marking was known by virtually everyone that was acquainted with the famous actor, and served as a positive identifying mark of Booth.
30 Statement of Mudd. NARA, M-599, reel 5, frames 0212 -0225.
31 Colonel and provost marshal, general defenses south of the Potomac.

CHAPTER 5

1 Mudd statement to Wells, NARA, M-599, reel 5, frames 0212-0225.
2 Louis J. Weichmann was an old schoolboy chum of John Surratt's and a boarder at Mary Surratt's boarding house in Washington. Weichmann became a key government witness who proved vital to the government's case supplying considerable detail about the comings and goings of John Surratt, Booth, and Mary Surratt highly reminiscent of John Dean's testimony a century later in the Watergate case. Weichmann has been criticized and occasionally vilified by supporters of Mary Surratt and Samuel Mudd as a liar and turncoat who turned state's witness to avoid prosecution. Weichmann's testimony, however, has held steadfast against considerable challenge. See *Trial*, I:69-110, I:135-136, I:369-390, II:42-44.
3 This memorandum detailing Booth's residency at the National Hotel in 1864 and 1865 was prepared by G. W. Bunker, the clerk of the National in anticipation of his testimony at the trial. Bunker's testimony covers the months of November and December, 1864. His testimony appears in *Trial*, I:29-32. The memoranda appears in, NARA, M-599, reel 15, frames 0262-0263. The actual register of the National Hotel is missing.
4 In the David Rankin Barbee papers housed in the Georgetown University Library is a letter written by John Wilkes Booth to J. Dominick Burch, proprietor of the tavern in Bryantown requesting Burch's help in retrieving an object (believed to be a pistol) which Booth left on the stage during his round trip. The letter is dated, Washington, November 14 (1864) further placing Booth in Washington on Monday the 14th.
5 Interview of Thomas Harbin by George Alfred Townsend, Cincinnati *Enquirer*, April 18, 1892.
6 Testimony of Thomas Gardiner, *Trial*, I:364.
7 The circumstances of this visit and the sequence of events was worked out by James O. Hall and appears in the book, *Come Retribution*. Hall originally misdated Booth's visit in December by three days, but in further research established Booth's visit between December 17 and December 22. Personal communication.

8   *Trial*, III:435.
9   Ibid.
10 Affidavit of Samuel A. Mudd dated August 28, 1865 in Laughlin, Clara, *The Death of Abraham Lincoln,* New York: Doubleday, Page & Company, 1909, 215-221. See Appendix 8.
11 See Appendix 7.
12 See Appendix 8.
13 Bunker memoranda.
14 Mudd had maintained that his only connection with Booth from the beginning was Booth's interest in purchasing land in Charles County. This was clearly a cover used by Booth and Mudd to explain their meetings.
15 *Trial*, II:258.
16 According to the testimony of Mary Simms, a former Mudd slave, John Surratt had visited the Mudd home on a dozen or more occasions and dined with Mudd in his home.
17 *Trial*, I:69-71.
18 In 1870, John Surratt gave a lengthy lecture at the courthouse in Rockville, Maryland in which he detailed his relationship with Booth and the events surrounding his involvement in the proposed capture of Lincoln. Surratt's *Rockville Lecture* is reprinted in its entirety in Weichmann, Louis J., *A True History of the Assassination of Abraham Lincoln and of the Conspiracy of 1865,* edited by Floyd E. Risvold, New York: Alfred A. Knopf, 1975, 428-440.
19 It appears that Jeremiah Mudd and Samuel Mudd separated for a period during the evening hours of December 23. The Pennsylvania House (also known as the Kimmel House) was where George Atzerodt bunked on his frequent visits to Washington and where he stayed the night of the assassination.
20 The time sequences and details for Booth's second visit to Charles County in December 1864 were worked out by James O. Hall.

CHAPTER 6

1   *Trial*, I:259.
2   Mudd Statement, NARA, M-599, reel 5, frames 0226-0239.
3   Mudd Statement, NARA, M-599, reel 5, frames 0226-0239.
4   Hardy testified that he had seen Booth in the Bryantown area on two separate occasions in November and December 1864. *Trial*, III:433.
5   *Trial*, III:420.
6   Mudd's role as a mail courier for the Confederacy is revealed by Samuel Cox, Jr. in his annotations of Thomas Jones' book, *J. Wilkes Booth.* Cox writes that the reason Mudd went into Bryantown on Saturday, April 15, was to mail letters he had, "...but a short time had gotten through the contraband mail for distribution...."
7   Jones' home, "Huckleberry," along with his farm is now a Catholic retreat known as "Loyola" operated by the Jesuit order.
8   Samuel Cox was not a colonel. He had briefly served as a captain of the local militia. The title of colonel was an honorary one among inhabitants of the region.
9   Statement of Oswell Swann, NARA, M-599, reel 6, frame 0227. Swann testified that Booth and Herold arrived at his cabin about nine p.m. and asked him to lead them to the home of William Burtles, a Confederate safehouse. Booth then changed his mind and instructed Swann to lead the two men to Samuel Cox's house for which they paid Swann twelve dollars.

10 Jones, Thomas A., *J. Wilkes Booth*. Laird & Lee, 1893. The book, long out of print, has been reprinted and may be obtained from the Surratt House Museum Gift Shop located in Clinton, Maryland.

11 Booth and Herold had been hidden in a pine thicket about one mile west of Cox's house by Cox's foreman, Frank Robey. Cox told Jones where to find the two fugitives. Jones, 73.

12 Booth's escape and eventual capture is detailed in: Steers, Edward, Jr. *The Escape and Capture of John Wilkes Booth*, Gettysburg: Thomas Publications, 1992.

13 Jones, 11.

14 Jones' book with Cox's annotations resides in The Maryland Historical Society. A photocopy of the annotations was obtained by James O. Hall. Photocopies were given by Mr. Hall to the writer and are quoted here.

15 According to Cox's annotations in the Jones book, mail drops were made in, "an old cedar stump on the knoll where E. J. Collis' house now stands...." This is well below Bryantown and would not be where Mudd would have dropped his mail. It is more likely that Mudd dropped his mail in Bryantown with the local postmaster who was also loyal to the Confederate cause.

16 In 1901 Osborn H. Oldroyd interviewed Samuel Cox, Jr. and was told the same account by Cox that appears in his annotations in Jones' book. Oldroyd published the account in his book, *Assassination of Abraham Lincoln*, privately published, Washington, D.C., 1901. See pages 265-269.

17 Pittman, Ben, *The Assassination of President Lincoln and the Trial of the Conspirators*, New York: Moore, Wilstach & Baldwin, 1865. See Appendix 7.

18 This affidavit also has Mudd acknowledging Booth's second visit to Charles County in December 1864, another fact he withheld from the authorities. See: Affidavit of Samuel A. Mudd in Laughlin, 215-220. See Appendix 2.

19 The Kimmel House or Pennsylvania Hotel was the same hotel where Mudd and his cousin stayed during their December, 1864 visit to Washington at the time Mudd introduced John Surratt to Booth. A stage coach line made a regular run between Washington and St. Mary's County stopping at the Kimmel House and the Bryantown Tavern.

20 Atzerodt's flight from Washington to the home of his cousin Hartman Richter and his subsequent capture is documented in the files of the NARA, M-619, reels 455 and 456. The documents appear in a pamphlet entitled *The Escape and Capture of George A. Atzerodt* by Edward Steers, Jr. and privately printed by the Surratt House Museum, Clinton, Maryland.

21 Hartranft Letters, Special Collections, Gettysburg College, Gettysburg, PA.

22 Atzerodt, *Lost Confession*.

23 Booth and Herold finally made the Virginia shore at a point where Gambo Creek empties into the Virginia side of the Potomac. Quesenberry's home was located a short distance from Gambo Creek on another creek by the name of Machodoc Creek.

24 Jones, 109-112.

25 Dr. Richard H. Stuart is the correct spelling. While the name is frequently spelled "Stewart" in the literature and in several of the original documents in the National Archives, "Stuart" is the spelling which appears on the doctor's tombstone at his home "Cedar Grove."

26 Statement of William Lucas, NARA, M-599, reel 5, frames 0144-0147.

27 Stuart was arrested on May 5 and imprisoned in the Old Capitol Prison in Washington. Released a month later, on June 7, Stuart returned home escaping the retribution that fell on several others.

28 Statement of Richard Stuart, NARA, M-599, reel 6, frames 0205-0211.
29 Ibid., (NARA, May 6, 1865).
30 Statement of William L. Bryant, NARA, M-519, reel 4, frame 0095. The correct spelling is Stuart. The spelling Stuart, suggests the statement was taken down by sound, and not written down by Bryant.

CHAPTER 7

1   The defendants included in the charges along with Mudd were, David E. Herold, George A. Atzerodt, Lewis Powell, Michael O'Laughlen, Edward Spangler, Samuel Arnold and Mary E. Surratt. Absent from this group was John H. Surratt (missing) and John Wilkes Booth (dead).
2   *Trial*, I:19.
3   *History Rewritten: The Case of Dr. Samuel A. Mudd*, written and directed by Paul Davis and produced by Fedoruk, Light Vision Films, 1995. This eighty minute video tape does an excellent job in presenting the case of Dr. Mudd from the perspective of his advocates. Copies of this video are available from the Surratt House Museum Gift Shop, Clinton, Maryland.
4   Mudd, Nettie, *The Life of Dr. Samuel A. Mudd*, New York and Washington: Neale Publishing Company, 1906, 131-132. Reprint. Linden, TN: Continental Book Company, 1975.
5   Ibid., 350.
6   Ibid., 144.
7   Mudd Voluntary Statement, NARA, M-599, reel 5, frames 0226 - 0239.
8   Letter from Mudd to O. A. Brownson (original in O. A. Brownson collection, University of Notre Dame Archives), reproduced in Mudd, Nettie.
9   Booth kept an incriminating letter written by Samuel Arnold in his personal belongings which resulted in Arnold being convicted, and he planted his bank book in Atzerodt's room at the Kirkwood implicating him. Booth also visited the Kirkwood earlier on Friday, April 14, leaving a personal card for Andrew Johnson in an effort to implicate Johnson should Atzerodt fail as Booth suspected he might. If Booth went down, he fully expected to take others with him including Mary Surratt and John Surratt.
10 Samuel Cox, Jr., in his annotations in Thomas Jones' book, quoted Mudd as telling him, "... and now the third time, (Booth) had come with a lie upon his tongue...." This further supports the fact that Booth had visited Mudd twice before at his home and not once as Mudd previously claimed.
11 William Burtles owned a house to the east of Mudd's which served as a safe house for Confederate operatives. Booth and Herold started out for Burtles' but got lost and came across Oswell Swann who they then asked to lead them to Samuel Cox's plantation instead.
12 Lieutenant Mortimer B. Ruggles, Private Absalom Bainbridge and Private Willie Jett. The three Confederate soldiers had recently been disbanded from Mosby's command and met Booth and Herold on Monday morning on the northern side of the Rappahannock River. Willie Jett took Booth to the farm of Richard Garrett. Herold went on to Bowling Green with the three soldiers and then to the home of Joseph Clarke where he spent the night. Herold returned to the Garrett farm on the afternoon of April 25 where he stayed with Booth until members of the 16th New York Cavalry arrived early Wednesday morning, April 26.
13 *Trial*, III, 433.

CHAPTER 8

1   Lincoln, *Works*, 518-537. Lincoln used this phrase in his Annual Message to Congress (37th Congress, third session) on December 1, 1862.

2   Weckesser, Elden C., *His Name Was Mudd*, North Carolina and London: McFarland & Company, Inc., Publishers, 1991, 199.

3   Mudd escaped the gallows by a single vote. The tribunal voted to hang Mudd five votes to four, but a hanging sentence required a two-thirds majority or six votes.

4   Mudd must bear responsibility for bringing Thomas Harbin and John H. Surratt into Booth's conspiracy. It was Dr. Mudd who specifically made the introductions of these two key members of the abduction conspiracy to Booth at prearranged meetings and it was John Surratt's participation that tied his mother, Mary Surratt, into the conspiracy. Without Mudd's active role and presumed credibility with Harbin and Surratt, they might never have agreed to join in Booth's plot and Mary Surratt and the three other men with her would not have wound up on the gallows.

5   Mudd, Nettie.

6   *Rewriting History: The Case of Dr. Samuel Mudd.*

7   McHale, John E., Jr., *Dr. Samuel A. Mudd and the Lincoln Assassination*, Parsippany, NJ: Dillon Press, 1995, 43-45.

8   Weckesser, 69.

9   Hartranft Letters, Gettysburg College Library, Gettysburg, PA. Photocopies in the files of James O. Hall.

10   McHale. Dr. Richard D. Mudd holds a Master's Degree in sociology, a PhD in history, and a doctorate in medicine from Georgetown University.

11   Ibid. There have been numerous gestures over the years by various bodies to honor or at least acknowledge Dr. Samuel A. Mudd and reverse the perception of his guilt. In 1961, a special plaque was affixed at Fort Jefferson honoring the doctor's efforts in the yellow fever epidemic. Several political bodies have passed resolutions in support of Mudd's innocence and even an elementary school and hospital room have been named after him.

12   Personal communication from Dr. Richard D. Mudd.

13   Letter from President Jimmy Carter to Dr. Richard D. Mudd, July 24, 1979, in the possession of Dr. Richard D. Mudd.

14   See appendix 4.

15   Jones, John Paul, ed., *Dr. Mudd and the Lincoln Assassination. The Case Reopened.* Conshohocken, PA: Combined Books, 1995.

16   This is discussed fully in Chapter Nine.

17   As discussed in Chapter Nine, Mudd was afforded full due process in the courts following his conviction. He appealed his case to the federal court for the Southern District of Florida where it was denied. The case was then appealed to the Supreme Court of the United States where arguments were heard, but the petition was dismissed before an opinion could be issued as the plaintiffs were pardoned by President Johnson making the petition moot. Mudd was not denied his rights in the American judicial system as most claim.

18   Jones, 274.

19   Also presenting the case for Dr. Mudd was the well-known defense attorney, F. Lee Bailey. Representing the military commission were John Jay Douglass, dean of the National College of District Attorneys and professor of law, University of Houston Law Center, former commandant of the Judge Advocate General's School and past president of the Army Judge Advocates Association; and John S. Jenkins, associate dean and lecturer, George Washington Univer-

sity National Law Center, former judge advocate general of the Navy and special counsel to the secretary of the Navy.

20 Two excellent articles discussing Mudd's guilt may be found in Jones: *The Curious Case of Dr. Mudd*, by Forest J. Bowman, and *The Case Against Dr. Samuel Mudd: Why His Family's Vanity Does Not Justify Rewriting Dr. Mudd's Story*, by Andrew C. Carington and Floyd E. Risvold.

21 Jones, 117-251.

22 See Appendix 11 for Congressman Hoyer's remarks from the floor of the House, and the complete text of the bill H.R. 1885.

23 U.S. Congress, House, Committee on National Security, Subcommittee on Military Personnel, *To direct the Secretary of the Army to set aside the conviction of Dr. Samuel A. Mudd by a military commission in 1865 for aiding, abetting, and assissting the conspirators who assassinated...*, 105th Cong., 1st Sess., 12 June, 1997.

24 Ibid., Section 2., paragraphs 1 and 2.

25 James O. Hall, letter to Angela Breeck, editor, *Maryland Independent*, 15 July, 1997, author's files.

26 And, for that matter, for John H. Surratt and Mary E. Surratt.

CHAPTER 9

1 The farm house which Dr. Mudd would purchase was built in 1830 and had become known as the Rock Hill Farm by the time Mudd acquired it.

2 Mudd, Nettie.

3 Jeremiah (Jere) Dyer would later marry Samuel Mudd's sister, Mary Clare Mudd, in 1867 while Mudd was still a prisoner at Fort Jefferson in the Dry Tortugas.

4 Weckesser.

5 Thomas Dyer Mudd was the father of Dr. Richard Dyer Mudd of Saginaw Michigan. Dr. Richard Mudd has mounted a considerable effort for over seventy years to reverse the judgment of the military tribunal and exonerate his grandfather.

6 Mary Simms, Elzee Eglent, Sylvester Eglent, Melvina Washington, Milo Simms and Rachel Spencer. See *Trial*, II:150,157,159,163,170 and 341.

7 Among the men identified was Captain Walter "Watt" Bowie, a prominent Prince George's County dignitary who rode with the famous Colonel John Mosby. Bowie was shot and killed after a raid near Rockville, Maryland in May 1864 referred to by local residents as the Battle of Rickett's Run.

8 *Trial*, II:157.

9 *Trial*, II: 154.

10 Weckesser, 125.

11 McHale, 79.

12 Mudd, Nettie, 128.

13 McHale, 93.

14 A description of these items may be found in the newsletters published by the Dr. Samuel A. Mudd Society entitled, *The Committee for the Restoration of the Dr. Samuel A. Mudd House, Inc.*, Vol. 1, No.8 and Vol. 1, No. 9, September, 1980 and December, 1980 respectively.

15 In 1936, John Houston directed the movie, *Prisoner of Shark Island* starring Warner Baxter based on the life of Dr. Mudd as seen through the eyes of Hollywood. While the movie was an historical farce, it elevated Dr. Mudd to a new folk hero status, truly the victim of a hysterical and brutal United States government that turned Fort Jefferson (Shark Island) into a "Devil's Island" for the sole purpose of torturing Dr. Mudd. In the movie, Dr. Mudd is not seen fashioning cabinetry at any time.

16 McHale, 102-114. Weckesser, 174-188.

17 The pardon is dated February 8, 1869. Mudd received official notification at Fort Jefferson thirty days later on March 8, 1869.

18 Arnold returned to his home in Baltimore and lived out his years in relative peace pausing only to write a book about his experiences. He died in 1906. Spangler returned to his old employer John T. Ford and eventually made his way to the home of Dr. Mudd in 1873 where he lived out the remainder of his years until his death in 1875. He was buried by Dr. Mudd in the old St. Peter's Cemetery across the road from the Mudd church. The grave was unmarked and remained so until 1985 when a joint effort of the Surratt Society and Dr. Samuel A. Mudd Society placed a gravestone on the alleged site.

19 Henry, 1870; Stella Marie, 1871; Edward Joseph, 1873; Rose De Lima, 1875; and Mary Eleanor (Nettie), 1878.

CHAPTER 10

1 This chapter is taken from an earlier version which appeared in the *Lincoln Herald* as Steers, Edward, Jr., "Inter Arma Silent Leges," *Lincoln Herald*, 83: No. 3, 719-730, fall, 1981.
"The law is silent among arms." This ominous maxim is taken from Attorney General James Speed's opinion provided to President Andrew Johnson dated July 1865. Speed maintained that this dictum was never wholly true as the object of the laws of war was to limit, as much as possible, injury to persons and property during war. See Speed, James F., *Opinion on the Constitutional Power of the Military to Try and Execute the Assassins of the President*, Government Printing Office, Washington, D.C. July, 1865.

2 Surratt was in Canada where he had been enroute on a mission for the Confederacy when Lincoln was assassinated. Friends quickly hid him and provided for him while the manhunt and subsequent trial took place. He eventually made his way to Europe, then the Vatican, where he briefly served as a Papal guard before being discovered. Taken into custody, he made a miraculous escape and sailed for Egypt only to be captured by United States authorities in Alexandria. He was returned to the United States where he was tried in civil court as a conspirator in Lincoln's murder. The jury failed to reach a verdict and Surratt was released when the government decided not to seek a new trial.

3 Interestingly, the original order is written in Secretary of War Edwin Stanton's own hand on War Department stationary. Stanton obviously made the decision to try the accused before a military court and drafted the executive order for Johnson to sign.

4 *Trial*, I:5.

5 War Department circular dated April 20, 1865. See Fleet, Betsy, "A Chapter of Unwritten History: Richard Bayard Garrett's Account of the Flight and Death of John Wilkes Booth." *The Virginia Magazine*, No. 4:387, 1963, 71. Also, Weckesser.

6 *Ex parte Milligan*, 4 Wall. 2:18 L.Ed. 281.

7 Arnold and Spangler filed a petition of habeas corpus with the Supreme Court in February 1869 as a result of their petition before the United States District Court of Southern Florida being denied. The Supreme Court agreed to hear the case and arguments were made before it by lawyers for the plaintiffs and the government. Andrew Johnson pardoned the two plaintiffs on March 1, 1869, and according to the court's calendar dated March 19, 1869, Chief Justice Salmon P. Chase dismissed the petition without a court ruling leaving the petition moot. For a full discussion of the hearing before the U.S. District Court for the Southern District of

Florida and the filing with the United States Supreme Court, see James E. T. Lange and Katharine DeWitt, Jr., "Mudd Habeas Corpus," *Surratt Courier*, 19, no. 1 (1994): 5-7.

8   Basler, Roy P., Marion D. Pratt, and Lloyd A. Dunlap, *The Collected Works of Abraham Lincoln*, 9 Volumes, New Brunswick, NJ: 1953, **IV**:344.

9   Lincoln, *Works*, **IV**:347.

10 The applicable clause is found in Article I, Section 9, paragraph 2 of the Constitution of the United States.

11 During this period in history justices of the Supreme Court served on circuit court duty while the Supreme Court was in recess. Chief Justice Taney received the Merryman petition while sitting as circuit court judge for the District of Baltimore during the April 1861 term. Taney's opinion is published in 17 Fed.Case 144.

12 Lincoln, *Works*, **IV**:344, 347, 364, 414, and Lincoln, *Works* supplement, 1832-1865, 109, 1974.

13 Lincoln, *Works*, **V**:436-437.

14 Neely, Mark E., *The Fate of Liberty*, New York: Oxford University Press, 1991. Neely, in a meticulous study of martial law and military commissions, concluded that such trials , "...were marked by procedural regularity," and that Judge Advocate General Joseph Holt was, "... a punctilious lawyer and military administrator who repeatedly overturned the decisions of trials by military commission (as well as courts-martial) for what can only be called legal technicalities." See Neely, 162.   While military justice in regard to civilians may have been viewed as harsh, Neely, in reviewing one hundred and eighty-four cases involving the death sentence which were sent to Lincoln between 1863 and 1865 for his approval, observed that Lincoln mitigated the punishment in eighty-nine of the cases or nearly one-half. See Neely, 165-166.

15 Copperhead was the name given to those Northern Democrats who actively supported the Confederate cause. While some merely believed in the right of a state to secede, others were more active in supporting (and even supplying) the Confederacy in word and deed.

16 *Ex parte Vallandigham*, 1 Wall. 243.

17 Pittman, *Trial*, 2.

18 Interestingly, the original draft of the Executive Order signed by Johnson is written in Stanton's own hand and appears on War Department stationary suggesting that Secretary of War Stanton was the originator of trying the accused before a military commission. While Stanton may have orchestrated the use of a military trial, there is no evidence that he orchestrated James Speed's opinion.

19 Speed, *Opinion*, 8.

20 *Ex parte Vallandigham*, 1 Wall. 243.

21 Speed, *Opinion*, 15.

22 Ibid.

23 Martial law came into effect throughout the United States for certain individuals and situations as a result of Lincoln's proclamation of September 24, 1862. The conditions of this proclamation were still in force at the time of Lincoln's assassination and the trial of the conspirators. Martial law was revoked by Andrew Johnson only after the trial and execution had taken place.

24 *Ex parte Milligan*, 4 Wall. 2, 18 L.Ed. 281.

25 Arrested with Milligan and tried by the military tribunal were William A. Bowles, Andrew Humphreys, Horace Heffren and Stephen Horsey.

26 According to Stanton biographer Frank A. Flower, Milligan's wife, who was an old childhood friend of Edwin Stanton, carried Milligan's written brief to Stanton

and pleaded for her husband's life. Stanton accepted Milligan's brief and told Mrs. Milligan that her husband would not be executed. Within hours, Governor Morton of Indiana received a dispatch from the War Department commuting the sentence. See, Flowers, Frank A., *Edwin McMasters Stanton*, New York: The Saalfield Publishing Company, 1906.

27   In a five to four vote the Court also ruled that the Congress had no power under the Constitution to authorize a military commission. The dissenting opinion, given by Chief Justice Salmon P. Chase, maintained that the war powers granted Congress authorized it to enact legislation establishing military commissions.

28   The question of Lincoln's suspension of the writ of habeas corpus became a moot point as a result of Congress' Act of March 1863, authorizing such suspension.

29   King, Willard L. *Lincoln's Manager David Davis.* Cambridge, MA: Harvard University Press, 263.

30   Salmon P. Chase papers, Department of History, Claremont Graduate School, Claremont, California.

31   The Court's records are missing, but the complete Boynton opinion may be found in a newspaper (unidentified) clipping in the *Lincoln Obsequies Scrapbook* located in the Library of Congress, Manuscript Division. The article purports to be a verbatim transcript of the opinion filed by Boynton for the United States District of Florida. The original case is cited in: 17 Fed. Case, 954. For a further discussion of Mudd's petition see Gary R. Planck, "Lincoln's Assassination: More "Forgotten" Litigation - ex parte Mudd (1868)," Lincoln *Herald*, 76, No. 2, 86-90, 1974.

32   The court's records are missing, but the complete Boynton opinion was discovered by James O. Hall in a newspaper (unidentified) clipping in the *Lincoln Obsequies Scrapbook* located in the Library of Congress, Manuscript Division. The article purports to be a verbatim transcript of the opinion filed by Boynton for the United States District of Florida. Subsequently the verbatim transcript of the case was published in the *Surratt Courier*. See James E. T. Lange and Katherine DeWitt, J., "Ex Parte Mudd Confirmed," *Surratt Courier*, 21, no. 3, (1996) pp. 4-8. The original case is cited in: 17 Fed.case, 954. For a further discussion of Mudd's petition see Gary R. Planck, "Lincoln's Assassination: More "Forgotten" Litigation—ex parte Mudd (18868)." *Lincoln Herald*, 76, no. 2, pp. 86-90 (1974).

33   The eleven Southern states were divided into five military districts along the following lines: West Virginia, Virginia; North and South Carolina; Georgia, Alabama, Florida; Mississippi and Arkansas; and Louisiana and Texas.

34   *Ex parte Garland*, 4 Wall. 333; Cummings vs, Missouri, 4 Wall. 277.

35   *Ex parte McCardle*, 6 Wall. 318.

36   *Ex parte McCardle*, 7 Wall. 506.

37   The eight consisted of Richard Quirin, George Dasch, Ernest Burger, Heinrich Heinck, Edward Kerling, Hermann Neubauer, Herbert Haupt and Werner Thiel. All eight saboteurs had lived in the United States previously and all eight spoke fluent English. Two of the eight were U. S. citizens. By June 27, 1942, they were standing trial before a military tribunal ordered by President Franklin Roosevelt. Leading the defense was army appointed counsel Colonel Robert Royall who promptly petitioned the Supreme Court for a writ of habeas corpus.

38   Proclamation No. 2561, July 2, 1942. 7 F.R. 5101, 56 Stat., 1964, "Enemies denied access to United States Courts," 10 U.S.C. 906.

39 *Ex parte Quirin*, 317, U.S. 1.

40 On August 3, 1942, the commission found the defendants guilty on all charges, and on August 8, all but Dasch and Burger were electrocuted in the District of Columbia jail. Dasch and Burger, who told everything to the FBI, received jail terms which were to be commuted to deportation at the end of the war.

41 *Ex parte Yamashita*, 327 U.S. 1.

42 The establishment of martial law over the domestic population as it existed during the Civil War did not end as a result of the Supreme Court ruling in *ex parte Milligan*. Shortly after the Japanese attack on Pearl Harbor in 1941, the governor of the Territory of Hawaii closed the civil courts and turned the government over to the commanding general of the department with the full approval of the president of the United States. Two years later, in February, 1944, the Supreme Court again invoked *ex parte Milligan* in ruling that martial law can only exist when the civil arm of the government becomes powerless because of invasion, insurrection or anarchy. Duncan v. Kahanamoku, 327 U.S. 304.

43 Powell served as a private in Mosby's command while O'Laughlen and Arnold served in the First Maryland Infantry; O'Laughlen in Company D, and Arnold in Company C. See John C. Brennan, "Bradley T. Johnson's Plan to Abduct President Lincoln," *Chronicles of St. Mary's*, vol. 22, no. 12, December, 1974. 421-425.

APPENDIX 6

1 Atzerodt, *Lost Confession*. See note 21, Chapter 2.

2 James Wood was an alias used by Lewis Powell. While boarding at the Surratt House, Powell represented himself as a Baptist minister which came naturally to him as his father was, in fact, a Baptist minister.

3 Louis J. Weichmann, a classmate and boyhood friend of John H. Surratt, Jr., boarded at the Surratt boarding house in Washington. He became an important witness for the government's case against John and Mary Surratt.

4 Thomas Harbin was a member of the Confederate Signal Service (Secret Service) and in charge of Virginia's north shore of the Potomac River. Mudd arranged a meeting between Harbin and Booth in December 1864, at Bryantown.

5 John Boyle, known locally as the Guerrilla Boyle, sometimes terrorized the area of Prince George's County and Charles County. Mudd claims that he first thought it was Boyle who banged on his door early Saturday morning when Booth and Herold arrived. The government at first thought it was Boyle who had attacked Seward on Friday evening. The truth is, Mudd nothing to fear from Boyle.

6 John H. Caldwell managed the grocery store of Matthews and Company in Georgetown. Matthews was a wholesale and retail dealer in "fine teas and choice groceries for the family." Atzerodt stopped here early Saturday morning while fleeing Washington. He pawned his revolver with Caldwell for $10.00 before proceeding on to the home of his cousin, Hartman Richter in Germantown, Montgomery County, Maryland where he was eventually captured early Thursday morning, April 20.

APPENDIX 9

1 NARA, M-619, reel 456, frames 0488 - 0490.

INDEX

The names of each of the major conspirators involved with John Wilkes Booth occur frequently throughout the text. Therefore, John Wilkes Booth, Samuel Arnold, George A. Atzerodt, Thomas Harbin, David Herold, Dr. Samuel A. Mudd, Michael O'Laughlen, Lewis Powell, Edman Spangler, John H. Surratt, Jr., and Mary Surratt are not listed in this index.